Dean Martin
A Complete Guide to the "Total Entertainer"

Dean Martin
A Complete Guide to the "Total Entertainer"

by
John Chintala

Chi Productions
1998

ISBN 0-9664735-0-7
Library of Congress Catalog Card Number: 98-93028

Published by Chi Productions
Exeter, PA

Printed in the United States of America

This is a limited first edition (# 242 of 500)

For:
Aunt Betty and Uncle Paul
and
Dean Martin
Thank you for my childhood

(NBC publicity photo)

Contents

(Paramount Pictures Corp. publicity photo)

Preface

He was the epitome of cool. If there was one word to describe Dean Martin, it had to be "cool." I first became aware of this while still a child. There was something about the *Gentle On My Mind* and *Door Is Still Open To My Heart* albums that my great uncle owned that reached out and grabbed my then-two-year-old attention. It was such a special treat to stay up past my bedtime on Thursday nights to watch Dean's television show. I laughed as he intentionally stumbled through the opening line of "Everybody Loves Somebody," slid down that ever-present fireman's pole, told the politically-incorrect jokes about his "drinking" and marital problems and then launched into song.

Perhaps as a result of his devil-may-care attitude, self-deprecating humor, and the uncanny ability to make singing and acting look so effortless, Dean's vast body of work has not been taken as seriously as that of many of his contemporaries. Hopefully this book will help to remedy that neglect.

Since this alleged "lazy" entertainer recorded some 600 songs, hosted 275 episodes of his own television show and racked up 200 other appearances on the small screen, starred in more than 50 motion pictures, was heard on over 100 radio programs and made countless nightclub appearances, the notion that Dean Martin "coasted" through his career is completely unfounded.

While you're looking through this book, play one of Dean's albums and listen to his voice glide effortlessly through *This Time I'm Swingin'*, or hear a proud man pay homage to his ancestry on *Italian Love Songs*. If you're in a romantic mood, both *Sleep Warm* and *Dream With Dean* can work wonders; or feel free to relive the "couch songs" that Dean performed in your living room (through the magic of a cathode ray tube) with Ken Lane and the Les Brown Orchestra on the *T. V. Show* album. And maybe, just maybe, you'll forget your troubles for a half hour. 'Cause Dino is singing, pally; and all is right with the world.

JPC

April 1998

Acknowledgments

Special thanks to the following individuals who helped make this work possible: Mom and Dad, my sisters Angela and Ann Marie, my two grandmothers, Tom Alexander, Lou and Gail Antonicello, Ed Baul, Tom Carswell, Susan Chokola, Dennis Coleman, Mark Dixon, Dan Einstein, Ray Faiola (CBS Audience Services), Anthony Ferrara, Kim Fuller, Ron Furmanek, Greg Garrison and Mary Scully, Mary Beth Holmes, Jeff Kline, Sandy Kruger, Steve Lang (Warner Bros. Records), Joseph J. Laredo, Chris Lewis, Pete Longo, Rachel McLaughlin, Dale Mikolaczyk, Jim Monaco, Dale Neidigh, Ed O'Brien, Ted Okuda, Sandy Oliveri, Peter Paul Oprisko II, the late Bill Osborn, Richard Pearson, Joe Peregrin, Cindy Plumlee, Robert Policastro, Frank Reda, Research Video (Paul Surratt and Bill DiCicco), Scott Sayers, Jim Schumacher (Capitol Records), Stephen Tufts, Richard Weize (Bear Family Records), Randy Yantek and Marc Zubatkin.

An extra special thanks to Bob Furmanek. Without his supreme generosity, this book would be much less than what it is now; it is an honor to call him "friend." My deepest gratitude and sincerest thanks.

The Library of Congress, Washington, D.C. (Gene DeAnna, Neil Gladd, Wynn Mathias and James Wolf)

The Lincoln Center of the Performing Arts, New York

The Museum of Television and Radio, New York (Kevin Scott)

Billboard chart information taken from Joel Whitburn's Record Research publications. Thanks to Joel Whitburn, Kim Bloxdorf and Joanne Wagner.

Cashbox chart information courtesy of George Albert. Thanks also to Pat Downey and Joanne Ricca.

Movie grosses courtesy of *Variety*. Thanks to Neal Vitale and Kristien Deiley.

Stills courtesy of Columbia Pictures, Las Vegas News Bureau, MGM/United Artists, NBC, Paramount Pictures, 20th Century Fox, Universal Pictures, and Warner Brothers.

For further information on Dean Martin, contact:

The Dean Martin Fan Center (Neil Daniels)
P. O. Box 660212
Arcadia, CA 91066-0212

The Dean Martin Association (Bernard Thorpe and Jayne Kempsey)
P. O. Box 80
Uckfield
East Sussex
TN22 1ZR
England

Certain sections (especially regarding various artists releases, magazine and sheet music covers, and home video releases) may contain omissions. Corrections and additions are welcomed and encouraged. E-mail information to: JohnChi500@aol.com

Chapter 1

Alphabetical Listing of Songs

(Note: The songwriters are listed in parentheses followed by any additional information.)

Absence Makes The Heart Grow Fonder
(Samuel M. Lewis, Harry Warren, Joseph Young)
Paul Weston Orchestra
Produced by Lee Gillette

Ain't Gonna Try Anymore
(Ballard)
Arranged and Conducted by Don Costa
Produced by Chuck Sagle

Ain't That A Kick In The Head
(Jimmy Van Heusen, Sammy Cahn)
Conducted by Nelson Riddle
Produced by Lee Gillette

Alabamy Bound
(Ray Henderson, Buddy DeSylva, Bud Green)
Arranged by Dave Cavanaugh
Produced by Voyle Gilmore

All I Do Is Dream Of You
(Nacio Herb Brown, Arthur Freed)
Arranged by Pete King
Produced by Lee Gillette
Orchestra Conducted by Frank Sinatra

All I Have To Give You Is My Love
(Jody Evans, Jeff Davis)
Conducted by Dick Stabile
Arranged by Gus Levene
Produced by Lee Gillette

All In A Night's Work
(Ruth Roberts, William Katz)
Produced by Kent Larsen
Orchestra Conducted by Nelson Riddle

All Of Me
(Seymour Simons, Gerald Marks)
Nat Brandwynne Orchestra

Almost Like Being In Love
(Alan Jay Lerner, Frederick Loewe)
Arranged by Van Alexander
Produced by Jimmy Bowen

Always In My Heart
(Lecuona, Gannon)
Arranged and Conducted by Don Costa

Always Together
(J. Sawyer, Peter DeAngelis)
Arranged by Ernie Freeman
Produced by Jimmy Bowen

Amor
(Gabriel Ruiz, Sunny Skylar)
Produced by Dave Cavanaugh
Arranged and Conducted by Nelson Riddle

Amor Mio
(Sammy Cahn, George Barrie)
Produced by Jimmy Bowen
Arranged by Larry Muhoberac

Angel Baby
(John Michael, Carl Niessen)
Conducted by Gus Levene
Produced by Lee Gillette

Any Man Who Loves His Mother
(Sammy Cahn, James Van Heusen)
Produced by Johnny Burke
Arranged and Conducted by Nelson Riddle

Any Time
(Lawson)
Produced by Chuck Sagle
Arranged and Conducted by Don Costa

April Again
(Glen D. Hardin)
Produced by Jimmy Bowen
Arranged and Conducted by Ernie Freeman

April In Paris
(Harburg, Duke)
Arranged and Conducted by Neal Hefti

Arrivederci, Roma
(Renato Rascal, Garinei, Giovanni, Carl Sigman)
Produced by Dave Cavanaugh
Conducted by Gus Levene

As You Are
(Billy Friedman, Herbert L. Miller)
Produced by Lee Gillette
Conducted by Dick Stabile
Arranged by Gus Levene

At Sundown
(Walter Donaldson)
Produced by Jimmy Bowen
Arranged by Van Alexander

Aw C'Mon
(Dave Gregory, Walter Byron)
Arranged and conducted by Dick Stabile
Produced by Lee Gillette

Baby It's Cold Outside
(Frank Loesser)
Produced by Lee Gillette
Conducted by Gus Levene

Baby-O
(Johnny Mercer, Johnny Rotella)
Conducted by Neal Hefti

Baby Obey Me
(Jay Livingston, Ray Evans)
Paul Weston Orchestra
Produced by Lee Gillette
Arranged by Bill Loose

Baby, Won't You Please Come Home
(Charles Warfield, Clarence Williams)
(1964 Version)
Produced by Jimmy Bowen

Baby, Won't You Please Come Home
(1966 Version)
Produced by Jimmy Bowen
Arranged by Ernie Freeman
Conducted by Les Brown

Baby, Won't You Please Come Home
(1973 Version)
Produced by Jimmy Bowen
Arranged by Ernie Freeman

Bamboozled
(Fred Ebb, Paul Klein)
Gus Levene Orchestra
Produced by Lee Gillette

Basin St. Blues
(Spencer Williams)
Produced by Voyle Gilmore
Arranged by Dave Cavanaugh
With Dick Stabile's Dixie Cats

Be An Angel
(Ketti Frings, Gale Anderson)
With the Nelson Riddle Orchestra
Produced by Lee Gillette

Beau James
(Herbert Baker)
Orchestra and Chorus conducted by Gus Levene
Produced by Lee Gillette

Be Honest With Me
(Gene Autry, Fred Rose)
With Paul Weston and His Dixie Eight
Produced by Lee Gillette

Bella Bella Bambina
(Bernice Ross, Addy Baron)
Produced by Kent Larson

Belle From Barcelona
(Louis Yule Brown, Dante De Paulo)
Produced by Lee Gillette
Conducted by Dick Stabile
Arranged by Gus Levene

Besame Mucho
(Velasquez, Skyler)
Arranged and Conducted by Don Costa

Beside You
(Ray Evans, Jerry Livingston)
Arranged by Bill Loose
Lou Busch Orchestra
Produced by Lee Gillette

Bet-I-Cha
(Jimmy White, Billy Talou)
Conducted by Dick Stabile
Produced by Lee Gillette

Better Than A Dream
(Betty Comden, Adolph Green, Jule Styne)
Adapted and Conducted by Andre Previn
Produced by Lee Gillette and John Palladino
Orchestrations by Alexander Courage and Pete King

Bianca
(Cole Porter)
Arranged by Skip Martin
Produced by Frank Sinatra
Conducted by Morris Stoloff

5

Birds and the Bees
(Herb Newman)
Produced by Jimmy Bowen
Arranged and Conducted by Ernie Freeman

Blue, Blue Day
(Don Gibson)
Arranged and Conducted by Don Costa
Produced by Chuck Sagle

Blue Christmas
(Hayes, Johnson)
Produced by Jimmy Bowen
Arranged and Conducted by Bill Justis

Blue Memories
(J. A. Balthrop)
Produced by Jimmy Bowen
Arranged by Larry Muhoberac
With the Jimmy Bowen Orchestra and Chorus

Blue Moon
(Rodgers, Hart)
Produced by Jimmy Bowen

Blue Smoke
(Rohu Auwahi)
Conducted by Dick Stabile
Arranged by Nelson Riddle
Produced by Lee Gillette

Bonne Nuit
(Jay Livingston, Ray Evans)
Conducted by Dick Stabile
Produced by Lee Gillette

Born To Lose
(Frankie Brown)
Produced by Jimmy Bowen
Arranged and Conducted by Ernie Freeman

Bouquet of Roses
(Nelson, Hilliard)
Produced by Jimmy Bowen
Arranged and Conducted by Marty Paich

Brahms' Lullaby
(Johannes Brahms)
Produced by Lee Gillette
Conducted by Frank Sinatra
Arranged by Pete King

Bumming Around
(P. Graves)
Produced by Jimmy Bowen
Arranged and Conducted by Ernie Freeman

Buona Sera
(Carl Sigman, Peter de Rose)
Orchestra and Chorus Conducted by Gus Levene
Produced by Lee Gillette

Buttercup Of Golden Hair
(Mitchell Tableporter)
Conducted by Gus Levene
Produced by Lee Gillette

By The Time I Get To Phoenix
(Jimmy Webb)
Produced by Jimmy Bowen
Arranged and Conducted by Ernie Freeman

Bye Bye Blackbird
(Ray Henderson, Mort Dixon)
Arranged by Matty Matlock
With Paul Weston and His Dixie Eight
Produced by Lee Gillette

Canadian Sunset
(Eddie Haywood, Norman Gimbel)
Produced by Lee Gillette
Conducted by Gus Levene

Candy Kisses
(George Morgan)
Produced by Jimmy Bowen
Arranged and Conducted by Marty Paich

Captured
(Hal David, Leon Carr)
Conducted by Gus Levene
Produced by Lee Gillette

Career
(Sammy Cahn, James Van Heusen)
Conducted by Gus Levene
Produced by Lee Gillette

Carolina In The Morning
(Walter Donaldson, Gus Kahn)
Produced by Lee Gillette
Arranged by Dave Cavanaugh
With Dick Stabile's Dixie Cats

Carolina Moon
(Joe Burke, Benny Davis)
Produced by Lee Gillette
Arranged by Dave Cavanaugh
With Dick Stabile's Dixie Cats

C'est Magnifique
(Cole Porter)
Arranged and Conducted by Neal Hefti

C'est Si Bon
(Betti, Seelen, Hornel)
Arranged and Conducted by Neal Hefti

Cha Cha Cha D'Amour
(Leo Johns, Henri Salvador)
Produced by Dave Cavanaugh
Arranged and Conducted by Nelson Riddle

Change of Heart
(John Rox)
Conducted by Dick Stabile

Cheatin' On Me
(Lew Pollack, Jack Yellin)
Gus Levene Orchestra and Chorus
Produced by Lee Gillette

Chee Chee-Oo Chee
(Saverio Seracini, John Turner, Geoffrey Parsons)
Conducted by Dick Stabile
Produced by Lee Gillette

Choo'N Gum
(Vic Mizzy, Mann Curtis)
With Paul Weston and His Dixie Eight
Produced by Lee Gillette

Christmas Blues
(Sammy Cahn, David Holt)
Conducted by Dick Stabile
Arranged by Gus Levene
Produced by Lee Gillette

Clinging Vine
(Shuman, Carr, Lane)
Produced by Jimmy Bowen
Arranged by Ernie Freeman

Come Back To Sorrento
(Ernesto deCurtis, G. B. deCurtis, Alice Mattulath)
Conducted by Dick Stabile
Arranged by Gus Levene
Produced by Lee Gillette

Come On Down
(Dino Martin, William Hinsche)
Produced by Dino Martin
Arranged by Billy Hinsche and Al Capps

Come Running Back
(Dick Glasser)
Produced by Jimmy Bowen
Arranged and Conducted by Billy Strange

Confused
(Ben Weisman)
Conducted by Dick Stabile
Arranged by Gus Levene
Produced by Lee Gillette

Corrine, Corrina
(Williams, Chatman, Parish)
Produced by Jimmy Bowen
Arranged and Conducted by Marty Paich

Crying Time
(Buck Owens)
Produced by Jimmy Bowen
Arranged by Jimmie Haskell
With the Jimmy Bowen Orchestra and Chorus

Cuddle Up A Little Closer
(Karl Hoschna, Otto Harbach)
Produced by Lee Gillette
Conducted by Frank Sinatra
Arranged by Pete King

Dame Su Amor
(Kusik, Ballard)
Conducted by Neal Hefti

Darktown Strutter's Ball
(Shelton Brooks)
Arranged by Dick Stabile
With Paul Weston and His Dixie Eight
Produced by Lee Gillette

Darling, Je Vous Aime Beaucoup
(Sosenko)
Arranged and Conducted by Neal Hefti

Day In The Country
(Sammy Fain, Paul Francis Webster)
Orchestra Conducted by Gus Levene
Produced by Lee Gillette

Day You Came Along
(A. Johnston, S. Coslow)
Produced by Jimmy Bowen
Strings by Alan Moore

Detour
(Paul Westmoreland)
Produced by Jimmy Bowen
Arranged and Conducted by Bill Justis
With the Jack Halloran Singers

Detroit City
(Danny Dill, Mel Tillis)
Produced by Jimmy Bowen
Arranged by Billy Strange
With the Jimmy Bowen Orchestra and Chorus

Dinah
(Harry Akst, Sam M. Lewis, Joe Young)
Arranged by Dave Cavanaugh
Produced by Voyle Gilmore
With Dick Stabile's Dixie Cats

Do It Yourself
(Betty Comden, Adolph Green, Jule Styne)
Produced by Lee Gillette and John Palladino
Adapted and Conducted by Andre Previn
Orchestrations by Alexander Courage and Pete King

Do You Believe This Town
(Williams, Nixon)
Produced by Jimmy Bowen
With the Jimmy Bowen Orchestra and Chorus
Arranged by Glen D. Hardin

Don't Be A Do-Badder Finale
(Sammy Cahn, James Van Heusen)
Produced by Sonny Burke
Arranged and Conducted by Nelson Riddle

Don't Give Up On Me
(Ben Peters)
Produced by Jimmy Bowen
Strings Arranged by Al DeLory and Alan Moore

Don't Let The Blues Make You Bad
(Billy Mize)
Produced by Jimmy Bowen

Don't Rock The Boat, Dear
(Harold Arlen, Ralph Blane)
Frank Devol Orchestra
Produced by Lee Gillette

Don't You Remember?
(Ace Dinning)
Conducted by Dick Stabile
Arranged by Dick Stabile
With The Herman McCoy Singers
Produced by Lee Gillette

Door Is Still Open To My Heart
(Chuck Willis)
Produced by Jimmy Bowen
Arranged by Ernie Freeman

Down Home
(Clark)
Produced by Jimmy Bowen
Arranged and Conducted by Bill Justis
With the Jack Halloran Singers

Down Home
(Gerry Goffin, Carole King)
Produced by Dino Martin
Arranged by Dino Martin, Billy Hinsche and Al Capps

Dream
(Johnny Mercer)
Produced by Lee Gillette
Conducted by Frank Sinatra
Arranged by Pete King

Dream A Little Dream Of Me
(Wilbur Schwandt, Fabian Andree, Gus Kahn)
Produced by Lee Gillette
Conducted by Frank Sinatra
Arranged by Pete King

Dreamy Old New England Moon
(Morty Berk, Frank Capano, Max C. Freedman)
Paul Weston Orchestra
With the Martingales
Produced by Lee Gillette

Drinking Champagne
(Bill Mack)
Produced by Jimmy Bowen
Strings Arranged by Al DeLory and Alan Moore

Drowning In My Tears
(Ken Lane, Irving Taylor)
Produced by Jimmy Bowen
Arranged and Conducted by Ernie Freeman

El Rancho Grande
(Ramos, Costello)
Arranged and Conducted by Don Costa

Empty Saddles In The Old Corral
(Billy Hill)
Produced by Jimmy Bowen

Everybody But Me
(Dave Burgess)
Produced by Jimmy Bowen
Arranged and Conducted by Bill Justis
With the Jack Halloran Singers

Everybody Loves Somebody
(Ken Lane, Irving Taylor)
(Small group Version)
Produced by Jimmy Bowen

Everybody Loves Somebody
("Hit" Version)
Produced by Jimmy Bowen
Arranged by Ernie Freeman

Everybody's Had The Blues
(Merle Haggard)
Produced by Jimmy Bowen
Strings Arranged by Al DeLory and Alan Moore

Every Minute, Every Hour
(Ken Lane, Irving Taylor)
Produced by Jimmy Bowen
Arranged by Ernie Freeman

Ev'ry Street's A Boulevard In Old New York
(Jule Styne, Bob Hilliard)
Arranged and Conducted by Walter Scharf

Face In A Crowd
(Redd, Torok)
Produced by Chuck Sagle
Arranged and Conducted by Don Costa

First Thing Ev'ry Morning
(J. Dean, R. Roberts)
Produced by Jimmy Bowen
Arranged and Conducted by Bill Justis
With the Jack Halloran Singers

5 Card Stud
(Washington, Jarre)
Arranged by Ernie Freeman

Fools Rush In
(Bloom, Mercer)
Produced by Jimmy Bowen

Forgetting You
(Buddy Kaye, Gary Bruce)
Orchestra and Chorus Conducted by Gus Levene
Produced by Lee Gillette

For Once In My Life
(R. Miller, O. Murden)
Produced by Jimmy Bowen
Arranged and Conducted by Ernie Freeman
With the Jimmy Bowen Orchestra and Chorus

For Sentimental Reasons
(William Best, Deek Watson)
Produced by Dave Cavanaugh
Arranged and Conducted by Nelson Riddle

For The Good Times
(Kris Kristofferson)
Produced by Jimmy Bowen
Arranged and Conducted by Ernie Freeman
With the Jimmy Bowen Orchestra and Chorus

For The Love Of A Woman
(William Hinsche)
(Listed on some pressings as being written by William Hinsche
    and Dino Martin)
Produced by Dino Martin and William Hinsche
Arranged by Dino Martin, William Hinsche and Al Capps

For You
(Joe Burke, Al Dubin)
Arranged and Conducted by Gus Levene
Produced by Lee Gillette

Free To Carry On
(Dale Bobbit, Jim Brody)
Produced by Jimmy Bowen
Arranged by Ernie Freeman

From Lover To Loser
(Warren, Kent)
Produced by Jimmy Bowen
Arranged and Conducted by Marty Paich

From The Bottom Of My Heart
(Danny Diminno, George Cardini)
Arranged and Conducted by Chuck Sagle

Fugue For Tinhorns
(Frank Loesser)
Arranged by Bill Loose
Conducted by Morris Stoloff

Gentle On My Mind
(John Hartford)
Produced by Jimmy Bowen
Arranged and Conducted by Ernie Freeman

Georgia On My Mind
(Hoagy Carmichael, Stuart Gorrell)
Produced by Lee Gillette
Arranged by Dave Cavanaugh
With Dick Stabile's Dixie Cats

Georgia Sunshine
(Jerry Hubbard)
Produced by Jimmy Bowen
Arranged and Conducted by Ernie Freeman
With the Jimmy Bowen Orchestra and Chorus

Get On With Your Livin'
(Ted Hamilton)
Produced by Jimmy Bowen
Arranged by Larry Muhoberac

Gigi
(Lerner, Loewe)
Arranged and Conducted by Neal Hefti

Gimme A Little Kiss
(Roy Turk, Jack Smith, Maleo Pinkard)
(1964 Version)
Produced by Jimmy Bowen

Gimme A Little Kiss
(1973 Version)
Produced by Jimmy Bowen
Arranged by Ernie Freeman

Girl Named Mary And A Boy Named Bill
(Jerry Livingston, Mack David)
Conducted by Dick Stabile
Produced by Lee Gillette

Give Me A Sign
(Grace Saxon, Barry Mirkin)
Gus Levene Orchestra
Produced by Lee Gillette

Giuggiola
(Nisa, Sammy Cahn, Corrado Lojacono)
Produced by Kent Larsen
Nelson Riddle Orchestra

Glory Of Love
(Billy Hill)
Produced by Jimmy Bowen

Go Go Go Go
(Jerry Livingston, Mack David)
Conducted by Dick Stabile
Arranged by Sid Feller
Produced by Lee Gillette

Good Mornin', Life
(Robert Allen, Joseph Meyer)
Conducted by Gus Levene
Produced by Lee Gillette

Goodnight, My Love
(Mack Gordon, Harry Revel)
Produced by Lee Gillette
Conducted by Frank Sinatra
Arranged by Pete King

Goodnight Sweetheart
(Ray Noble, Jimmy Campbell, Reg Connelly, Rudy Vallee)
Produced by Lee Gillette
Conducted by Frank Sinatra
Arranged by Pete King

Grazie, Prego, Scusi
(Marchelti, Mogol, Prete, Reizner)
Produced by Jimmy Bowen

Green, Green Grass Of Home
(Curly Putnam)
Produced by Jimmy Bowen
Conducted by Ernie Freeman
Arranged by Billy Strange

Guess Who
(Jo Anne Belvin)
Produced by Jimmy Bowen
Arranged by Larry Muhoberac
With the Jimmy Bowen Orchestra and Chorus

Guys and Dolls
(Frank Loesser)
Produced by Frank Sinatra
Arranged by Bill Loose
Conducted by Morris Stoloff

17

Hammer and Nails
(Dick Glasser)
Produced by Jimmy Bowen
Arranged and Conducted by Bill Justis
With the Jack Halloran Singers

Hands Across The Table
(Delettre, Parish)
Produced by Jimmy Bowen

Hangin' Around
(Chip Hardy, Rick Carnes, Janis Carnes)
Produced by Jimmy Bowen
Strings Arranged by Al DeLory and Alan Moore

Hangin' Around With You
(Al Stillman, Ray Doll, Bernard Maltin)
Conducted by Dick Stabile
Arranged by Nelson Riddle and Dick Stabile
Produced by Lee Gillette

Happy Feet
(Roy Ross, Al Stillman)
With Paul Weston and His Dixie Eight
Produced by Lee Gillette

Have A Heart
(Ken Lane, Irving Taylor)
Produced by Jimmy Bowen
Arranged and Conducted by Ernie Freeman

Have A Little Sympathy
(Sammy Gallop, Ben Weisman)
Paul Weston Orchestra
Produced by Lee Gillette

Hear My Heart
(Buddy Lester)
Produced by Lee Gillette

Heart Over Mind
(Mel Tillis)
Produced by Jimmy Bowen
Arranged by Billy Strange
With the Jimmy Bowen Orchestra and Chorus

18

Heaven Can Wait
(Eddie De Lange, Jimmy Van Heusen)
Produced by Lee Gillette
Arranged and Conducted by Nelson Riddle

Here Comes My Baby
(D. West, B. West)
Produced by Jimmy Bowen
Arranged and Conducted by Ernie Freeman

Here We Go Again
(Russell Steagull, Don Lanier)
Produced by Jimmy Bowen
Arranged by Glen D. Hardin
With the Jimmy Bowen Orchestra and Chorus

He's Got You
(Hank Cochran)
Produced by Jimmy Bowen

Hey, Brother, Pour The Wine
(Ross Bagdasarian)
Conducted by Dick Stabile
Arranged by Gus Levene
Produced by Lee Gillette

Hey, Good Lookin'
(Hank Williams)
Produced by Chuck Sagle
Arranged and Conducted by Don Costa

Hit The Road To Dreamland
(Harold Arlen, Johnny Mercer)
Produced by Lee Gillette
Conducted by Frank Sinatra
Arranged by Pete King

Hold Me
(Jack Little, David Oppenheim, Ira Schuster)

Hollywood Or Bust
(Sammy Fain, Paul Francis Webster)
Orchestra Conducted by Gus Levene
Produced by Lee Gillette

Home
(Van Steeden, H. Clarkson, J. Clarkson)
Produced by Jimmy Bowen
Arranged by Ernie Freeman
Orchestra Conducted by Les Brown

Hominy Grits
(Smiley Burnette)
Conducted by Dick Stabile
Arranged by Nelson Riddle
Produced by Lee Gillette

Honey
(Bob Russell)
Produced by Jimmy Bowen
Arranged and Conducted by Ernie Freeman

Houston
(Lee Hazlewood)
Produced by Jimmy Bowen
Arranged and Conducted by Bill Justis
With the Jack Halloran Singers

How Do You Speak To An Angel
(Jule Styne, Bob Hilliard)
Arranged and Conducted by Walter Scharf

How D'Ya Like Your Eggs In The Morning?
(Sammy Cahn, Nicholas Brodszky)
Conducted by Dick Stabile
Arranged by Billy May
Produced by Lee Gillette

How Sweet It Is
(Joe Cooper, Harry Tobias)
Conducted by Gus Levene
Produced by Lee Gillette

Humdinger
(Edna Lewis, Irving Fields)
Conducted by Gus Levene
Produced by Lee Gillette

Hundred Years From Today
(Victor Young, Ned Washington, Joseph Young)
Produced by Dave Cavanaugh
Arranged and Conducted by Nelson Riddle

I Ain't Gonna Lead This Life No More
(Ervin Drake)
Conducted by Gus Levene
Produced by Lee Gillette

I Can Give You What You Want Now
(Carl Belew, Van Givens)
Produced by Jimmy Bowen
Arranged by Larry Muhoberac
With the Jimmy Bowen Orchestra and Chorus

I Can't Believe That You're In Love With Me
(Clarence Gaskill, Jimmy McHugh)
Produced by Lee Gillette
Arranged and Conducted by Nelson Riddle

I Can't Give You Anything But Love
(Jimmy McHugh, Dorothy Fields)
Arranged and Conducted by Gus Levene
Produced by Lee Gillette

I Can't Help It If I'm Still In Love With You
(Hank Williams)
Produced by Jimmy Bowen
Arranged and Conducted by Marty Paich

I Can't Help Remembering You
(Bert Kaempfert, Herbert Rehbein, Jimmy Bowen)
Produced by Jimmy Bowen
Arranged by Billy Strange
Conducted by Ernie Freeman

I Cried For You
(A. Freed, G. Arnheim, A. Lyman)
Produced by Jimmy Bowen
Strings by Alan Moore

I Don't Care If The Sun Don't Shine
(Mack David)
With Paul Weston and His Dixie Eight
Produced by Lee Gillette

I Don't Know What I'm Doing
(J. A. Balthrop)
Produced by Jimmy Bowen
Arranged by Larry Muhoberac
With the Jimmy Bowen Orchestra and Chorus

I Don't Know Why
(Fred Ahlert, Roy Turk)
(1957 Version)
Arranged and Conducted by Gus Levene
Produced by Lee Gillette

I Don't Know Why
(1964 Version)
Produced by Jimmy Bowen

I Don't Know Why
(1973 Version)
Produced by Jimmy Bowen
Arranged and Conducted by Ernie Freeman

I Don't Think You Love Me Anymore
(Lanier, Thacker)
Produced by Jimmy Bowen
Arranged and Conducted by Ernie Freeman

I Feel A Song Coming On
(Jimmy McHugh, Dorothy Fields, George Oppenheimer)
Dick Stabile Orchestra
Arranged by Nelson Riddle
Produced by Lee Gillette

I Feel Like A Feather In The Breeze
(Mack Gordon, Harry Ravel)
Conducted by Dick Stabile
Arranged by Nelson Riddle
Produced by Lee Gillette

I Got The Sun In The Morning
(Irving Berlin)
Nat Brandwynne Orchestra

I Have But One Heart
(Johnny Farrow, Marty Symes)
Produced by Dave Cavanaugh
Conducted by Gus Levene

I Know A Dream When I See One
(Mack David, Jerry Livingston)
Conducted by Dick Stabile
Arranged by Gus Levene
Produced by Lee Gillette

I Know I Can't Forget
(Audrey Allison, Vivian Keith)
Conducted by Gus Levene
Produced by Lee Gillette

I Like Them All
(Ebb, Klein, Coleman)
(Listed in Bear Family set as being written by Arthur Schwartz
  and Sammy Cahn)
Conducted by Dick Stabile
Produced by Lee Gillette

I Love Paris
(Cole Porter)
Arranged and Conducted by Neal Hefti

I Love The Way You Say Goodnight
(Eddie Pola, George Wyle)
Lou Busch Orchestra
Arranged by Bill Loose
Produced by Lee Gillette

I Love You Much Too Much
(Don Raye, Alex Olshanetsky, Chaim Towber)
Produced by Dave Cavanaugh
Arranged and Conducted by Nelson Riddle

I Met A Girl
(Betty Comden, Adolph Green, Jule Styne)
Produced by Lee Gillette and John Palladino
Adapted and Conducted by Andre Previn
Orchestra by Alexander Courage and Pete King

I Never Had A Chance
(Irving Berlin)
Conducted by Gus Levene
Produced by Lee Gillette

I Passed Your House Tonight
(Don Raye, Lew Spence)
Arranged and Conducted by Dick Stabile
Produced by Lee Gillette

I Ran All The Way Home
(Bennie Benjamin, George Weiss)
Arranged and Conducted by Dick Stabile
Produced by Lee Gillette

I Still Get A Thrill Thinking Of You
(Fred J. Coots, Benny Davis)
Produced by Lee Gillette

I Take A Lot Of Pride In What I Am
(Merle Haggard)
Produced by Jimmy Bowen
Arranged by Glen D. Hardin
With the Jimmy Bowen Orchestra and Chorus

I Walk The Line
(Johnny Cash)
Produced by Chuck Sagle
Arranged and Conducted by Don Costa

I Want You
(Murray Rich, Bob Greely)
Arranged by Gus Levene
Produced by Lee Gillette

I Will
(Dick Glasser)
Produced by Jimmy Bowen
Arranged and Conducted by Bill Justis
With the Jack Halloran Singers

I Wish You Love
(Charles Trenet, Albert A. Beach)
Produced by Dave Cavanaugh
Arranged and Conducted by Nelson Riddle

I Wonder Who's Kissing Her Now
(W. M. Hough, Frank R. Adams, J. E. Howard)
Produced by Jimmy Bowen
Arranged by Van Alexander

I'd Cry Like A Baby
(Sammy Gallup, Howard Steiner)
Arranged by Gus Levene
Dick Stabile Orchestra
Produced by Lee Gillette

I'll Always Love You
(Jay Livingston, Ray Evans)
Arranged by Bill Loose
Paul Weston Orchestra
Produced by Lee Gillette

I'll Be Home For Christmas
(Gannon, Kent, Ram)
Produced by Jimmy Bowen

I'll Be Seeing You
(Kahal, Fain)
Produced by Jimmy Bowen
Arranged and Conducted by Ernie Freeman

I'll Gladly Make The Same Mistake Again
(Sammy Cahn, David Holt)
Conducted by Dick Stabile
Arranged by Gus Levene
Produced by Lee Gillette

I'll Hold You In My Heart
(Arnold, Horton, Dilbeck)
Produced by Jimmy Bowen
Arranged and Conducted by Ernie Freeman

I'll Buy That Dream
(Magidson, Wrubel)
Produced by Jimmy Bowen

I'm Confessin'
(Al J. Neiburg, Doc Daugherty, Ellis Reynolds)
(1964 Version)
Produced by Jimmy Bowen

I'm Confessin'
(1973 Version)
Produced by Jimmy Bowen
Arranged by Ernie Freeman

I'm Forever Blowing Bubbles
(Jean Kenbrovin, John William Kellette)
Produced by Jimmy Bowen
Arranged by Van Alexander

I'm Gonna Change Everything
(Zanetis)
Produced by Jimmy Bowen
Arranged and Conducted by Marty Paich

I'm Gonna Paper All My Walls With Your Love Letters
(Teddy Powell, Bernie Wayne)
With Paul Weston and His Dixie Eight
Produced by Lee Gillette

I'm Gonna Steal You Away
(Fred Spielman, Buddy Kaye)
Conducted by Dick Stabile
With the Nuggets
Produced by Lee Gillette

I'm In Love With You
(Don Raye, Gene DePaul)
Frank DeVol Orchestra
Produced by Lee Gillette

I'm Living In Two Worlds
(Jan Crutchfield)
Produced by Jimmy Bowen
Arranged and Conducted by Bill Justis

I'm Not The Marrying Kind
(Lalo Schifrin, Howard Greenfield)
Produced by Jimmy Bowen
Arranged by Bill Justis

I'm Sitting On Top Of The World
(Lewis, Young, Henderson)
Produced by Jimmy Bowen
Arranged by Van Alexander

I'm So Lonesome I Could Cry
(Hank Williams)
Produced by Chuck Sagle
Arranged and Conducted by Don Costa

I'm Yours
(Johnny Green, E. Y. Harburg)
Conducted by Dick Stabile
Arranged by Gus Levene
Produced by Lee Gillette

I've Got My Love To Keep Me Warm
(Irving Berlin)
Produced by Lee Gillette
Conducted by Gus Levene

I've Grown Accustomed To Her Face
(Frederick Loewe, Alan Jay Lerner)
(1960 Version)
Produced by Lee Gillette
Arranged and Conducted by Nelson Riddle

I've Grown Accustomed To Her Face
(1966 Version)
Produced by Jimmy Bowen
Arranged by Ernie Freeman
Orchestra Conducted by Les Brown

If
(Tolchard Evans, Stanley J. Damerell, Robert Hargreaves)
Arranged by Lou Busch
With the Lou Busch Orchestra
Produced by Lee Gillette

If I Could Sing Like Bing
(Victor G. David)
Conducted by Dick Stabile
Arranged by Gus Levene
With the Herman McCoy Singers
Produced by Lee Gillette

If I Ever Get Back To Georgia
(Baker Knight)
Produced by Jimmy Bowen

If I Had You
(J. Shapiro, J. Campbell, R. Connelly)
(1966 Version)
Produced by Jimmy Bowen
Arranged by Ernie Freeman
Orchestra Conducted by Les Brown

If I Had You
(1978 Version)
Produced by Jimmy Bowen
Strings by Alan Moore

If I Should Love Again
(J. Fred Coots, Mickey Alpert)
Conducted by Dick Stabile
Arranged by Sid Feller
Produced by Lee Gillette

If Love Is Good To Me
(Fred Speilman, Redd Evans)
Produced by Dave Cavanaugh
Arranged and Conducted by Nelson Riddle

If This Isn't Love
(Burton Lane, "Yip" Harburg)
With the Hi-Lo's
Arranged by Warren Barker and Gene Puerling

If You Ever Get Around To Loving Me
(Baker Knight)
Produced by Jimmy Bowen
With the Jimmy Bowen Orchestra and Chorus
Arranged by Jimmie Haskell

If You Knew Susie
(B. G. DeSylva, Joseph Meyer)
Produced by Jimmy Bowen

If You Were The Only Girl
(Ayer, Grey)
Produced by Jimmy Bowen

Imagination
(Jimmy Van Heusen, Johnny Burke)
Produced by Lee Gillette
Arranged and Conducted by Nelson Riddle

In A Little Spanish Town
(Wayne, Lewis, Young)
Arranged and Conducted by Don Costa

In Love Up To My Heart
(Chester Lester)
Produced by Jimmy Bowen
Strings Arranged by Al DeLory and Alan Moore

In Napoli
(Carmen Vitale, Robert Mellin)
Conducted by Dick Stabile
Produced by Lee Gillette

In The Chapel In The Moonlight
(Billy Hill)
Produced by Jimmy Bowen
Arranged and Conducted by Ernie Freeman

In The Cool, Cool, Cool Of The Evening
(Johnny Mercer, Hoagy Carmichael)
Dick Stabile Orchestra
Produced by Lee Gillette

In The Misty Moonlight
(Cindy Walker)
Produced by Jimmy Bowen
Arranged by Ernie Freeman

Innamorata
(Jack Brooks, Harry Warren)
Conducted by Dick Stabile
Produced by Lee Gillette

Invisible Tears
(Ned and Sue Miller)
Produced by Jimmy Bowen
Arranged and Conducted by Ernie Freeman
With the Jimmy Bowen Orchestra and Chorus

Is It True What They Say About Dixie
(Irving Caeser, Sammy Lerner, Gerald Marks)
Produced by Voyle Gilmore
Arranged by Dave Cavanaugh
With Dick Stabile's Dixie Cats

It Just Happened That Way
(Fred Carter, Jr.)
Produced by Jimmy Bowen
Arranged by Ernie Freeman

It Keeps Right On A-Hurtin
(Johnny Tillotson)
Produced by Jimmy Bowen
Arranged by Glen D. Hardin
With the Jimmy Bowen Orchestra and Chorus

It Looks Like Love
(Sammy Fain, Paul Francis Webster)
Orchestra Conducted by Gus Levene
Produced by Lee Gillette

It Takes So Long To Say Goodbye
(Larry Shay, Haven Gillespie)
Gus Levene Orchestra
Produced by Lee Gillette

It Won't Cool Off
(Sammy Cahn, Ken Lane)
Produced by Lee Gillette
Conducted by Gus Levene

It's A Good Day
(Peggy Lee, David Barbour)
Produced by Jimmy Bowen
Arranged by Van Alexander

It's Easy To Remember
(Richard Rodgers, Lorenz Hart)
Arranged and Conducted by Gus Levene
Produced by Lee Gillette

It's Magic
(Jule Styne, Sammy Cahn)
Produced by Jimmy Bowen
Strings by Alan Moore

It's The Talk Of The Town
(Livingston, Symes, Neiburg)
Produced by Jimmy Bowen
Arranged by Ernie Freeman
Orchestra Conducted by Les Brown

It's 1200 Miles From Palm Springs To Texas
(Ray Ryan, Sammy Cahn, James Van Heusen)

Jingle Bells
(Traditional)
Produced by Jimmy Bowen

Johnny Get Your Girl
(Mann Curtis, Vic Mizzy)
Paul Weston Orchestra
Arranged by Bill Loose
Produced by Lee Gillette

June In January
(Leo Robin, Ralph Rainger)
Produced by Lee Gillette
Conducted by Gus Levene

Just A Little Bit South Of North Carolina
(Sammy Skyler, Bette Cannon, Arthur Shaftel)
Produced by Lee Gillette
Arranged by Dave Cavanaugh
With Dick Stabile's Dixie Cats

Just A Little Lovin'
(Clements, Arnold)
Produced by Jimmy Bowen
Arranged and Conducted by Marty Paich

Just Close Your Eyes
(Baum, Rotella)
Conducted by Neal Hefti

Just For Fun
(Jay Livingston, Ray Evans)
Paul Weston Orchestra
Produced by Lee Gillette

Just Friends
(Klenner, Lewis)
Produced by Jimmy Bowen
Arranged by Ernie Freeman
Orchestra Conducted by Les Brown

Just In Time
(Jule Styne, Betty Comden, Adolph Green)
(Album Version)
Produced by Lee Gillette
Arranged and Conducted by Nelson Riddle

Just In Time
(Soundtrack Version)
Produced by Lee Gillette and John Palladino
Adapted and Conducted by Andre Previn
Orchestrations by Alexander Courage and Pete King

Just Kiss Me
(Jesse Stone)
Conducted by Gus Levene
Produced by Lee Gillette

Just One More Chance
(Arthur Johnston, Sam Coslow)
Conducted by Dick Stabile
Arranged by Nelson Riddle
Produced by Lee Gillette

Just Say I Love Her
(Jack Val, Jimmy Dale, Martin Kalmanoff, Sam Ward)
Produced by Dave Cavanaugh
Conducted by Gus Levene

Just The Other Side Of Nowhere
(Kris Kristofferson)
Produced by Jimmy Bowen
Arranged by Larry Muhoberac
With the Jimmy Bowen Orchestra and Chorus

King Of The Road
(Roger Miller)
Produced by Jimmy Bowen
Arranged and Conducted by Ernie Freeman

Kiss
(Haven Gillespie, Lionel Newman)
Conducted by Dick Stabile
Arranged by Nelson Riddle
Produced by Lee Gillette

Kiss The World Goodbye
(Kris Kristofferson)
Produced by Jimmy Bowen
Arranged by Larry Muhoberac
With the Jimmy Bowen Orchestra and Chorus

L. A. Is My Home
(Jack Latimer, Jacki Altier)
Produced by Jimmy Bowen

La Giostra
(Ellstein, Manning)
Produced by Jimmy Bowen
Arranged by Gus Levene

La Paloma
(Y-Radier)
Arranged and Conducted by Don Costa

La Vie En Rose
(Louiguy, David, Piaf)
Arranged and Conducted by Neal Hefti

Lady With The Big Umbrella
(David Nelson, Danny Goodman)
Conducted by Dick Stabile
Produced by Lee Gillette

Last Roundup
(Billy Hill)
Produced by Jimmy Bowen

Last Time I Saw Paris
(Kern, Hammerstein II)
Arranged and Conducted by Neal Hefti

Lay Some Happiness On Me
(Jean Chapel, Bob Jennings)
Produced by Jimmy Bowen
Arranged by Ernie Freeman

Let It Snow, Let It Snow, Let It Snow
(Jule Styne, Sammy Cahn)
(1959 Version)
 Produced by Lee Gillette
Conducted by Gus Levene

Let It Snow, Let It Snow, Let It Snow
(1966 Version)
Produced by Jimmy Bowen

Let Me Go Lover
(Jenny Lou Carlson, Al Hill)
Orchestra and Chorus Conducted by Dick Stabile
Produced by Lee Gillette

Let Me Know
(Mitchell Tableporter)
Produced by Lee Gillette

Let Me Love You Tonight
(Rene Touzet, Mitchell Parish)
Produced by Dave Cavanaugh
Arranged and Conducted by Nelson Riddle

Let's Be Friendly
(Sammy Fain, Paul Francis Webster)
Orchestra Conducted by Gus Levene
Produced by Lee Gillette

Let's Put Out The Lights
(Herman Hupfeld)
Produced by Lee Gillette
Conducted by Frank Sinatra
Arranged by Pete King

Little Did We Know
(Peter Fadden, Matt Terry)
Conducted by Dick Stabile
Arranged by Gus Levene
Produced by Lee Gillette

Little Green Apples
(Bob Russell)
Produced by Jimmy Bowen
With the Jimmy Bowen Orchestra and Chorus
Arranged by Glen D. Hardin

Little Lovely One
(Tommy Boyce, Bobby Hart)
Produced by Jimmy Bowen
Arranged and Conducted by Bill Justis
With the Jack Halloran Singers

Little Ole Wine Drinker, Me
(Mills, Jennings)
Produced by Jimmy Bowen
Arranged by Bill Justis
Conducted by Ernie Freeman

Little Voice
(Lester, Gluck)
Produced by Jimmy Bowen
Arranged by Ernie Freeman

Long, Long Ago
(Marvin Fisher, Roy Alfred)
Conducted by Billy May
Arranged by Nelson Riddle
Produced by Lee Gillette

Look
(Bob Russell)
Conducted by Dick Stabile
Produced by Voyle Gilmore

Louise
(Richard A. Whiting, Leo Robin)

Louise
(1953 Version)
Conducted by Dick Stabile
Arranged by Gus Levene
Produced by Lee Gillette

Love Is All That Matters
(Sammy Cahn, Arthur Schwartz)
Conducted by Dick Stabile
Produced by Lee Gillette

Love, Love, Love
(McRae, Wyche, David)
Produced by Jimmy Bowen
Arranged and Conducted by Bill Justis
With the Jack Halloran Singers

Love Me, Love Me
(Vincent de Chiarra, Bill Walker)
Arranged by Gus Levene
Dick Stabile Orchestra
With the Herman McCoy Singers
Produced by Lee Gillette

Love Me, My Love
(Phil Medley, Vic Abrams)
Produced by Lee Gillette
Conducted by Gus Levene

Love Put A Song In My Heart
(Ben Peters)
Produced by Jimmy Bowen
Strings Arranged by Al DeLory and Alan Moore

Love Thy Neighbor
(M. Gordon, H. Revel)
Produced by Jimmy Bowen
Strings by Alan Moore

Love (Your Spell Is Everywhere)
(Edmund Goulding, Elsie Janis)
Produced by Dave Cavanaugh
Arranged and Conducted by Nelson Riddle

Lucky Song
(Harry Warren, Jack Brooks)
Conducted by Dick Stabile
Produced by Lee Gillette

Luna Mezzo Mare
(Paolo Citorello)
Conducted by Dick Stabile
Arranged by Sidney Schwartz
Produced by Lee Gillette

(Ma Come Bali) Bella Bimba
(Marilou Harrington, Oscar Demejo)
Conducted by Dick Stabile
Produced by Lee Gillette

Magician
(Jay Milton)
Conducted by Gus Levene
Produced by Lee Gillette

Magic Is The Moonlight
(Grever, Pasquale)
Arranged and Conducted by Don Costa

Make It Rain
(Billy Mize)
Produced by Jimmy Bowen
With the Jimmy Bowen Orchestra and Chorus
Arranged by Glen D. Hardin

37

Make The World Go Away
(Hank Cochran)
Produced by Jimmy Bowen
Arranged by Billy Strange
With the Jimmy Bowen Orchestra and Chorus

Makin' Love Ukelele Style
(Paul Weirick, Charlie Hayes)
Conducted by Gus Levene
Produced by Lee Gillette

Mama Roma
(Henry, Weiss)
Arranged and Conducted by Gus Levene

Mambo Italiano
(Bob Merrill)
Conducted by Dick Stabile
Produced by Lee Gillette

Mam'selle
(Gordon, Goulding)
Arranged and Conducted by Neal Hefti

Manana
(Peggy Lee, Dave Barbour)
Arranged and Conducted by Don Costa

Man Who Plays The Mandolino
(Alan Bergman, Marilyn Keith, Nisa Fanciulli)
Conducted by Gus Levene
Produced by Lee Gillette

Marry Me
(Les Reed, Barry Mason)
Produced by Jimmy Bowen
Arranged and Conducted by Ernie Freeman
With the Jimmy Bowen Orchestra and Chorus

Marshmallow World
(Sigman, De Rose)
Produced by Jimmy Bowen
Arranged and Conducted by Ernie Freeman

Maybe
(Allan Flynn and Frank Madden)
(Listed on some pressings as being written by George and
  Ira Gershwin)
Arranged and Conducted by Gus Levene
Produced by Lee Gillette

Meanderin'
(Cy Coben, Charles Green, George Botsford)
Conducted by Dick Stabile
Arranged by Nelson Riddle
Produced by Lee Gillette

Mean To Me
(Roy Turk, Fred E. Ahlert)
Produced by Lee Gillette
Arranged and Conducted by Nelson Riddle

Memories Are Made Of This
(Terry Gilkyson, Rich Dehr, Frank Miller)
Conducted by Dick Stabile
With the Easy Riders
Produced by Lee Gillette

Memory Lane
(Con Conrad, Larry Spier, B. G. DeSylva)

Me 'N' You 'N' The Moon
(Sammy Cahn, James Van Heusen)
Orchestra Conducted by Dick Stabile
Produced by Lee Gillette

Middle Of The Night Is My Crying Time
(Wooley)
Produced by Jimmy Bowen
Arranged and Conducted by Marty Paich

Million And One
(Yvonne Delaney)
Produced by Jimmy Bowen
Arranged and Conducted by Bill Justis

Mimi
(Richard Rodgers, Lorenz Hart)
Arranged and Conducted by Neal Hefti

Mississippi Dreamboat
(Roy Stanley, Mel Leven)
Conducted by Dick Stabile
Produced by Voyle Gilmore

Mississippi Mud
(Harry Baris)
Produced by Lee Gillette
Arranged by Dave Cavanaugh
With Dick Stabile's Dixie Cats

Mister Booze
(Sammy Cahn, James Van Heusen)
Produced by Sonny Burke
Arranged and Conducted by Nelson Riddle

Money Burns A Hole In My Pocket
(Jule Styne, Bob Hilliard)
(45 Single Version)
Arranged and Conducted by Gus Levene
Produced by Lee Gillette

Money Burns A Hole In My Pocket
(EP Version)
Arranged and Conducted by Walter Scharf

Money Is A Problem
(Nicholas Brodszky, Sammy Cahn)
Conducted by Gus Levene
Produced by Lee Gillette

Money Song
(Harold Rome)
Mario R. Armengol Orchestra
With Jerry Lewis
Produced by Lee Gillette

Muskrat Ramble
(Edward Ory, Ray Gilbert)
With Paul Weston and His Dixie Eight
Produced by Lee Gillette

My First Country Song
(Conway Twitty)
Produced by Jimmy Bowen
Strings Arranged by Al DeLory and Alan Moore
With Conway Twitty

My Guiding Star
(Jule Styne, Betty Comden, Adolph Green)
Adapted and Conducted by Andre Previn
Produced by John Palladino

My Heart Cries For You
(Sigman, Faith)
Produced by Chuck Sagle
Arranged and Conducted by Don Costa

My Heart Has Found A Home Now
(Dick Stabile, Ruth Hughes Aarons)
Conducted by Dick Stabile
Arranged by Nelson Riddle
Produced by Lee Gillette

My Heart Is An Open Book
(David, Pockriss)
Produced by Jimmy Bowen
Arranged and Conducted by Ernie Freeman

My Heart Reminds Me
(Camillo Bargoni, Al Stillman, Paul Siegel)
Produced by Dave Cavanaugh
Conducted by Gus Levene

My Melancholy Baby
(Burnett, Norton, Watson)
Produced by Jimmy Bowen

My One and Only Love
(Guy Wood, Robert Mellin)
Produced by Dave Cavanaugh
Arranged and Conducted by Nelson Riddle

My Own, My Only, My All
(Jay Livingston, Ray Evans)
Paul Weston Orchestra
Arranged by Bill Loose
Produced by Lee Gillette

My Rifle, My Pony, And Me
(Dimitri Tiomkin, Paul Francis Webster)
Orchestra Conducted by Gus Levene
Produced by Lee Gillette

My Shoes Keep Walking Back To You
(Ross, Wills)
Produced by Jimmy Bowen
Arranged and Conducted by Ernie Freeman

My Sugar's Gone
(Warren, Kent)
Produced by Jimmy Bowen
Arranged and Conducted by Marty Paich

My Woman, My Woman, My Wife
(Marty Robbins)
Produced by Jimmy Bowen
Arranged by John Bahler
With the Jimmy Bowen Orchestra and Chorus

Napoli
(Carmen Lombardo, Danny Di Minno)
Conducted by Gus Levene
Produced by Lee Gillette

Naughty Lady Of Shady Lane
(Sid Tepper, Roy C. Bennett)
Conducted by Dick Stabile
Produced by Lee Gillette

Never Before
(Mack David, Jerry Livingston)
Conducted by Dick Stabile
Arranged by Gus Levene
Produced by Lee Gillette

Nevertheless
(Bert Kalmar, Harry Ruby)
Arranged and Conducted by Gus Levene
Produced by Lee Gillette

Night Is Young and You're So Beautiful
(Dana Suesse, Billy Rose, Irving Kahal)
Hal Kanner Orchestra

Night Train To Memphis
(Beasley Smith, Marvin Hughes, Owen Bradley)
Conducted by Dick Stabile
Arranged by Nelson Riddle
Produced by Lee Gillette

Nobody But A Fool
(Bill Anderson)
Produced by Jimmy Bowen

Nobody's Baby Again
(Baker Knight)
Produced by Jimmy Bowen
Arranged by Ernie Freeman

Non Dimenticar
(P. G. Redi, Michele Galdieri, Shelly Dobbins)
Produced by Dave Cavanaugh
Conducted by Gus Levene

Not Enough Indians
(Baker Knight)
Produced by Jimmy Bowen
Arranged and Conducted by Ernie Freeman

Object of My Affection
(Pinky Tomlin, Coy Poe, Jimmie Grier)
Arranged and Conducted by Gus Levene
Produced by Lee Gillette

Off Again, On Again
(Marilyn Keith, Alan Bergman, Lew Spence)
Produced by Lee Gillette

Oh Boy, Oh Boy, Oh Boy, Oh Boy, Oh Boy
(Armando Fragna, Dorcas Cochran)
Conducted by Dick Stabile
Arranged by Nelson Riddle
Produced by Lee Gillette

Oh Marie
(Eduardo di Capua)
(1947 Version)

Oh Marie
(1952 Version)
Conducted by Dick Stabile
Arranged by Nelson Riddle
Produced by Lee Gillette

Old Bones
(John Hadley)
Produced by Jimmy Bowen
Strings Arranged by Al DeLory and Alan Moore

Old Yellow Line
(Henson, Bowen, Smith)
Produced by Jimmy Bowen
Arranged by Bill Justis
With the Jack Halloran Singers

Oldest Established Permanent Floating Crap Game In New York
(Frank Loesser)
Produced by Frank Sinatra
Arranged by Billy May
Conducted by Morris Stoloff

On An Evening In Roma
(Sandro Taccani, Umberto Bertini, Nanette Frederics)
(1959 Version)
Orchestra and Chorus Conducted by Gus Levene
Produced by Lee Gillette

On An Evening In Roma
(1962 Version)
Produced by Dave Cavanaugh
Conducted by Gus Levene

On The Street Where You Live
(Frederick Loewe, Alan Jay Lerner)
Produced by Lee Gillette
Arranged and Conducted by Nelson Riddle

On The Sunny Side Of The Street
(Dorothy Fields, Jimmy McHugh)
Produced by Jimmy Bowen

Once A Day
(Bill Anderson)
Produced by Jimmy Bowen
Arranged by Billy Strange
With the Jimmy Bowen Orchestra and Chorus

Once In A While
(Michael Edwards, Bud Green)
(1957 Version)
Arranged and Conducted by Gus Levene
Produced by Lee Gillette

Once In A While
(1978 Version)
Produced by Jimmy Bowen
Strings by Alan Moore

Once In Love With Amy
(Frank Loesser)
Produced by Lee Gillette

Once Upon A Time
(Benny Carter, John V. Moen)
Conducted by Gus Levene
Produced by Lee Gillette

One Cup Of Happiness
(Baker Knight)
Produced by Jimmy Bowen
Arranged by Jimmie Haskell
With the Jimmy Bowen Orchestra and Chorus

One Foot In Heaven
(David Roth, Ervin Drake, Frances Aycock)
Hal Kanner Orchestra

One I Love Belongs To Somebody Else
(Jones, Kahn)
Produced by Jimmy Bowen
Arranged by Ernie Freeman
Orchestra Conducted by Les Brown

One Lonely Boy
(Baker Knight)
Produced by Jimmy Bowen
Arranged and Conducted by Billy Strange

One More Time
(Al Hill, Horst Heinz Henning)
Conducted by Dick Stabile
Arranged by Gus Levene
Produced by Lee Gillette

Only Forever
(James V. Monaco, Johnny Burke)
(1957 Version)
Arranged and Conducted by Gus Levene
Produced by Lee Gillette

Only Forever
(1978 Version)
Produced by Jimmy Bowen
Strings By Alan Moore

Only Trust Your Heart
(Nicholas Brodszky, Sammy Cahn)
Orchestra and Chorus Conducted by Gus Levene
Produced by Lee Gillette

Open Up The Doghouse
(Marvin Fisher, Roy Alfred)
Conducted by Billy May
Arranged by Nelson Riddle
Produced by Lee Gillette
With Nat King Cole

(Open Up The Door) Let The Good Times In
(Torok, Redd)
Produced by Jimmy Bowen
Arranged by Bill Justis

Out In The Cold Again
(Ted Koehler, Rube Bloom)
Produced by Lee Gillette
Conducted by Gus Levene

Outta My Mind
(Lew Spence, Alan Bergman, Marilyn Keith)
Conducted by Gus Levene
Produced by Lee Gillette

Pardners
(Sammy Cahn, James Van Heusen)
Orchestra Conducted by Dick Stabile
Produced by Lee Gillette

Pardon
(Carmen Lombardo, Danny Di Minno)
Produced by Dave Cavanaugh
Conducted by Gus Levene

Party Dolls and Wine
(Joe Bob Barnhill)
Produced by Jimmy Bowen
Arranged by Larry Muhoberac
With the Jimmy Bowen Orchestra and Chorus

Peace On Earth/Silent Night
(Traditional)
Produced by Sonny Burke
Arranged and Conducted by Vic Schoen

Peddler Man
(Nicholas Brodszky, Jack Lawrence)
Conducted by Dick Stabile
Arranged by Gus Levene
Produced by Lee Gillette

Peddler's Serenade
(Jimmy Eaton, J. J. Corvo, Paul McGrane)
Conducted by Lou Busch
With the Starlighters
Produced by Lee Gillette

Pennies From Heaven
(Arthur Johnston, Johnny Burke)
Conducted by Dick Stabile
Produced by Lee Gillette

Perfect Mountain
(Gene Thomas)
Produced by Jimmy Bowen
Arranged by Ernie Freeman
With the Jimmy Bowen Orchestra and Chorus

Place In The Shade
(Baker Knight)
Produced by Jimmy Bowen
Arranged and Conducted by Ernie Freeman

Please Don't Talk About Me When I'm Gone
(Sam Stept, Sidney Clarke)
Produced by Lee Gillette
Arranged and Conducted by Nelson Riddle

Poor People Of Paris
(Lawrence, Monnot)
Arranged and Conducted by Neal Hefti

Powder Your Face With Sunshine
(Carmen Lombardo, Stanley Rochinski)
Paul Weston Orchestra
Produced by Lee Gillette

Pretty As A Picture
(Johnny Anz)
Conducted by Dick Stabile
Arranged by Gus Levene
Produced by Lee Gillette

Pretty Baby
(Egbert Van Alstyne, Tony Jackson, Gus Kahn)
Arranged and Conducted by Gus Levene
Produced by Lee Gillette

Pride
(Walker, Stanton)
Produced by Jimmy Bowen
Arranged and Conducted by Ernie Freeman

Professor, Professor
(Gene De Paul, Sammy Cahn)
Conducted by Gus Levene
Produced by Lee Gillette

Promise Her Anything
(Roy Alfred)
Conducted by Gus Levene
Produced by Lee Gillette

Rain
(Eugene Ford)
Paul Weston Orchestra
Produced by Lee Gillette

Rainbows Are Back In Style
(Dave Burgess)
Produced by Jimmy Bowen
Arranged and Conducted by Ernie Freeman

Raindrops Keep Falling On My Head
(Burt Bacharach, Hal David)
Produced by Jimmy Bowen
Arranged and Conducted by Ernie Freeman
With the Jimmy Bowen Orchestra and Chorus

Raining In My Heart
(Boudleaux Bryant, Felice Bryant)
Produced by Jimmy Bowen
Arranged and Conducted by Ernie Freeman
With the Jimmy Bowen Orchestra and Chorus

Ramblin' Rose
(Noel and Joe Sherman)
Produced by Jimmy Bowen
Arranged by Van Alexander

Red Roses For A Blue Lady
(Tepper, Bennett)
Produced by Jimmy Bowen
Arranged and Conducted by Ernie Freeman

Red Sails In The Sunset
(Kimmy Kennedy, Hugh Williams)
Produced by Jimmy Bowen

Relax-Ay-Voo
(Sammy Cahn, Arthur Schwartz)
Conducted by Dick Stabile
Produced by Lee Gillette

Release Me
(Miller, Williams, Yount)
Produced by Jimmy Bowen
Conducted by Ernie Freeman
Arranged by H. B. Barnum

(Remember Me) I'm The One Who Loves You
(Stuart Hamblen)
Produced by Jimmy Bowen
Arranged and Conducted by Ernie Freeman

Return To Me
(Carmen Lombardo, Danny Di Minno)
(1958 Version)
Orchestra and Chorus Conducted by Gus Levene
Produced by Lee Gillette

Return To Me
(1961 Version)
Produced by Dave Cavanaugh
Conducted by Gus Levene

Ridin' Into Love
(Dino N. Crocetti, Louis Yule Brown, Mack Gray)
Conducted by Dick Stabile
Produced by Lee Gillette

Right Kind Of Woman
(Baker Knight)
Produced by Jimmy Bowen
Arranged by Larry Muhoberac
With the Jimmy Bowen Orchestra and Chorus

Rio Bravo
(Dimitri Tiomkin, Paul Francis Webster)
Orchestra Conducted by Gus Levene
Produced by Lee Gillette

River Seine
(Roberts, Holt, LaFarge)
Arranged and Conducted by Neal Hefti

Rockin' Alone In An Old Rockin Chair
(Miller)
Produced by Jimmy Bowen
Arranged and Conducted by Marty Paich

Room Full Of Roses
(Spencer)
Produced by Chuck Sagle
Arranged and Conducted by Don Costa

Rudolph The Red-Nosed Reindeer
(Johnny Marks)
Produced by Lee Gillette
Conducted by Gus Levene

Sailor's Polka
(Mack David, Jerry Livingston)
Arranged and conducted by Dick Stabile
Produced by Lee Gillette

Sam's Song
(Elliott, Quadling)
Conducted by Billy May
Produced by Sammy Cahn and Jimmy Van Heusen
With Sammy Davis, Jr.

Santa Lucia
(Neapolitan Folk Song)

Second Chance
(Guy Wood, Ben Raleigh)
Conducted by Dick Stabile
Arranged by Nelson Riddle
Produced by Lee Gillette

Second Hand Rose
(Howard)
Produced by Jimmy Bowen
Arranged and Conducted by Marty Paich

Send Me Some Lovin'
(Price, Marascalco)
Produced by Jimmy Bowen
Arranged and Conducted by Ernie Freeman

Send Me The Pillow You Dream On
(Hank Locklin)
Produced by Jimmy Bowen
Arranged and Conducted by Ernie Freeman

Senza Fine
(Paoli, Wilder)
Produced by Jimmy Bowen
Neal Hefti Orchestra

Shades
(Lee Hazlewood)
Produced by Jimmy Bowen
Arranged and Conducted by Billy Strange

She's A Little Bit Country
(Harlan Howard)
Produced by Jimmy Bowen
Arranged and Conducted by Ernie Freeman
With the Jimmy Bowen Orchestra and Chorus

Shoulder To Shoulder
(Dallas Frazier)
Produced by Jimmy Bowen
Strings Arranged by Al DeLory and Alan Moore

Shutters and Boards
(Audie Murphy, Scott Turner)
Produced by Chuck Sagle
Arranged and Conducted by Don Costa

Side By Side
(Harry Woods)
Produced by Jimmy Bowen

Siesta Fiesta
(Barkan, Raleigh)
Produced by Jimmy Bowen

Silent Night
(Traditional)
Produced by Jimmy Bowen

Silver Bells
(Jay Livingston, Ray Evans)
Produced by Jimmy Bowen

Simpatico
(Sammy Cahn, Arthur Schwartz)
Conducted by Dick Stabile
Produced by Lee Gillette

Since I Met You Baby
(Ivory Joe Hunter)
Produced by Jimmy Bowen
Strings by Al DeLory and Alan Moore

Singing The Blues
(Endsley)
Produced by Chuck Sagle
Arranged and Conducted by Don Costa

Sleep Warm
(Marilyn Keith, Alan Bergman, Lew Spence)
Produced by Lee Gillette
Conducted by Frank Sinatra
Arranged by Pete King

Sleepy Time Gal
(Auge Lorenzo, Richard A. Whiting, J. R. Alden, Raymond B. Egan)
(1957 Version)
Arranged and Conducted by Gus Levene
Produced by Lee Gillette

Sleepy Time Gal
(1959 Version)
Produced by Lee Gillette
Conducted by Frank Sinatra
Arranged by Pete King

Small Exception Of Me
(Tony Hatch, Jackie Trent)
Produced by Jimmy Bowen
Arranged by Larry Muhoberac
With the Jimmy Bowen Orchestra and Chorus

Smile
(Charles Chaplin, John Turner, Geoffrey Parsons)
(1964 Version)
Produced by Jimmy Bowen

Smile
(1973 Version)
Produced by Jimmy Bowen
Arranged by Van Alexander

Snap Your Fingers
(Martin, Lanetis)
Produced by Jimmy Bowen
Arranged and Conducted by Bill Justis
With the Jack Halloran Singers

Sneaky Little Side Of Me
(Baker Knight)
Produced by Jimmy Bowen
Arranged by Jimmie Haskell
With the Jimmy Bowen Orchestra and Chorus

So Long Baby
(Gene Cross)
Produced by Jimmy Bowen
Arranged by Ernie Freeman

Sogni D'Oro
(Lew Spence, Marilyn Keith, Alan Bergman)
Conducted by Gus Levene
Produced by Lee Gillette

Solitaire
(King Guion, Renee Borek, Carl Nutter)
Arranged and Conducted by Dick Stabile
Produced by Lee Gillette

Somebody Loves You
(Peter de Rose and Charles Tobias)
(Listed on some pressings as being written by Gershwin, DeSylva,
 MacDonald)
Produced by Dave Cavanaugh
Arranged and Conducted by Nelson Riddle

Someday
(Jimmy Hodges)
Produced by Lee Gillette
Arranged and Conducted by Nelson Riddle

Somewhere There's A Someone
(Baker Knight)
Produced by Jimmy Bowen
Arranged by Ernie Freeman

Sophia
(George and Ira Gershwin)
Produced by Jimmy Bowen
Arranged and Conducted by Ernie Freeman

South Of The Border
(Jimmy Kennedy, Michael Carr)
(1962 Version)
Arranged and Conducted by Don Costa

South Of The Border
(1966 Version)
Produced by Jimmy Bowen

Sparklin' Eyes
(Shirley Wolfe, Sy Soloway)
Conducted by Nelson Riddle
Produced by Lee Gillette

S'posin
(Denniker, Razaf)
Produced by Jimmy Bowen
Arranged by Ernie Freeman
Conducted by Les Brown

Standing On The Corner
(Frank Loesser)
Dick Stabile Orchestra and Chorus
Produced by Voyle Gilmore

55

Story Of Life
(Anna Sosenko, Stella Unger, Fred Spielman)
Produced by Kent Larsen
Nelson Riddle Orchestra

Street Of Love
(Dino Crocetti, Louis Yule Brown)
Conducted by Dick Stabile
Produced by Lee Gillette

Style
(Sammy Cahn, James Van Heusen)
Produced by Sonny Burke
Arranged and Conducted by Nelson Riddle
With Frank Sinatra and Bing Crosby

Sun Is Shining
(D. Deal, C. Deal)
Produced by Jimmy Bowen
With the Jimmy Bowen Orchestra and Chorus
Arranged by Glen D. Hardin

Sway
(Pablo Beltran Ruiz, Norman Gimbel)
Conducted by Dick Stabile
Arranged by Gus Levene
Produced by Lee Gillette

Sweet, Sweet Lovable You
(Dick Glasser)
Produced by Jimmy Bowen

Sweetheart
(Barry and Maurice Gibb)
Produced by Jimmy Bowen
Arranged and Conducted by Ernie Freeman
With the Jimmy Bowen Orchestra and Chorus

Sweetheart Of Sigma Chi
(Byron D. Stokes, Dudleigh Vernor)
Nat Brandwynne Orchestra

Take Good Care Of Her
(Warren, Kent)
Produced by Jimmy Bowen
Arranged and Conducted by Marty Paich

Take Me
(Bloom, David)
Produced by Jimmy Bowen
Arranged by Gus Levene

Take Me In Your Arms
(Adapted by Joe Lilley)
Produced by Dave Cavanaugh
Conducted by Gus Levene

Take These Chains From My Heart
(Rose, Heath)
Produced by Jimmy Bowen
Arranged and Conducted by Ernie Freeman

Tangerine
(Schertz, Inger, Mercer)
Arranged and Conducted by Don Costa

Tarra Ta-Larra Ta-Lar
(Marty Symes, Johnny Farrow)
Produced by Lee Gillette

Ten Thousand Bedrooms
(Nicholas Brodszky, Sammy Cahn)
Conducted by Gus Levene
Produced by Lee Gillette

Terrible, Tangled Web
(Billy Mize)
Produced by Jimmy Bowen

Test Of Time
(Jimmy Van Huesen, Sammy Cahn)
Conducted by Dick Stabile
Produced by Lee Gillette

That Certain Party
(Gus Kahn, Walter Donaldson, Dean Martin, Jerry Lewis)
With Mario R. Armengol Orchestra
With Jerry Lewis
Produced by Lee Gillette

That Lucky Old Sun
(Haven Gillespie, Beasley Smith)
Paul Weston Orchestra
Produced by Lee Gillette

That Old Clock On The Wall
(Ken Lane, Irving Taylor)
Produced by Jimmy Bowen
Arranged by Ernie Freeman

That Old Gang Of Mine
(M. Dixon, R. Henderson, B. Rose)
Produced by Jimmy Bowen
Strings by Alan Moore

That Old Time Feeling
(Baker Knight)
Produced by Jimmy Bowen
Arranged and Conducted by Ernie Freeman

That's All I Want From You
(Fritz Rutter)
Orchestra and Chorus Conducted by Dick Stabile
Produced by Lee Gillette

That's Amore
(Harry Warren, Jack Brooks)
Arranged by Gus Levene
Dick Stabile Orchestra
Produced by Lee Gillette

That's What I Like
(Jule Styne, Bob Hilliard)
(45 RPM Version)
Conducted by Dick Stabile
Arranged by Gus Levene
Produced by Lee Gillette

That's What I Like
(EP Version)
Arranged and Conducted by Walter Scharf

That's When I See The Blues
(Belew, Blake, Stevenson)
Produced by Jimmy Bowen
Arranged and Conducted by Ernie Freeman

There's My Lover
(Sid Lippman, Sylvia Dee)
Conducted by Dick Stabile
Arranged by Nelson Riddle
Produced by Lee Gillette

There's No Tomorrow
(Eduardo Di Capua, Al Hoffman, Leo Corday, Leon Carr)
Produced by Dave Cavanaugh
Conducted by Gus Levene

The Wind, The Wind
(Sammy Cahn, Jimmy Van Heusen)
Orchestra Conducted by Dick Stabile
Produced by Lee Gillette

Things
(Bobby Darin)
(1962 Version)
Produced by Chuck Sagle
Arranged and Conducted by Don Costa

Things
(1967 Version)
(With Nancy Sinatra)
Produced by Billy Strange

Things We Did Last Summer
(Jule Styne, Sammy Cahn)
(1959 Version)
Produced by Lee Gillette
Conducted by Gus Levene

Things We Did Last Summer
(1966 Version)
Produced by Jimmy Bowen
Arranged by Ernie Freeman
Conducted by Les Brown

Think About Me
(Lewis, Williams, Harrison)
Produced by Jimmy Bowen
Arranged by Ernie Freeman

Thirty More Miles To San Diego
(Casey Anderson)
Produced by Jimmy Bowen
Arranged by Bill Justis

3 Wishes
(Jack Elliott, Harold Spina)
Paul Weston Orchestra
With the Martingales
Produced by Lee Gillette

Tie A Yellow Ribbon
(Larry Brown, Irwin Levine)
Produced by Jimmy Bowen
Arranged by Ernie Freeman

Tik-A-Tee, Tik-A-Tay
(Andre, Feola, Lama)
Conducted by Neal Hefti

'Til I Find You
(Katy Estes, Anita Kerr)
Conducted by Dick Stabile
Arranged by Nelson Riddle
Produced by Lee Gillette

Tips Of My Fingers
(Bill Anderson)
Produced by Jimmy Bowen
Arranged by Glen D. Hardin
With the Jimmy Bowen Orchestra and Chorus

Today Is Not The Day
(Mary Taylor)
Produced by Jimmy Bowen

Together Again
(Buck Owens)
Produced by Jimmy Bowen
Arranged by Billy Strange
With the Jimmy Bowen Orchestra and Chorus

Tonda Wanda Hoy
(Mack David, Jerry Livingston)
Conducted by Lou Busch
With the Starlighters
Produced by Lee Gillette

Tracks Of My Tears
(Marv Tarplin, William Moore, William Robinson)
Produced by Dino Martin and Billy Hinsche
Arranged by Dino Martin,William Hinsche, and Al Capps

Tricche Tracche
(Phil Tuminello)
Conducted by Gus Levene
Produced by Lee Gillette

True Love
(Cole Porter)
Produced by Lee Gillette
Arranged and Conducted by Nelson Riddle

Try Again
(Otto Kollman, Johnny May)
Conducted by Dick Stabile
Arranged by Gus Levene
Produced by Lee Gillette

Turn The World Around
(Ben Peters)
Produced by Jimmy Bowen
Arranged by Glen D. Hardin
With the Jimmy Bowen Orchestra and Chorus

Turn To Me
(Larry Kusik, Eddie Snyder)
Produced by Jimmy Bowen
Conducted by Ernie Freeman
Arranged by Bill Justis

Tu Sei Bella, Signorina
(Danny Thomas)
Conducted by Gus Levene
Produced by Lee Gillette

Twilight On The Trail
(Sidney Mitchell, Louis Alter)
Produced by Jimmy Bowen
Strings by Alan Moore

Two Loves Have I
(Vincent Scotto, Georges Koger, Henri Eugene Varna, Harry Trivers,
   Jack Murray)
Produced by Dave Cavanaugh
Arranged and Conducted by Nelson Riddle

Two Sleepy People
(Frank Loesser, Hoagy Carmichael)
Conducted by Dick Stabile
Produced by Lee Gillette

Under The Bridges Of Paris
(Vincent Scatto, Doris Cochran)
Conducted by Dick Stabile
Produced by Lee Gillette

Until The Real Thing Comes Along
(Mann Holiner, Saul Chaplin, Alberta Nichols, Sammy Cahn,
   L. E. Freeman)
Produced by Lee Gillette
Arranged and Conducted by Nelson Riddle

Until
(Sylvia Dee, Sid Lippman, Salve D'Esposito)
Arranged and Conducted by Dick Stabile
Produced by Lee Gillette

Via Veneto
(Schwab)
Arranged and Conducted by Gus Levene

Vieni Su
(Johnny Cola)
(1949 Version)
Paul Weston Orchestra
Produced by Lee Gillette

Vieni Su
(1962 Version)
Produced by Dave Cavanaugh
Conducted by Gus Levene

Volare
(Domenico Modugno, Milgliacci, Mitchell Parish)
Orchestra Conducted by Gus Levene
Produced by Lee Gillette

Waiting For The Robert E. Lee
(Lewis F. Muir, L. Wolfe Gilbert)
Produced by Lee Gillette
Arranged by Dave Cavanaugh
With Dick Stabile's Dixie Cats

Walk On By
(K. Hayes)
Produced by Jimmy Bowen
Arranged and Conducted by Ernie Freeman

Walkin' My Baby Back Home
(Roy Turk, Fred Ahlert)

Wallpaper Roses
(Spina, Robertson)
Produced by Jimmy Bowen
Arranged and Conducted by Ernie Freeman

Watching The World Go By
(Jean Senn, Sunny Skyler)
Dick Stabile Orchestra
Produced by Lee Gillette

Way Down Yonder In New Orleans
(Henry Creamer, Turner Layton)
Produced by Lee Gillette
Arranged by Dave Cavanaugh
With Dick Stabile's Dixie Cats

We Never Talk Much
(Sammy Cahn, Nicholas Brodszky)
Dick Stabile Orchestra
Arranged by Billy May
Produced by Lee Gillette

We Open In Venice
(Cole Porter)
Produced by Frank Sinatra
Arranged by Billy May
Conducted by Morris Stoloff
With Frank Sinatra and Sammy Davis, Jr.

We'll Sing In The Sunshine
(Gale Garnett)
Produced by Jimmy Bowen
Arranged by Ernie Freeman

Wedding Bells
(Claude Boone)
Produced by Jimmy Bowen
Arranged and Conducted by Ernie Freeman

Welcome To My Heart
(Bert Kaempfert, Rehbein, Pockriss, Vance)
Produced by Jimmy Bowen
Arranged and Conducted by Ernie Freeman

Welcome To My World
(Winkler, Hathcock)
Produced by Jimmy Bowen
Arranged and Conducted by Ernie Freeman

Wham! Bam! Thank You Ma'am!
(Hank Penny)
Conducted by Lou Busch
With the Starlighters
Produced by Lee Gillette

What A Difference A Day Made
(Grever, Adams)
Arranged and Conducted by Don Costa

What Can I Say After I Say I'm Sorry
(Donaldson, Lyman)
Produced by Jimmy Bowen
Arranged by Ernie Freeman
Orchestra Conducted by Les Brown

What Could Be More Beautiful
(Sid Lippman, Hector Marchese)
Conducted by Dick Stabile
Arranged by Gus Levene
Produced by Lee Gillette

What's Yesterday
(Peter Andreoli, Tony Bruno, Vincent Poncia, Jr.)
Produced by Jimmy Bowen
Arranged by Larry Muhoberac
With the Jimmy Bowen Orchestra and Chorus

When It's Sleepy Time Down South
(Leon and Otis Rene, Clarence Muse)
Produced by Lee Gillette
Arranged by Matty Matlock
With Dick Stabile's Dixie Cats

When The Red, Red Robin Comes Bob, Bob, Bobbin' Along
(Harry Woods)
Produced by Jimmy Bowen
Arranged by Van Alexander

When You Pretend
(Harry Warren, Jack Brooks)
Conducted by Dick Stabile
Produced by Lee Gillette

When You're Smiling
(Larry Shay, Mark Fisher, Joe Goodwin)
Conducted by Dick Stabile
Arranged by Nelson Riddle
Produced by Lee Gillette

Where Can I Go Without You
(Victor Young, Peggy Lee)
Dick Stabile Orchestra
Produced by Lee Gillette

Where The Blue And Lonely Go
(Warren, Verissimo, Silva, Sagle)
Produced by Jimmy Bowen
With the Jimmy Bowen Orchestra and Chorus
Arranged by Glen D. Hardin

Which Way Did My Heart Go
(Gene Carroll, Rose, Sid Wayne)
Nat Brandwynne Orchestra

White Christmas
(Irving Berlin)
(1959 Version)
Produced by Lee Gillette
Conducted by Gus Levene

White Christmas
(1966 Version)
Produced by Jimmy Bowen

Who Was That Lady?
(Sammy Cahn, James Van Heusen)
Produced by Lee Gillette
Gus Levene Orchestra

Who's Got The Action
(Jack Brooks, George Duning)
Arranged and Conducted by Chuck Sagle

Who's Sorry Now
(Ted Snyder, Harry Ruby, Bert Kalmar)
Orchestra Conducted by Lou Busch
Produced by Lee Gillette

Who's Your Little Who-Zis
(Al Goering, Ben Bernie, Walter Hirsch)
Conducted by Dick Stabile
Arranged by Nelson Riddle
Produced by Lee Gillette

Winter Romance
(Sammy Cahn, Ken Lane)
Produced by Lee Gillette
Conducted by Gus Levene

Winter Wonderland
(Felix Bernard, Dick Smith)
(1959 Version)
Produced by Lee Gillette
Conducted by Gus Levene

Winter Wonderland
(1966 Version)
Produced by Jimmy Bowen

With My Eyes Wide Open I'm Dreaming
(Mack Gordon, Harry Revel)
Dick Stabile Orchestra
Arranged by Gus Levene
Produced by Lee Gillette

Without A Word Of Warning
(M. Gordon, H. Revel)
Produced by Jimmy Bowen
Strings by Alan Moore

Won't You Surrender
(Kay Twomey, Fred Wise, Ben Weisman, Ivan Mogull)
Conducted by Dick Stabile
Arranged by Nelson Riddle
Produced by Lee Gillette

Wrap Your Troubles In Dreams
(Harry Barris, Billy Moll, Ted Koehler)
Produced by Lee Gillette
Conducted by Frank Sinatra
Arranged by Pete King

Write To Me From Naples
(Alex Alstone, Jimmy Kennedy)
Conducted by Gus Levene
Produced by Lee Gillette

You and Your Beautiful Eyes
(Mack David, Jerry Livingston)
Conducted by Lou Busch
Arranged by Henry Beau
Produced by Lee Gillette

You Belong To Me
(Pee Wee King, Redd Stewart, Chilton Price)
Dick Stabile Orchestra
Produced by Lee Gillette

You Better Move On
(Arthur Alexander)
Produced by Jimmy Bowen
Arranged by Ernie Freeman

You Can't Love 'Em All
(Jimmy Van Heusen, Sammy Cahn)
Orchestra and Chorus Conducted by Gus Levene
Produced by Lee Gillette

You I Love
(Sammy Cahn, Nicholas Brodszky)
Conducted by Gus Levene
Produced by Lee Gillette

You Look So Familiar
(Harry Warren, Jack Brooks)
Conducted by Dick Stabile
Produced by Lee Gillette

You Made Me Love You
(Joseph McCarthy, James V. Monaco)
Produced by Jimmy Bowen
Arranged by Van Alexander

You Was
(Sonny Burke, Paul Francis Webster)
Paul Weston Orchestra
Produced by Lee Gillette
With Peggy Lee

You Were Made For Love
(Ralph Freed, Grace Saxon)
Gus Levene Orchestra
Produced by Lee Gillette

You'll Always Be The One I Love
(Skylar, Freeman)
Produced by Jimmy Bowen
Arranged and Conducted by Ernie Freeman

You're Breaking My Heart
(Pat Genaro, Sunny Skylar)
Produced by Dave Cavanaugh
Conducted by Gus Levene

You're Nobody 'Til Somebody Loves You
(Russ Morgan, Larry Stock, James Cavanaugh)
(1960 Version)
Produced by Lee Gillette
Arranged and Conducted by Nelson Riddle

You're Nobody 'Til Somebody Loves You
(1964 Version)
Produced by Jimmy Bowen
Arranged and Conducted by Ernie Freeman

You're The Best Thing That Ever Happened To Me
(Jim Wetherly)
Produced by Jimmy Bowen
Arranged by Ernie Freeman

You're The Reason I'm In Love
(J. Morrow)
Produced by Jimmy Bowen
Arranged and Conducted by Bill Justis
With the Jack Halloran Singers

You're The Right One
(Jack Brooks, Harry Warren)
Conducted by Dick Stabile
Produced by Lee Gillette

You've Got Me Crying Again
(Isham Jones, Charles Newman)
Arranged and Conducted by Gus Levene
Produced by Lee Gillette

You've Still Got A Place In My Heart
(Leon Payne)
(LP Version)
Produced by Jimmy Bowen

You've Still Got A Place In My Heart
(45 Version)
Produced by Jimmy Bowen
Arranged by Glen D. Hardin

Young and Foolish
(Albert Hague, Arnold B. Horwith)
Conducted by Dick Stabile
Produced by Lee Gillette

Your Other Love
(Doc Pomus, Mort Shuman)
Produced by Jimmy Bowen

Zing-A Zing-A Boom
(Black, Out e Ze Maria, Glen Moore)
Paul Weston Orchestra
Produced by Lee Gillette

Chapter 2

Recording Sessions

The following is a chronological listing of Dean Martin's recording sessions from 1946 to 1985. The format is as follows: date, studio, time, musicians, master number, take number, title, single/EP release number, LP/CD release number. All studios are located in Los Angeles unless indicated.

July 1946
Personnel: Nat Brandwynne (piano) and his Orchestra

2035A	Which Way Did My Heart Go	2035
2035X	All Of Me	2035
2036A	I Got The Sun In The Morning	2036
2036X	Sweetheart of Sigma Chi	2036

October 1947
WOR Studios, NY
Personnel: Jerry Jerome Orchestra (Cliff White: guitar; Cedric Wallace: bass; Cozy Cole: drums; Jimmy Rivers: piano; Johnny Mince: clarinet)

3142	Oh Marie	1088	5936
		705	1310
3143	Walking My Baby Back Home	1088	5936
		705	1310
		27	

November 1947
Personnel: Unknown

3229		Santa Lucia	1116 705 27	5936
3230		Hold Me	1116 705 27	5936 1310
3231		Memory Lane		5936
3232		Louise	27	5936

November 1947 (?)
Personnel: Hal Kanner Orchestra

124A		One Foot In Heaven	124	
124B		The Night Is Young And You're So Beautiful	124	

September 13, 1948
(Music Tracks Recorded September 9, 1948)
Personnel: Mario R. Armengol Orchestra

3494	4	The Money Song (With Jerry Lewis)	15249	113
3495	4 (M) 1 (V)	That Certain Party (With Jerry Lewis)	15249	91633 113

November 22, 1948
Personnel: Unknown

3550	2	Tarra Ta-Larra Ta-Lar	15329	
3600	2	Once In Love With Amy	15329	3057 2001

December 14, 1948
Personnel: Unknown

| 3587 | 10 (M) | You Was (With Peggy Lee) | 15349 | 98409 |
| | 4 (V) | | | 113 |

December 17, 1948
(Music Tracks Recorded December 15, 1948)
Personnel: Paul Weston Orchestra

3805	11(M)	Powder Your Face With Sunshine	15351	91633
	4 (V)			98409
				113
3806	2	Absence Makes The Heart Grow Fonder	15351	3136
3807		The Gal Who's Got My Heart	UNRELEASED	
		{Orchestration Only; No Vocals Recorded}		

January 26, 1949
Radio Records
2 PM-5 PM
Personnel: George Van Eps: guitar; John Ryan: bass; Nick Fatool: drums;
Milton Raskin: piano; Lenny Hartman: saxophone; Herbert Haymer:
saxophone; Hank Lawson: saxophone; Matty Matlock: saxophone; Fred
Stulce: saxophone; Carl Loeffler: trombone; William Schaefer: trombone;
Allan Thompson: trombone; Charles Griffin: trumpet; George Seaberg:
trumpet; Zeke Zarchy: trumpet

3906	2	Have A Little Sympathy	15395
3907	2	Johnny Get Your Girl	15395

March 9, 1949
Radio Records
2 PM-5 PM
Personnel: George Van Eps: guitar; John Ryan: bass; Nick Fatool: drums;
Milton Raskin: piano; May Cambern: harp; Artmut Kafton: cello; Joseph
Saxon: cello; Maurice Perlmutter: viola; Paul Robyn: viola; Raymond Cerf:
violin; Sam Cytron: violin; George Kast: violin; Murray Kellner: violin;
Sam Middleman: violin; Paul Nero: violin; Raoul Poliakin: violin; Julius
Schachter: violin; Paul Shure: violin; Lenny Hartman: saxophone; Herbert
Haymer: saxophone; Hank Lawson: saxophone; Matty Matlock: saxophone;
Fred Stulce: saxophone; William Schaefer: trombone; Allan Thompson:
trombone; Ziggy Elman: trumpet; Irving Goodman: trumpet; Zeke Zarchy:
trumpet

4089	1 (M) 3 (V)	Dreamy Old New England Moon (With the Martingales)	549	98409
4090	2	Three Wishes (With the Martingales)	549	

June 20, 1949
Personnel: Paul Weston Orchestra

4520	2	Just For Fun	691	113
4558	3	My Own, My Only, My All	691	

August 12, 1949
Capitol Studios
8 PM-11 PM
Personnel: George Van Eps: guitar; John Ryan: bass; Nick Fatool: drums;
Milton Raskin: piano; Sam Cytron: violin; George Kast: violin; Dan Lube:
violin; Samuel Middleman: violin; Raoul Poliakin: violin; Felix Slatkin:
violin; Morty Friedman: saxophone; Lenny Hartman: saxophone; Hank
Lawson: saxophone; Matty Matlock: saxophone; Fred Stulce: saxophone;
Ziggy Elman: trumpet

4873	5	That Lucky Old Sun	726	3057 2001 434 5234
4874	5	Vieni Su	726	

March 3, 1950
Capitol Studios
8:30 PM-Midnight
Personnel: George Van Eps: guitar; John Ryan: bass; Nick Fatool: drums;
Milton Raskin: piano; Hank Lawson: saxophone; Matty Matlock:
saxophone; Edward Miller: saxophone; Jack Stacey: saxophone; Fred
Stulce: saxophone; Robert McGarity: trombone; William Schaefer:
trombone; Allan Thompson: trombone; Ziggy Elman: trumpet; Clyde
Hurley: trumpet; George Seaberg: trumpet

5604	4	Rain	937	3136 5235
5605	4	Zing-A Zing-A Boom	937	

5606	2	I'm Gonna Paper All My Walls With Your Love Letters	948	5036 94306 98409
5607	6	Muskrat Ramble	948	94306

March 28, 1950
Capitol Studios
1:30 PM-4:30 PM
Personnel: George Van Eps: guitar; Larry Breen: bass; Nick Fatool: drums; Milton Raskin: piano; Matty Matlock: clarinet; Edward Miller: saxophone; Fred Stulce: saxophone; Robert McGarity: trombone; Clyde Hurley, Jr.: trumpet

5662	2	I Don't Care If The Sun Don't Shine	981	94306
5699	2	Choo'N Gum	981	
5606	3	Be Honest With Me	1002	3057 2001 434 94306
5607	3	I Still Get A Thrill Thinking Of You	1002	3057 2001 434

April 27, 1950
Capitol Studios
6:30 PM-10 PM
Personnel: George Van Eps: guitar; John Ryan: bass; Nick Fatool: drums; Jack Turner: drums; Milton Raskin: piano; Matty Matlock: clarinet; Edward Miller: saxophone; Robert McGarity: trombone; Clyde Hurley, Jr.: trumpet

5919	2	Bye Bye Blackbird	1052	94306
5920	6	Happy Feet	1052	94306

April 28, 1950
Capitol Studios
6 PM-9 PM
Personnel: Al Hendrickson: guitar; John Ryan: bass; Nick Fatool: drums; Jack Turner: drums; Milton Raskin: piano; Frank Messina: accordion; Hank Lawson: saxophone; Matty Matlock: saxophone; Fred Stulce: saxophone;

Edward Miller: saxophone; Eddie Kusby: trombone; Robert McGarity: trombone; Ziggy Elman: trumpet; Clyde Hurley, Jr.: trumpet; Mannie Klein: trumpet

5923	3	Baby Obey Me	1028	
5924	3	I'll Always Love You	1028	5036
			1682	3175
				494
				8115
				91633
				1100
				106526
				98409
				8371
				8259
				113
				17761
5925	3	Darktown Strutter's Ball		94306
5926		Rockabye Your Baby With A Dixie Melody	UNRELEASED	

(Note: The master to this track has been lost.)

July 6, 1950
Capitol Studios
1 PM-4:30 PM
Personnel: Barney Kessel: guitar; Harry Babasin: bass; Milton Holland: drums; Arnold Ross: piano; Robert McGarity: trombone; Collen Satterwhite: trombone; Marion Childers, Jr.: trumpet; Ray Linn: trumpet; George Seaberg: trumpet; Skeets Herfurt: woodwinds; Jerome Kasper: woodwinds; Julkes Kinsler: woodwinds; Ted Romersa: woodwinds

6311	3	I'm In Love With You (With Margaret Whiting)	1160	113
6312	5	Don't Rock The Boat, Dear (With Margaret Whiting)	1160	113

July 31, 1950
Capitol Studios
8 PM-11:30 PM
Personnel: Allan Reuss: guitar; Phil Stephens: bass; Nick Fatool: drums; Frank Messina: accordion; Edwin Cole: piano; Heinie Beau: clarinet; Morty Friedman: saxophone; Hoyt Bohannon: trombone; Eddie Kusby: trombone; Robert McGarity: trombone; Clyde Hurley, Jr.: trumpet

6467	3	Tonda Wanda Hoy (With the Starlighters)	1358	
6468	4	Who's Sorry Now (With the Starlighters)	1458	3057 2001 434 5235
6469	4	Wham! Bam! Thank You, Ma'am! (With the Starlighters)	1139	
6470	4	Peddler's Serenade (With the Starlighters)	1139	

December 2, 1950
Capitol Studios
7:15 PM-11:15 PM
Personnel: George Van Eps: guitar; Phil Stephens: bass; Nick Fatool: drums; Stanley Ellison: accordion; George Greeley: piano; Cy Bernard: cello; Kurt Reher: cello; Harry Bluestone: violin; Mischa Russell: violin; Felix Slatkin: violin; Marshall Sosson: violin; Skeets Herfurt: saxophone; Jerome Kasper: saxophone; Jules Kinsler: saxophone; Ted Romersa: saxophone; Robert McGarity: trombone; Ziggy Elman: trumpet

6886	4	If	1342	3057 2001 434 5233 91633 8259 113
6887	6	Beside You (With the Starlighters)	1458	5059
6888	7	I Love The Way You Say Goodnight (With the Starlighters)	1342	5036 3175 494
6889	15	You And Your Beautiful Eyes (With the Starlighters)	1358	

April 9, 1951
Capitol Studios
4 PM-8:30 PM
Personnel: Allan Reuss: guitar; Morty Corb: bass; Ray Toland: drums; Ernest
Hughes: piano; William Hamilton, Jr.: saxophone; Robert Lawson:
saxophone; Ed Rosa: saxophone; Joe Stabile: saxophone; Si Zentner:
trombone; Ralph Muzillo: trumpet; Uan Rasey: trumpet; Joe Triscari:
trumpet; Ziggy Elman: trumpet

7324	8	We Never Talk Much (With Helen O'Connell)	1575	
7325	5	How D'Ya Like Your Eggs In The Morning? (With Helen O'Connell)	1575	113
7326	5	In The Cool, Cool, Cool Of The Evening	1703	3136 5231
7327	9	Bonne Nuit	1703	

June 20, 1951
New York City
Personnel: Unknown

7254	9	Luna Mezzo Mare	1724 481	
7255	13	Pennies From Heaven		5018 3136 5235
7256	7	Go Go Go Go	1724	

August 29, 1951
Capitol Studios
8 PM-11 PM
Personnel: Allan Reuss: guitar; Morty Corb: bass; Ray Toland: drums; Lou
Brown: piano; Reuben Marcus: viola; Ed Bergman: violin; John DeVoogt:
violin; Anatol Kaminsky: violin; Armond Kaproff: violin; Joe Livote: violin;
Dan Lube: violin; Jerry Reisler: violin; Don Cole: horn; Vincent DeRosa:
horn; Jack Aiken: saxophone; Robert Lawson: saxophone; Ed Rosa:
saxophone; Joe Stabile: saxophone; Harold Steinfeld: saxophone

7478	7	Aw C'mon	1797
7479	10	Hangin' Around With You	1797

7480	5	Solitaire	1817	2815
				2212
				98409

| 7481 | 10 | My Heart Has Found A Home Now | 1938 | |

September 15, 1951
Capitol Studios
7:30 PM-10:30 PM
Personnel: Vincent Terri: guitar; Morty Corb: bass; Ray Toland: drums; Lou
    Brown; piano; Jack Aiken: saxophone; Robert Lawson: saxophone; Ed
    Rosa: saxophone; Joe Stabile: saxophone; Harold Steinfeld: saxophone; Ray
    Heath: trombone; Joe Howard: trombone; Robert Lawson: trombone; Jerry
    Rose: trombone; Virgil Evans: trumpet; Ray Linn: trumpet; George Seaberg:
    trumpet

| 7973 | 5 | (Ma Come Bali) Bella Bimba | 1811 | |

| 9020 | 6 | Sailor's Polka | 1901 | |

| 9021 | 9 | I Ran All The Way Home | 1817 | 5059 |

| 9022 | 7 | Meanderin' | 1811 | |

November 5, 1951
Capitol Studios
7 PM-11 PM
Personnel: Jack Marshall: guitar; Vincent Terri: guitar; Norman Seelig: bass;
    Ray Toland: drums; Lou Brown: piano; Alan Harshman: viola; Armond
    Kaproff: viola; Louis Kievman: viola; Alex Beller: violin; Emil Briano:
    violin; John DeVoogt: violin; Nick Pisani: violin; Joseph Quadri: violin;
    Gerald Vinci: violin; Vincent DeRosa: horn; Jack Aiken: saxophone; Robert
    Lawson: saxophone; Ed Rosa: saxophone; Joe Stabile: saxophone

| 9282 | 7 | As You Are | 1921 | |

| 9292 | 9 | Blue Smoke | 1885 | |

| 9293 | 8 | Night Train To Memphis | 1885 | 98409 |

November 19, 1951
Capitol Studios
6 PM-9:30 PM

Personnel: Jack Rose: guitar; Vincent Terri: guitar; Norman Seelig: bass; Ray
 Toland: drums; Lou Brown: piano; Alan Harshman: viola; Armond Kaproff:
 viola; Louis Kievman: viola; John Augustine: violin; Victor Bay: violin;
 Emil Briano: violin; John DeVoogt: violin; Nick Pisani: violin; Gerald
 Vinci: violin; Vincent DeRosa: horn; Jack Aiken: saxophone; Robert
 Lawson: saxophone; Ed Rosa: saxophone; Joe Stabile: saxophone; Virgil
 Evans: trumpet

9318	6	Until You Love Someone	1938	5036
				3175
				494

| 9319 | 6 | Oh Boy, Oh Boy, Oh Boy, Oh Boy, Oh Boy | 1921 | |

9320	6	Come Back To Sorrento	2140	T-401
			481	494
			DU 2601	2601
				2815
				3175
				378
				2941
				46627
				1029
				1100
				77383
				37571
				8371
				113

| 9321 | 6 | Never Before | 1901 | 5059 |
| | | | | 113 |

January 21, 1952
Capitol Studios
9 PM-1 AM

Personnel: Alvino Rey: guitar; Morty Corb: bass; Ray Toland: drums; Lou
 Brown: piano; Armond Kaproff: cello; Cy Bernard: cello; Ann Stockton:
 harp; Alan Harshman: viola; Reuben Marcus: viola; John Augustine: violin;
 Victor Bay: violin; Emil Briano: violin; John DeVoogt: violin; Nick Pisani:
 violin; Joseph Quadri: violin; Jerry Reisler: violin; Gerald Vinci: violin; Ted
 Nash: woodwind

9625	5	When You're Smiling	1975	450
				2001
				2941
				T-401
				1047
				3089
				5233
				8115
				1100
				106526
				113
9626	7	Won't You Surrender	2001	
9627	7	All I Have To Give You	1975	5036
9628	13	Pretty As A Picture	2001	98409

April 8, 1952
Capitol Studios
8 PM-12:45 AM
Personnel: Vincent Terri: guitar; Norman Seelig: bass; Ray Toland: drums; Lou Brown: piano; Armond Kaproff: cello; Alan Harshman: viola; Louis Kievman: viola; John Augustine: violin; Emil Briano: violin; John DeVoogt: violin; Nick Pisani: violin; Vincent DeRosa: horn; Jack Aiken: saxophone; Lenny Hartman: saxophone; Robert Lawson: saxophone; Ed Rosa: saxophone; Ray Heath: trombone; Si Zentner: trombone; Pete Candoli: trumpet; Virgil Evans: trumpet; Manuel Stevens: trumpet

9871	8	Oh Marie	2140	T-401
			481	3136
			1682	2941
				98409
				113
9937	3	I Passed Your House Tonight	2071	
9938	17	Bet-I-Cha	2071	

June 12, 1952
Capitol Studios
8 PM-11:30 PM
Personnel: Dick Stabile: saxophone; Vincent Terri: guitar; Norman Seelig: bass;
    Ray Toland: drums; Lou Brown: piano; Armond Kaproff: cello; Ray
    Kramer: cello; Helen Bliss: harp; Alan Harshman: viola; Louis Kievman:
    viola; John Augustine: violin; Harry Bluestone: violin; Emil Briano: violin;
    John DeVoogt: violin; Nick Pisani: violin; Joseph Quadri: violin

10272	6	You Belong To Me	2165	91633
				8155
				1177
				8304
				1100
				77383
				9389
				106526
				98409
				8371
				8259
				113
				17761
10273	9/10	Kiss	2319	
10274	21	What Could Be More Beautiful	2319	5059
10275	8	Little Did We Know	2378	5018
				3136

July 2, 1952
Capitol Studios
7 PM-10 PM and 11:30 PM-1:30 AM
Personnel: Vincent Terri: guitar; Morty Corb: bass; Frank Carlson: drums; Ray
    Toland: drums; Lou Brown: piano; Robert Lawson: saxophone; Ed Rosa:
    saxophone; Victor Hamman: trombone; Eddie Kusby: trombone; Carl
    Loeffler: trombone; William Haeferen: trombone; Virgil Evans: trumpet;
    Micky Mangano: trumpet; Manuel Stevens: trumpet; Joe Triscari: trumpet

10173	6	Susan		98409
10174	12	Peanut Vendor		98409
10352	5	I Know A Dream When I See One	2240	

10353	17	Second Chance	2240	5059
10354	2	Hominy Grits	2165	94306

November 20, 1952
Capitol Studios
5 PM-8 PM and 9:30 PM-12:30 AM
Personnel: Vincent Terri: guitar; Norman Seelig: bass; Ray Toland: drums; Lou
  Brown: piano; Armond Kaproff: cello; Elias Friede: cello; Helen Bliss:
  harp; Louis Kievman: viola; Reuben Marcus: viola; John Augustine: violin;
  Victor Bay: violin; John DeVoogt: violin; Nick Pisani: violin; Joseph
  Quadri: violin; Mischa Russell: violin

10836	5	Just One More Chance	450
			2001
			2941
			401
			3089
			1177
10837	5	I'm Yours	434
			2001
			2815
			2941
			401
			3057
			2601
			46627
			37571
			98409
10838	2	With My Eyes Wide Open I'm Dreaming	401
			2941
			5233
			1177
			8371

10839	6	There's My Lover	2378	5059
10840	2	A Girl Named Mary and a Boy Named Bill	401	

Personnel: Vincent Terri: guitar; Morty Corb: bass; Ray Toland: drums; Lou
  Brown: piano; Jules Jacob: saxophone; Robert Lawson: saxophone; Ted
  Nash: saxophone; Ed Rosa: saxophone; Ray Heath: trombone; Eddie
  Kusby: trombone; Paul Tanner: trombone; Conrad Gozzo: trumpet; Joe
  Dolney: trumpet; James Roselli: trumpet

10841	4	Louise	401
			2941
			5232
			29385
			113

10842	2	Who's Your Little Who-Zis	401
			2941

10843	7	I Feel Like A Feather In The Breeze	401
			2941
			5233

10844	11	I Feel A Song Coming On	401
			2941
			5232

May 4, 1953
Capitol Studios
8 PM-Midnight
Personnel: Vincent Terri: guitar; Phil Stephens: bass; Ray Toland: drums; Bernie
    Mattinson: xylophone; Lou Brown: piano; Armond Kaproff: cello; Al
    Harshman: viola; Louis Kievman: viola; Leonard Atkins: violin; Victor Bay:
    violin; John DeVoogt: violin; Carl LaMagna: violin; Nick Pisani: violin;
    Gerald Vinci: violin

11532	11	'Til I Find You	2485	5059

11533	2	Don't You Remember?	2555	2051
			939	2815
				1047
				3307

11534	10	If I Could Sing Like Bing	2555	113

11535	5	Love Me, Love Me	2485	2815
				2212
				91633
				8259
				113

August 13, 1953
Capitol Studios
8:30 PM-12:30 AM
Personnel: Vincent Terri: guitar; Phil Stephens: bass; Ray Toland: drums; Max
    Gralnick: marimbas; Ralph Hansell: marimbas; Jack Rose: marimbas;
    Ernest Felice: accordion; Buddy Cole: piano; Jack Dumont: saxophone;
    Chuck Gentry: saxophone; Herman Gunkler: saxophone; David Harris:
    saxophone; Marshall Cram: trombone; Joe Howard: trombone; George
    Roberts: trombone; Elmer Smithers: trombone; Virgil Evans: trumpet;
    Maurice Harris: trumpet; Manuel Stevens: trumpet; Charles Zimmerman:
    trumpet

11693	2	I Want You	Music Track Only	
11694	6	That's Amore	2589	2815
			481	378
			1580	2941
			DU 2601	T-401
			6011	2601
			44153	5235
			9058	46627
			6076	8115
				91633
				1029
				1100
				10733
				9098
				77383
				9389
				106526
				37571
				98409
				8371
				8259
				113
				17761
				11243
11695	5	You're The Right One	2589	113
11697	7	I'd Cry Like A Baby		98409

September 3, 1953
New York City
Personnel: Unknown

20187	8	Where Can I Go Without You		5006
20188	4	If I Should Love Again	2640	5036

October 5, 1953
Capitol Studios
7 PM-11 PM
Personnel: Bob Bain: guitar; Joe Comfort: bass; Frankie Carlson: drums; Alvin Stoller: drums; Walter Weschler: piano; Cy Bernard: cello; Eleanor Slatkin: cello; Ann Stockton: harp; Paul Robyn: viola; David Sterkin: viola; Victor Bay: violin; Alex Beller: violin; Harry Bluestone: violin; Walter Edelstein: violin; Nathan Ross: violin; Mischa Russell: violin; Paul Shure: violin; Felix Slatkin: violin; Gerald Vinci: violin; Harry Klee: saxophone; Champ Webb: saxophone; Milton Bernhart: trombone; Pullman Pederson: trombone; George Roberts: trombone; Si Zentner: trombone; Pete Candoli: trumpet

11943	8	Christmas Blues	2640	93115
				57688

December 23, 1953
Capitol Studios
8:30 PM-?
Personnel: Bob Bain: guitar; Jack Marshall: guitar; Phil Stephens: bass; Ray Toland: drums; Lou Brown: piano; Armond Kaproff: cello; Al Harshman: viola; Louis Kievman: viola; Leonard Atkins: violin; Victor Bay: violin; John DeVoogt: violin; Dan Lube: violin; Nick Pisani: violin; Gerald Vinci: violin; Chuck Gentry: saxophone; Skeets Herfurt: saxophone; Ed Rosa: saxophone; Champ Webb: saxophone; Marshall Cram: trombone; Ray Heath: trombone; Tom Pederson: trombone; Pete Candoli: trumpet; Conrad Gozzo: trumpet; Micky Mangano: trumpet

12132	4	Hey, Brother, Pour The Wine	2749	2815
			2037	2212
				2601
				378
				46627
				37571
				98409
12133	4	Money Burns A Hole In My Pocket	2818	91633
				113

12134	6	Moments Like This		15781
12135	1	That's What I Like	2870	2815
				2212
				5059

December 24, 1953
Capitol Studios
Personnel: Bob Bain: guitar; Jack Marshall: guitar; Phil Stephens: bass; Ray
    Toland: drums; Lou Brown: piano; Armond Kaproff: cello; Al Harshman:
    viola; Louis Kievman: viola; Leonard Atkins: violin; Victor Bay: violin;
    John DeVoogt: violin; Dan Lube: violin; Nick Pisani: violin; Gerald Vinci:
    violin; Chuck Gentry: saxophone; Skeets Herfurt: saxophone; Ed Rosa:
    saxophone; Champ Webb: saxophone; Marshall Cram: trombone; Ray
    Heath: trombone; Tom Pederson: trombone; Pete Candoli: trumpet; Conrad
    Gozzo: trumpet; Micky Mangano: trumpet

11696	2	I Want You		5018
11697	11	I'd Cry Like A Baby	2749	91633
			2038	

April 20, 1954
Paramount Studios
Personnel: Walter Scharf Orchestra

12811	How Do You Speak To An Angel	533	113
12813	Ev'ry Street's A Boulevard In Old New York (With Jerry Lewis)	533	98409 113
12841	Money Burns A Hole In My Pocket	533	
12842	That's What I Like	533	

April 22, 1954
Capitol Studios
1:30 PM-6 PM
Personnel: Laurindo Almeida: guitar; Vincent Terri: guitar; Norman Seelig:
    bass; Joe Guerrero: drums; Milton Holland: drums; Ray Toland: drums;
    Ernest Felice: accordion; Lou Brown: piano; Armond Kaproff: cello; Louis
    Kievman: viola; Joe Reilich: viola; Harry Bluestone: violin; Emil Briano:
    violin; John DeVoogt: violin; Nick Pisani: violin; Joseph Quadri: violin;
    Darrell Terwilliger: violin; Jack Aiken: saxophone; Robert Lawson:
    saxophone; Ed Rosa: saxophone; Joe Stabile: saxophone; Virgil Evans:
    trumpet; Maurice Harris: trumpet; Mannie Klein: trumpet

12571	6	Belle From Barcelona	3011	
12572	6	Sway	2818	2815
				2601
				2212
				378
				8115
				46627
				91633
				1029
				77383
				9389
				106526
				37571
				8371
				113
				17761
12573	8	Under The Bridges Of Paris	3036	
12574	12/13	Peddler Man	2870	2815
				2212
12608	6	I Never Had A Chance		15781

August 12, 1954
Capitol Studios
1 PM-4:30 PM
Personnel: Bob Bain: guitar; Vincent Terri: guitar; Norman Seelig: bass; Ray
    Toland: drums; Ernest Felice: accordion; Lou Brown: piano; Virgil Gates:
    cello; Louis Kievman: viola; Irving Manning: viola; Harry Bluestone:
    violin; Sam Caplan: violin; John DeVoogt: violin; Harold Lieberman: violin;
    Dan Lube: violin; Darrell Terwilliger: violin; Jack Aiken: saxophone;
    Robert Lawson: saxophone; Ed Rosa: saxophone; Joe Stabile: saxophone;
    Ryland Weston: saxophone; Virgil Evans: trumpet; Conrad Gozzo: trumpet;
    Ralph Muzillo: trumpet

12908	5	Confused	3011	
12909	4	One More Time	2911	5059
12910	6	Try Again	2911	2815
				2212
				5059

12911	5	I'll Gladly Make The Same Mistake Again	3988	98409
			1027	

September 7, 1954
Capitol Studios
2 PM-5 PM
Personnel: John Collins: guitar; Charles Harris: bass; Lee Young: drums; Lou
Brown: piano; Chuck Gentry: saxophone; Skeets Herfurt: saxophone; Harry
Klee: saxophone; Ted Nash: saxophone; Eddie Kusby: trombone; Murray
McEachern: trombone; Si Zentner: trombone; John Best: trumpet; Conrad
Gozzo: trumpet; Mannie Klein: trumpet

13011	13	Open Up The Doghouse	2985	98409
		(With Nat King Cole)		113
				11243

13012	2	Long, Long Ago	2985	113
		(With Nat King Cole)		

September 30, 1954
Capitol Studios
2 PM-5 PM
Personnel: Vincent Terri: guitar; Phil Stephens: bass; Ray Toland: drums; Lou
Brown: piano; Gus Bivona: saxophone; Edward Miller: saxophone; Joe
Howard: trombone; Tom Pederson: trombone; Lloyd Ulyate: trombone;
Virgil Evans: trumpet; Mannie Klein: trumpet; Charles Teagarden: trumpet

12705		Mississippi Mud	576
			2333
			5230
			94306

12717	2	When It's Sleepy Time Down South	576
			2333
			5235
			94306

13029	6	Carolina Moon	576
			2333
			94306

13030		Way Down Yonder In New Orleans	576
			2333
			5230
			94306

October 7, 1954
Capitol Studios
2:30 PM-5:30 PM
Personnel: Vincent Terri: guitar; Phil Stephens: bass; Ray Toland: drums; Lou
Brown: piano; Gus Bivona: saxophone; Edward Miller: saxophone; Joe
Howard: trombone; Tom Pederson: trombone; George Roberts: trombone;
Lloyd Ulyate: trombone; Virgil Evans: trumpet; Mannie Klein: trumpet;
Charles Teagarden: trumpet

13050	8	Just A Little Bit South Of North Carolina	576
			2333
			94306
13051	6	Georgia On My Mind	576
			2333
			94306
			1177
			8371
			113
13056	14	Waiting For The Robert E. Lee	576
			2333
			94306
13057	3	Carolina In The Morning	576
			2333
			5235
			94306
			984095
			113

November 26, 1954
Capitol Studios
8 PM-12:30 AM
Personnel: Laurindo Almeida: guitar; Jack Marshall: guitar; Morty Corb: bass;
Frankie Carlson: drums; Frank Flynn: marimba; Chico Guerrero: drums;
Ray Toland: drums; Ernest Felice: accordion; Lou Brown: piano; Virgil
Cates: cello; Al Harshman: viola; Irving Manning: viola; Harry Bluestone:
violin; Sam Caplin: violin; John DeVoogt: violin; Sebastian Mercurto:
violin; Nick Pisani: violin; Gerald Vinci: violin; Ed Rosa: saxophone;
Milton Bernhart: trombone; Hoyt Bohannon: trombone; Eddie Kusby:
trombone

13208	3	Let Me Go Lover	9123	3136
13209	5	Naughty Lady Of Shady Lane	9123	

13210	10	Mambo Italiano	9123	113
13211	8	That's All I Want From You	9123	3136
				5234

December 28, 1954
Capitol Studios
4 PM-7:30 PM
Personnel: Bob Bain: guitar; Joe Comfort: bass; Frankie Carlson: percussion;
Frank Flynn: percussion; Lou Singer: percussion; Lou Brown: piano; Cy
Bernard: cello; Victor Gottlieb: cello; Kathryn Julye: harp; Victor Bay:
violin; Alex Beller: violin; Walter Edelstein: violin; Henry Hill: violin; Felix
Slatkin: violin; Paul Sure: violin; Gerald Vinci: violin; John Cave: horn;
Vincent DeRosa: horn; Morris Bercov: saxophone; Alex Gershunoff:
saxophone; Champ Webb: saxophone; Harold Diner: trombone; Pullman
Pederson: trombone; William Schaefer: trombone; Bob Graham, Jack
Gruberman, John Gustavson, Gene Lanham, Ray Linn, Jr., Gil Mershon,
Bill Reeve, Robert Wacker: vocal chorus

13387	7	Young And Foolish	3036	3136
				5230
				113

February 4, 1955
Capitol Studios
3 PM-6 PM
Personnel: Vincent Terri: guitar; Phil Stephens: bass; Ray Toland: drums; Lou
Brown: piano; Charles Butler: saxophone; Ed Rosa: saxophone; Milton
Bernhart: trombone; Joe Howard: trombone; George Roberts: trombone;
Lloyd Ulyate: trombone; Virgil Evans: trumpet; Conrad Gozzo: trumpet;
Charles Teagarden: trumpet

13548		Basin Street Blues		576
				2333
				5231
				94306
				113
13549	4	Is It True What They Say About Dixie		576
				2333
				94306
				113
13550	6	Dinah		576
				94306

13551		Alabamy Bound		576
				2333
				5234
				94306

April 20, 1955
Capitol Studios
8:30 PM-12:30 AM
Personnel: Laurindo Almeida: guitar; Jack Marshall: guitar; Norman Seelig: bass; Frankie Carlson: drums; Bernie Mattison: drums; Ray Toland: drums; Lou Brown: piano; Ernest Felice: accordion; Virgil Gates: cello; Armond Kaproff: cello; Irving Manning: viola; Jack Rose: viola; Leonard Atkins: violin; Sam Caplin: violin; John DeVoogt: violin; Harold Lieberman: violin; Sebastian Mercurto: violin; Nick Pisani: violin; Darrell Terwilliger: violin; Gerald Vinci: violin; Ed Rosa: saxophone; Milton Bernhart: trombone; Ray Heath: trombone; Joe Howard: trombone; George Roberts: trombone; Betty Allan, Lee Gotch, Gene Lanham, Dorothy McCarthy, Gil Mershon, Robert Wacker, Norma Zimmer: vocal chorus

13722	4	Chee Chee-Oo Chee		15781
13723	10	In Napoli	3238	5018
				98409
13724	8	Lady With The Big Umbrella	3352	
13725	5	I Like Them All	3238	
			701	

April 25, 1955
Capitol Studios
9 PM-12:30 AM
Personnel: Jack Marshall: guitar; Vincent Terry: guitar; Norman Seelig: bass; Frankie Carlson: drums; Bernie Mattison: drums; Ray Toland: drums; Lou Brown: piano; Edwin Carver: accordion; Virgil Gates: cello; Armond Kaproff: cello; Louis Kievman: viola; Irving Manning: viola; Sam Caplin: violin; John DeVoogt: violin; Harold Lieberman: violin; Dan Lube: violin; Sebastian Mercurto: violin; Nick Pisani: violin; Darrell Terwilliger: violin; Gerald Vinci: violin; Ed Rosa: saxophone; Ray Heath: trombone; Joe Howard: trombone; Eddie Kusby: trombone; George Roberts: trombone; Gene Lanham, Gil Mershon, Betty Noyes, Virginia Rees, Robert Wacker, Norma Zimmer: vocal chorus

13741	10	Chee Chee-Oo Chee	3133	5018
13742	5	Love Is All That Matters	3153	5036

92

13743	7	Simpatico	3153	

13744	3	Ridin' Into Love	3133	
			701	

April 27, 1955
Capitol Studios
2 PM-5:30 PM
Personnel: Vincent Terry: guitar; Norman Seelig: bass; Bernie Mattison: drums; Ray Toland: drums; Lou Brown: piano; Jack Aiken: saxophone; Leo Anthony: saxophone; Ed Rosa: saxophone; Babe Russin: saxophone; Joe Stabile: saxophone; Ray Heath: trombone; Joe Howard: trombone; Eddie Kusby: trombone; John Best: trumpet; Virgil Evans: trumpet; Anthony Terran: trumpet

13749	15	Relax-Ay-Voo (With Line Renaud)	3196	

13750	8	Two Sleepy People (With Line Renaud)	3196	

13751	5	I Know Your Mother Loves You		15781

October 28, 1955
Capitol Studios
2 PM-5 PM
Personnel: Jack Marshall: guitar; Phil Stephens: bass; Ray Toland: drums; Frank Flynn: xylophone; Lou Brown: piano; Leonard Atkins: violin; Emil Briano: violin; Sam Caplin: violin; John DeVoogt: violin; Dan Lube: violin; Nick Pisani: violin; Joseph Quadri: violin; Darrell Terwilliger: violin; Gerald Vinci: violin; Ed Rosa: saxophone; Babe Russin: saxophone; Joe Stabile: saxophone; Jack Teagarden: trombone; Virgil Evans: trumpet; Conrad Gozzo: trumpet; Ray Linn, Jr.: trumpet; Anthony Terran: trumpet; Easy Riders-Terry Gilkyson, Richard Dehr, Frank Miller: vocal chorus

14643	9	Memories Are Made Of This	3295	378
		(With the Easy Riders)	701	2601
			1580	2212
			DU 2601	8115
			6011	5232
			9058	46627
			6076	91633
				1029
				1100
				10733
				77383
				9389
				1065265

				37571
				98409
				8371
				8259
				113
				17761
				11243
14658	4	Change Of Heart	3295	
			701	
14668	10	When You Pretend		15781
14669	7	Lucky Song	702	

November 18, 1955
Capitol Studios
2 PM-5 PM
Personnel: Jack Marshall: guitar; Norman Seelig: bass; John Cyr: drums; Ray Toland: drums; Lou Brown: piano; Leonard Atkins: violin; Emil Briano: violin; Sam Caplan: violin; John DeVoogt: violin; Dan Lube: violin; Carl LaMagna: violin; Nick Pisani: violin; Joseph Quadri: violin; Gerald Vinci: violin; Emmett Callen: saxophone; Ed Rosa: saxophone; Joe Stabile: saxophone; Joe Howard: trombone; Virgil Evans: trumpet; Conrad Gozzo: trumpet; Maurice Harris: trumpet; Anthony Terran: trumpet

14707	5	When You Pretend	702	450
				2001
				3089
14708	5	You Look So Familiar	702	450
				2001
				3089
14709	4	Innamorata	3352	450
			702	2001
				3089
				5230
				91633
				1100
				77383
				9389
				37571
				8259
				113

February 8, 1956
(Orchestration only; no vocals recorded)

15026	Children's Songs From Italy Part 1	UNRELEASED
15027	Children's Songs From Italy Part 2	UNRELEASED

March 7, 1956
Capitol Tower
5 PM-8 PM
Personnel: Jack Marshall: guitar; Speedy West: steel guitar; Norman Seelig: bass; Frankie Carlson: drums; Irving Cottler: drums; Ray Toland: drums; Dominic Frontiere: accordion; Lou Brown: piano; Ennio Bolognini: cello; Gus Levene: cello; Harold Lieberman: viola; Irving Manning: viola; Leonard Atkins: violin; Sam Caplan: violin; John DeVoogt: violin; Paul Israel: violin; Nick Pisani: violin; Darrell Terwilliger: violin; Jack Aiken: saxophone; Robert Lawson: saxophone; Ted Nash: saxophone; Joe Stabile: saxophone; Karl DeKarske: trombone; James Henderson: trombone; Joe Howard: trombone; Murray McEachern: trombone

15176	8	The Look	3577	1047
				2815
15177	14	Mississippi Dreamboat	3521	
15178	6	Standing On The Corner	3414	2051
				3307
				2815
				2212
				140
				8115
				91633
				1177
				1100
				77383
				106526
				37571
				8371
				113
				17761
15179	3	Street Of Love	3468	5036
15180	9	Watching The World Go By	3414	5235
				91633

May 15, 1956
Capitol Tower
8 PM-11 PM
Personnel: Vincent Terri: guitar; Speedy West: steel guitar; Norman Seelig: bass; John Cyr: drums; Ray Toland: drums; Lou Brown: piano; Ennio Bolognini: cello; Gus Levene: cello; Cesare Pascarella: cello; Harold Lieberman: viola; Louis Kievman: viola; Sam Caplan: violin; John DeVoogt: violin; Alexander Neiman: violin; Nick Pisani: violin; Darrell Terwilliger: violin; Gerald Vinci: violin; George Fields: harmonica; Jack Aiken: saxophone; Robert Lawson: saxophone; Ed Rosa: saxophone; Joe Stabile: saxophone; Ray Heath: trombone; James Henderson: trombone; Joe Howard: trombone

15474		Pardners (With Jerry Lewis)	752	113

May 22, 1956
Capitol Tower
8 PM-Midnight
Personnel: Vincent Terri: guitar; Norman Seelig: bass; John Cyr: drums; Ray Toland: drums; Lou Brown: piano; Armond Kaproff: cello; Ray Kramer: cello; Gus Levene: cello; Maxine Johnson: viola; Louis Kievman: viola; Emil Briano: violin; Sam Caplan: violin; John DeVoogt: violin; Dan Lube: violin; Nick Pisani: violin; Darrell Terwilliger: violin; George Fields: harmonica; Jack Aiken: saxophone; Robert Lawson: saxophone; Ed Rosa: saxophone; Joe Stabile: saxophone; Ray Heath: trombone; James Henderson: trombone; Joe Howard: trombone

15481	19	Test Of Time	3521	450
				2001
				1047
				3089
15482	7	Me 'N' You 'N' The Moon	752	
15483	13	The Wind, The Wind	752	
15484	8	I'm Gonna Steal You Away (With the Nuggets)	3468	98409

August 20, 1956
Capitol Tower
2 PM-6 PM
Personnel: Jack Marshall: guitar; Alvino Rey: guitar; Mike Rubin: bass; Norman Seelig: bass; Frankie Carlson: drums; Frank Flynn: drums; Lou Brown: piano; Cy Bernard: cello; Armond Kaproff: cello; Alvin Dinken: viola; Jack Rose: viola; Victor Bay: violin; Harry Bluestone: violin; Jacques Gasselin: violin; Mischa Russell: violin; Paul Shure: violin; Felix Slatkin: violin; Marshall Sosson: violin;

96

Gerald Vinci: violin; Skeets Herfurt: saxophone; Jules Kinsler: saxophone; Champ Webb: saxophone; Herbert Harper: trombone; Eddie Kusby: trombone; Si Zentner: trombone

15850	10	Bamboozled	3680	
15851	8	Give Me A Sign	3577	
15852	6	Captured	3648	
15853	4	I Know I Can't Forget	3604	1047

November 26, 1956
Capitol Tower
2 PM-5 PM
Personnel: Jack Marshall: guitar; Joe Comfort: bass; Frankie Carlson: drums; Geoffrey Clarkson: piano; Kurt Reher: cello; Alvin Dinken: viola; Louis Kievman: viola; Israel Baker: violin; Erno Neufeld: violin; Nick Pisani: violin; Felix Slatkin: violin; Marshall Sosson: violin; Gerald Vinci: violin; Joe Howard: trombone; Murray McEachern: trombone; Pullman Pederson: trombone; Conrad Gozzo: trumpet; Micky Mangano: trumpet; Cecil Read: trumpet; Morris Bercov: woodwinds; Chuck Gentry: woodwinds; Ted Nash: woodwinds; Wilbur Schwartz: woodwinds

16026	11	I Never Had A Chance	3718	5006
16027	4	It Looks Like Love	806	450 2001 3089
16028	4	Let's Be Friendly	806	
16029	7	Just Kiss Me	3604	

December 6, 1956
Capitol Tower
3 PM-6:30 PM
Personnel: Jack Marshall: guitar; Jack Rose: mandolin; Abe Luboff: bass; Lou Singer: drums; Fred Travers: accordion; Buddy Cole: piano; Kurt Reher: cello; Kathryn Julye: harp; Louis Kievman: viola; Victor Arno: violin; Benny Gill: violin; William Miller: violin; Joseph Pepper: violin; John Cave: horn; Vincent DeRosa: horn; Richard Perissi: horn; Alexander Gershunoff: woodwinds; Ethmer Roten: woodwinds; Champ Webb: woodwinds; James Williamson: woodwinds

16227	1	A Day In The Country	806	450
				2001
				3089

| 16228 | 7 | Hollywood Or Bust | 806 | |

| 16229 | 16 | Man Who Plays The Mandolino | 3648 | 2212 |
| | | | | 2815 |

January 28, 1957
Capitol Tower
2 PM-5:45 PM
Personnel: Alvino Rey: guitar; Vincent Terri: guitar; Joe Comfort: bass; Nick
Fatool: drums; Buddy Cole: piano; Matty Matlock: clarinet; Chuck Gentry:
saxophone; Edward Miller: saxophone; Moe Schneider: trombone; Dick
Cathcart: trumpet

16531	5	Nevertheless		849
				5235
				1177
				8304
				8371

16532	5	I Can't Give You Anything But Love	3718	450
				2001
				849
				3089
				5230
				113

16533	1	It's Easy To Remember		849
				2815
				2601
				5232
				8115
				46627
				106526
				8371
				113

16534	2	Pretty Baby		849
				140
				5232
				37571

| 16539 | 3 | Sleepy Time Gal | | 849 |

| 16540 | 2 | For You | 849 |

January 30, 1957
Capitol Tower
2:15 PM-6:45 PM
Personnel: Alvino Rey: guitar; Vincent Terri: guitar; Joe Comfort: bass; Nick
    Fatool: drums; Buddy Cole: piano; Matty Matlock: clarinet; Chuck Gentry:
    saxophone; Edward Miller: saxophone; Moe Schneider: trombone; Dick
    Cathcart: trumpet

| 16527 | 5 | Maybe | 849 |

16528	5	Once In A While	849
			5230
			1177
			8304
			1100
			8371

| 16529 | 2 | I Don't Know Why | 849 |
| | | | 1100 |

16530	5	Object Of My Affection	494
			849
			3175
			5231

| 16545 | 11 | Only Forever | 849 |
| | | | 5231 |

| 16546 | 17 | You've Got Me Crying Again | 849 |

February 5, 1957
Capitol Tower
9 PM-1:30 AM
Personnel: Bob Bain: guitar; Alvino Rey: guitar; Joe Comfort: bass; Nick
    Fatool: drums; Buddy Cole: piano; Heinie Beua: reeds; Fred Falensby:
    reeds; Skeets Herfurt: reeds; Robert Lawson: reeds; Babe Russin: reeds;
    Hoyt Bohannon: trombone; Murray McEachern: trombone; George Roberts:
    trombone; Pete Candoli: trumpet; Conrad Gozzo: trumpet; Micky Mangano:
    trumpet

| 16567 | 6 | Money Is A Problem | 840 |

16570	8	You I Love	840	494
				3175
				5036
				8259

| 16571 | 8 | 10,000 Bedrooms | 840 | |

| 16572 | 13 | Only Trust Your Heart | 3680 | 98409 |
| | | | 840 | |

May 22, 1957
Capitol Tower
2 PM-5:30 PM
Personnel: Jack Rose: guitar; Vincent Terri: guitar; Joe Comfort: bass; Frankie
    Carlson: drums; Lou Singer: drums; Carl Fortina: accordion; Buddy Cole:
    piano; Heinie Beau: saxophone; Buddy Collette: saxophone; Skeets Herfurt:
    saxophone; Robert Lawson: saxophone; Murray McEachern: trombone;
    George Roberts: trombone; Lloyd Ulyate: trombone; Pete Candoli: trumpet;
    Conrad Gozzo: trumpet; Micky Mangano: trumpet

| 17073 | 6 | Beau James | 3752 | 98409 |

| 17074 | 3 | Promise Her Anything | 3787 | 1047 |

| 17075 | 10 | Tricche Tracche | 3787 | |

| 17076 | 4 | Write To Me From Naples | 3752 | 1047 |
| | | | | 2815 |

October 24, 1957
Capitol Tower
8 PM-10:45 PM
Personnel: Bob Bain: guitar; Jack Marshall: guitar; Alvino Rey: guitar; Allan
    Reuss: ukelele; Rollie Bundock: bass; Roy Harte: drums; Buddy Cole:
    piano; Ken Lane: piano

| 17707 | 10 | Good Mornin', Life | 3841 | 98409 |

| 17708 | 4 | Makin' Love Ukelele Style | 3841 | 1047 |

17716	6	Cheatin' On Me		494
				5018
				3175

January 23, 1958
Capitol Tower
2 PM-5:30 PM
Personnel: Alvino Rey: guitar; Howard Roberts: guitar; Jack Rose: guitar; Joe
 Comfort: bass; Frankie Carlson: drums; Lou Singer: drums; Domino
 Frontiere: accordion; Ken Lane: piano; Jim Arkatov: cello; Kurt Reher:
 cello; Virginia Majewski: viola; David Sterkin: viola; Victor Bay: violin;
 Kurt Dieterle: violin; Natalie Kaproff: violin; Erno Neufeld: violin; Nick
 Pisani: violin; Lou Raderman: violin; Mischa Russell: violin; Heinie Beau:
 saxophone; Chuck Gentry: saxophone; Skeets Herfurt: saxophone; Babe
 Russin: saxophone; Ray Heath: trombone; George Roberts: trombone;
 Lloyd Ulyate: trombone; Conrad Gozzo: trumpet; Micky Mangano:
 trumpet; Cecil Read: trumpet

18520	8	Return To Me	3894	2051
			939	1047
			1580	3307
			6048	8115
			6256	91633
				1029
				77383
				9389
				106526
				37571
				98409
				8371
				8259
				113
				11243
				17761
18252	5	Buona Sera	939	1047
				2815
				8371
18253	6	Forgetting You	3894	
			939	
18283	4	Tu Sei Bella, Signorina	4518	

18290	8	Angel Baby	3988	1047
			1027	8115
				91633
				1177
				106526
				8371
				8259
				17761

March 21, 1958

	8	It's 1200 Miles From Palm Springs To Texas	2160	98409

June 20, 1958
Capitol Tower
8 PM-11:30 PM
Personnel: Bob Bain: guitar; Alvino Rey: guitar; Joe Mondragon: bass; Frankie Carlson: drums; Lou Singer: drums; John Duffy: organ; Paul Smith: piano; Mahlon Clark: saxophone; Babe Russin: saxophone; Milton Bernhart: trombone; Marshall Cram: trombone; George Roberts: trombone; William Schaefer: trombone; Larry Sullivan: trumpet

19438	10	You Were Made For Love	4124	494
				3175
				5036
19439	7	Once Upon A Time	4065	
19440	8	Outta My Mind	4028	
			1027	
19441	5	Magician	4065	

July 14, 1958
Capitol Tower
11:30 AM-12:30 PM
Personnel: Alton Hendrickson: guitar; Alvino Rey: guitar; Joe Mondragon: bass; Ralph Hansell: drums; Milton Holland: drums; Bernie Mattison: drums; John Duffy: organ; Ken Lane: piano; Kathryn Julye: harp

19593	11	Volare	4028	2815
			1027	378
			1580	1047
			DU 2601	2601
			6048	5234
			6256	8115
				46627
				91633
				1029
				1100
				10733
				9098
				77383
				9389
				106526
				37571
				98409
				8371
				8259
				113
				17761
				11243

September 15, 1958
Capitol Tower
9 PM-12:30 AM
Personnel: Bob Bain: guitar; Alvino Rey: guitar; Jack Rose: guitar; Abe Luboff: bass; John Cyr: drums; Lou Singer: drums; Carl Fortina: accordion; Rex Koury: piano; Ken Lane: piano; Kurt Reher: cello; Eleanor Slatkin: cello; Louis Kievman: viola; David Sterkin: viola; David Frisina: violin; Joseph Livoti: violin; Dan Lube: violin; Erno Neufeld: violin; Mischa Russell: violin; Felix Slatkin: violin; Marshall Sosson: violin; Gerald Vinci: violin

30113	7	Rio Bravo	4174	5006
30114	8	It Takes So Long To Say Goodbye	4124	5006
30115	8	On An Evening In Roma	4222	91633
				77383
				98409
				113
30116	10	My Rifle, My Pony And Me	4174	113
			1063	

October 13, 1958
Capitol Tower
10 PM-1 AM
Personnel: Al Viola: guitar; Joe Comfort: bass; Alvin Stoller: drums; Ken Lane: piano; Bill Miller: piano; Elizabeth Greensporn: cello; Ed Lustgarten: cello; Kathryn Julye: harp; Alvin Dinken: viola; Louis Kievman: viola; Victor Arno: violin; Harry Bluestone: violin; Jacques Gasselin: violin; Seymour Kramer: violin; Carl LaMagna: violin; Dan Lube: violin; Amerigo Marino: violin; Paul Shure: violin; Jack Cave: French horn; Herman Gunkler: saxophone; Dale Issenhuth: saxophone; Jules Jacobs: saxophone; Abraham Most: saxophone; Ted Nash: saxophone

30354	7	Dream	1150
			2241
			8115
			29389
			1029
			1100
			106526
			37500
			8371
30355	6	Dream A Little Dream Of Me	1150
			2241
			2297
			3465
			8115
			29389
			1029
			1177
			1100
			106526
			37500
			113
30356	10	Goodnight Sweetheart	1150
			2241
			2297
			3465
			5231
			29389
			1029
			37500

30357	4	Cuddle Up A Little Closer		1150
				2241
				2297
				3465
				5234
				29389
				37500
				113

October 14, 1958
Capitol Tower
10 PM-1 AM
Personnel: Al Viola: guitar; Joe Comfort: bass; Alvin Stoller: drums; Ken Lane: piano; Bill Miller: piano; Elizabeth Greensporn: cello; Kurt Reher: cello; Stella Castellucci: harp; Alexander Neiman: viola; Paul Robyn: viola; Victor Arno: violin; James Getzoff: violin; Dan Lube: violin; Amerigo Marino: violin; Alex Murray: violin; Erno Neufeld: violin; Paul Shure: violin; Gerald Vinci: violin; Vincent DeRosa: French horn; Herman Gunkler: saxophone; Dale Issenhuth: saxophone; Jules Jacobs: saxophone; Abraham Most: saxophone; Ted Nash: saxophone

30400	15	Sleep Warm	987	1150
				2241
				2297
				37500

30401	14	Let's Put Out The Lights		1150
				2241
				2297
				3465
				5233
				1029
				37500

30402	5	Brahms' Lullaby		1150
				2241
				2297
				3465
				5231
				37500

30403	19	Goodnight, My Love	1150
			2241
			2297
			3465
			5234
			37500

October 15, 1958
Capitol Tower
10 PM-Midnight
Personnel: Al Viola: guitar; Joe Comfort: bass; William Richmond: drums;
 Ken Lane: piano; Bill Miller: piano; Elizabeth Greensporn: cello; Eleanor
 Slatkin: cello; Kathryn Julye: harp; Alvin Dinkin: viola; Paul Robyn: viola;
 Victor Arno: violin; Dan Lube: violin; Amerigo Marino: violin; Louis
 Raderman: violin; Paul Shure: violin; Felix Slatkin: violin; Marshall
 Sosson: violin; Gerald Vinci: violin; Gus Bivona: saxophone; Dale
 Issenhuth: saxophone; Jules Jacobs: saxophone; Abraham Most: saxophone;
 Wilbur Schwartz: saxophone; Joe Howard: trombone; Murray McEachern:
 trombone; George Roberts: trombone; Frank Beach: trumpet; Conrad
 Gozzo: trumpet; D. McMichle: trumpet

30147	6	Sleepy Time Gal	1150
			2241
			2297
			3465
			5232
			29389
			1029
			37500

30148	3	Wrap Your Troubles In Dreams	1150
			2241
			2297
			3465
			5232
			29389
			1029
			37500

30149	5	All I Do Is Dream Of You	987	1150
				2241
				2297
				3465
				5233
				8115
				29389
				1029
				8304
				106526
				37500
				98409
				8371
30150	1	Hit The Road To Dreamland		1150
				2241
				2297
				3465
				5230
				29389
				1029
				37500

January 1959

		My Rifle, My Pony and Me (With Ricky Nelson)	2262

May 13, 1959
Capitol Tower
8 PM-Midnight

Personnel: Bobby Gibbons: guitar; Alvino Rey: guitar; Jack Rose: guitar; Red Callender: bass; Ralph Hansell: drums; Carl Fortina: accordion; James Rowles: piano; Armond Kaproff: cello; Eleanor Slatkin: cello; Donald Cole: viola; David Sterkin: viola; Victor Bay: violin; Kurt Dieterle: violin; Marvin Limonik: violin; Joseph Livoti: violin; Dan Lube: violin; Jerry Reisler: violin; Isadore Roman: violin; Felix Slatkin: violin; Harry Zagon: violin; Skeets Herfurt: saxophone; Jules Kinsler: saxophone; Ed Rosa: saxophone; William Ulyate: saxophone; Marshal Cram: trombone; Joe Howard: trombone; George Roberts: trombone; Lloyd Ulyate: trombone; Conrad Gozzo: trumpet; Mannie Klein: trumpet; Larry Sullivan: trumpet

31662	14	Sogni D'Oro	4472	
31663	14	Napoli		15959

31664	15	You Can't Love 'Em All	4222	434
				2001
				3057
31665	6	How Sweet It Is	4472	5018
31678	8	Off Again, On Again		5006

May 15, 1959
Capitol Tower
6:30 PM-9:30 PM
Personnel: Bobby Gibbons: guitar; Tony Rizzi: guitar; Red Callender: bass;
John Cyr: drums; Alvin Stoller: drums; James Rowles: piano; Marshal
Cram: trombone; Joe Howard: trombone; William Smiley: trombone;
Lloyd Ulyate: trombone

31691	11	Humdinger	4420	
31692	6	I Ain't Gonna Lead This Life No More	4287	434
				2001
				3057
31693	11	Love Me, My Love	4328	5006
				91633
31694	3	Buttercup Of Golden Hair	4391	

July 29, 1959
Capitol Tower
8 PM-11:30 PM
Personnel: Bobby Gibbons: guitar; Red Callender: bass; Lou Singer: drums;
James Rowles: piano; Kurt Reher: cello; Eleanor Slatkin: cello; Donald
Cole: viola; Virginia Majewski: viola; David Sterkin: viola; Victor Bay:
violin; John DeVoogt: violin; Nathan Kaproff: violin; Joseph Livoti: violin;
Dan Lube: violin; Erno Neufeld: violin; Jerry Reisler: violin; Felix Slatkin:
violin; Gerald Vinci: violin; Arnold Koblentz: oboe; Ted Nash: saxophone

32147	8	Things We Did Last Summer	1285
			2343
			91285
			93115
			29389

32148	7	Winter Wonderland		1285
				2343
				91285
				93115
				57688
32149	7	White Christmas	57889	1285
				2343
				93115
				57688
32150	4	Canadian Sunset		140
				1285
				2343
				91285
				5231
				93115
				37571

August 4, 1959
Capitol Tower
7:30 PM-11 PM
Personnel: Bobby Gibbons: guitar; Red Callender: bass; Lou Singer: drums;
    Ray Sherman: piano; Kurt Reher: cello; Eleanor Slatkin: cello; Kathryn
    Julye: harp; Donald Cole: viola; Alvin Dinkin: viola; Virginia Majewski:
    viola; Victor Bay: violin; John DeVoogt: violin; Nathan Kaproff: violin;
    Joseph Livoti: violin; Dan Lube: violin; Erno Neufeld: violin; Jerry Reisler:
    violin; Ralph Schaefer: violin; Felix Slatkin: violin; Gerald Vinci: violin;
    Arnold Koblentz: oboe; Mahlon Clark: saxophone; Skeets Herfurt:
    saxophone; Eddie Kusby: saxophone; Ronald Langinger: saxophone;
    Mannie Klein: trumpet

32161	10	A Winter's Romance	1285
			91285
			93115
			57688
32162	6	June In January	378
			1285
			2343
			2601
			91285
			5234
			93115
			46627
			29389

32163	7	It Won't Cool Off		1285
				2343
				91285
				93115
				57688

32164	8	I've Got My Love To Keep Me Warm		1285
				2343
				91285
				93115
				57688
				113

August 6, 1959
Capitol Tower
8 PM-11:30 PM
Personnel: Bobby Gibbons: guitar; Red Callender: bass; Lou Singer: drums; James Rowles: piano; Edward Ross: accordion; Kurt Reher: cello; Eleanor Slatkin: cello; Kathryn Julye: harp; Donald Cole: viola; Alvin Dinkin: viola; Virginia Majewski: viola; Israel Baker: violin; Victor Bay: violin; John DeVoogt: violin; Nathan Kaproff: violin; Joseph Livoti: violin; Dan Lube: violin; Erno Neufeld: violin; Jerry Reisler: violin; Felix Slatkin: violin; James Briggs: saxophone; Mahlon Clark: saxophone; Harry Klee: saxophone

32191	12	Out In The Cold Again		1285
				2343
				91285
				93115
				57688

32192	15	Baby It's Cold Outside		1285
				2343
				91285
				93115
				57688
				113

32193	4	Rudolph The Red-Nosed Reindeer	57889	1285
				2343
				93115
				57688

32194	15	Let It Snow, Let It Snow, Let It Snow	1285
			2343
			91285
			93115
			57688

August 31, 1959
Capitol Tower
2 PM-5 PM
Personnel: Alvino Rey: guitar; Tony Rizzi: guitar; Jack Rose: guitar; Red
   Callender: bass; Nick Fatool: drums; Ralph Hansell: drums; Carl Fortina:
   accordion; James Rowles: piano; Kurt Reher: cello; Louis Kievman: viola;
   David Sterkin: viola; Victor Bay: violin; Kurt Dieterle: violin; Benny Gill:
   violin; Nathan Kaproff: violin; Joseph Livoti: violin; Erno Neufeld: violin;
   Nick Pisani: violin; Marshall Sosson: violin; William Vandenburg: violin;
   Harry Zagon: violin; Chuck Gentry: saxophone; Skeets Herfurt: saxophone;
   Babe Russin: saxophone; Marshal Cram: trombone; Conrad Gozzo:
   trumpet; Carroll Lewis: trumpet; Micky Mangano: trumpet

32304	17	Professor, Professor	4361	
32305	4	Napoli	4361	
32306	2	Career	4287	5006
32307	5	Who Was That Lady?	4328	5018

May 9, 1960

33702	2	Do It Yourself		1435
				92060
33704	5	Better Than A Dream (With Judy Holliday)		1435
				92060
33705	2	I Met A Girl		1435
				92060
33706	5	Just In Time (With Judy Holliday)		1435
				92060
				113
33715	1	My Guiding Star	145	98409

May 9, 1960
Capitol Tower
8 PM-11 PM
Personnel: Al Hendrickson: guitar; Joe Comfort: bass; Irv Cottler: drums; Bill
   Miller: piano; Ed Lustgarten: cello; Eleanor Aller Slatkin: cello; Stanley
   Harris: viola; Paul Robyn: viola; Victor Bay: violin; Alex Beller: violin;
   Harry Bluestone: violin; Jacques Gasselin: violin; Dan Lube: violin; Gerald
   Vinci: violin; Buddy Collette: saxophone; Plas Johnson: saxophone; Harry
   Klee: saxophone; Joseph Koch: saxophone; Ronnie Lang: saxophone;
   Russell Brown: trombone; Dick Noel: trombone; Tom Pederson: trombone;
   Thomas Shepard: trombone; Pete Candoli: trumpet; Donald Fagerquist:
   trumpet; Carroll Lewis: trumpet; Shorty Sherock: trumpet

33744	4	Someday	524
			1442
			2051
			2241
			3283
			8115
			29389
			1100
			106526
33745	9	On The Street Where You Live	524
			1442
			2051
			2241
			3283
			5233
33746	8	I've Grown Accustomed To Her Face	140
			524
			1442
			2051
			2241
			3283
			5232
			8115
			8304
			57005
			1100
			106526
			37571
			8371
			113

112

33747	4	Imagination	524
			1442
			2051
			2241
			3307
			5230
			29389
			8304

May 10, 1960
Capitol Tower
8 PM-11 PM

Personnel: Al Hendrickson: guitar; Joe Comfort: bass; Alvin Stoller: drums; Bill Miller: piano; Ed Lustgarten: cello; Eleanor Slatkin: cello; Alvin Dinken: viola; Paul Robyn: viola; Victor Bay: violin; Alex Beller: violin; Dan Lube: violin; Felix Slatkin: violin; Marshall Sosson: violin; Gerald Vinci: violin; Buddy Collette: saxophone; Plas Johnson: saxophone; Harry Klee: saxophone; Joseph Koch: saxophone; Wilbur Schwartz: saxophone; Russell Brown: trombone; Dick Noel: trombone; Tom Pederson: trombone; Thomas Shepard: trombone; Pete Candoli: trumpet; Conrad Gozzo: trumpet; Carroll Lewis: trumpet; Shorty Sherock: trumpet

33804	5	Until The Real Thing Comes Along	1442
			2051
			2241
			3283
			5234
			29389
			57005
			98409

33805	4	Please Don't Talk About Me When I'm Gone	524
			1442
			2051
			2241
			3283
			5234
			29389

33806	5	You're Nobody 'Til Somebody Loves You	378
			524
			1442
			2241
			2601
			2815
			5230

				8115
				46627
				29389
				1029
				8304
				57005
				1100
				77383
				106526
				37571
				8371
				8259
				113
				17761
				11243
33807	4	Ain't That A Kick In The Head	4420	434
				2001
				3057
				91633
				98409
				11243
33808	6	Mean To Me		524
				1442
				2241
				29389
				113

May 17, 1960
Capitol Tower
8 PM-11 PM
Personnel: Al Hendrickson: guitar; Joe Comfort: bass; Alvin Stoller: drums; Bill Miller: piano; Jacques Gasselin: cello; Ed Lustgarten: cello; Eleanor Slatkin: cello; Alvin Dinken: viola; Paul Robyn: viola; Victor Arno: violin; Victor Bay: violin; Alex Beller: violin; Dan Lube: violin; Marshall Sosson: violin; Buddy Collette: saxophone; Plas Johnson: saxophone; Harry Klee: saxophone; Joseph Koch: saxophone; Wilbur Schwartz: saxophone; Russell Brown: trombone; Dick Noel: trombone; Thomas Shepard: trombone; Pete Candoli: trumpet; Carroll Lewis: trumpet; Dale McMickle: trumpet; Shorty Sherock: trumpet

33847	4	Just In Time	DU 2601	378
				4391	524
				1442
				2051

			2212
			2241
			2601
			2815
			3283
			5235
			8115
			46627
			29389
			1029
			1177
			57005
			8304
			1100
			106526
			37571
			98409
			8371
			8259
33848	2	True Love	524
			1442
			2051
			2241
			3283
			5231
			1100
			113
33849	8	Heaven Can Wait	1442
			2051
			2241
			3283
			5234
33850	3	I Can't Believe That You're In Love With Me	524
			1442
			2051
			2241
			3283
			5231
			29389
			1177
			57005

115

December 12, 1960
Capitol Tower
8:30 PM-Midnight
Personnel: Bob Bain: guitar; Bobby Gibbons: guitar; Joe Comfort: bass; Alvin
  Stoller: drums; Bill Miller: piano; Ossip Giskin: cello; Ed Lustgarten: cello;
  Eleanor Slatkin: cello; Kathryn Julye: harp; Paul Robyn: viola; Barbara
  Simon: viola; Victor Arno: violin; Israel Baker: violin; Alex Beller: violin;
  Jacques Gasselin: violin; James Getzoff: violin; Dan Lube: violin; Erno
  Neufeld: violin; Felix Slatkin: violin; Gerald Vinci: violin; Buddy Collette:
  saxophone; Harry Klee: saxophone; Joseph Koch: saxophone; Abraham Most:
  saxophone; Dick Nash: trombone; Dick Noel: trombone; Tom Pederson:
  trombone; Thomas Shepard: trombone

35075	6	The Story Of Life		15959
35076	6	Bella Bella Bambina		15959
35077	31	Giuggiola	4570	
35078	3	Sparklin' Eyes	4518	5018

December 13, 1960
Capitol Tower
8 PM-9:40 PM
Personnel: Bob Bain: guitar; Bobby Gibbons: guitar; Joe Comfort: bass; Alvin
  Stoller: drums; Bill Miller: piano; Ossip Giskin: cello; Ed Lustgarten: cello;
  Eleanor Slatkin: cello; Kathryn Julye: harp; Paul Robyn: viola; Barbara
  Simon: viola; Alex Beller: violin; James Getzoff: violin; Murray Kellner: vio-
  lin; Joseph Livoti: violin; Dan Lube: violin; Erno Neufeld: violin; Felix Slatkin:
  violin; Gerald Vinci: violin; Buddy Collette: saxophone; Harry Klee: saxophone; Joseph Koch: saxophone; Abraham Most: saxophone; Dick Noel:
  trombone; Jimmy Priddy: trombone; William Schaefer: trombone; Thomas
  Shepard: trombone

35083	8	Let Me Know	15959
35084	2	Be An Angel	15959
35085	5	Hear My Heart	15959

February 10, 1961
Capitol Tower
8 PM-11 PM
Personnel: Bobby Gibbons: guitar; Al Hendrickson: guitar; Joe Comfort: bass; Irv
  Cottler: drums; James Rowles: piano; Ossip Giskin: cello; Armond Kaproff:
  cello; George Neikrug: cello; Kathryn Julye: harp; Alvin Dinkin: viola; Barbara
  Simon: viola; Victor Arno: violin; Victor Bay: violin; Alex Beller: violin;
  George Devron: violin; David Frisina: violin; Jacques Gasselin: violin; James

Getzoff: violin; Dan Lube: violin; Erno Neufeld: violin; Paul Shure: violin; Buddy Collette: saxophone; Harry Klee: saxophone; Joseph Koch: saxophone; Wilbur Schwartz: saxophone; Dick Nash: trombone; Dick Noel: trombone; George Roberts: trombone; Thomas Shepard: trombone

35351	4	All In A Night's Work	4551	450
				2001
				3089
35352	3/6	The Story Of Life	4570	5006
35353	3/4	Giuggiola		15959
35354	5	Hear My Heart		5006
				5233

February 15, 1961
Capitol Tower
8:30 PM-11:30 PM
Personnel: Bobby Gibbons: guitar; Al Hendrickson: guitar; Joe Comfort: bass; Irv Cottler: drums; Donn Trenner: piano; Armond Kaproff: cello; Ed Lustgarten: cello; Eleanor Slatkin: cello; Kathryn Julye: harp; Alvin Dinkin: viola; Barbara Simon: viola; Victor Arno: violin; Victor Bay: violin; Alex Beller: violin; Jacques Gasselin: violin; Dan Lube: violin; Erno Neufeld: violin; Paul Shure: violin; Marshall Sosson: violin; Gerald Vinci: violin; Justin Gordon: saxophone; Joseph Koch: saxophone; Abraham Most: saxophone; Wilbur Schwartz: saxophone; George Arus: trombone; Tom Pederson: trombone; George Roberts: trombone; Thomas Shepard: trombone

35404	4	Be An Angel		5006
				98409
35405	6	Bella Bella Bambina	4551	
35406	3	Let Me Know		494
				3175
				5018

September 6, 1961
Capitol Tower
8 PM-11 PM
Personnel: Bob Bain: guitar; Al Hendrickson: guitar; Allan Reuss: guitar; Murray Shapinsky: bass; Nick Fatool: drums; Lou Singer: drums; Ken Lane: piano; Carl Fortina: accordion; Justin DiTullo: cello; Ray Kramer: cello; Ed Lustgarten: cello; Kurt Reher: cello; Ann Stockton: harp; Alvin Dinkin: viola; Al Harshman: viola; Virginia Majewski: viola; Paul Robyn:

viola; Victor Arno: violin; Israel Baker: violin; Kurt Dieterle: violin; James Getzoff: violin; Benny Gill: violin; Anatol Kaminski: violin; Nathan Kaproff: violin; Joseph Livoti: violin; Dan Lube: violin; Louis Raderman: violin; Marshall Sosson: violin; Harry Zagon: violin

36411	1	Arrivederci, Roma	SU 1659	140
				525
				1659
				2242
				2815
				5232
				56
				9098
				4563
				37571
				8371
				113
36428	3	There's No Tomorrow		1659
				2242
				2815
				1177
				56
				9098
				525
				4563
				8371
				8259
				113
36436	8	Return To Me	DU 2601	378
				525
				1659
				2242
				2601
				2815
				5232
				46627
				56
				9098
				4563
				1100
36443	2	Non Dimenticar	SU 1659	1659
				2051

				2242
				2815
				3307
				1177
				1100
				9098
				77383
				525
				4563
				98409
				8371
				113
36444	9	I Have But One Heart	SU 1659	1659
				2051
				2242
				2815
				3307
				9098
				525
				4563
				8371
				113

September 7, 1961
Capitol Tower
8 PM-11 PM

Personnel: Bob Bain: guitar; Al Hendrickson: guitar; Allan Reuss: guitar; Murray Shapinsky: bass; Nick Fatool: drums; Lou Singer: drums; Ken Lane: piano; Carl Fortina: accordion; Naoum Banditzky: cello; Justin DiTullo: cello; Armond Kaproff: cello; Ed Lustgarten: cello; Ann Stockton: harp; Alvin Dinkin: viola; Louis Kievman: viola; Virginia Majewski: viola; Paul Robyn: viola; Victor Arno: violin; Israel Baker: violin; Kurt Dieterle: violin; Jacques Gasselin: violin; Anatol Kaminski: violin; Nathan Kaproff: violin; Joseph Livoti: violin; Dan Lube: violin; Louis Raderman: violin; Mischa Russell: violin; Harry Zagon: violin

36449	6	You're Breaking My Heart	1659
			2242
			2815
			1177
			56
			1100
			9098
			525
			4563

119

				8371
				113
36450	4	On An Evening In Roma	SU 1659	1659
			EAP 1659	2242
				2815
				525
				4563
				8371
36451	7	Pardon		1659
				2242
				2815
				4563
36452	4	Just Say I Love Her	SU 1659	140
			EAP 1659	525
				1659
				2242
				2815
				8115
				1177
				1100
				9098
				106526
				4563
				37571
				8371

September 8, 1961
Capitol Tower
8 PM-11 PM
Personnel: Bob Bain: guitar; Al Hendrickson: guitar; Allan Reuss: guitar;
Murray Shapinsky: bass; Nick Fatool: drums; Lou Singer: drums; Ken
Lane: piano; Carl Fortina: accordion; Justin DiTullo: cello; Armond
Kaproff: cello; Ed Lustgarten: cello; Ray Kramer: cello; Ann Stockton:
harp; Joseph DiFiore: viola; Louis Kievman: viola; Virginia Majewski:
viola; Paul Robyn: viola; Victor Arno: violin; Israel Baker: violin; Kurt
Dieterle: violin; Jacques Gasselin: violin; James Getzoff: violin; Benny Gill:
violin; Anatol Kaminski: violin; Nathan Kaproff: violin; Joseph Livoti:
violin; Dan Lube: violin; Mischa Russell: violin; Harry Zagon: violin

36453	10	Take Me In Your Arms	SU 1659	1659
				2242
				2815
				5233
				525

				4563
				8371
36454	4	My Heart Reminds Me	EAP 1659	1659
				2242
				2815
				4563
36455	11	Vieni Su	SU 1659	140
			EAP 1659	525
				1659
				2242
				2815
				4563
				37571

December 18, 1961
Capitol Tower
5:30 PM-8:30 PM
Personnel: Tony Reyes: bass; Fred Aguirre: drums; Carlos Mejia: drums; Ramon
    Rivera: drums; Eddie Cano: piano; Ken Lane: piano; Gene Cipriano:
    saxophone; Dale Issenhuth: saxophone; Harry Klee: saxophone; Joseph
    Koch: saxophone; Wilbur Schwartz: saxophone; Carroll Lewis: trumpet;
    Henry Miranda: trumpet; Al Rojo: trumpet; Shorty Sherock: trumpet

36853	4	Love (Your Magic Spell Is Everywhere)	1702
			2242
			5230
36854	9	Cha Cha Cha D'Amour	140
			1702
			2242
			8115
			57005
			106526
36879	4	Amor	1702
			2242
			113
36887	7	Two Loves Have I	1702
			2242
			5231

December 19, 1961
Capitol Tower
8 PM-11 PM
Personnel: Al Hendrickson: guitar; Tommy Tedesco: guitar; Tony Reyes: bass;
Fred Aguirre: drums; Carlos Mejia: drums; Ramon Rivera: drums; Eddie
Cano: piano; Ken Lane: piano; Victor Gottleib: cello; Armond Kaproff:
cello; Eleanor Slatkin: cello; Alvin Dinkin: viola; Virginia Majewski: viola;
Barbara Simon: viola; Victor Arno: violin; Victor Bay: violin; Alex Beller:
violin; David Frisina: violin; James Getzoff: violin; Benny Gill: violin; Dan
Lube: violin; Erno Neufeld: violin; Nathan Ross: violin; Felix Slatkin:
violin; Harry Klee: saxophone

| 36898 | 6 | I Love You Much Too Much | 1702 |
| | | | 2242 |

| 36899 | 6 | Let Me Love You Tonight | 1702 |
| | | | 2242 |

36921	3	My One And Only Love	140
			1702
			2051
			2242
			3307
			57005
			37571
			113

36922	6	I Wish You Love	1702
			1177
			2242
			57005
			8371
			113

December 20, 1961
Capitol Tower
5:30 PM-8:30 PM
Personnel: Al Hendrickson: guitar; Tommy Tedesco: guitar; Tony Reyes: bass;
Fred Aguirre: drums; Carlos Mejia: drums; Ramon Rivera: drums; Eddie
Cano: piano; Ken Lane: piano; Gene Cipriano: saxophone; Justin Gordon:
saxophone; Harry Klee: saxophone; Wilbur Schwartz: saxophone; Carroll
Lewis: trumpet; Henry Miranda: trumpet; Al Rojo: trumpet; Shorty
Sherock: trumpet

36946	7	If Love Is Good To Me	140
			1702
			2051

			2242 3307 37571	
36947	9	For Sentimental Reasons	1702 2242	
36948	9	Somebody Loves You	1702 2242 5235 57005 98409	
36949	3	A Hundred Years From Today	1702 2051 2242 3307 5233 113	

February 13, 1962

(Note: Dean Martin's estate own the rights to his recordings from this point forward. As such, all information regarding take numbers and session personnel is currently unavailable.)

857	Senza Fine	20140	
858	Dame Su Amour	20082	
859	Baby-O	20082 S-191	6130
860	Just Close Your Eyes	20058 SR 6130	6130
861	Tik-A-Tee, Tik-A-Tay	20058	6028

February 26, 1962

912	C'est Si Bon	20072 40016	6021
913	Poor People Of Paris	20072 40017	6021

914	River Seine	40018	6021
915	I Love Paris	40020	6021
916	Last Time I Saw Paris	40018	6021
917	Mimi	40017	6021
918	April In Paris	40016	6021
919	Darling, Je Vous Aime Beaucoup		6021
920	Gigi	40020	6021
921	La Vie en Rose		6021
922	C'est Magnifique	40019	6021
923	Mam'selle	40019	6021

July 27, 1962

17286	Remote at Lake Tahoe	UNRELEASED	

August 28-30, 1962

1428	Manana		6054
1429	South Of The Border	40045	6054
1430	Tangerine	40045	6054
1431	In A Little Spanish Town	20116 40045	6054
1432	El Rancho Grande		6054
1433	What A Difference A Day Made	40045	6054
1434	Always In My Heart		6054
1435	Magic Is The Moonlight	40045	6054
1436	Besame Mucho	40045	6054

1437	From The Bottom Of My Heart	20116	
1438	Who's Got The Action?	20116	
		20140	
1439	La Paloma		6054

October 22, 1962

1510	Sam's Song (With Sammy Davis, Jr.)	20128	6188

November 26-December 2, 1962

(16 shows were recorded when Dean, Frank Sinatra and Sammy Davis, Jr. performed at the Villa Venice in Chicago. 57 reels of tape exist from these appearances. The master numbers are T 3208 through T 3264.)

December 1962

1605	Anytime	40046	6061
		SR 6201	6201
			6213
			5228
			93929
1606	Room Full Of Roses	40046	6061
			6201
			5228
			56
1607	My Heart Cries For You	S-192	6061
		SR 6130	6201
			5228
			55
1608	I'm So Lonesome I Could Cry		6061
			6201
			5228
			55
1609	Shutters And Boards	S-191	6061
		40046	6130
1610	Singing The Blues	40046	6061

1611	Ain't Gonna Try Anymore	20150 SR 6213	6061 6213
1612	Face In A Crowd	20150 40046 SR 6130 S-194	6061 6130
1613	Things	SR 6130 S-194	6061 6130
1614	Blue, Blue Day		6061 6201 5268
1615	Hey, Good Lookin'	40046	6061 10733
1616	I Walk The Line	40046	6061 6201 5268 93929

April 22, 1963

2011	My Sugar's Gone	20194	6085 6140
2012	Candy Kisses		6085 6201 5268 93929
2013	Take Good Care Of Her		6085
2014	I Can't Help It If I'm Still In Love With You	SR 6201	6085 6201 55 10733

April 23, 1963

2015	I'm Gonna Change Everything		6085 6140

			5228
			10733
2016	Bouquet Of Roses	0466	6085
		SR 6201	6201
			5268
			93929
2017	From Lover To Loser		6085
			6130
2018	Rockin' Alone In An Old Rocking Chair		6085

April 24, 1963

2019	Second Hand Rose	SR 6201	6085
			6201
2020	Corrine, Corrina	SR 6130	6085
		S-193	6130
			5228
2021	Middle Of The Night Is My Crying Time	20194	6085
			6140
2022	Just A Little Lovin'	SR 6201	6085
			6201
			93929

July 10, 1963

2149	We Open In Venice (With Frank Sinatra and Sammy Davis, Jr.)		2017
			46013

July 18, 1963

2188	Guys and Dolls (With Frank Sinatra)	2016	45014
			46013
2196	Guys and Dolls Reprise (With Frank Sinatra)		2016
			45014
			46013

July 25, 1963

2155	Bianca		2017

July 29, 1963

2184	Fugue For Tinhorns (With Frank Sinatra and Bing Crosby)	20217	2016 45014 46013
2185	Oldest Established Permanent Floating Crap Game In New York (With Frank Sinatra and Bing Crosby)	20217	2016 45014 46013

August 13, 1963

2159	If This Isn't Love (With The Hi-Lo's)		2015

August 27, 1963

2224	Peace On Earth - Silent Night		50001

September 5, 1963

2299	Via Veneto	20215
2300	Mama Roma	20215

September 6-8, 1963

(Note: Six shows were recorded when Dean appeared with Frank Sinatra and Sammy Davis, Jr. at the Sands in Las Vegas; 12 reels of tape exist from these performances. "The Summit" comedy routine that appears on Frank Sinatra's *A Man And His Music* LP was recorded during these dates. The master numbers are T 3314 through T 3325.)

December 17, 1963

2476	Grazie, Prego, Scusi	0252	
2477	Marina	UNRELEASED	
2478	Take Me		6140
2479	La Giostra	0252	

March 12-15, 1964
Personnel: Irving Cottler: drums; Barney Kessel: guitar; Ken Lane: piano;
    Red Mitchell: bass

2662	My Melancholy Baby		6123
2663	Smile	SR 6123	6123
2664	I'm Confessin'	SR 6123	6123
2665	Baby, Won't You Please Come Home	SR 6123	6123
2666	I Don't Know Why	SR 6123	6123
2667	Fools Rush In		6123
2668	I'll Buy That Dream	SR 6123	6123
2669	Blue Moon		6123
2670	If You Were The Only Girl		6123
2671	Gimme A Little Kiss	SR 6123	6123
2672	Everybody Loves Somebody		6123
2673	Hands Across The Table		6123

April 10, 1964

2631	Style (With Frank Sinatra and Bing Crosby)		2021 46013
2632	Mister Booze (With Frank Sinatra, Bing Crosby, and Sammy Davis, Jr.)		2021 46013
2633	Don't Be A Do-Badder Finale (With Frank Sinatra, Bing Crosby and Sammy Davis, Jr.)		2021 46013
2634	Any Man Who Loves His Mother		2021

April 16, 1964

2703	Everybody Loves Somebody	0281 S-190	6130 6301

		SR 6130	246
		0709	305
			56
			10733
2704	Your Other Love	S-190	6130
2705	Siesta Fiesta	S-193	6130
2706	A Little Voice	0281	6130
		S-192	

RECORDING DATES UNKNOWN

2990	Everybody Loves Somebody	UNRELEASED
2991	Everybody Loves Somebody	UNRELEASED

August 7, 1964

2914	So Long Baby		6140
2915	Door Is Still Open To My Heart	0307	6140
		0718	6320
			246
			305
			10733
			55
2916	You're Nobody 'Til Somebody Loves You	0333	6140
		0717	6146
		SR 6301	6301
			305
			10733
			246
2917	Every Minute, Every Hour	0307	6140
		SR 6301	6301
			305

August 24, 1964

2932	We'll Sing In The Sunshine	6140
		5228

2933	Clinging Vine		6140
2934	Always Together		6140
2935	In The Misty Moonlight	0640	6140
		0735	6320
		SR 6320	93929
			305
			10733
			55

October 23, 1964

3013	Everybody Loves Somebody (Spanish Version)	UNRELEASED

RECORDING DATES UNKNOWN

3022	Everybody Loves Somebody	UNRELEASED
3026	Door Is Still Open To My Heart	UNRELEASED

November 3, 1964

3035	Have A Heart		6146
3036	You'll Always Be The One I Love	0333	6146
		SR 6301	6301
			246
			305
			56
3037	Wedding Bells		6146
			5228
3038	Sophia		200

December 22, 1964

3140	Send Me The Pillow You Dream On	0344	6146
		0718	6320
		SR 6320	5268
			305
			93929

"Sophia" promo 45 (Reprise PRO 200)
(Author's collection)

			10733
			246
3141	I'll Be Seeing You	0344	6146
			5228
3142	Send Me Some Lovin'		6146
3144	In The Chapel In The Moonlight	0601	6146
		0730	6250
		SR 6250	6301
		SR 6320	305
			93929
			56
3145	I'll Hold You In My Heart		6146
			5268
			55
3146	My Heart Is An Open Book		6146

April 13, 1965
United
8 PM-11 PM

H 3308	(Remember Me) I'm The One Who Loves You (Note: This version was 2:53 in length.)	UNRELEASED	
H 3309	Here Comes My Baby	SR 6170	6170
			5228
H 3310	Welcome To My World	0601	6170
		SR 6250	6250
			5268
			55

April 15, 1965
United
8 PM-11 PM

H 3308-RE	(Remember Me) I'm The One Who Loves You	0369	6170
		0717	6301
		SR 6170	246
			305
			10733

H 3311	Birds And The Bees	SR 6170	6170 6301 305
H 3312	I Don't Think You Love Me Anymore		6170
H 3313	My Shoes Keep Walking Back To You	SR 6170	6170 5268
H 3314	Born To Lose		6170 55

April 16, 1965
United
8 PM-11 PM

H 3315	King Of The Road	SR 6170 SR 6320	6170 6320 5268 305 10733
H 3316	Take These Chains From My Heart		6170 5268 55
H 3317	Walk On By	SR 6170	6170 5268
H 3318	Bumming Around	0393 SR 6301	6170 6301 93929 305
H 3319	Red Roses For A Blue Lady		6170 5228 10733

July 2, 1965

H 3622	Love, Love, Love		6181
H 3623	Houston	0393 0714 SR 6181	6181 6301 246

			305
			10733
H 3624	Little Lovely One	SR 6181	6181

September 15, 1965
United
8 PM-11 PM

H 3740	I Will	0415	6181
		0714	6320
		SR 6181	246
			305
			10733
H 3741	Down Home	SR 6181	6181
H 3742	Old Yellow Line	0672	6181
			6320
			305

September 20, 1965
United
8 PM-11 PM

H 3743	First Thing Ev'ry Morning	SR 6181	6181
			5268
H 3744	Everybody But Me		6181
			5228
H 3745	You're The Reason I'm In Love	0415	6181
			93929

October 5, 1965
United
8 PM-11 PM

H 3746	Hammer And Nails		6181
H 3747	Snap Your Fingers	SR 6181	6181
H 3748	Detour		6181
			93929

135

January 11, 1966
United
8 PM-11 PM

J 3966	Somewhere There's A Someone	0443	6201
		0711	6320
		SR 6201	246
			305
			56
J 3967	That Old Clock On The Wall	0443	6201
			93929
J 3968	Leave A Light In Your Window	UNRELEASED	
	(Written by: Barry Mann/Cynthia Weil)		

January 26, 1966
United
8:30 PM-11:30 PM

J 3991	South Of The Border		6211
			93929
J 3992	Empty Saddles In The Old Corral	SR 6211	6211
J 3993	Red Sails In The Sunset	SR 6211	6211
			93929
J 3994	On The Sunny Side Of The Street	SR 6211	6211
			93929

January 27, 1966
United
8:30 PM-11:30 PM

J 3997	Glory Of Love	SR 6211	6211
			6320
			93929
			305
			10733
J 3999	Side By Side	SR 6211	6211
			93929
J 4000	If You Knew Susie		6211

J 4001	Last Roundup	SR 6211	6211

March 26, 1966
United
3 PM-6 PM

J 4158	Come Running Back	0466 0711	6213 6301 246 305
J 4159	Shades	0500 SR 6213	6213
J 4160	One Lonely Boy	0765	6213
J 4161	Terrible, Tangled Web		6213

April 11, 1966
United
8:30 PM-11:30 PM

J 4196	Don't Let The Blues Make You Bad	SR 6123	6213
J 4197	Nobody But A Fool		6213 5228
J 4198	I'm Living In Two Worlds	SR 6123	6213 5268
J 4199	Today Is Not The Day	SR 6123	6213

June 30, 1966
United
8 PM-11 PM

J 4409	A Million And One	0500 0709 SR 6213	6213
J 4411	Marshmallow World	0542	6222

August 17, 1966
United
7 PM-11 PM

J 4472	Nobody's Baby Again	0516	6242
			6301
			246
			305

| J 4473 | It Just Happened That Way | 0516 | 6242 |
| | | | 246 |

| J 4474 | White Christmas | | 6222 |

September 20, 1966
United
7 PM-10 PM and 10:30 PM-Midnight

J 4512	Winter Wonderland		6222
J 4513	Let It Snow, Let It Snow, Let It Snow		6222
J 4514	Jingle Bells		6222
J 4515	Things We Did Last Summer		6222
			6233
J 4516	Blue Christmas	0542	6222
J 4517	Silent Night		6222
J 4518	I'll Be Home For Christmas		6222
J 4519	Silver Bells	247	6222

October 19, 1966
Western
7 PM-Midnight
Personnel: Les Brown Orchestra; Ken Lane: piano

J 4573	The One I Love Belongs To Somebody Else		6233
			56
J 4574	Baby, Won't You Please Come Home		6233

J 4575	If I Had You		6233 5228
J 4576	I've Grown Accustomed To Her Face		6233
J 4577	It's The Talk Of The Town		6233
J 4578	Just Friends		6233
J 4579	S'posin		6233
J 4580	What Can I Say After I Say I'm Sorry		6233 5228
J 4581	Home		6233

November 11, 1966
United
7 PM-11:30 PM

J 4611	I'm Not The Marrying Kind	0538	6242
J 4614	Thirty More Miles To San Diego		6242
J 4616	(Open Up The Door) Let The Good Times In	0538 0703	6242 6320 305
J 4617	Pride		6250 5228

March 13, 1967
Western
7 PM-11 PM

K 4860	You've Still Got A Place In My Heart	SR 6320	6242 6320 305 55
K 4861	Sweet, Sweet Lovable You		6242
K 4862	Think About Me	0571	6242
K 4863	Lay Some Happiness On Me	0571	6242

		0703	6320
		SR 6320	93929
			305
K 4864	He's Got You		6242
K 4865	If I Ever Get Back To Georgia		6242

June 23, 1967
United
7:30 PM-Midnight

K 6043	Little Ole Wine Drinker, Me	0608	6250
		0730	6320
		SR 6250	305
		SR 6320	10733
K 6056	Turn To Me		6250
K 6057	Release Me	SR 6250	6250
			55
K 6058	I Can't Help Remembering You	0608	6250
			6301
			305
K 6059	Green, Green Grass Of Home	SR 6250	6250
			5268
			55
K 6060	A Place In The Shade		6250
K 6061	Wallpaper Roses	0640	6250
		SR 6250	93929

September 20, 1967

K 6161	Things (With Nancy Sinatra)	6277
		6409
	(Note: Nancy Sinatra overdubbed her vocal onto the original master 1613. Dean's vocal is the same.)	6057

February 13, 1968
United

L 6446   You've Still Got A Place In My Heart   0672

(Note: Glen D. Hardin arranged and overdubbed different choral backing vocals and instrumentation onto the original master K 4860 creating a more "commercial-sounding" single. Dean's vocal is the same as the version found on the *Happiness Is Dean Martin* LP.)

RECORDING DATE UNKNOWN

6338   Various Radio and Promo Spots   UNRELEASED

May 13, 1968

6339   I Don't Know If The World Outside Tomorrow   UNRELEASED

6340   Love Is Forever   UNRELEASED

6341   You're The Only One That Makes My Life Worth Living   UNRELEASED

6342   Once In My Life   UNRELEASED

6343   To Keep A Roof Over My Head   UNRELEASED

June 11, 1968

6344   Remembering   UNRELEASED

6346   Jam   UNRELEASED

6347   My First Night Alone   UNRELEASED

June 27, 1968
United
5 PM-8 PM

L 6652   By The Time I Get To Phoenix   SR 6330   6330
                                                                     10733

L 6653	Gentle On My Mind	0812	6330
			5268
			10733
L 6654	Rainbows Are Back In Style	0780	6330
		SR 6330	
L 6655	Honey	SR 6330	6330

June 28, 1968
United

L 6656	That's When I See The Blues	0812	6330
L 6657	Welcome To My Heart		6330
L 6658	Drowning In My Tears	0841	6330
L 6659	Not Enough Indians	0780	6330
		0735	
		SR 6330	
L 6660	That Old Time Feeling	0761	6330
		SR 6330	
L 6661	April Again	0761	6330
		SR 6330	

July 23, 1968
United

| L 6739 | 5 Card Stud | 0765 | |

June 11, 1969
TTG
8 PM-11 PM

M 7323	Do You Believe This Town		6338
M 7324	Where The Blue And Lonely Go		6338
M 7372	Make It Rain		6338

M 7373	Sneaky Little Side Of Me		6338

M 7382	Sun Is Shining		6338

June 12, 1969
TTG
8 PM-11 PM

M 7377	Crying Time	0857	6338
			5228
			56

M 7378	I Take A Lot Of Pride In What I Am	0841	6338
			5268
			10733

M 7379	If You Ever Get Around To Loving Me		6338

M 7380	One Cup Of Happiness	0857	6338

M 7381	Little Green Apples		6338
			5228
			10733

January 8, 1970
Columbia
7 PM-10 PM

N 17990	Down Home	0893

N 17991	For The Love Of A Woman	0915

January 9, 1970
Columbia
7 PM-10 PM

N 17992	Tracks Of My Tears	0915

N 17993	Come On Down	0893

May 27, 1970
TTG
7 PM-11 PM

N 18647	Make The World Go Away	LLP 119	6403
			5268
			10733
N 18648	Together Again	LLP 119	6403
N 18649	Detroit City	0955	6403
			10733
N 18650	Once A Day		6403
N 18651	Heart Over Mind		6403
			5268

May 28, 1970
TTG
7 PM-11 PM

N 18652	Turn The World Around	0955	6403
		LLP 119	
N 18653	Here We Go Again	0934	6403
		LLP 119	
N 18654	Tips Of My Fingers		6403
			5268
N 18655	It Keeps Right On A-Hurtin	LLP 119	6403
N 18656	My Woman, My Woman, My Wife	0934	6403
		LLP 119	10733

August 18, 1970
Western
7 PM-10 PM

| N 18954 | I'm Gonna Sit Right Down And Write Myself A Letter | UNRELEASED |
| N 18957 | Come Live With Me | UNRELEASED |

N 18958	Smoke		UNRELEASED
N 18959	Bidin' My Time		UNRELEASED

September 29, 1970
United

N 19136	Invisible Tears		6428
N 19137	Raindrops Keep Fallin On My Head		6428 10733
N 19138	For Once In My Life		6428 10733
N 19139	Raining In My Heart	1004	6428
N 19140	Sweetheart		6428

September 30, 1970
United

N 19145	Georgia Sunshine	0973	6428
N 19146	A Perfect Mountain		6428
N 19147	Marry Me		6428
N 19148	For The Good Times	0973	6428 10733
N 19149	She's A Little Bit Country	1004	6428 5268

April 12, 1971
Hollywood Sound
3 PM-6 PM

PCA 0293	Right Kind Of Woman	1060	2053
PCA 0294	Do You Think It's Time (Written by: Baker Knight)		UNRELEASED

145

| PCA 0295 | I Can Remember | UNRELEASED |
| | (Written by: Baker Knight) | |

November 16, 1971
United
5 PM-Midnight

PCA 0907	I Don't Know What I'm Doing		2053
PCA 0908	Small Exception Of Me		2053
PCA 0909	Party Dolls And Wine	LLP 179	2053
PCA 0910	Blue Memories	LLP 179	2053
PCA 0911	I Can Give You What You Want Now	1085 LLP 179	2053

November 17, 1971
United

PCA 0912	Kiss The World Goodbye		2053
PCA 0913	Just The Other Side Of Nowhere	LLP 179	2053
PCA 0914	Guess Who	1085 LLP 179	2053
PCA 0915	Right Kind Of Woman (Note: Listed in Reprise files as "deleted.")	UNRELEASED	
PCA 0916	What's Yesterday	1060 LLP 179	2053

December 21, 1972
Hollywood Sound
8 PM-11:30 PM

QCA 3655	I'm Sitting On Top Of The World	LLP 228	2113
QCA 3656	Smile	1166	2113
QCA 3657	When The Red, Red Robin Comes Bob, Bob, Bobbin' Along		2113

QCA 3658	Ramblin' Rose	LLP 228	2113
			10733
QCA 3659	Get On With Your Livin'	1166	2174
QCA 3660	I Wonder Who's Kissing Her Now	LLP 228	2113
			56

December 22, 1972
Hollywood Sound
8:30 PM-12:30 AM

QCA 3661	It's A Good Day	LLP 228	2113
QCA 3662	At Sundown	LLP 228	2113
QCA 3663	You Made Me Love You	1141	2113
QCA 3664	Almost Like Being In Love	LLP 228	2113
QCA 3665	I'm Forever Blowing Bubbles		2113
QCA 3666	Amor Mio	1141	2174

July 25, 1973
Hollywood Sound
7 PM-Midnight

RCA 4136	Gimme A Little Kiss		2174
RCA 4137	Baby, Won't You Please Come Home		2174
RCA 4138	I'm Confessin'	LLP 252	2174
RCA 4139	I Don't Know Why	LLP 252	2174

July 26, 1973
Hollywood Sound
7 PM-Midnight

| RCA 4140 | Free To Carry On | 1178 | 2174 |
| | | LLP 252 | |

RCA 4141	Tie A Yellow Ribbon	LLP 252	2174
			10733
RCA 4142	You Better Move On		2174
RCA 4143	You're The Best Thing That Ever Happened To Me	1178 LLP 252	2174

August 10, 1973
Hollywood Sound

| RCA 4172 | I'll Hold Out My Hand | UNRELEASED |

November 22, 1974
Hollywood Sound
5 PM-8 PM and 9 PM-12:30 AM

SCA 5183	Twilight On The Trail	2267
SCA 5184	Love Thy Neighbor	2267
SCA 5185	Without A Word Of Warning	2267
SCA 5186	That Old Gang Of Mine	2267

November 25, 1974
Hollywood Sound

SCA 7825	If I Had You	2267
SCA 7826	It's Magic	2267
SCA 7827	I Cried For You	2267
SCA 7828	Day You Came Along	2267
SCA 7829	Only Forever	2267
SCA 7830	Once In A While	2267

January 17, 1983
Masterfonics Sound

| BTN 1712 | Love Put A Song In My Heart | 23870 |

| BTN 1738 | Everybody's Had The Blues (With Merle Haggard) | | 23870 |

January 18, 1983
Masterfonics Sound

| BTN 1711 | My First Country Song (With Conway Twitty) | 29584 | 23870 |

January 19, 1983
Masterfonics Sound

| BTN 1713 | Old Bones | | 23870 |

| BTN 1714 | Drinking Champagne | 29480 52662 | 23870 |

January 20, 1983
Masterfonics Sound

| BTN 1739 | Don't Give Up On Me | | 23870 |

| BTN 1740 | Shoulder To Shoulder | | 23870 |

January 21, 1983
Masterfonics Sound

| BTN 1741 | Since I Met You Baby | 29480 | 23870 |

| BTN 1742 | In Love Up To My Heart | | 23870 |

| BTN 1846 | Hangin' Around | 29584 | 23870 |

July 1985

| MC 18550 | L. A. Is My Home | 52662 | |

(Paramount Pictures Corp. publicity photo)

Chapter 3

American Discography

(Note: The format is as follows: record label, number, date released and titles.)

SINGLES

Diamond

2035	1946	Which Way Did My Heart Go/All Of Me
2036	1946	I Got The Sun In The Morning/Sweetheart Of Sigma Chi

Apollo

1088	1947	Oh Marie/Walking My Baby Back Home
1116	1948	Santa Lucia/Hold Me

Embassy

124	1949	One Foot In Heaven/The Night Is Young And You're So Beautiful

Capitol

15249	10/18/48	The Money Song/That Certain Party (With Jerry Lewis)
15329	12/27/48	Once In Love With Amy/Tarra Ta-Larra Ta-Lar
15349	1/17/49	You Was (With Peggy Lee)/Someone Like You (Peggy Lee Only)

15351	1/17/49	Powder Your Face With Sunshine/Absence Makes The Heart Grow Fonder
15395	2/28/49	Have A Little Sympathy/Johnny Get Your Girl
545	4/11/49	Dreamy Old New England Moon/3 Wishes
		(Note: All of the above were released on 78 RPM only.)
691		My Own, My Only, My All/Just For Fun (Note: This was released as a 78 RPM on 7/18/49 and as Dean's first 45 RPM on 8/15/49.)
726	9/12/49	Vieni Su/That Lucky Old Sun
937	4/3/50	Zing-A Zing-A Boom/Rain
948	4/10/50	Muskrat Ramble/I'm Gonna Paper All My Walls With Your Love Letters
981	5/1/50	I Don't Care If The Sun Don't Shine/Choo'N Gum
1002	5/10/50	I Still Get A Thrill Thinking Of You/Be Honest With Me
1028	5/22/50	I'll Always Love You/Baby Obey Me
1052	6/5/50	Happy Feet/Bye Bye Blackbird
1139	8/7/50	Wham! Bam! Thank You, Ma'am!/Peddler's Serenade
1160	8/21/50	I'm In Love With You/Don't Rock The Boat, Dear (With Margaret Whiting)
1342	12/11/50	If/I Love The Way You Say Goodnight
1358	1/15/51	You And Your Beautiful Eyes/Tonda Wanda Hoy
1458	4/2/51	Beside You/Who's Sorry Now
1575	6/18/51	We Never Talk Much/How D'ya Like Your Eggs In The Morning (With Helen O'Connell)
1703	7/16/51	Bonne Nuit/In The Cool, Cool, Cool Of The Evening
1724	7/30/51	Go Go Go Go/Luna Mezzo Mare

1797	9/24/51	Hangin' Around With You/Aw C'Mon
1811	10/8/51	(Ma Come Bali) Bella Bimba/Meanderin'
1817	10/15/51	Solitaire/I Ran All The Way Home
1885	12/3/51	Blue Smoke/Night Train To Memphis
1901	12/10/51	Never Before/Sailor's Polka
1921	1/7/52	Oh Boy! Oh Boy! Oh Boy! Oh Boy! Oh Boy!/As You Are
1938	1/21/52	Until/My Heart Has Found A Home Now
1975	2/18/52	When You're Smiling/All I Have To Give You
2001	3/10/52	Won't You Surrender/Pretty As A Picture
2071	5/5/52	I Passed Your House Tonight/Bet-I-Cha
2140	6/30/52	Come Back To Sorrento/Oh Marie
2165	7/28/52	You Belong To Me/Hominy Grits
2240	10/6/52	Second Chance/I Know A Dream When I See One
2319	12/29/52	Kiss/What Could Be More Beautiful
2378	2/23/53	Little Did We Know/There's My Lover
2485	6/1/53	Love Me, Love Me/'Til I Find You
2555	8/10/53	Don't You Remember?/If I Could Sing Like Bing
2589	9/14/53	That's Amore/You're The Right One
2640	11/2/53	The Christmas Blues/If I Should Love Again
2749	3/8/54	Hey, Brother, Pour The Wine/I'd Cry Like A Baby
2818	5/24/54	Sway/Money Burns A Hole In My Pocket
2870	7/19/54	That's What I Like/Peddler Man
2911	9/6/54	One More Time/Try Again

153

2985   11/29/54 Long, Long Ago/Open Up The Doghouse
                            (With Nat King Cole)

3011   12/27/54 Belle From Barcelona/Confused

3036   2/7/55   Young And Foolish/Under The Bridges Of Paris

3133   5/30/55   Chee Chee-Oo Chee/Ridin' Into Love

3153   6/13/55   Love Is All That Matters/Simpatico

3196   8/1/55   Relax-Ay-Voo/Two Sleepy People (With Line Renaud)

3238   9/19/55   I Like Them All/In Napoli

3295   11/28/55 Memories Are Made Of This/Change Of Heart

3352   2/13/56   Innamorata/The Lady With The Big Umbrella

3414   4/30/56   Standing On The Corner/Watching The World Go By

3468   6/25/56   I'm Gonna Steal You Away (With The Nuggets)/Street Of
                            Love

3521   8/27/56   Mississippi Dreamboat/The Test Of Time

3577   10/29/56 Give Me A Sign/The Look

3604   12/24/56 I Know I Can't Forget/Just Kiss Me

3648   2/18/57   The Man Who Plays The Mandolino/Captured

3680   4/1/57   Only Trust Your Heart/Bamboozled

3718   5/13/57   I Never Had A Chance/I Can't Give You Anything But Love

3752   7/1/57   Write To Me From Naples/Beau James

3787   9/2/57   Promise Her Anything/Tricche Tracche

3841   11/25/57 Good Mornin', Life/Makin' Love Ukelele Style
                            (Note: This is Dean's last known release
                            on 78 RPM)

3894   2/17/58   Return To Me/Forgetting You

3988	6/9/58	Angel Baby/I'll Gladly Make The Same Mistake Again
4028	8/11/58	Volare/Outta My Mind (Issued with a picture sleeve)
4065	10/6/58	Magician/Once Upon A Time
4124	1/12/59	You Were Made For Love/It Takes So Long To Say Goodbye
4174	3/30/59	Rio Bravo/My Rifle, My Pony And Me
4222	6/8/59	On An Evening In Roma/You Can't Love 'Em All (Issued with a picture sleeve)
4287	10/5/59	I Ain't Gonna Lead This Life No More/Career
4328	1/4/60	Love Me, My Love/Who Was That Lady?
4361	3/28/60	Professor, Professor/Napoli
4391	6/20/60	Just In Time/Buttercup Of Golden Hair
4420	8/8/60	Ain't That A Kick In The Head/Humdinger
4472	11/14/60	Sogni D'Oro/How Sweet It Is
4518	2/13/61	Sparklin' EyesTu Sei Bella, Signorina
4551	4/3/61	All In A Night's Work/Bella Bella Bambina
4570	5/22/61	Giuggiola/Story Of Life

Capitol Reissues

1682	3/16/53	Oh Marie/I'll Always Love You
6011	1/1/62	Memories Are Made Of This/That's Amore
6048	4/6/64	Return To Me/Volare
44153	4/13/88	That's Amore/It Must Be Him (By Vikki Carr) (Issued with a picture sleeve)
57889	1992	Rudolph The Red-Nosed Reindeer/White Christmas

Capitol Promotional

Note: A special white label 78 RPM exists with Dean "introducing" Just For Fun and My Own, My Only My All (master 4254)

726	1949	Vieni Su/A Yore A Dopey Gal ("B"-side by Red Ingle & The Natural Seven)
10842	1953	Who's Your Little Who-Zis/Flip side by Jane Froman. (Note: Exists as a yellow-label promo 78 RPM)
2037-38	1954	Hey Brother Pour The Wine/I'd Cry Like A Baby (7" that plays at 78 RPM)
2870	1954	That's What I Like (Same song on both sides)
3604	1956	Just Kiss Me (Same song on both sides)
3988	1958	Angel Baby (Same song on both sides)
PRO 987	1959	Sleep Warm/All I Do Is Dream Of You (Issued with a picture sleeve)
PRO 1609	1960	I Met A Girl (Issued with a picture sleeve)

American Pie

9058	That's Amore/Memories Are Made Of This

Collectables

6076	1993	Memories Are Made Of This/That's Amore
6256	1995	Volare/Return To Me

Reprise

20058	2/15/62	Tik-A-Tee, Tik-A-Tay/Just Close Your Eyes
20072	4/25/62	C'est Si Bon/Poor People Of Paris (Note: According to Reprise files, this single was pressed "for release in England only.")
20082	5/8/62	Baby-O/Dame Su Amor

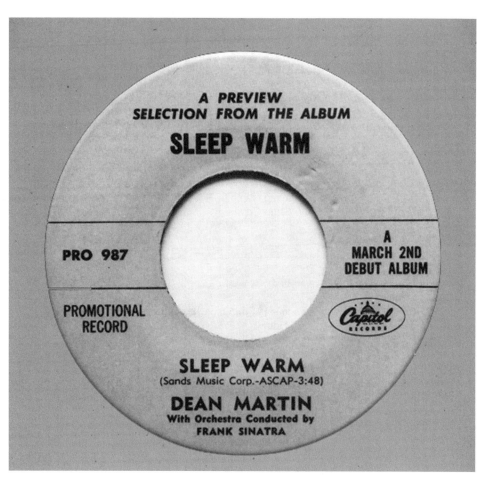

"Sleep Warm" promo 45 (Capitol PRO 987)
(Oprisko Family collection)

20116	9/24/62	Who's Got The Action?/From The Bottom Of My Heart (Issued with a picture sleeve)
20116	1962	From The Bottom Of My Heart/In A Little Spanish Town
20128	1962	Sam's Song (With Sammy Davis, Jr.)/Me And My Shadow (Frank Sinatra and Sammy Davis, Jr.) (Issued with a picture sleeve)
20140	1962	Senza Fine/Who's Got The Action
20150	2/5/63	Ain't Gonna Cry Anymore/Face In A Crowd
20194	7/25/63	My Sugar's Gone/Corrine, Corrina
20194	1963	My Sugar's Gone/Middle Of The Night Is My Crying Time
20215	9/5/63	Via Veneto/Mama Roma
20217	1963	Fugue For Tinhorns/Oldest Established Permanent Floating Crap Game In New York (With Frank Sinatra and Bing Crosby) (Issued with a picture sleeve)
0252	1964	La Giostra/Grazie, Prego, Scusi
0281	5/64	Everybody Loves Somebody/A Little Voice
0307	8/25/64	The Door Is Still Open To My Heart/Every Minute, Every Hour
0333	11/64	You're Nobody 'Til Somebody Loves You/You'll Always Be The One I Love
0344	2/65	Send Me The Pillow You Dream On/I'll Be Seeing You
0369	5/65	(Remember Me) I'm The One Who Loves You/Born To Lose
0393	7/65	Houston/Bumming Around
0415	9/29/65	I Will/You're The Reason I'm In Love
0443	1/13/66	Somewhere There's A Someone/That Old Clock On The Wall

0466	4/11/66	Come Running Back/Bouquet Of Roses
0500	6/30/66	A Million And One/Shades
0516	8/31/66	Nobody's Baby Again/It Just Happened That Way
0538	11/16/66	(Open Up The Door) Let The Good Times In/I'm Not The Marrying Kind
0542	11/29/66	Blue Christmas/Marshmallow World
0571	3/23/67	Lay Some Happiness On Me/Think About Me
0601	1967	In The Chapel In The Moonlight/Welcome To My World
0608	7/5/67	Little Ole Wine Drinker, Me/I Can't Help Remembering You
0640	1967	In The Misty Moonlight/Wallpaper Roses
0672	1968	You've Still Got A Place In My Heart/Old Yellow Line
0761	7/11/68	April Again/That Old Time Feeling
0765	7/31/68	5 Card Stud/One Lonely Boy
0780	9/25/68	Not Enough Indians/Rainbows Are Back In Style
0812	1/23/69	Gentle On My Mind/That's When I See The Blues
0841	7/2/69	I Take A Lot Of Pride In What I Am/Drowning In My Tears
0857	9/11/69	One Cup Of Happiness/Crying Time
0893	2/6/70	Come On Down/Down Home
0915	4/17/70	For The Love Of A Woman/Tracks Of My Tears
0934	7/1/70	My Woman, My Woman, My Wife/Here We Go Again
0955	9/16/70	Detroit City/Turn The World Around
0973	11/11/70	Georgia Sunshine/For The Good Times

1004	3/24/71	She's A Little Bit Country/Raining In My Heart
1060	12/8/71	What's Yesterday/Right Kind Of Woman
1085	3/27/72	Guess Who/I Can Give You What You Want Now
1141	2/28/73	Amor Mio/You Made Me Love You
1166	7/5/73	Get On With Your Livin'/Smile
1178	10/3/73	You're The Best Thing That Ever Happened To Me/Free To Carry On

Reprise Reissues

0703	1967	Lay Some Happiness On Me/(Open Up The Door) Let The Good Times In
0709	1967	Everybody Loves Somebody/A Million And One
0711	1967	Come Running Back/Somewhere There's A Someone
0714	1967	Houston/I Will
0717	1967	(Remember Me) I'm The One Who Loves You/You're Nobody 'Til Somebody Loves You
0718	1967	The Door Is Still Open To My Heart/Send Me The Pillow You Dream On
0730	1968	Little Ole Wine Drinker, Me/In The Chapel In The Moonlight
0735	1969	In The Misty Moonlight/Not Enough Indians

Reprise Promotional

PRO 200	1965	Sophia (Same song on both sides)
PRO 247	10/28/66	Silver Bells (Same song on both sides)
PRO 345	7/30/69	*I TAKE A LOT OF PRIDE IN WHAT I AM* Radio Spot
PRO 415	8/5/70	*MY WOMAN, MY WOMAN, MY WIFE* Radio Spot
1141	1973	Amor Mio (Stereo/Mono)

My Woman, My Woman, My Wife Radio Spot promo 45 (Reprise PRO 415)
(Author's collection)

| 1166 | 1973 | Get On With Your Livin' (Stereo/Mono) |

Warner Brothers

| 29584 | 6/8/83 | My First Country Song (With Conway Twitty)/Hangin' Around |
| 29480 | 9/28/83 | Since I Met You Baby/Drinking Champagne |

MCA

| 52662 | 1985 | L. A. Is My Home/Drinking Champagne |

Special Promotional

| HB 2160 | 1958 | It's 1200 Miles From Palm Springs To Texas (Note: This was made for airplay in Palm Springs during "Circus Week," April 16-20, 1958. The label erroneously shows the title as "It's 1200 Miles From Texas To Palm Springs.") |

Reprise Compact 33 Stereo Singles

40016	5/9/62	C'est Si Bon/April In Paris
40017		Mimi/Poor People Of Paris
40018		River Seine/Last Time I Saw Paris
40019		Mam'selle/C'est Magnifique
40020		Gigi/I Love Paris
S-190	10/64	Everybody Loves Somebody/Your Other Love
S-191		Shutters And Boards/Baby-O
S-192		My Heart Cries For You/A Little Voice
S-193		Siesta Fiesta/Corrine, Corrina
S-194		Things/Face In A Crowd

EXTENDED PLAYS

Lloyds
705   1951   *DEAN MARTIN*
               Oh Marie; Walking My Baby Back Home; Santa
               Lucia; Hold Me

18 Top Hits
BR-27   1951   *DEAN MARTIN*
               Walking My Baby Back Home; Hold Me; Louise;
               Santa Lucia

Capitol
EAP 401   1953   *DEAN MARTIN SINGS*
               2 Volume EP Set. Same as H-401.

EBF 401   1/12/53 *DEAN MARTIN SINGS*
               Exists as both a gatefold double pocket and a box set
               EP. Same as H-401.

EAP 481   12/7/53 *SUNNY ITALY*
               That's Amore; Oh Marie; Come Back To Sorrento;
               Luna Mezzo Mare

EAP 533   6/7/54   *LIVING IT UP*
               Money Burns A Hole In My Pocket; That's What I
               Like; How Do You Speak To An Angel; Ev'ry Street's
               A Boulevard In Old New York
               (With Jerry Lewis)

EAP 9123 12/13/54 *DEAN MARTIN*
               Let Me Go, Lover; Naughty Lady Of Shady Lane;
               Mambo Italiano; That's All I Want From You

EAP 401   1/3/55   *DEAN MARTIN SINGS*
               2 Volume EP Set. Same as H-401.

EAP 576   8/1/55   *SWINGIN' DOWN YONDER*
               3 Volume EP Set. Same as T-576

EAP 701   12/12/55 *MEMORIES ARE MADE OF THIS*
               Memories Are Made Of This; I Like Them All;
               Change Of Heart; Ridin' Into Love

EAP 702   12/26/55   *ARTISTS AND MODELS*
Innamorata; Lucky Song; You Look So Familiar;
When You Pretend

EAP 752   6/25/56   *PARDNERS*
Pardners (With Jerry Lewis); Me 'N' You 'N' The
Moon; Buckskin Beauty (Jerry Lewis Only); The
Wind, The Wind

EAP 806   1/21/57   *HOLLYWOOD OR BUST*
Hollywood Or Bust; Let's Be Friendly; It Looks Like
Love; A Day In The Country

EAP 840   2/25/57   *TEN THOUSAND BEDROOMS*
Ten Thousand Bedrooms; Money Is A Problem; Only
Trust Your Heart; You I Love

EAP 849   6/17/57   *PRETTY BABY*
3 Volume EP Set. Same as T-849

EAP 939   4/21/58   *RETURN TO ME*
Return To Me; Don't You Remember; Forgetting You;
Buona Sera

EAP 1027 8/11/58   *VOLARE*
Volare; Outta My Mind; Angel Baby; I'll Gladly Make
The Same Mistake Again

EAP 1285 11/16/59 *A WINTER ROMANCE*
3 Volume EP Set. Same as T-1285

MA1-1580 2/20/61   *DEAN MARTIN*
That's Amore; Memories Are Made Of This; Volare;
Return To Me

EAP 1659 1961   *DINO-ITALIAN LOVE SONGS*
On An Evening In Roma; My Heart Reminds Me; Just
Say I Love Her; Vieni Su

Capitol Jukebox
SU 1659   4/4/66   *ITALIAN LOVE SONGS*
Just Say I Love Her; Arrivederci, Roma; Non
Dimenticar; Vieni Su; Take Me In Your Arms; I Have
But One Heart

164

DU 2601   1966   *THE BEST OF DEAN MARTIN*
That's Amore; Return To Me; Volare; Memories Are
Made Of This; Just In Time; Come Back To Sorrento

Reprise Jukebox

40045   3/26/63   *DINO LATINO*
Tangerine; South Of The Border; In A Little Spanish
Town; What A Difference A Day Made; Magic Is The
Moonlight; Besame Mucho

40046   3/26/63   *COUNTRY STYLE*
Any Time; Room Full Of Roses; I Walk The Line; Hey,
Good Lookin'; Singing The Blues; Face In A Crowd;
Shutters and Boards

SR 6123   8/64   *DREAM WITH DEAN*
I Don't Know Why; Baby, Won't You Please Come
Home; I'm Confessin'; Gimmie A Little Kiss; I'll Buy
That Dream; Smile
(Note: Also exists as a white label promo.)

SR 6130   8/64   *EVERYBODY LOVES SOMEBODY*
Everybody Loves Somebody; Corrine, Corrina; Face In
A Crowd; Just Close Your Eyes; Things; My Heart
Cries For You
(Note: Also exists as a white label promo.)

SR 6170   8/18/65   *(REMEMBER ME) I'M THE ONE WHO LOVES YOU*
Walk On By; King Of The Road; (Remember Me) I'm
The One Who Loves You; Here Comes My Baby; My
Shoes Keep Walking Back To You; Birds And The
Bees

SR 6181   1/6/66   *HOUSTON*
Houston; Snap Your Fingers; Little Lovely One; I Will;
The First Thing Ev'ry Morning; Down Home

SR 6201   3/66   *SOMEWHERE THERE'S A SOMEONE*
Second Hand Rose; Bouquet Of Roses; Just A Little
Lovin'; Somewhere There's A Someone; I Can't Help
It; Any Time

SR 6211   3/23/66   SILENCERS
Glory Of Love; Empty Saddles In The Old Corral; Side

By Side; On The Sunny Side Of The Street; The Last
Round Up; Red Sails In The Sunset

SR 6213   8/29/66   *HIT SOUND OF DEAN MARTIN*
Don't Let The Blues Make You Bad; A Million And
One; I'm Living In Two Worlds; Shades; Today Is Not
The Day; Ain't Gonna Try Anymore

SR 6250   8/67   *WELCOME TO MY WORLD*
Little Ole Wine Drinker, Me; Green, Green Grass Of
Home; Wallpaper Roses; In The Chapel In The
Moonlight; Welcome To My World; Release Me

SR 6301   5/3/68   *DEAN MARTIN'S GREATEST HITS VOL. 1*
Everybody Loves Somebody; You're Nobody 'Til
Somebody Loves You; In The Chapel In The
Moonlight; Every Minute, Every Hour; Bumming
Around; You'll Always Be The One I Love

SR 6320   1968   *DEAN MARTIN'S GREATEST HITS VOL. 2*
In The Misty Moonlight; Send Me The Pillow You
Dream On; Little Ole Wine Drinker, Me; Lay Some
Happiness On Me; You've Still Got A Place In My
Heart; King Of The Road

SR 6330   1968   *GENTLE ON MY MIND*
That Old Time Feeling; Welcome To My Heart; By The
Time I Get To Phoenix; Gentle On My Mind; That's
When I See The Blues; April Again

LLP 119   1970   *MY WOMAN, MY WOMAN, MY WIFE*
Here We Go Again; Make The World Go Away; It
Keeps Right On A-Hurtin; My Woman, My Woman,
My Wife; Turn The World Around; Together Again

LLP 179   2/23/72   *DINO*
Guess Who; Just The Other Side Of Nowhere; What's
Yesterday; Blue Memories; I Can Give You What You
Want Now; Party Dolls And Wine

LLP 228   10/15/73   *SITTIN' ON TOP OF THE WORLD*
I Wonder Who's Kissing Her Now; At Sundown;
Almost Like Being In Love; It's A Good Day;
Ramblin' Rose; I'm Sitting On Top Of The World

LLP 252   6/74   *YOU'RE THE BEST THING THAT EVER HAPPENED*
                   TO ME
                   I Don't Know Why; Tie A Yellow Ribbon;
                   I'm Confessin'; You're The Best Thing That
                   Ever Happened To Me; Free To Carry On

ALBUMS

Capitol

H-401   1/12/53   *DEAN MARTIN SINGS (10" LP)*
                    Who's Your Little Who-Zis; I'm Yours; I Feel A Song
                    Comin' On; With My Eyes Wide Open I'm Dreaming;
                    Just One More Chance; Louise; I Feel Like A Feather
                    In The Breeze; A Girl Named Mary And A Boy Named
                    Bill

T-401   4/4/55   *DEAN MARTIN SINGS (12" LP)*
                    Same eight songs as above plus: When You're Smiling;
                    Oh Marie; Come Back To Sorrento; That's Amore
                            (Note: First pressing cover is red and shows a
                            large photo of Dean's face. The album was
                            reissued in the early 1960s and shows a
                            drawing of Dean holding a cigarette.)

T-576   8/1/55   *SWINGIN' DOWN YONDER*
                    Carolina Moon; Waiting For The Robert E. Lee; When
                    It's Sleepy Time Down South; Mississippi Mud;
                    Alabamy Bound; Dinah; Carolina In The Morning;
                    Way Down Yonder In New Orleans; Georgia On My
                    Mind; Just A Little Bit South Of North Carolina; Basin
                    St. Blues; Is It True What They Say About Dixie

T-849   6/17/57   *PRETTY BABY*
                    I Can't Give You Anything But Love; Only Forever;
                    Sleepy Time Gal; Maybe; I Don't Know Why; Pretty
                    Baby; You've Got Me Crying Again; Once In A While;
                    The Object Of My Affection; For You; It's Easy To
                    Remember; Nevertheless

T-1047   8/25/58   *THIS IS DEAN MARTIN*
                    Volare; Write To Me From Naples; Test Of Time; Don't
                    You Remember; The Look; Return To Me; Buona
                    Sera; I Know I Can't Forget; Angel Baby;

167

When You're Smiling; Makin' Love Ukelele Style; Promise Her Anything

T/ST 1150 3/2/59   *SLEEP WARM*
Sleep Warm; Hit The Road To Dreamland; Dream; Cuddle Up A Little Closer; Sleepy Time Gal; Good Night Sweetheart; All I Do Is Dream Of You; Let's Put Out The Lights And Go To Sleep; Dream A Little Dream Of Me; Wrap Your Troubles In Dreams; Goodnight, My Love; Brahms' Lullaby

T/ST 1285 11/16/59 *A WINTER ROMANCE*
A Winter Romance; Let It Snow, Let It Snow, Let It Snow; Things We Did Last Summer; I've Got My Love To Keep Me Warm; June In January; Canadian Sunset; Winter Wonderland; Out In The Cold Again; Baby It's Cold Outside; Rudolph The Red-Nosed Reindeer; White Christmas; It Won't Cool Off

T/ST 1442 10/3/60   *THIS TIME I'M SWINGIN'*
I Can't Believe That You're In Love With Me; True Love; You're Nobody 'Til Somebody Loves You; On The Street Where You Live; Imagination; Until The Real Thing Comes Along; Please Don't Talk About Me When I'm Gone; I've Grown Accustomed To Her Face; Someday; Mean To Me; Heaven Can Wait; Just In Time

T/ST 1659 2/5/62   *DINO - ITALIAN LOVE SONGS*
Just Say I Love Her; Arrivederci, Roma; My Heart Reminds Me; You're Breaking My Heart; Non Dimenticar; Return To Me; Vieni Su; On An Evening In Roma; Pardon; Take Me In Your Arms; I Have But One Heart; There's No Tomorrow

T/ST 1702 11/5/62   *CHA CHA DE AMOR*
Somebody Loves You; My One And Only Love; Love (Your Spell Is Everywhere); I Wish You Love; Cha Cha Cha D'Amour; A Hundred Years From Today; I Love You Much Too Much; For Sentimental Reasons; Let Me Love You Tonight; Amor; Two Loves Have I; If Love Is Good To Me

DT 1047   9/3/63   *THIS IS DEAN MARTIN*
Electronically enhanced reissue of T-1047

T/DT 2212 11/30/64 *HEY BROTHER POUR THE WINE*
Hey, Brother, Pour The Wine; Sway; Try Again; Man
Who Plays The Mandolino; Memories Are Made Of
This; Peddler Man; Standing On The Corner; Love Me,
Love Me; That's What I Like; Solitaire; Just In Time

T/ST 2297 4/12/65 *DEAN MARTIN SINGS/FRANK SINATRA CONDUCTS*
Same as ST 1150; "Dream" is deleted from this release.

T/DT 2333 5/31/65 *SOUTHERN STYLE*
Same as T 576; "Dinah" is deleted from this release.
An acetate test pressing of this release exists with the
title shown as *SOUTHERN COMFORT.*

T/STT 2343 10/4/65 *HOLIDAY CHEER*
Same as ST 1285; "A Winter Romance" is deleted from
this release. Cover slicks exist with the title shown as
BABY IT'S COLD OUTSIDE and some labels were
pressed with this title as well.

T/ST 91285 1965 *WINTER ROMANCE*
Same as ST 1285; "Rudolph The Red-Nosed Reindeer"
and "White Christmas" are deleted from this release.
(Issued through the Capitol Record Club
only.)

T/DT 2601 10/3/66 *BEST OF DEAN MARTIN*
That's Amore; You're Nobody 'Til Somebody Loves
You; Volare; It's Easy To Remember; Sway; Return
To Me; Memories Are Made Of This; June In January;
Come Back To Sorrento; Just In Time; I'm Yours; Hey,
Brother, Pour The Wine

DTCL 2815 10/2/67 *DEAN MARTIN DELUXE SET*
(3 Record Set)
Entire LP's of ST 1659 and DT 2212. The
third album is a combination of tracks from
DT 2601 and DT 1047 and contains: That's
Amore; Volare; It's Easy To Remember; June
In January; Come Back To Sorrento; I'm
Yours; Write To Me From Naples; Don't You
Remember?; The Look; Buona Sera

169

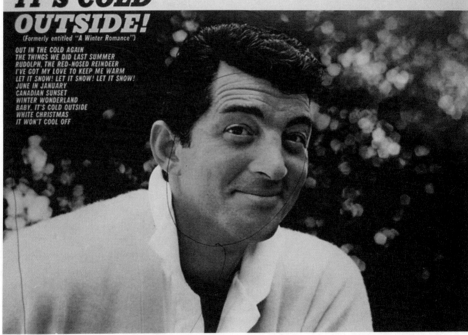

Baby It's Cold Outside LP cover slick (unreleased) (Capitol 2343)
(The markings were made by the Capitol art department.)
(Bob Furmanek collection)

DT 2941   9/16/68   *DEAN MARTIN FAVORITES*
Electronically enhanced reissue of T-401; "A Girl Named Mary And A Boy Named Bill" is deleted from this release.

SKAO 140 1/13/69   *BEST OF DEAN MARTIN VOL. 2*
Just Say I Love Her; If Love Is Good To Me; Standing On The Corner; Vieni Su; Cha Cha Cha D'Amour; Arrivederci, Roma; I've Grown Accustomed To Her Face; Canadian Sunset; Pretty Baby; My One And Only Love
(Note: The Capitol Record Club version 8-0140 was issued in a single pocket, not gatefold, jacket.)

DKAO 378 10/20/69 *DEAN MARTIN'S GREATEST*
Same as DT 2601; "It's Easy To Remember" and "I'm Yours" are deleted from this release.

STBB 523 7/13/70   *RETURN TO ME/YOU'RE NOBODY 'TIL SOMEBODY LOVES YOU*
(2 Record Set)
Same as ST 1659 and ST 1442; "My Heart Reminds Me," "Pardon," "Heaven Can Wait" and "Until The Real Thing Comes Along" are deleted from this release.

SF 524   7/13/70   *YOU'RE NOBODY 'TIL SOMEBODY LOVES YOU*
Same as ST 1442; "Heaven Can Wait" and "Until The Real Thing Comes Along" are deleted from this release.

SF 525   7/13/70   *RETURN TO ME*
Same as ST 1659; "My Heart Reminds Me" and "Pardon" are deleted from this release.

SY 4563   1/1/73   *ITALIAN LOVE SONGS*
Same as ST 1659

SM 2601 6/15/75   *BEST OF DEAN MARTIN*
Same as DT 2601; "It's Easy To Remember" and "June In January" are deleted from this release. Some Capitol Record Club pressings (DT 8-2601) were also issued with only ten tracks.

171

SM 2343   10/15/75 *HOLIDAY CHEER*
                        Same as STT 2343

SM 1659   5/15/77   *ITALIAN LOVE SONGS*
                        Same as ST 1659

SLB 8371   1984   *MEMORIES ARE MADE OF THIS (2-12")*
                        That's Amore; There's No Tomorrow; I've Grown
                        Accustomed To Her Face; With My Eyes Wide Open
                        I'm Dreaming; I Have But One Heart; Angel Baby;
                        Dream; You're Nobody 'Til Somebody Loves You;
                        Arrivederci, Roma; I Wish You Love; Nevertheless;
                        Just Say I Love Her; Return To Me; On An Evening In
                        Roma; You Belong To Me; Memories Are Made Of
                        This; Volare; Take Me In Your Arms; Just In Time;
                        Georgia On My Mind; Sway; I'll Always Love You;
                        Buona Sera; Standing On The Corner; Non Dimenticar;
                        All I Do Is Dream Of You; Once In A While; Come
                        Back To Sorrento; It's Easy To Remember; You're
                        Breaking My Heart

Reprise

R/R9 6021 4/62   *FRENCH STYLE*
                        C'est Si Bon; April In Paris; Mimi; Darling, Je Vous
                        Aime Beaucoup; La Vie En Rose; Poor People Of
                        Paris; River Seine; Last Time I Saw Paris; Mam'selle;
                        C'est Magnifique; Gigi; I Love Paris

R/R9 6054 11/27/62 *DINO LATINO*
                        El Rancho Grande; Manana; Tangerine; South Of The
                        Border; In A Little Spanish Town; What A Difference A
                        Day Made; Magic Is The Moonlight; Always In My
                        Heart; Besame Mucho; La Paloma

R/R9 6061 1/14/63 *COUNTRY STYLE*
                        I'm So Lonesome I Could Cry; Face In A Crowd;
                        Things; Room Full Of Roses; I Walk The Line; My
                        Heart Cries For You; Any Time; Shutters And Boards;
                        Blue, Blue Day; Singing The Blues; Hey Good
                        Lookin'; Ain't Gonna Try Anymore
                              (Note: "Blue, Blue Day" differs on the stereo
                              and mono releases.)

R/R9 6085 6/10/63 *DEAN TEX MARTIN RIDES AGAIN*
I'm Gonna Change Everything; Candy Kisses; Rockin' Alone In An Old Rocking Chair; Just A Little Lovin'; I Can't Help It If I'm Still In Love With You; My Sugar's Gone; Corrine, Corrina; Take Good Care Of Her; Middle Of The Night Is My Crying Time; From Lover To Loser; Bouquet Of Roses; Second Hand Rose

R/RS 6123 8/4/64 *DREAM WITH DEAN*
I'm Confessin'; Fools Rush In; I'll Buy That Dream; If You Were The Only Girl; Blue Moon; Everybody Loves Somebody; I Don't Know Why; Gimme A Little Kiss; Hands Across The Table; Smile; My Melancholy Baby; Baby, Won't You Please Come Home

R/RS 6130 8/4/64 *EVERYBODY LOVES SOMEBODY*
Everybody Loves Somebody; Your Other Love; Shutters And Boards; Baby-O; A Little Voice; Things; My Heart Cries For You; Siesta Fiesta; From Lover To Loser; Just Close Your Eyes; Corrine, Corrina; Face In A Crowd

R/RS 6140 10/3/64 *THE DOOR IS STILL OPEN TO MY HEART*
The Door Is Still Open To My Heart; We'll Sing In The Sunshine; I'm Gonna Change Everything; Middle Of The Night Is My Crying Time; Every Minute, Every Hour; Clinging Vine; In The Misty Moonlight; Always Together; My Sugar's Gone; You're Nobody 'Til Somebody Loves You; Take Me; So Long Baby

R/RS 6146 2/2/65 *DEAN MARTIN HITS AGAIN*
You're Nobody Til Somebody Loves You; I'll Hold You In My Heart; Have A Heart; My Heart Is An Open Book; You'll Always Be The One I Love; In The Chapel In The Moonlight; Send Me The Pillow You Dream On; Send Me Some Lovin'; Wedding Bells; I'll Be Seeing You
(Note: Early pressings listed "Mack Gray" as Dean's manager on the back cover. Later pressings omitted this paragraph.)

173

R/RS 6170 8/2/65 *(REMEMBER ME) I'M THE ONE WHO LOVES YOU*
(Remember Me) I'm The One Who Loves You; King Of The Road; Welcome To My World; My Shoes Keep Walking Back To You; Born To Lose; Birds And The Bees; Walk On By; Red Roses For A Blue Lady; Take These Chains From My Heart; Here Comes My Baby; I Don't Think You Love Me Anymore; Bumming Around

(Note: Early pressings did not list "Birds And The Bees" on the back cover; "Walk On By" is erroneously credited to Burt Bacharach and Hal David; the back cover picture of Dean did not include any background detail.)

R/RS 6181 11/65 *HOUSTON*
Houston; The First Thing Ev'ry Morning; Hammer And Nails; Little Lovely One; Love, Love, Love; Down Home; I Will; Snap Your Fingers; Everybody But Me; Old Yellow Line; Detour; You're The Reason I'm In Love

(Note: Some copies came with a sticker on the shrink wrap that said "Contains 'I Will'.")

R/RS 6201 3/8/66 *SOMEWHERE THERE'S A SOMEONE*
Somewhere There's A Someone; Any Time; Blue, Blue Day; I'm So Lonesome I Could Cry; Candy Kisses; I Can't Help It If I'm Still In Love With You; That Old Clock On The Wall; Bouquet Of Roses; I Walk The Line; Just A Little Lovin'; Room Full Of Roses; Second Hand Rose

R/RS 6211 4/66 *SINGS SONGS FROM THE SILENCERS*
Glory Of Love; Empty Saddles In The Old Corral; Last Roundup; Side By Side; South Of The Border; Red Sails In The Sunset; If You Knew Susie; On The Sunny Side Of The Street

(Plus 4 instrumental selections)

R/RS 6213 7/26/66 *HIT SOUND OF DEAN MARTIN*
A Million And One; Don't Let The Blues Make You Bad; Any Time; One Lonely Boy; I'm Living In Two Worlds; Come Running Back; Shades; Today Is Not The Day; Terrible, Tangled Web; Nobody But A Fool; Ain't Gonna Try Anymore

R/RS 6222 10/11/66 *DEAN MARTIN CHRISTMAS ALBUM*
White Christmas; Jingle Bells; I'll Be Home For
Christmas; Blue Christmas; Let It Snow, Let It Snow,
Let It Snow; Marshmallow World; Silver Bells; Winter
Wonderland; Things We Did Last Summer; Silent
Night

R/RS 6233 11/7/66 *DEAN MARTIN TV SHOW*
If I Had You; What Can I Say After I Say I'm Sorry;
The One I Love Belongs To Somebody Else; S'posin;
It's The Talk Of The Town; Baby, Won't You Please
Come Home; I've Grown Accustomed To Her Face;
Just Friends; Things We Did Last Summer; Home

R/RS 6242 5/2/67 *HAPPINESS IS DEAN MARTIN*
Lay Some Happiness On Me; Think About Me; I'm
Not The Marrying Kind; If I Ever Get Back To
Georgia; It Just Happened That Way; (Open Up The
Door) Let The Good Times In; You've Still Got A
Place In My Heart; Sweet, Sweet Lovable You; He's
Got You; Thirty More Miles To San Diego; Nobody's
Baby Again

R/RS 6250 8/15/67 *WELCOME TO MY WORLD*
In The Chapel In The Moonlight; Release Me; I Can't
Help Remembering You; Turn To Me; Wallpaper
Roses; Little Ole Wine Drinker, Me; Green, Green
Grass Of Home; A Place In The Shade; Pride; Welcome
To My World
(Note: Some copies came with a sticker on
the shrink wrap that said "Contains 'Little Ole
Wine Drinker, Me' and 'In The Chapel In The
Moonlight'.")

SQBO 93929 1968 *ON THE SUNNY SIDE (2-12")*
Side By Side; I Walk The Line; In The Misty
Moonlight; Lay Some Happiness On Me; Release Me;
In The Chapel In The Moonlight; Just A Little Lovin';
Bumming Around; Red Sails In The Sunset; You're
The Reason I'm In Love; Glory Of Love; Any Time;
Send Me The Pillow You Dream On; On The Sunny
Side Of The Street; That Old Clock On The Wall;
Detour; Candy Kisses; Wallpaper Roses;

South Of The Border; Bouquet Of Roses
(Capitol Record Club release.)

RS 6301   5/13/68   *DEAN MARTIN'S GREATEST HITS VOL. 1*
Everybody Loves Somebody; You're Nobody 'Til
Somebody Loves You; In The Chapel In The
Moonlight; Houston; (Remember Me) I'm The One
Who Loves You; I Can't Help Remembering You;
Nobody's Baby Again; Every Minute, Every Hour;
Bumming Around; You'll Always Be The One I Love;
Come Running Back; The Birds And The Bee
(Note: Mono copies of this album exist only
as white label promos.)

RS 6320   8/13/68   *DEAN MARTIN'S GREATEST HITS VOL. 2*
The Door Is Still Open To My Heart; I Will; Send Me
The Pillow You Dream On; Little Ole Wine Drinker,
Me; You've Still Got A Place In My Heart; In The
Misty Moonlight; Lay Some Happiness On Me; (Open
Up The Door) Let The Good Times In; Somewhere
There's A Someone; Glory Of Love; King Of The
Road; Old Yellow Line

RS 6330   12/17/68   *GENTLE ON MY MIND*
Not Enough Indians; That Old Time Feeling; Honey;
Welcome To My Heart; By The Time I Get To
Phoenix; Gentle On My Mind; That's When I See The
Blues; Rainbows Are Back In Style; Drowning In My
Tears; April Again
(Note: There is one known mono stock copy
in existence.)

RS 6338   8/7/69   *I TAKE A LOT OF PRIDE IN WHAT I AM*
I Take A Lot Of Pride In What I Am; Make It Rain;
Where The Blue And Lonely Go; If You Ever Get
Around To Loving Me; Do You Believe This Town;
One Cup Of Happiness; Sun Is Shining (On Everybody
But Me); Sneaky Little Side Of Me; Crying Time;
Little Green Apples

Gentle On My Mind mono LP (Reprise R 6330)
(Author's collection)

2RS 5528 1970 *DEAN MARTIN SONGBOOK VOLUMES 1 AND 2*
(2-12")

Honey; Nobody But A Fool; Corrina, Corrina;
Wedding Bells; Here Comes My Baby;
Release Me; We'll Sing In The Sunshine;
Room Full Of Roses; My Heart Cries For
You; Any Time; I'm Gonna Change
Everything; What Can I Say After I Say I'm
Sorry; Everybody But Me; Pride; Little Green
Apples; Red Roses For A Blue Lady; I'm So
Lonesome I Could Cry; If I Had You; Crying
Time; I'll Be Seeing You

(RCA Record Club release.)

(Note: On this release, the
opening introduction to
"I'll Be Seeing You" is
deleted as is the closing
applause segment from
"Little Green Apples.")

RS 6403 8/25/70 *MY WOMAN, MY WOMAN, MY WIFE*

My Woman, My Woman, My Wife; Once A Day; Here
We Go Again; Make The World Go Away; Tips Of My
Fingers; Detroit City; Together Again; Heart Over
Mind; Turn The World Around; It Keeps Right On
A-Hurtin

RS 6428 2/2/71 *FOR THE GOOD TIMES*

For The Good Times; Marry Me; Georgia Sunshine;
Invisible Tears; Raindrops Keep Falling On My Head;
A Perfect Mountain; Raining In My Heart; She's A
Little Bit Country; For Once In My Life; Sweetheart

2RS 5268 1971 *DEAN MARTIN COUNTRY (2-12")*

Welcome To My World; Heart Over Mind; She's A
Little Bit Country; Take These Chains From My Heart;
Candy Kisses; I Walk The Line; I'll Hold You In My
Heart; My Shoes Keep Walking Back To You; I'm
Living In Two Worlds; King Of The Road; Bouquet Of
Roses; Send Me The Pillow You Dream On; I Take A
Lot Of Pride In What I Am; Tips Of My Fingers;
Green, Green Grass Of Home; Gentle On My Mind;
First Thing Ev'ry Morning;

178

Make The World Go Away; Blue, Blue Day;
Walk On By
(RCA Record Club release.)

MS 2053   1/18/72   *DINO*

What's Yesterday; Small Exception Of Me; Just The
Other Side Of Nowhere; Blue Memories; Guess Who;
Party Dolls And Wine; I Don't Know What I'm Doing;
I Can Give You What You Want Now; Right Kind Of
Woman; Kiss The World Goodbye
(Note: Some pressings list "I Can Give You
What You Want Now" as "I CAN'T Give..."
on the front cover.)

MS 2113   5/29/73   *SITTIN' ON TOP OF THE WORLD*

I'm Sitting On Top Of The World; I Wonder Who's
Kissing Her Now; Smile; Ramblin' Rose; Almost Like
Being In Love; It's A Good Day; At Sundown; When
The Red, Red Robin Comes Bob, Bob, Bobbin' Along;
You Made Me Love You; I'm Forever Blowing
Bubbles

MS 2174   12/14/73   *YOU'RE THE BEST THING THAT EVER HAPPENED
TO ME*

Free To Carry On; You're The Best Thing
That Ever Happened To Me; I'm Confessin';
Amor Mio; You Better Move On; Tie A
Yellow Ribbon; Baby, Won't You Please
Come Home; I Don't Know Why; Gimme A
Little Kiss; Get On With Your Livin'

MSK 2267 10/20/78   *ONCE IN A WHILE*

Twilight On The Trail; Love Thy Neighbor; Without A
Word Of Warning; That Old Gang Of Mine; The Day
You Came Along; It's Magic; If I Had You; Only
Forever; I Cried For You; Once In A While

Reprise Promotional

PRO 246   10/25/66   *DEAN MARTIN RADIO STATION SAMPLER/DEAN
MARTIN MONTH*

Everybody Loves Somebody; The Door Is
Still Open To My Heart; You're Nobody 'Til
Somebody Loves You; You'll Always Be The
One I Love; Send Me The Pillow You Dream
On; (Remember Me)

179

I'm The One Who Loves You; Houston; I
Will; Somewhere There's A Someone; Come
Running Back; It Just Happened That Way;
Nobody's Baby Again

Warner Brothers
23870   6/15/83   *NASHVILLE SESSIONS*

Old Bones; Everybody's Had The Blues (With Merle
Haggard); Don't Give Up On Me; In Love Up To My
Heart; Shoulder To Shoulder; Since I Met You Baby;
My First Country Song (With Conway Twitty);
Drinking Champagne; Hangin' Around; Love Put A
Song In My Heart

(Note: Some copies came with a sticker on
the shrink wrap that said, "Includes: 'My First
Country Song', 'Since I Met You Baby',
"Shoulder To Shoulder', 'Everybody's Had
The Blues'.")

Heartland Music
1100   *GOLDEN MEMORIES (2-12")*

I Don't Know Why; Someday; When You're Smiling;
I've Grown Accustomed To Her Face; True Love;
That's Amore; Once In A While; Innamorata; Non
Dimenticar; Volare; You Belong To Me; Just Say I
Love Her; Dream A Little Dream Of Me; Just In Time;
Return To Me; Come Back To Sorrento; You're
Nobody 'Til Somebody Loves You; Dream; Standing
On The Corner; You're Breaking My Heart; Memories
Are Made Of This; I'll Always Love You
(Mail-order release).

(Note: The first few seconds of
"You're Nobody 'Til Somebody
Loves You" are cut on this release.)

Longines Symphony
SYS 5230-34   *MEMORIES ARE MADE OF THIS* (5-12" with booklet)

You're Nobody 'Til Somebody Loves You; Innamorata;
Imagination; I Can't Give You Anything But Love;
Way Down Yonder In New Orleans; Hit The Road To
Dreamland; Love (Your Magic Spell Is Everywhere);
Once In A While; Mississippi Mud; Young And
Foolish; Goodnight Sweetheart; Two

Loves Have I; Canadian Sunset; Brahms' Lullaby;
Basin Street Blues; True Love; I Can't Believe That
You're In Love With Me; Object Of My Affection; In
The Cool, Cool, Cool Of The Evening; Only Forever;
Wrap Your Troubles In Dreams; Sleepy Time Gal; I
Feel A Song Coming On; It's Easy To Remember;
Memories Are Made Of This; Return To Me; I've
Grown Accustomed To Her Face; Louise; Arrivederci,
Roma; Pretty Baby; All I Do Is Dream Of You; On The
Street Where You Live; Hear My Heart; I Feel Like A
Feather In The Breeze; A Hundred Years From Today;
Take Me In Your Arms; Let's Put Out The Lights; With
My Eyes Wide Open I'm Dreaming; When You're
Smiling; Cuddle Up A Little Closer; Goodnight, My
Love; Heaven Can Wait; Volare; That Lucky Old Sun;
Until The Real Thing Comes Along; Please Don't Talk
About Me When I'm Gone; June In January; That's All
I Want From You; Alabamy Bound
(Mail-order release)

SYS 5235   *THAT'S AMORE*
That's Amore; Somebody Loves You; Who's Sorry
Now; Rain; Pennies From Heaven; Just In Time;
Carolina In The Morning; Nevertheless; When It's
Sleepy Time Down South; Watching The World Go By
(Mail-order release)

Pair
PDL2 1029 1983   *DREAMS AND MEMORIES (2-12")*
Memories Are Made Of This; Dream; Volare; Hit The
Road To Dreamland; You're Nobody 'Til Somebody
Loves You; Wrap Your Troubles In Dreams; Come
Back To Sorrento; Sleepy Time Gal; Just In Time;
Dream A Little Dream Of Me; That's Amore; Let's Put
Out The Lights; Return To Me; All I Do Is Dream Of
You; Sway; Goodnight Sweetheart

Pickwick
PC/SPC 3057   *YOU CAN'T LOVE 'EM ALL*
You Can't Love 'Em All; I'm Yours; That Lucky Old
Sun; Be Honest With Me; I Still Get A Thrill Thinking
Of You; Who's Sorry Now; I Ain't Gonna

Lead This Life No More; Once In Love With Amy; If; Ain't That A Kick In The Head

PC/SPC 3089   *I CAN'T GIVE YOU ANYTHING BUT LOVE*
I Can't Give You Anything But Love; Innamorata; All In A Night's Work; You Look So Familiar; It Looks Like Love; Just One More Chance; When You're Smiling; When You Pretend; The Test Of Time; A Day In The Country

SPC 3136   *YOUNG AND FOOLISH*
Young And Foolish; Oh Marie; Little Did We Know; Pennies From Heaven; Let Me Go Lover; That's All I Want From You; In The Cool, Cool, Cool Of The Evening; Rain; Absence Makes The Heart Grow Fonder

SPC 3175   *YOU WERE MADE FOR LOVE*
You Were Made For Love; I'll Always Love You; You I Love; Until You Love Someone; Cheatin' On Me; Object Of My Affection; I Love The Way You Say Goodnight; Let Me Know; Come Back To Sorrento

SPC 3283   *DEAN MARTIN DELUXE*
Same as ST 1442; "Mean To Me," "Imagination," and "You're Nobody 'Til Somebody Loves You" are deleted from this release.

SPC 3307   *I HAVE BUT ONE HEART*
I Have But One Heart; Don't You Remember?; Return To Me; My One And Only Love; A Hundred Years From Today; Standing On The Corner; Imagination; Non Dimenticar; If Love Is Good To Me

SPC 3465   *DEAN MARTIN SINGS/SINATRA CONDUCTS*
Same as ST 1150; "Dream" and "Sleep Warm" are deleted from this release.

PTP 2001   *DEAN MARTIN SWINGIN'*
2 record set release of 3057 and 3089

PTP 2051   *DEAN MARTIN*
2 record set release of 3283 and 3307

Sears

SP/SPS 434   *I'M YOURS*
              Same as SPC 3057

SP/SPS 450   *JUST ONE MORE CHANCE*
              Same as SPC 3089

SPS 494   *I'LL ALWAYS LOVE YOU*
              Same as SPC 3175

Silver Eagle

10733   1988   *DEAN MARTIN GREATEST HITS (2-12")*
                   You're Nobody 'Til Somebody Loves You; The Door Is
                   Still Open To My Heart; That's Amore; Turn To Me;
                   Volare; Everybody Loves Somebody; Make The World
                   Go Away; (Remember Me) I'm The One Who Loves
                   You; I'm Gonna Change Everything; I Will; Little Ole
                   Wine Drinker, Me; Send Me The Pillow You Dream
                   On; Houston; Ramblin' Rose; I Take A Lot Of Pride In
                   What I Am; Memories Are Made Of This; Red Roses
                   For A Blue Lady; In The Misty Moonlight; I Can't
                   Help It If I'm Still In Love With You; Glory Of Love
                   (Mail-order release)

10733-2   1988   *DEAN MARTIN FAVORITE SONGS*
                   For The Good Times; Honey; Raindrops Keep Falling
                   On My Head; By The Time I Get To Phoenix; Tie A
                   Yellow Ribbon; King Of The Road; Hey, Good
                   Lookin'; Little Green Apples; For Once In My Life;
                   Detroit City; Gentle On My Mind; My Woman, My
                   Woman, My Wife
                   (Mail-order release)
                                    (Note: There was a TV commercial
                                    made to promote these albums. It
                                    showed still photos of Dean as well
                                    as clips from the 1983 London
                                    concert.)

Suffolk Marketing

SML1-55 1984   *HEART-TOUCHING TREASURY*
                  My Heart Cries For You; I'll Hold You In My Heart;
                  Release Me; Green, Green Grass Of Home; Born To
                  Lose; Welcome To My World; In The Misty Moonlight;
                  I'm So Lonesome I Could Cry; Take These Chains

183

From My Heart; I Can't Help It If I'm Still In Love
With You; The Door Is Still Open To My Heart; You've
Still Got A Place In My Heart
(Mail-order release.)

SML1-56   1984   *FAMOUS LOVE SONGS*
Everybody Loves Somebody; Somewhere There's A
Someone; I Wonder Who's Kissing Her Now; Crying
Time; The One I Love Belongs To Somebody Else;
You're Breaking My Heart; Return To Me; Arrivederci
Roma; There's No Tomorrow; Room Full Of Roses; In
The Chapel In The Moonlight; You'll Always Be The
One I Love
(Mail-order release.)
(Note: There was a TV commercial
made for these albums in which
Dean is shown lip-synching several
of the songs.)

Tee Vee/Capitol
SLB 8115   1978   *20 GREAT HITS (2-12")*
Memories Are Made Of This; That's Amore; I've
Grown Accustomed To Her Face; Just Say I Love Her;
All I Do Is Dream Of You; Volare; Standing On The
Corner; Just In Time; You Belong To Me; Angel Baby;
You're Nobody 'Til Somebody Loves You; Cha Cha
Cha D'Amour; Dream A Little Dream Of Me; I'll
Always Love You; It's Easy To Remember; Sway;
Someday; Return To Me; When You're Smiling; Dream

Tower
T/DT 5006 10/11/65 *LUSH YEARS*
Love Me, My Love; Be An Angel; Off Again, On
Again; Where Can I Go Without You; Hear My
Heart; I Never Had A Chance; Rio Bravo; Career;
Story Of Life; It Takes So Long To Say Goodbye

T/DT 5018 3/7/66 *RELAXIN'*
Little Did We Know; Pennies From Heaven; Napoli;
Chee Chee-Oo Chee; I Want You; Sparklin' Eyes;
Cheatin' On Me; Let Me Know; How Sweet It Is;
Who Was That Lady

T/DT 5036 8/2/66   *HAPPY IN LOVE*
> Love Is All That Matters; I Love The Way You Say Goodnight; I'll Always Love You; You I Love; All I Have To Give You Is My Love; Until You Love Someone; If I Should Love Again; Street Of Love; You Were Made For Love; I'm Gonna Paper All My Walls With Your Love Letters

T/DT 5059 8/7/67   *LIKE NEVER BEFORE*
> I Ran All The Way Home; What Could Be More Beautiful; Second Chance; There's My Lover; 'Til I Find You; Never Before; Try Again; Beside You; That's What I Like; One More Time

PROPOSED ALBUM RELEASES

Capitol
1494   *THE LOVERS OF ROME*
> (Note: Front cover slicks of this release exist. It might have been a working title for *ITALIAN LOVE SONGS*, but no further information is available.)

Reprise
6127   *BING, DINO 'N' DIXIE*
> (Note: Front cover slicks of this proposed release exist.)

6189   *OLD TIME RELIGION*
> (Note: "Project canceled" according to Reprise files.)

REEL-TO-REEL

Capitol
Y2T 2241 4/12/65 *SLEEP WARM/THIS TIME I'M SWINGIN*
> Same as ST 1150 and ST 1442

Y2T 2242 5/3/65 *ITALIAN LOVE SONGS/CHA CHA DE AMOR*
> Same as ST 1659 and ST 1702

Bing, Dino 'N' Dixie LP cover slick (unreleased) (Reprise R9/R 6127)
(Bob Furmanek collection)

(Note: There are 2 different front covers to the reel-to-reel version of *The Best of Dean Martin.* First pressings picture an out-take from the *Italian Love Songs* photo sessions. Second pressings picture the standard LP photo cover.)

Reprise
ST 305   *GREATEST HITS VOL. 1 AND 2*
                           Same as RS 6301 and RS 6320

CASSETTE

Capitol
4XL 8304 1982   *ALL I DO IS DREAM OF YOU*
                         (Reissued as *YOU'RE NOBODY 'TIL SOMEBODY LOVES YOU* in 1990)
                               I've Grown Accustomed To Her Face; Just In Time; Imagination; Nevertheless; You're Nobody 'Til Somebody Loves You; All I Do Is Dream Of You; You Belong To Me; Once In A While

4XL 9098 1984   *SINGS ITALIAN FAVORITES*
                         Just Say I Love Her; Arrivederci, Roma; You're Breaking My Heart; Return To Me; There's No Tomorrow; That's Amore; I Have But One Heart; Volare; Non Dimenticar

4XL 9389 1986   *GREATEST HITS*
                         Memories Are Made Of This; Sway; Return To Me; I'll Always Love You; Innamorata; That's Amore; Standing On The Corner; You Belong To Me; Volare

4XL 57005 1988   *YOU'RE NOBODY 'TIL SOMEBODY LOVES YOU*
                         You're Nobody 'Til Somebody Loves You; Just In Time; I Wish You Love; I Can't Believe That You're In Love With Me; Cha Cha Cha D'Amour; I've Grown Accustomed To Her Face; My One And Only Love; Until The Real Thing Comes Along; Somebody Loves You

COMPACT DISCS

Capitol

CDP 46627 2/10/88 *BEST OF DEAN MARTIN*
> Same as T 2601

CDP 91633 10/25/89 *CAPITOL COLLECTOR'S SERIES*
> That Certain Party (With Jerry Lewis); Powder Your Face With Sunshine; I'll Always Love You; If; You Belong To Me; Love Me, Love Me; That's Amore (With studio chatter); I'd Cry Like A Baby; Sway (With studio chatter); Money Burns A Hole In My Pocket; Memories Are Made Of This; Innamorata; Standing On The Corner; Watching The World Go By (With studio chatter); Return To Me; Angel Baby; Volare; On An Evening In Roma (With studio chatter); Love Me, My Love; Ain't That A Kick In The Head (With studio chatter)

CDP 93155 11/08/89 *A WINTER ROMANCE*
> Same as ST 1285
>
> Bonus Track: The Christmas Blues and there is studio chatter preceding Baby It's Cold Outside and It Won't Cool Off.

CDP 94306 6/24/91 *SWINGIN' DOWN YONDER*
> Same as T 576
>
> Bonus Tracks: Hominy Grits; I'm Gonna Paper All My Walls With Your Love Letters; Muskrat Ramble; Be Honest With Me; I Don't Care If The Sun Don't Shine; Bye Bye Blackbird; Happy Feet; Darktown Strutter's Ball and there is studio chatter preceding I'm Gonna Paper All My Walls With Your Love Letters and Be Honest With Me.

CDP 29389   8/1/95 *SPOTLIGHT ON DEAN MARTIN*
> All I Do Is Dream Of You; Please Don't Talk About Me When I'm Gone; Things We Did Last Summer; Mean To Me; Wrap Your Troubles In Dreams; Imagination; Sleepy Time Gal; You're Nobody 'Til Somebody Loves You; Dream; Someday; June In January; I Can't Believe That You're In Love With Me; Dream A Little Dream Of Me; Just In Time; Cuddle Up A Little Closer; Until The Real Thing

> Comes Along; Hit The Road To Dreamland; Goodnight
> Sweetheart

CDP 37500 4/16/96 *SLEEP WARM*
> Same as ST 1150

CDP 37571 4/16/96 *THAT'S AMORE: THE BEST OF DEAN MARTIN*
> That's Amore; You're Nobody 'Til Somebody Loves
> You Volare; Sway; Return To Me; Memories Are Made
> Of This; Come Back To Sorrento; Just In Time; I'm
> Yours; Hey, Brother, Pour The Wine; Just Say I Love
> Her; If Love Is Good To Me; Standing On The Corner;
> Vieni Su; Innamorata; Arrivederci, Roma; I've Grown
> Accustomed To Her Face; Canadian Sunset; Pretty
> Baby; My One And Only Love

CDP 98409 6/11/96 *DEAN MARTIN - THE CAPITOL YEARS* (2 CD Set)
> Memories Are Made Of This; Powder Your Face With
> Sunshine; You Was (With Peggy Lee); Dreamy Old
> New England Moon; I'm Gonna Paper All My Walls
> With Your Love Letters; I'll Always Love You;
> Solitaire; Night Train To Memphis; Pretty As A Picture;
> Oh Marie; You Belong To Me; Susan; Peanut Vendor;
> I'm Yours; That's Amore; I'd Cry Like A Baby; Hey,
> Brother, Pour The Wine; Ev'ry Street's A Boulevard In
> Old New York (With Jerry Lewis); I'll Gladly Make
> The Same Mistake Again; Open Up The Doghouse
> (With Nat King Cole); Carolina In The Morning; In
> Napoli; Innamorata; I'm Gonna Steal You Away (With
> the Nuggets); Only Trust Your Heart; Beau James;
> Good Mornin', Life; Return To Me; It's 1200 Miles
> From Palm Springs To Texas; Volare; On An Evening
> In Roma; All I Do Is Dream Of You; Live Medley:
> (You Made Me Love You/It Had To Be
> You/Nevertheless/I'm Gonna Sit Right Down And
> Write Myself A Letter); My Guiding Star; Until The
> Real Thing Comes Along; Ain't That A Kick In The
> Head; Just In Time; Be An Angel; Non Dimenticar;
> Somebody Loves You
>> (Note: This release also contains a brief
>> spoken introduction to "Memories Are Made
>> Of This" by Dean.)

Capitol Promo-Only Release
DPRO 11243 1996 *DEAN MARTIN - THE CAPITOL YEARS SAMPLER*
Open Up The Doghouse (With Nat King Cole); Ain't That A Kick In The Head; Memories Are Made Of This; Live Medley; That's Amore; You're Nobody 'Til Somebody Loves You; Volare; Return To Me

Cema
17761 *THAT'S AMORE*
Memories Are Made Of This; Standing On The Corner; That's Amore; Sway; I'll Always Love You; You're Nobody 'Til Somebody Loves You; Return To Me; Volare; Angel Baby; You Belong To Me

57688 1992 *SEASON'S GREETINGS*
White Christmas; Let It Snow, Let It Snow, Let It Snow; Baby It's Cold Outside; Winter Romance; Winter Wonderland; I've Got My Love To Keep Me Warm; Rudolph The Red-Nosed Reindeer; Christmas Blues; Out In The Cold Again; It Won't Cool Off

Curb
77383 1990 *ALL-TIME GREATEST HITS*
That's Amore; Sway; You Belong To Me; Memories Are Made Of This; Return To Me; Volare; Standing On The Corner; Innamorata; On An Evening In Roma; You're Nobody 'Til Somebody Loves You; Non Dimenticar; Come Back To Sorrento

Good Music Record Company
106526 *20 GREAT HITS*
Same as SLB 8115

Heartland Music
1100 1990 *GOLDEN MEMORIES*
Same as LP

Pair
PCD 1029 1983 *DREAMS AND MEMORIES*
Same as LP; CD issued with 2 different covers

PCD 1177 1987 *HAPPY HOUR WITH DEAN MARTIN*
Non Dimenticar; You Belong To Me; I Wish You Love;
Just In Time; Just Say I Love Her; Standing On The
Corner; Just One More Chance; I Can't Believe That
You're In Love With Me; You're Breaking My Heart;
Georgia On My Mind; Once In A While; Angel Baby;
With My Eyes Wide Open I'm Dreaming; There's No
Tomorrow; Nevertheless; Dream A Little Dream Of Me

Ranwood
8259 1997 *LOVE SONGS BY DEAN MARTIN*
That's Amore; Memories Are Made Of This; Return To
Me; I'll Always Love You; Angel Baby; You Belong To
Me; Just In Time; Volare; Innamorata; If; You I Love;
Love Me, Love Me; There's No Tomorrow; You're
Nobody 'Til Somebody Loves You

Reader's Digest
113 1997 *THE CAPITOL YEARS* (3 CD Set)
That's Amore; I'll Always Love You; You Belong To
Me; Standing On The Corner; Return To Me; Sway; If;
Powder Your Face With Sunshine; Love Me, Love Me;
Memories Are Made Of This; There's No Tomorrow;
Oh Marie; You're Breaking My Heart; On An Evening
In Roma; Mambo Italiano; I Have But One Heart;
Non Dimenticar; Volare; Come Back To Sorrento;
Arrivederci, Roma; Basin Street Blues; Open Up The
Doghouse (With Nat King Cole); Georgia On My
Mind; Baby It's Cold Outside; Long, Long Ago (With
Nat King Cole); Just In Time (With Judy Holliday);
Don't Rock The Boat, Dear (With Margaret Whiting);
You Was (With Peggy Lee); I'm In Love With You
(With Margaret Whiting); How D'Ya Like Your Eggs
In The Morning (With Helen O'Connell); Money
Burns A Hole In My Pocket; My Rifle, My Pony And
Me; Never Before; Innamorata; You're The Right One;
Just For Fun; The Money Song (With Jerry Lewis);
Ev'ry Street's A Boulevard In Old New York (With
Jerry Lewis); That Certain Party (With Jerry Lewis);
Pardners (With Jerry Lewis); My One And Only Love;
Cuddle Up A Little Closer; True Love; I Wish You

191

Love; Dream A Little Dream Of Me; Amor; I've Grown Accustomed To Her Face; I've Got My Love To Keep Me Warm; Mean To Me; Young And Foolish; How Do You Speak To An Angel; If I Could Sing Like Bing; It's Easy To Remember; You're Nobody 'Til Somebody Loves You; A Hundred Years From Today; I Can't Give You Anything But Love; Is It True What They Say About Dixie; Carolina In The Morning; Louise; When You're Smiling

Silver Eagle

SED 10733   1988   *GREATEST HITS*
Same as LP

SED 10733   1988   *FAVORITE SONGS*
Same as LP

UNAUTHORIZED AMERICAN RELEASE

BAMA 2864 1996   *DINO AT THE SANDS*
Parody Medley: Bourbon From Heaven/It's All Right With Me; June In January; You Must Have Been A Beautiful Baby; Memories Are Made Of This; That's Amore; Medley: You Made Me Love You/It Had To Be You/Nevertheless; On A Slow Boat To China; Medley: Volare/On An Evening In Roma; Mr. Wonderful
Bonus Track: Radio ad for Pete Epsteen's Pontiac dealership in Chicago, IL

SPECIAL FOREIGN RELEASES

Bear Family

BCD 15781   1997   *MEMORIES ARE MADE OF THIS*
This is an 8-CD set released in Germany. It contains all of Dean's recordings from 1946 through 1955. Additionally, the following songs were issued for the first time ever on this set:
Moments Like This
I Never Had A Chance
(Master 12608)
Chee Chee-Oo Chee (Master 13722)
I Know Your Mother Loves You
When You Pretend (Master 14668)

CD's #7 and #8 contain the following songs taken directly from the motion picture soundtracks: Just For Fun; Donkey Serenade (With Jerry Lewis); My Own, My Only, My All; Here's To Love (With Jerry); Baby Obey Me (With Jerry and Corinne Calvet); Singing A Vagabond Song (With Jerry); I'll Always Love You; Santa Lucia/ Fiddle And Guitar Band (With Jerry); Tonda Wanda Hoy; You And Your Beautiful Eyes (With Polly Bergen); Too Ra Loo Ra Loo Ra; Ballin' The Jack (With Polly); I'm In The Mood For Love; Today, Tomorrow, Forever; Sailor's Polka; Old Calliope (With Jerry); Never Before; Parachute Jump; Big Blue Sky Is The Place For Me; I Know A Dream When I See One; Keep A Little Dream Handy (With Jerry); I'm Yours; Who's Your Little Who-Zis (With Jerry); With My Eyes Wide Open I'm Dreaming; I Feel A Song Coming On (With Jerry); A Girl Named Mary And A Boy Named Bill (With Polly); I Feel Like A Feather In The Breeze; Just One More Chance (With Jerry); Who's Your Little Who-Zis (With Jerry); I Don't Care If The Sun Don't Shine; You Hit The Spot; What Have You Done For Me Lately (With Jerry); San Domingo/The Bongo Bingo (With Jerry and Carmen Miranda); When Someone Wonderful Thinks You're Wonderful; Enchilada Man (With Jerry and Carmen); What Wouldcha Do Without Me (With Jerry); That's Amore (With Jerry); You're The Right One; It's A Whistle-In Kinda Morning; What Wouldcha Do Without Me (With Jerry); Love Is The Same All Over The World; Moments Like This; I

193

Only Have Eyes For You; That's
What I Like; How Do You Speak To
An Angel; Money Burns A Hole
In My Pocket; Ev'ry Street's A
Boulevard In Old New York (With
Jerry); It's A Big, Wide, Wonderful
World; Hey Punchinello (With
Jerry); Relax-Ay-Voo (With Jerry);
I Know Your Mother Loves You;
Love Is All That Matters; Face The
Music; Simpatico; I Like To Hike;
Artists And Models; When You
Pretend (With Jerry); You Look
So Familiar; The Lucky Song;
Innamorata; Artists And Models
(With Jerry); When You Pretend
(With Jerry, Shirley MacLaine and
Dorothy Malone)

BCD 15959   1998   *RETURN TO ME*

This is an 8-CD set released in Germany. It contains
all of Dean's recordings from 1956 through
1961. Additionally, the following songs
were issued for the first time ever on this set:
Napoli (Master 31663)
Story Of Life (Master 35075)
Bella Bella Bambina (Master 35076)
Let Me Know (Master 35083)
Be An Angel (Master 35084)
Hear My Heart (Master 35085)
Giuggiola (Master 35353)
CD #7 contains the following songs taken directly
from the motion picture soundtracks:
The Wind, The Wind; Pardners
(With Jerry Lewis); Me 'N' You 'N'
The Moon; Pardners (With Jerry);
Hollywood Or Bust (With Jerry);
A Day In The Country (With Jerry);
Let's Be Friendly; The Wild And
Wooly West (With Jerry and Pat
Crowley); It Looks Like Love (With
Pat Crowley); Hollywood Or Bust;
Ten Thousand Bedrooms; Only Trust
Your Heart (With Anna-Maria
Alberghetti); You I Love; You I Love

(With Anna-Maria); Money Is A Problem (With Jules Munshin); How About You/Blue Moon; My Rifle, My Pony And Me (With Ricky Nelson); Cindy (With Ricky and Walter Brennan); Who Was That Lady; Just Do It; Better Than A Dream (With Judy Holliday); I Met A Girl (With Judy Holliday); Just In Time; Ain't That A Kick In The Head; May The Lord Bless You Real Good

CD #8 contains the following songs taken directly from original radio broadcasts:

My Melancholy Baby; Till Then; If I Knew Then; There'll Be A Hot Time In The Town Of Berlin; My Melancholy Baby; Someday; Peg O' My Heart; Everybody Loves Somebody; On A Slow Boat To China; Ramblin' Rose Of Mine; Here I'll Stay; I'll String Along With You; I Wonder Who's Kissing Her Now; About A Quarter To Nine; Somewhere Along The Way; For Me And My Gal; If You Were The Only Girl; Glow Worm; Because You're Mine; Deep Purple; My Lady Loves To Dance; It Takes Two To Tango; Why Don't You Believe Me; It's Beginning To Look A Lot Like Christmas; To See You Is To Love You; Silver Bells; Silent Night; Don't Let The Stars Get In Your Eyes; Heart And Soul; You'd Be Surprised

RECORD COMPANY INNERSLEEVES

Capitol

1953   The Famous 1600 Series
           Lists Dean's 1682 - Oh Marie/I'll Always Love You

1960   Pictures *BELLS ARE RINGING* Soundtrack W 1435
           (black and white)

1960   Pictures *BELLS ARE RINGING* Soundtrack SW 1435
            (color)

1961   Capitol 7" Compact 33
            Pictures Dean's EP 1580

1961   Pictures black and white caricature of
            ITALIAN LOVE SONGS ST 1659

1965   Pictures *DEAN MARTIN SINGS/SINATRA CONDUCTS*
            ST 2297

1965   Pictures *HEY, BROTHER, POUR THE WINE* DT 2212

1966   Pictures *THE BEST OF DEAN MARTIN* DT 2601

Reprise

1962   Pictures *FRENCH STYLE* R9 6021

1964   Lists *FRENCH STYLE* 6021; *DINO LATINO* 6054;
            COUNTRY STYLE 6061; RIDES AGAIN 6085;
            ROBIN AND THE 7 HOODS 2021; *DREAM*
            WITH DEAN 6123 and the unreleased
            BING, DINO 'N' DIXIE 6127

1964   Lists *FRENCH STYLE* 6021; *DINO LATINO* 6054;
            COUNTRY STYLE 6061; *RIDES AGAIN* 6085;
            ROBIN AND THE 7 HOODS 2021; *DREAM*
            WITH DEAN 6123; *EVERYBODY LOVES*
            SOMEBODY 6130 and *DOOR IS STILL OPEN*
            TO MY HEART 6140

1965   Pictures *DREAM WITH DEAN* 6123; *EVERYBODY*
            LOVES SOMEBODY 6130; *DOOR IS STILL*
            OPEN TO MY HEART 6140 and *HITS AGAIN*
            6146

1965   Pictures *EVERYBODY LOVES SOMEBODY* 6130;
            DOOR IS STILL OPEN TO MY HEART 6140;
            (REMEMBER ME) I'M THE ONE WHO LOVES
            YOU 6170 and *HOUSTON* 6181

1966   Pictures *EVERYBODY LOVES SOMEBODY* 6130;
        HITS AGAIN 6146; *HOUSTON* 6181;
        SOMEWHERE THERE'S A SOMEONE 6201
        and *SINGS SONGS FROM THE SILENCERS* 6211

1967   Pictures *HIT SOUND* 6213; *TV SHOW* 6233 and
        HAPPINESS IS 6242

1967   Pictures *HIT SOUND* 6213; *HAPPINESS IS* 6242 and
        WELCOME TO MY WORLD 6250

1968   Pictures *WELCOME TO MY WORLD* 6250;
        GREATEST HITS, VOL. 1 6301; and
        GREATEST HITS, VOL. 2 6320

1969   Lists Dean's name as one of Reprise Records'
        "Makers Of Fine Music"

1970   Pictures caricature of Dean

(NBC publicity photo)

Chapter 4

Various Artists Releases

(Note: The format is as follows: label, number, album title, song or
songs performed by Dean.)

ALBUMS

Capitol

H 9112   *TODAY'S TOP HITS VOLUME VII* (10")
          You Belong To Me

H 9116   *TODAY'S TOP HITS VOLUME XI* (10")
          That's Amore

H 9117   *TOP HITS OF 1954* (10")
          Hey, Brother, Pour The Wine

T 830   *GOLD RECORD*
          That's Amore

T 913   *TODAY'S TOP HITS*
          Memories Are Made Of This

T 945   *JUST FOR VARIETY VOLUME 2*
          Money Burns A Hole In My Pocket

T 946   *JUST FOR VARIETY VOLUME 3*
          That's Amore

T 949   *JUST FOR VARIETY VOLUME 6*
         Memories Are Made Of This

T 950   *JUST FOR VARIETY VOLUME 7*
         Who's Your Little Who-Zis

T 951   *JUST FOR VARIETY VOLUME 8*
         I Like Them All

T 953   *JUST FOR VARIETY VOLUME 10*
         Just One More Chance

T 967   *JUST FOR VARIETY VOLUME 13*
         Mambo Italiano

CSD 1001   *FIRESTONE 5 STAR FIESTA*
         Memories Are Made Of This
         Return To Me
             (Note: This release was only available in November and December of 1961. Initial press run of 100,000 copies.)

T 1007   *JUST FOR VARIETY VOLUME 15*
         Naughty Lady Of Shady Lane

ST 1435   *BELLS ARE RINGING*
         I Met A Girl
         Do It Yourself
         Just In Time (With Judy Holliday)
         Better Than A Dream (With Judy Holliday)

T 1488   *GREAT SMASH HITS*
         That's Amore

T 1622   *SEASON'S GREETINGS*
         Rudolph The Red-Nosed Reindeer

T 2474   *CAMP!*
         Powder Your Face With Sunshine

STBB 2979   *BEST OF CHRISTMAS* (2 -12")
         Rudolph The Red-Nosed Reindeer

SL 6568   *ZENITH PRESENTS BEST OF THE POPULAR VOCAL FAVORITES*
         Canadian Sunset
         Arrivederci, Roma

SL 6603   *GREAT SONG STYLISTS*
                    Arrivederci, Roma

SL 6648   *BEST OF THE GREAT POPULAR VOCALISTS*
                    Canadian Sunset

SL 6659   *CHRISTMAS GIFT OF MUSIC VOL. 3*
                    Let It Snow, Let It Snow, Let It Snow

SL 6679   *CHRISTMAS THE SEASON OF MUSIC*
                    Winter Wonderland

SL 6688   *CHRISTMAS MUSIC FESTIVAL*
                    White Christmas

SL 6706   *LEGENDARY SONG STYLISTS*
                    Canadian Sunset

SL 6754   *ZENITH PRESENTS DEAN MARTIN/*
                GLEN CAMPBELL
                    I've Got My Love To Keep Me Warm
                    Arrivederci, Roma
                    There's No Tomorrow
                    Mean To Me
                    Just In Time

SL 6808   *MUSICAL MILESTONES*
                    Memories Are Made Of This

SLC 6874   *GREAT SUPERSTARS* (3-12")
                    Same as SL 6754

SL 6881   *MERRY MUSIC CHRISTMAS*
                    Baby It's Cold Outside
                    Winter Wonderland
                    I've Got My Love To Keep Me Warm
                    Rudolph The Red-Nosed Reindeer
                    White Christmas

SL 6884   *CHRISTMAS AMERICA*
                    Winter Wonderland

SL 6923   *LET'S CELEBRATE CHRISTMAS*
                    White Christmas

SL 6925   *CHRISTMAS WITH BING, NAT, DEAN*
                 Winter Wonderland
                 White Christmas

SL 6941   *SONGS OF LOVE*
                 I Wish You Love

SLDR 6955   *MEMORIES ARE MADE OF THESE* (4-12")
                 Memories Are Made Of This
                 Canadian Sunset

SL 8006   *JOY PRESENTS POP HITS OF THE '50s*
                 That's Amore

SL 8072   *FAMILY CHRISTMAS*
                 White Christmas

SLB 8098   *FROM ITALY WITH LOVE* (2-12")
                 Arrivederci, Roma
                 Return To Me
                 That's Amore

SL 8100   *POPULAR CHRISTMAS CLASSICS*
                 White Christmas

SL 8107   *SPANISH FEELINGS*
                 Sway

SL 8321   *MAGIC OF CHRISTMAS*
                 Rudolph The Red-Nosed Reindeer

W 9028   *MERRY CHRISTMAS TO YOU* (16 track version)
                 Christmas Blues

T 9030   *MERRY CHRISTMAS TO YOU* (12 track version)
                 Christmas Blues

T 9130   *TODAY'S TOP HITS VOL. 14*
                 Memories Are Made Of This

SM 11833   *BEST OF CHRISTMAS VOL. 1*
                 Let It Snow, Let It Snow, Let It Snow

SM 11834   *BEST OF CHRISTMAS VOL. 2*
                 Rudolph The Red-Nosed Reindeer

SNX 16389   *BEST OF CHRISTMAS VOL. 2*
                    Rudolph The Red-Nosed Reindeer

SL 57065   *THE CHRISTMAS SONGS VOL. 2*
                    Baby It's Cold Outside

SLB 57054   *THE CHRISTMAS SONGS* (2-12")
                    Rudolph The Red-Nosed Reindeer
                    White Christmas

SNP 90494   *CHRISTMAS STOCKING*
                    Rudolph The Red-Nosed Reindeer
                       (Capitol Record Club release)

SNP 91017   *SILVER YEARS*
                    Volare
                       (Capitol Record Club release)

SWBB 93810   *THE MAGIC OF CHRISTMAS* (2-12")
                    White Christmas

STBB 93245   *SOUNDS OF CHRISTMAS* (2-12")
                    Rudolph The Red-Nosed Reindeer

SQBE 94406   *CHRISTMAS CAROUSEL* (2-12")
                    Let It Snow, Let It Snow, Let It Snow

Note: A Capitol test pressing exists (dated 4/2/75) with 5 songs by Sandler and Young on one side and the following songs by Dean on the other:
                    For Sentimental Reasons
                    If Love Is Good To Me
                    My One And Only Love
                    I Wish You Love
                    Cha Cha Cha D'Amour

Capitol Promotional-Only Releases
197/198   *THE CAPITOL STORY* (7")
                    That's Amore
                    (Excerpt only)

Recorded Highlights of Glen Wallichs Day promo 10" (Capitol PRO 215)
(Oprisko Family collection)

215-218   *RECORDED HIGHLIGHTS OF GLEN WALLICHS*
           DAY (9/27/54)
               (2-10")
                         Dean was the Master of Ceremonies at this
                         luncheon for Capitol Record's president.
                         That's Amore
                         Try Again
                         (Excerpts only)

254/255   *THE CAPITOL RECORD-A SOUVENIR OF THE CAPITOL*
           TOWER
               (7")
                         Memories Are Made Of This
                         (Excerpt only)

727-730   *CHRISTMAS AROUND THE WORLD*
           DECEMBER 1958 (2-12")
                         Christmas Blues

967-970   *SOUNDS UNLIMITED-NEW ALBUM PREVIEW FOR*
           MARCH 1959
               (2-12")
                         Hit The Road To Dreamland
                         Wrap Your Troubles In Dreams

1063/1064 My Rifle, My Pony and Me/Rio Bravo
           (7" with picture sleeve)
                         (Also contains De Guello by Nelson Riddle)

1298/1299 *NEW PREVIEW ALBUMS (NOVEMBER 1959)*
           A Winter's Romance

1390/1391 *TRIBUTE TO JIMMY McHUGH -*
           I FEEL A SONG COMING ON
           I Feel A Song Coming On

1585/1586 *REACH FOR A STAR JULY 1960*
           Better Than A Dream

1665/1666 *REACH FOR A STAR OCTOBER 1960*
                         I Can't Believe That You're In Love With Me
                         Please Don't Talk About Me When I'm Gone

           (Note: In late 1960, Dean was one of many Capitol acts
           shown on a generic picture sleeve used for the company's
           "Can you find the Capitol mystery artist?" promotion.)

1958/1959 *GREAT NEW RELEASES FROM THE SOUND CAPITOL*
           OF THE WORLD FEBRUARY 1962
                         Just Say I Love Her
                         Vieni Su

205

2195/2196   *NINE FOR NOVEMBER 1962*
                Somebody Loves You
                I Love You Much Too Much

2505-2508   *INSTANT HITS-JANUARY 1964* (2-12")
                Volare
                Memories Are Made Of This
                       (Note: These are specially edited versions
                       clocking in at approximately one minute
                       each.)

2821/2822   *GREAT NEW RELEASES FROM THE SOUND CAPITOL*
              OF THE WORLD APRIL 1965
                All I Do Is Dream Of You
                Wrap Your Troubles In Dreams

2879/2880   *GREAT NEW RELEASES FROM THE SOUND CAPITOL*
              OF THE WORLD JUNE 1965
                Carolina In The Morning

3029/3030   *SILVER PLATTER SERVICE DECEMBER 1962*
                Christmas Blues

3085/3086   *SILVER PLATTER SERVICE*
                Promise Her Anything

3137/3138   *SILVER PLATTER SERVICE JANUARY/FEBRUARY 1965*
                Standing On The Corner

3147-3150   *SILVER PLATTER SERVICE APRIL 1965*
                Dream A Little Dream Of Me
                Wrap Your Troubles In Dreams
                Sleepy Time Gal
                Hit The Road To Dreamland

3179/3180   *SILVER PLATTER SERVICE DECEMBER 1965*
                Rudolph The Red-Nosed Reindeer

3211/3212   *SILVER PLATTER SERVICE*
                Promise Her Anything

4155/4156   *STEREO SAMPLER OCTOBER 1966*
                You're Nobody 'Til Somebody Loves You

4174-4177   *REMEMBER HOW GREAT* (2-12")
       Memories Are Made Of This
       You're Nobody 'Til Somebody Loves You

4210/4211   *MUSIC FOR CHRISTMAS SHOPPERS ONLY*
       Although Dean's *Holiday Cheer* album is pictured
       on the cover, this record does not contain any Dean
       Martin tracks.

4411/4412   *25 YEAR SILVER ANNIVERSARY*
       Memories Are Made Of This
       (Excerpt Only)

4724/4725   *CAPITOL HITS THROUGH THE YEARS*
       That's Amore
       Memories Are Made Of This
       Return To Me
       Volare
       (Excerpts only)

Pickwick

SPC 1009   *I'LL BE HOME FOR CHRISTMAS*
       Rudolph The Red-Nosed Reindeer

SPC 3253   *STAR SHINE*
       I'm Yours

SH 3303   *THE STARS AND THE HITS* (3-12")
       I'm Yours

SPC 3462   *LITTLE DRUMMER BOY*
       White Christmas

Reprise

246   Four For Texas/Foolish Pride by Dorsey Burnette (7" with
       picture sleeve)
          (Note: Dean, Frank Sinatra, Anita Ekberg
          and Ursula Andress are shown on the pic-
          ture sleeve of this release.)

2FS 1016   *SINATRA: A MAN AND HIS MUSIC*
       The Summit (Comedy routine with Frank Sinatra and
          Sammy Davis, Jr.)
       The Oldest Established Permanent Floating Crap
          Game In New York (With Frank Sinatra
          and Bing Crosby)

FS 2015 *REPRISE MUSICAL REPERTORY THEATRE PRESENTS*
     FINIAN'S RAINBOW
       If This Isn't Love (With The Hi-Los)

FS 2016 *REPRISE MUSICAL REPERTORY THEATRE PRESENTS*
     GUYS AND DOLLS
       Fugue For Tinhorns (With Frank Sinatra
        and Bing Crosby)
       The Oldest Established Permanent Floating
        Crap Game In New York (With
        Frank Sinatra and Bing Crosby)
       Guys And Dolls (With Frank Sinatra)
       Guys and Dolls Reprise (With Frank Sinatra)

FS 2017 *REPRISE MUSICAL REPERTORY THEATRE PRESENTS*
     KISS ME KATE
       We Open In Venice (With Frank Sinatra and
        Sammy Davis, Jr.)
       Bianca
        (Note: First pressings of the
        above 3 albums were issued in
        gatefold covers.)

FS 2019 REPRISE REPERTORY THEATRE BOX SET
       A 4-record set comprising the above 3 albums as
       well as FS 2018 *SOUTH PACIFIC* which does not
       contain any songs by Dean.

FS 2021 ROBIN AND THE SEVEN HOODS
       Any Man Who Loves His Mother
       Style (With Frank Sinatra and Bing Crosby)
       Mister Booze (With Frank Sinatra, Bing Crosby and
        Sammy Davis, Jr.)
       Don't Be A Do-Badder Finale (With Frank Sinatra,
        Bing Crosby and Sammy Davis, Jr.)

R9 6028 *ALL-STAR SPECTACULAR*
       Tik-A-Tee, Tik-A-Tay

RS 6188 *THE SAMMY DAVIS, JR. SHOW*
       Sam's Song (With Sammy Davis, Jr.)

RS 6277 *MOVIN' WITH NANCY*
       Things (With Nancy Sinatra)

SR 6277 *MOVIN' WITH NANCY* (7" jukebox EP)
       Things (With Nancy Sinatra)

RS 6409　　　　*NANCY'S GREATEST HITS*
　　　　　　　　Things (With Nancy Sinatra)

RS 50001　　　*FRANK SINATRA AND HIS FRIENDS WANT YOU TO*
　　　　　　　　HAVE YOURSELF A MERRY LITTLE CHRISTMAS
　　　　　　　　　　　Peace On Earth - Silent Night
　　　　　　　　　　　(Note: First pressings picture a
　　　　　　　　　　　Christmas tree and Frank Sinatra's
　　　　　　　　　　　face on the front cover. The sec-
　　　　　　　　　　　ond pressing shows individual
　　　　　　　　　　　black and white photos of the
　　　　　　　　　　　artists on the front cover. The third
　　　　　　　　　　　pressing illustrates a giant wreath
　　　　　　　　　　　on the front cover.)

Reprise Promotional-Only Releases

RD-6　　　　　*SPRING TONIC FOR YOUR PROFIT PICTURE* (One-sided)
　　　　　　　　April In Paris

RD-7　　　　　*THE 74,000,000 TALENT BONANZA* (Special
　　　　　　　　Demonstration Record, July 1962)
　　　　　　　　　　　(Note: Dean is listed on the cover, but is
　　　　　　　　　　　not on the album.)

RD-9　　　　　*LOOK WHO'S COMING TO YOUR HOUSE* (January 1963)
　　　　　　　　My Heart Cries For You
　　　　　　　　I'm So Lonesome I Could Cry

PRO 177　　　*MEET YOUR NEW SALESMEN - THE MOST POPULAR*
　　　　　　　　RECORDING STARS IN THE WORLD
　　　　　　　　　　　(7" EP with picture sleeve)
　　　　　　　　　　　Everybody Loves Somebody
　　　　　　　　　　　(Excerpt only)
　　　　　　　　　　　　　Narrated by Gary Owens
　　　　　　　　　　　　　Presented by Creative
　　　　　　　　　　　　　Record Service

PRO-252　　　*WARNER BROS./REPRISE ARTIST VOICE TRACKS*
　　　　　　　　(3 Dean Martin Voice Tracks)

PRO-A-775　　*THE WARNER BROTHERS RECORDS 20TH ANNIVERSARY*
　　　　　　　　ALBUM IN SOUND PICTURE (6-12")
　　　　　　　　　　　Everybody Loves Somebody
　　　　　　　　　　　Only 3,000 copies made

Ajazz

519　　　　　　*FRANK SINATRA THROUGH THE YEARS VOLUME 4*
　　　　　　　　Medley with Frank and Mickey Rooney

209

Warner Bros./Reprise Voice Tracks promo 45 (Reprise PRO 252)
(Author's collection)

Audition
33-5936   *DEAN MARTIN SINGS/NICOLINI LUCCHESI PLAYS*
            Walking My Baby Back Home
            Santa Lucia
            Hold Me
            Louise
            Memory Lane
            Oh Marie

Beautiful Music Company
3-128   *ROMANCE ALBUM*
            Return To Me

Brigade
P 1310   *DINO, GORDON AND BOB SING*
            (With Gordon MacRae and Bob Eberly)
            Walking My Baby Back Home
            Oh Marie
            Hold Me
                        (Note: Walking My Baby Back
                        Home and Hold Me are shortened
                        versions.)

Casablanca
SPNB 1296   *HERE'S JOHNNY-MAGIC MOMENTS FROM THE
            TONIGHT SHOW*
            Comedy segments

Collector's Edition
CE-505   *ALL-TIME CHRISTMAS FAVORITES*
            White Christmas
            Marshmallow World
            Silver Bells
            Winter Wonderland
            Silent Night

Columbia Musical Treasury
3P 6306   *MERRY CHRISTMAS* (3-12")
            Let It Snow, Let It Snow, Let It Snow

2P 7285   *MERRY CHRISTMAS* (2-12")
            Let It Snow, Let It Snow, Let It Snow

Columbia Special Products/Brookville Records

P2-12925   *ARRIVEDERCI ROMA* (2-12")
                   That's Amore
                   Volare

Decca

79224   *CHRISTMAS SEALS FOR 1962*
                   (Note: This is a public service radio show for TB.
                   Dean's program is on one side; the flip side contains
                   a show by Patti Page.)

79235   *CHRISTMAS SEALS FOR 1962*
                   (Note: Same show as above, but this release has
                   Dean's and Patti Page's programs on one side and
                   shows by Si Zentner and Vaughn Monroe on the
                   other.)

79240   *CHRISTMAS SEAL CAMPAIGN 1962*
                   Thirty-second spot by Dean

Diamond

D-7   *MANHATTAN AT MIDNIGHT* (4-record 78 RPM box set)
                   2005 Brooks Brothers
                   2022 Nick Lucas
                   2035 Dean Martin
                   2039 Vera Massey

Harmony

HS 11286   *HITS FROM FINIAN'S RAINBOW*
                   If This Isn't Love (With The Hi-Lo's)

HS 11374   *GUYS AND DOLLS*
                   Fugue For Tinhorns (With Frank Sinatra and Bing
                           Crosby)
                   Oldest Established Permanent Floating Crap Game
                           In New York
                                   (With Frank Sinatra and Bing
                                   Crosby)
                   Guys and Dolls (With Frank Sinatra)

Heartland Music

1071-1074   *UNFORGETTABLE FIFTIES* (4-12")
                   That's Amore

1082-4   *THOSE WONDERFUL YEARS*
                   Memories Are Made Of This

Jimmy McHugh
400   *MUSIC BY JIMMY McHUGH* (7" 33 1/3 issued with title sleeve)

        I Feel A Song Coming On

Latimer
247-17   *FRANKIE, DINO, AND SAMMY*

        (Summit Meeting at the 500 Club; Atlantic City, New Jersey)

        (Note: Issued with three different paste-on covers)

Lifetime
LT21   *HOME FOR CHRISTMAS* (4-12")

        White Christmas

Longines
93926   *MILLION DOLLAR SELLERS VOL. 2*

        Memories Are Made Of This

Longines/Capitol Special Markets
SYS 5826   *CHRISTMAS WITH THE STARS*

        Rudolph The Red-Nosed Reindeer

Memorabilia
MLP 714   *WHEN RADIO WAS KING*

        Dean Martin and Jerry Lewis Radio Show

            First Show on the Air 1948; Guest Star: Lucille Ball

MGM
12920   Just In Time by Maurice Chevalier (7" 45 RPM with picture sleeve) Sleeve illustrates Dean and Judy Holliday.

National Mask and Puppet Corporation
        (Note: Contains an excerpt from the first Martin and Lewis radio show. This was included with the Martin and Lewis puppets. It is a 7" colored vinyl release that plays at 78 RPM and has caricatures of Dean and Jerry on the label.)

Radiola
MR 110   *DEAN MARTIN AND JERRY LEWIS ON RADIO*

        Guest: Lucille Ball (December 22, 1948)

        Guest: William Bendix (February 27, 1949)

RCA
DML3-0258   *COUNTRY MUSIC CAVALCADE: FOR THE GOOD TIMES* (3-12")

        Memories Are Made Of This

Reader's Digest

030   *REMEMBERING THE '50s AND '60s*
          That's Amore
          Memories Are Made Of This

038   *MEMORIES ARE MADE OF THIS -*
              GREAT STARS OF THE '50s (7-12")
                  Memories Are Made Of This
                  That's Amore
                  Return To Me
                  Standing On The Corner
                  You Belong To Me
                  I'll Always Love You

150   *I'VE HEARD THAT SONG BEFORE* (7-12")
          Powder Your Face With Sunshine

Retrospect

509   *SINATRA, BASIE AND FRIENDS*
          Frank and Some Friends
              (Excerpt from 1965 Dismas House concert)

Roast

1002   *FOSTER BROOKS ROASTS*
          Excerpts of Brooks' appearances on Dean's televised
          roasts.

Stetson

8120   *BELLS ARE RINGING*
          Same as ST 1435

Suffolk Marketing

1-96   *50 CHRISTMAS FAVORITES*
          Let It Snow, Let It Snow, Let It Snow

1-99   *50 TIMELESS RECORDING CLASSICS*
          Everybody Loves Somebody

17693   *50 OF THE MOST LOVED RECORDS OF YOUR LIFE*
          Return To Me

Talking Book

58007   *LOOK MAGAZINE DECEMBER 26, 1967*
          (10" that plays at 16 2/3.)
                  (Note: Contains an interview with Dean on
                  side one and an interview with playwright
                  Tom Stoppard on the other.)

Time-Life
STL 131   *THE FAMILY CHRISTMAS COLLECTION*
                     Winter Wonderland

No Labels Indicated
SPO-145   My Guiding Star (7" 45 RPM)
                     (Note: This is an unauthorized release. The song is from the film *Bells Are Ringing,* but is not included on the soundtrack album. The flip side is a song by Barbra Streisand and Larry Blyden.)

JB-2262   My Rifle, My Pony and Me (7" 45 RPM)
                     (Note: This is a one-sided single released in conjunction with the film *Rio Bravo.* It features John Wayne introducing Dean and Ricky Nelson who sing My Rifle, My Pony and Me.)

BS 17   *BIG SOUND STARS INTERNATIONAL INC. PRESENTS RADIO TEMPERATURE READINGS 100-109*
                     Dean informs us that it's 108 degrees.

248-50   *THE MARTIN AND LEWIS SHOW*
                     Box set of 3 red vinyl 45 RPM's issued by NBC to promote the Martin and Lewis radio show. It contains the entire show from 6/28/49 starring John Carradine. Before Dean sings Candy Kisses, an announcer makes a sales pitch for network affiliates to carry the show.

Military-Related Releases
AFD 123-4   *ARMED FORCES RECORDS* (Colored Vinyl)
                     Try Again

156   *U.S. AIR FORCE PRESENTS MUSIC IN THE AIR* (45 RPM)
                     Sparklin' Eyes

189-192   *NATIONAL GUARD SESSION WITH MARTIN BLOCK*
                     (Note: This is a four-part interview show with Dean conducted by Martin Block. Suggested air dates were September 12, 19, and 26 and October 3, 1965.)

                                GUARD SESSION #189
                                  Bumming Around
                                (Remember Me) I'm The One
                                Who Loves You
                                Here Comes My Baby

GUARD SESSION #190
> The Birds And The Bees
> Everybody Loves Somebody
> Born To Lose

GUARD SESSION #191
> I Don't Think You Love Me
> > Anymore
> Memories Are Made Of This
> Walk On By

GUARD SESSIONS #192
> King Of The Road
> That's Amore
> Red Roses For A Blue Lady

2683-84   *ARMED FORCES RADIO SERVICE*
> Hominy Grits
> You Belong To Me

3101-02   *ARMED FORCES RADIO SERVICE*
> Kiss
> What Could Be More Beautiful

P-5983   *ARMED FORCES RADIO AND TELEVISION* (16")
> Good Morning, Life
> Forgetting You
> Makin' Love Ukelele Style

75-103/104   *DEPARTMENT OF THE TREASURY PRESENTS THE*
GRAMMY TREASURE CHEST
> > The Oldest Established Permanent Floating
> > Crap Game In New York (With
> > Frank Sinatra and Bing Crosby)

(Note: In addition to the radio commercials issued for nearly every Dean movie, special interview and sales pitch excerpts with Dean are known to exist for *My Friend Irma; At War With The Army; That's My Boy; 10,000 Bedrooms; Who Was That Lady; All In A Night's Work; Toys In The Attic; Robin and the 7 Hoods; Kiss Me, Stupid; The Silencers; Murderers' Row; The Ambushers; The Wrecking Crew; Airport;* and *Showdown.*)

EXTENDED PLAYS

Capitol
EBF 9112   *TODAY'S TOP HITS BY TODAY'S TOP ARTISTS*
              (2-7" EP Box Set)
                      You Belong To Me

Victory
BG 1031   *TOP HITS*
                      Walking My Baby Back Home   (Red Vinyl)

Popular
PO 4   Oh Marie

1035   Oh Marie
              (Note: Both 45 RPM and 78 RPM versions are
              known to exist.)

PO 2210   Oh Marie
              (Note: Both 45 RPM and 78 RPM versions are
              known to exist.)

REEL-TO-REEL

Capitol
Y2A1   *SHOWCASE OF STARS*
              Let's Put Out The Lights and Go To Sleep

Y2T 2405   *SEASON'S GREETINGS/FAVORITE SONGS OF CHRISTMAS*
              Rudolph The Red-Nosed Reindeer

Y2T 2600   *CAPITOL ALL-STAR FAVORITES VOLUME 1*
              Cha Cha Cha D'Amour

Reprise
S9-1   *STEREO SAMPLER*
              In A Little Spanish Town

S9-2   *THE WORLD'S GREATEST ARTISTS AND THEIR BIG HITS*
              You're Nobody 'Til Somebody Loves You
                      (Manufactured by "STEREOTAPE" -
                      contains both Reprise and Dot artists.)

American Airlines
#7   Send Me The Pillow You Dream On
           You're Nobody 'Til Somebody Loves You
           You'll Always Be The One I Love

#36	In The Chapel In The Moonlight
	Let It Snow, Let It Snow, Let It Snow
	S'posin
	Winter Wonderland
	Baby, Won't You Please Come Home

| #59 | I Take A Lot Of Pride In What I Am |
| | Cryin' Time |

| #64 | (Open Up The Door) Let The Good Times In |
| | King Of The Road |

#69	Bumming Around
	Everybody Loves Somebody
	You'll Always Be The One I Love

| #78 | Sweetheart |
| | For The Good Times |

CASSETTE

Capitol
9237   *WHITE CHRISTMAS*

Winter Wonderland; White Christmas; Rudolph The Red-Nosed Reindeer; Let It Snow, Let It Snow, Let It Snow

(Note: Also contains songs by Peggy Lee)

Radio Spirits
2087   *MARTIN AND LEWIS SHOW*

Contains the radio broadcasts from 10/7/49 and 10/14/49 (with guest Dorothy Kirsten.)

2096   *MARTIN AND LEWIS SHOW*

Contains the radio broadcasts from 12/21/51 (with guest Helen O'Connell) and 12/28/51 (with guest Dale Evans.)

2124   *MARTIN AND LEWIS SHOW*

Contains the radio broadcasts from 11/9/51 (with guest Danny Thomas) and 11/16/51 (with guest Shelley Winters.)

16" TRANSCRIPTIONS

76023   *1954 AMERICAN CANCER SOCIETY - A TRIBUTE TO PETER DeROSE*
> Songs by Dean, Bing Crosby, The Ames Brothers

GRC 4290   *1957 HEART FUND (FEBRUARY 1-28)*
> Spot by Dean

GRC 4723   *1958 HEART FUND*
> Spot by Dean

GRC 5225   *1959 HEART FUND (FEBRUARY 1-28)*
> Spot by Dean

#547   *HERE'S TO VETERANS*
> (Spot announcement by Dean)

#557   *HERE'S TO VETERANS*
> (Your Insurance Beneficiaries)

PRIVATE RELEASES

FRIARS CLUB ROASTS
> Jack Benny 2/14/57
> Lucy and Desi Arnaz 11/23/58
> Dean Martin 11/8/59
> Gary Cooper 1/8/61
> Mervyn Leroy 10/22/61

2253-2254   *SHARE BOOMTOWN PARTY 1959*

RADIO PROGRAMS

LEE ARNOLD ON A COUNTRY ROAD
> My First Country Song played on various dates including:
> > 7/30/83

THE GREAT SOUNDS
> Dean Martin song played on many shows including the following dates:
> > 4/10/87
> > 7/9/88
> > 12/30/88

7/22/89
8/5/89
8/19/89
3/20/90

THE SOUNDS OF SINATRA
Dean/Frank duets played on many shows

WILLIAM B. WILLIAMS' MAKE-BELIEVE BALLROOM
Volume 2   That's Amore
            Sway
Volume 5   Is It True What They Say About Dixie?
Volume 6   Until The Real Thing Comes Along
Volume 7   Dinah
Volume 12   Imagination
Volume 15   There's No Tomorrow
Volume 16   With My Eyes Wide Open I'm
            Dreaming
Volume 21   The Object Of My Affection
Volume 22   The Object Of My Affection
Volume 23   Just One More Chance
            Carolina Moon

LINER NOTES "WRITTEN" by DEAN

656   *JOEY BISHOP SINGS COUNTRY AND WESTERN*
             Joey Bishop
             ABC Records

MD 1009   *THE GOLDDIGGERS*
             (Self-titled)
             Metromedia Records

SE 4340   *RIGHT NOW!*
             Lainie Kazan
             MGM Records

SE 4385   *LAINIE KAZAN*
             (Self-titled)
             MGM Records

6101   *AN EVENING AT DINO'S LODGE*
             Jack Elton (piano) and Steve LaFever (bass)
             Ultimate Records

RS 6171   *THE RHYTHM AND BLUES ALBUM*
Trini Lopez
Reprise Records

NON-VOCAL SOUNDTRACK RELEASES

DL 8719   *THE YOUNG LIONS*
Music by Hugo Friedhofer
Main Title; Ski Run; Christian And Francoise - Michael's Theme; Hope And Noah; The Captain's Lady; North African Episode; Parisian Interlude; Berlin Aftermath; A Letter From Noah; River Crossing; Death Of Christian And End Title
Decca Records

SW 1109   *SOME CAME RUNNING*
Music by Elmer Bernstein
Prelude; To Love And Be Loved; Dave's Double Life; Dave And Gwen; Fight; Gwen's Theme; Ginny; Short Noise; Live It Up; Tryst; Seduction; Smitty's Place; Rejection; Pursuit; Finale
Capitol Records

R9 2013   *SERGEANT'S 3*
Music by Billy May
Lazy Day In Medicine Band; The Sergeants 3 March; Desert Battle; Mount Of The Skulls; Sergeant Boswell's Rock; Mighty Wagon Roll; Ballad Of The Sergeants 3; Blue Bugle March; Beethoven's Night In The West; Girls Of The Antler Bar; Ambush
Reprise Records

CT-GD 1   *TOYS IN THE ATTIC*
Music by George Duning
Main Title - Lilly Enters; Lilly Phones; Carrie Remembers; Carrie Excited; The Attic - Julian; Lilly And Julian; The Presents; More Presents; The New Ring; Lilly Goes Home; Morning At Bernier's - Lilly Returns; Carrie Disturbed; Anna's Accusations; Julian, Don't Go; Do It!; Evil Carrie - Dock Rumble; Who Told Him?; Goodbye Carrie - End Theme
Citadel Records

TFS 3143   *WHAT A WAY TO GO!*
Music by Nelson Riddle
"Get Acquainted" and "Happy Houseboat"
by Styne, Comden, Green
Main Title; Louisa's Theme; Fabulous Penthouse; Get Acquainted; Love In The Garret; Happy Houseboat; Giggling Girls; Blue Flutes; 707 in 3/4 Time; Accidentally On Purpose; Chameleon Girl; End Title
20th Century
Fox Records

OS 6420   *SONS OF KATIE ELDER*
Music by Elmer Bernstein
Main Title; Texas Is A Woman (Recited by John Wayne); Elders' Fight; Dangerous Journey; Trouble In Town; Return To Town; Sons Of Katie Elder (Sung by Johnny Cash); Rebuked; Memories Of Clearwater; Sheriff Ambushed; Katie's Bible; Hastings Ranch
Columbia Records

LSO 1120   *SILENCERS*
Music by Elmer Bernstein
Main Title From The Silencers; The Silencers (Sung by Vikki Carr); Santiago (Sung by Vikki Carr); Tina's Waltz; Big "O"; Blast-Off Minus 3; Matt Helm's Blues; Spy Chase; Early To Bed; Promise Her Anything; A Little Tipsy; Showgirl Walk; Tung-Tze
RCA Records

COSO 5003   MURDERERS' ROW
Music by Lalo Schifrin
"I'm Not The Marrying Kind" and "Suzie's Theme" by Lalo Schifrin and Howard Greenfield
Murderers' Row; The Pin; I'm Not The Marrying Kind; Suzie's Theme; Dual Controls; Solaris; The Pendulum; Iron Head; Double Feature; Frozen Dominique; No Dining Allowed; I'm Not The Marrying Kind
Colgems Records

OS 3140   *HOW TO SAVE A MARRIAGE - AND RUIN YOUR LIFE*
Music by Michel Legrand
Opening Title - Winds Of Change (Sung by The Ray Conniff Singers); Overture; Second Honeymoon; Who Is It, Darling?; The Sunny Side; Punch And Judy Waltz; Winds

222

Of Change (Instrumental); S'Il Vous Plait
Bossa Nova; Thinking Voices; Main Theme
In Jazz; Slotkin's Monologue; End Title -
Winds Of Change (Sung by The Ray
Conniff Singers)
Columbia Records

PR 5026   *BANDOLERO!*
Music by Jerry Goldsmith
Main Title; The Trap; El Jefe; The Bait;
Ambushed; Sabinas; Dee's Proposal;
Across The River; A Bad Day For Hanging;
A Better Way
Project 3 Records

DL 79173   *AIRPORT*
Music by Alfred Newman
Airport; Airport Love Theme; Inez' Theme;
Guerrero's Goodbye; Ada Quonsett,
Stowaway!; Mel And Tanya; Airport Love
Theme; Joe Patroni: Plane Or Plows?;
Triangle!; Inez - Lost Forever; Emergency
Landing!; Airport
Decca Records

COMPACT DISCS

Capitol

29385   *SINGING IN THE RAIN - CAPITOL SINGS HOLLYWOOD*
Louise

29386   *IT'S MAGIC - CAPITOL SINGS SAMMY CAHN*
Things We Did Last Summer
Ain't That A Kick In The Head

31774   *HOORAY FOR LOVE - CAPITOL'S GREAT GENTLEMEN
OF SONG VOL. 1*
Imagination

31775   *PENNIES FROM HEAVEN - CAPITOL'S GREAT
GENTLEMEN OF SONG VOL. 2*
Until The Real Thing Comes Along

32566   *AN AFFAIR TO REMEMBER - CAPITOL SINGS HARRY
WARREN*
That's Amore

32567   *I HEAR MUSIC - CAPITOL SINGS FRANK LOESSER*
Once In Love With Amy

32592   *STARDUST - CAPITOL SINGS HOAGY CARMICHAEL*
In The Cool, Cool, Cool Of The Evening
Two Sleepy People (With Line Renaud)

35972   *ULTRA LOUNGE VOLUME 5 - WILD, COOL AND SWINGIN'*
Ain't That A Kick In The Head

37595   *ULTRA LOUNGE VOLUME 9 - CHA CHA DE AMOUR*
Sway
Cha Cha Cha D'Amour

38376   *ULTRA LOUNGE: LEOPARD SKIN PACKAGE*
Cha Cha Cha D'Amour

42183   *BEST CHRISTMAS EVER*
Let It Snow, Let It Snow, Let It Snow

52559   *ULTRA LOUNGE - CHRISTMAS COCKTAILS*
I've Got My Love To Keep Me Warm

53411   *ULTRA LOUNGE VOLUME 15 - WILD, COOL AND
SWINGIN' TOO*
Just In Time

79241   *CAPITOL 50TH ANNIVERSARY BOX SET*
(8 COMPACT DISCS)
Memories Are Made Of This
That's Amore

80180   *ROUTE 66 - CAPITOL SINGS COAST TO COAST*
When It's Sleepy Time Down South

80181   *FAR AWAY PLACES - CAPITOL SINGS AROUND
THE WORLD*
Arrivederci, Roma
Canadian Sunset

89587   *HAPPY HOLIDAYS - CAPITOL SINGS CHRISTMAS*
Baby It's Cold Outside
White Christmas

90231   *MOONSTRUCK SOUNDTRACK*
That's Amore

90592   *MEMORIES ARE MADE OF THIS*
Memories Are Made Of This

92050   *BELLS ARE RINGING SOUNDTRACK*
         Do It Yourself
         Better Than A Dream (With Judy Holliday)
         I Met A Girl
         Just In Time (With Judy Holliday)

96361   *ANYTHING GOES - CAPITOL SINGS COLE PORTER*
         True Love

96791   *TOO MARVELOUS FOR WORDS - CAPITOL SINGS*
         JOHNNY MERCER
         In The Cool, Cool, Cool Of The Evening

97458   *BEST OF CHRISTMAS*
         Rudolph The Red-Nosed Reindeer

97459   *MERRY CHRISTMAS, BABY - ROMANCE AND REINDEER*
         FROM CAPITOL
         A Winter Romance
         Let It Snow, Let It Snow, Let It Snow

98475   *AND THE WINNER IS...CAPITOL SINGS THE BEST*
         MOVIE SONGS
         Baby It's Cold Outside

98477   *PUTTIN' ON THE RITZ - CAPITOL SINGS IRVING BERLIN*
         I've Got My Love To Keep Me Warm

98478   *ISN'T IT ROMANTIC - CAPITOL SINGS RODGERS*
         AND HART
         It's Easy To Remember

98670   *MEMORIES ARE MADE OF THIS*
         That's Amore
         Memories Are Made Of This

99692   *LET IT SNOW - CUDDLY CHRISTMAS CLASSICS FROM*
         CAPITOL
         Christmas Blues
         I've Got My Love To Keep Me Warm

99777   *NAT KING COLE BOX SET*
         Open Up The Doghouse (With Nat King Cole)

Capitol Promo-Only
DPRO 11170   *SPOTLIGHT ON PART 2*
         Just In Time
         Dream

DPRO 79176   *CAPITOL 50TH ANNIVERSARY SAMPLER*
Memories Are Made Of This

DPRO 79338   *GREAT POP VOCALISTS VOLUME 1, DISC 4*
That's Amore
(Note: This is part of the World Business
Class Collector's Series available exclu-
sively through Northwest Airlines.)

DPRO 79346   *CAPITOL COLLECTOR'S SERIES SAMPLER*
Memories Are Made Of This

DPRO 79385   *CAPITOL CHRISTMAS SAMPLER*
A Winter's Romance
Baby It's Cold Outside

Reprise
45014   *GUYS AND DOLLS*
Fugue For Tinhorns (With Frank Sinatra and Bing
Crosby)
The Oldest Established Permanent Floating Crap
Game In New York (With Frank Sinatra
and Bing Crosby)
Guys and Dolls (With Frank Sinatra)
Guys and Dolls Reprise (With Frank Sinatra)

1016   *SINATRA: A MAN AND HIS MUSIC*
The Oldest Established Permanent Floating Crap
Game In New York (With Frank Sinatra
and Bing Crosby)
The Summit (Comedy routine with Frank Sinatra
and Sammy Davis, Jr.)

46013   *FRANK SINATRA - THE COMPLETE REPRISE STUDIO
RECORDINGS*
We Open In Venice (With Frank Sinatra and
Sammy Davis, Jr.)
Guys and Dolls (With Frank Sinatra)
Fugue For Tinhorns (With Frank Sinatra and Bing
Crosby)
Oldest Established Permanent Floating Crap Game
In New York (With Frank Sinatra and Bing
Crosby)
Style (With Frank Sinatra and Bing Crosby)
Mister Booze (With Frank Sinatra, Bing Crosby and
Sammy Davis, Jr.)
Don't Be A Do-Badder Finale (With Frank Sinatra,
Bing Crosby and Sammy Davis, Jr.)

A&M
540424   *THINGS TO DO IN DENVER WHEN YOU'RE DEAD*
                       SOUNDTRACK
                             You're Nobody 'Til Somebody Loves You

Beautiful Music Company
50 CHRISTMAS CLASSICS
Jingle Bells

HITS OF BROADWAY
Just In Time

LET A SONG BE YOUR UMBRELLA
Wrap Your Troubles In Dreams

POP MUSIC MEMORIES
Memories Are Made Of This

CBS Special Products
AGK 46849   *THE SOCIETY OF SINGERS PRESENT A GIFT OF MUSIC*
                         VOLUME 1
                             Everybody Loves Somebody

AK 67881   *SOCIETY OF SINGERS PRESENT AN ALL-STAR CHRISTMAS*
                       Rudolph The Red-Nosed Reindeer

Cema
17478   *IT'S CHRISTMAS TIME*
                 White Christmas
                       (An Avon Special Product)

18653   *HALLMARK CD*
                 Memories Are Made Of This
                       (Note: Sold for $9.95 in Hallmark stores)

19472   *BIG HITS OF THE '50s*
                 Memories Are Made Of This

56796   *YOU'RE ALL I WANT FOR CHRISTMAS*
                 Baby It's Cold Outside

57556   *NOW THAT'S ITALIAN*
                 Arrivederci, Roma
                 Volare
                 That's Amore

57570   *HAPPY HOLIDAYS, VOL. 26*
                  White Christmas

57901   *BEST LOVED SONGS OF CHRISTMAS - DEAN MARTIN*
                  AND AL MARTINO
                              Let It Snow, Let It Snow, Let It Snow
                              White Christmas
                              Baby It's Cold Outside
                              Winter Wonderland
                              Rudolph The Red-Nosed Reindeer

57903   *HAPPY HOLIDAYS*
                  Winter Wonderland

57904   *FAVORITE SONGS OF CHRISTMAS*
                  White Christmas

57905   *CHRISTMAS SONG FESTIVAL*
                  Let It Snow, Let It Snow, Let It Snow

57907   *SING WE NOEL*
                  Rudolph The Red-Nosed Reindeer

57983   *THE GREAT STARS SING THE GREAT SONGS OF*
                  CHRISTMAS
                  White Christmas

Collectables
2512   *THE ULTIMATE CHRISTMAS ALBUM VOLUME 2*
                  Let It Snow, Let It Snow, Let It Snow

Columbia
57767   *COCKTAIL HOUR*
                  When You're Smiling

Curb
77351   *CHRISTMAS ALL TIME GREATEST RECORDS*
                  Rudolph The Red-Nosed Reindeer

77354   *GREAT RECORDS OF THE DECADE - '50s HITS POP*
                  VOLUME 1
                              Memories Are Made Of This

Dining Discs (RCA Special Products)
1241   *CUCINA AMORE*
                  That's Amore

EMI
52498   *STRIPTEASE SOUNDTRACK*
             Return To Me

EMI-Capitol Special Markets
72438-19182   *HAPPY HOLIDAYS, VOL. 31*
             Rudolph The Red-Nosed Reindeer

Epic
57560   *BRONX TALE SOUNDTRACK*
             Ain't That A Kick In The Head

Flashback
FB 72709   *SENTIMENTAL FAVORITES*
             That's Amore

Geffen
24970   *FLIRTING WITH DISASTER SOUNDTRACK*
             Cha Cha Cha D'Amour

GNP/Crescendo
2234   *RIDIN' WEST*
             My Rifle, My Pony and Me

Hollywood Records
62091   *SWINGERS SOUNDTRACK*
             You're Nobody 'Til Somebody Loves You

62102   *DONNIE BRASCO SOUNDTRACK*
             Return To Me

JCI
7001   *THOSE WONDERFUL YEARS: TENDERLY*
             That's Amore

7007   *THOSE WONDERFUL YEARS: BECAUSE OF YOU*
             Memories Are Made Of This

K-Tel
3209   *ITALIAN LOVE SONGS*
             That's Amore

Laserlight
15 463   *CHRISTMAS FAVORITES*
                Jingle Bells
                            (Note: This is not the Reprise version; it is
                            from a Martin and Lewis radio show.)

MCA
11389   *CASINO SOUNDTRACK*
                You're Nobody 'Til Somebody Loves You

Oglio
25162   *THE COOLEST CHRISTMAS*
                Let It Snow, Let It Snow, Let It Snow

One-Way
18082   *CHRISTMAS WITH BING CROSBY, NAT KING COLE
                AND DEAN MARTIN*
                            White Christmas
                            Winter Wonderland
                            Let It Snow, Let It Snow, Let It Snow

Original Sound
8884   *21 ROCK AND ROLL HITS AT THE MOVIES*
                That's Amore

Radio Spirits
                THE MARTIN AND LEWIS SHOW
                            9-CD set containing 18 Martin and Lewis radio
                            shows from 1949.   Guests include: Lucille Ball,
                            William Bendix, Madeleine Carroll, Peter Lorre,
                            Burl Ives, Arthur Treacher, John Garfield, Henry
                            Fonda, Marilyn Maxwell, Tony Martin, John
                            Carradine, Ralph Bellamy, Frances Langford,
                            William Boyd, Burt Lancaster, Victor Moore, Billie
                            Burke, Jane Russell.

Reader's Digest
03 1534   *20 YEARS OF #1 HITS (1940-1959)*
                Memories Are Made Of This

Realm
7960   *SOCIETY OF SINGERS PRESENTS THE BEST OF THE
                GOLDEN VOICES VOL. 1*
                            Everybody Loves Somebody

Restless

72946　　　*L. A. CONFIDENTIAL SOUNDTRACK*
　　　　　　　Christmas Blues
　　　　　　　Powder Your Face With Sunshine

Rhino

71251　　　*SENTIMENTAL JOURNEY VOLUME 3 (1950-1954)*
　　　　　　　That's Amore

71252　　　*SENTIMENTAL JOURNEY VOLUME 4 (1954-1959)*
　　　　　　　Memories Are Made Of This

71580　　　*POP MEMORIES 1955-59*
　　　　　　　Memories Are Made Of This

71802　　　*BILLBOARD POP MEMORIES 1955-1959*
　　　　　　　Memories Are Made Of This

71803　　　*IT'S A BEAUTIFUL CHRISTMAS*
　　　　　　　White Christmas
　　　　　　　Rudolph The Red-Nosed Reindeer

72239　　　*COCKTAIL MIX VOLUME 3: SWINGIN' SINGLES*
　　　　　　　Ain't That A Kick In The Head

72413　　　*SENTIMENTAL FAVORITES*
　　　　　　　That's Amore

72557　　　*JACKPOT! THE LAS VEGAS STORY*
　　　　　　　That's Amore

72577　　　*EH PAISANO! - ITALIAN-AMERICAN CLASSICS*
　　　　　　　That's Amore

Rhino Promo-Only

71803　　　*IT'S A BEAUTIFUL CHRISTMAS*
　　　　　　　White Christmas
　　　　　　　Rudolph The Red-Nosed Reindeer

Rogers & Webster

　　　　　　　REMEMBERING THE '50s
　　　　　　　Memories Are Made Of This

Sandy Hook
2098   *MAE WEST ON THE AIR*
                 (Excerpt from Dean's May 3, 1959 TV show)

Smithsonian Institution/Radio Spirits
         OLD TIME RADIO SHOWBIZ TEAMS
            Four-CD set that contains the Martin and Lewis
            radio show from 1/4/52.

Sundazed
6057   *MOVIN' WITH NANCY*
            Things (With Nancy)

Time-Life

         CHRISTMAS MEMORIES
            The Christmas Blues

         #1 HITS OF THE '50s
            Memories Are Made Of This

         SPIRIT OF CHRISTMAS
            Rudolph The Red-Nosed Reindeer

         THE 40 GREATEST LOVE SONGS
            Return To Me

         THE MANY MOODS OF ROMANCE
            You Belong To Me

         YOUR HIT PARADE 1956
            Memories Are Made Of This

         YOUR HIT PARADE 1958
            Return To Me

         YOUR HIT PARADE - THE FABULOUS '50s
            Sway

         YOUR HIT PARADE - THE MID '50s
            That's Amore

         YOUR HIT PARADE - UNFORGETTABLE '50s
            I'll Always Love You

TVT
6810   *GRUMPIER OLD MEN SOUNDTRACK*
              That's Amore

No Label Or Number Indicated
              FRANK SINATRA - AN AMERICAN LEGEND
              CD issued in book written by Nancy Sinatra.
              Contains excerpt from The Summit comedy routine
              found on Sinatra's *A MAN AND HIS MUSIC* album.

Private Pressings

Jazz Hour
1033/1034   *FRANK SINATRA, DEAN MARTIN, SAMMY DAVIS, JR. AT*
              THE VILLA VENICE, CHICAGO (2 CD SET)
              Volume 1:
                            When You're Smiling/Lady Is A Tramp
                                  (Parodies)
                            I Left My Heart In San Francisco
                            I'm Gonna Sit Right Down And Write
                                  Myself A Letter
                            Volare/On An Evening In Roma
              Volume 2:
                            Excerpts in Medleys:
                            I Can't Give You Anything But Love
                            Pennies From Heaven
                            Embraceable You
                            Where Or When
                            Parodies:
                                  You Are Too Beautiful
                                  Love Walked In
                                  Carolina In The Morning
                                  Please Be Kind
                                  Dancing With Tears In My Eyes
                                  Try A Little Tenderness
                            Birth Of The Blues (With Frank Sinatra and
                                  Sammy Davis, Jr.)
                            Sam's Song (With Sammy Davis, Jr.)

Shine Box
61170   *FRANK SINATRA SPECTACULAR*
              King Of The Road
              Everybody Loves Somebody
              Volare/On An Evening In Roma
              You're Nobody 'Til Somebody Loves You
                    (From the Dismas House concert.)

No Label Listed

MAC 200   *A SWINGIN' NIGHT AT THE SABRE ROOM*
(With Frank Sinatra)
(Note: Recorded live at the Sabre Room, Chicago on June 7, 1977; Dean's 60th birthday. This release was limited to 1,000 and contains a silk-screened image of Dean and Frank on the disc.)

     When You're Smiling/Pennies From Heaven (Parodies)
     Everybody Loves Somebody
     Bad, Bad Leroy Brown
     Welcome To My World
     Brother, Can You Spare a Dime
     That's Amore
     Medley With Frank: I Can't Give You Anything But Love; Pennies From Heaven; Embraceable You; Where Or When; Oh Marie; When You're Smiling
     The Oldest Established Permanent Floating Crap Game In New York (With Frank)

MAG 500   FRANK AND DEAN'S HOLLYWOOD PARTY
(Note: This is the 1959 SHARE Boomtown Party Show.)

     Almost Like Being In Love (Parody)
     They Didn't Believe Me
     Medley: You Made Me Love You/It Had To Be You/Nevertheless
     I'm Gonna Sit Right Down And Write Myself A Letter
     Medley with Frank: Too Marvelous For Words; A Foggy Day In London Town; When You're Smiling; Come Fly With Me; I Can't Give You Anything But Love
     We're Glad That We're Italian (With Frank)

Chapter 5

Chart Positions and Awards

(Note: The format is as follows: date song debuted, peak position, weeks on chart.)

BILLBOARD CHARTS

Hot 100 Singles

12/4/48	22	1	That Certain Party (With Jerry Lewis)
2/19/49	10	4	Powder Your Face With Sunshine
9/2/50	11	16	I'll Always Love You
2/10/51	14	6	If
9/6/52	12	10	You Belong To Me
7/4/53	25	2	Love Me, Love Me
11/14/53	2 (2 weeks)	22	That's Amore
4/24/54	21	4	I'd Cry Like A Baby
7/24/54	15	10	Sway
7/24/54	23	4	Money Burns A Hole In My Pocket (B-side of above)
11/23/55	1 (6 weeks)	24	Memories Are Made Of This
2/29/56	27	12	Innamorata
5/9/56	29	15	Standing On The Corner
5/23/56	83	2	Watching The World Go By (B-side of above)
3/29/58	4	21	Return To Me
7/5/58	30	9	Angel Baby
8/10/58	15	13	Volare
7/19/59	59	13	On An Evening In Roma
12/1/62	91	6	From The Bottom Of My Heart
12/22/62	94	3	Sam's Song (With Sammy Davis, Jr.)
6/27/64	1 (1 week)	15	Everybody Loves Somebody

9/26/64	6	11	Door Is Still Open To My Heart
12/12/64	25	9	You're Nobody 'Til Somebody Loves You
12/26/64	64	5	You'll Always Be The One I Love
			(B-side of above)
2/20/65	22	9	Send Me The Pillow You Dream On
5/22/65	32	7	(Remember Me) I'm The One Who Loves You
8/7/65	21	9	Houston
10/30/65	10	10	I Will
2/12/66	32	8	Somewhere There's A Someone
5/7/66	35	7	Come Running Back
7/23/66	41	7	A Million And One
10/8/66	60	6	Nobody's Baby Again
12/17/66	55	6	(Open Up The Door) Let The Good Times In
4/29/67	55	5	Lay Some Happiness On Me
7/8/67	25	7	In The Chapel In The Moonlight
8/19/67	38	6	Little Ole Wine Drinker, Me
12/2/67	46	7	In The Misty Moonlight
3/23/68	60	7	You've Still Got A Place In My Heart
11/2/68	43	9	Not Enough Indians
8/9/69	75	4	I Take A Lot Of Pride In What I Am

Bubbling Under The Hot 100

1/18/60	107	4	Love Me, My Love
3/30/63	128	1	Face In A Crowd
10/10/64	123	2	Every Minute, Every Hour
			(B-side of Door Is Still Open To My Heart)
8/10/68	105	4	April Again
8/10/68	104	2	That Old Time Feeling (B-side of above)
9/14/68	107	1	Five Card Stud
2/22/69	103	3	Gentle On My Mind
10/25/69	107	3	One Cup Of Happiness
7/4/70	123	1	For The Love Of A Woman
8/1/70	110	3	My Woman, My Woman, My Wife
10/31/70	101	2	Detroit City
1/23/71	118	1	Georgia Sunshine

Easy Listening Singles

7/4/64	1 (8 weeks)	14	Everybody Loves Somebody
9/26/64	1 (1 week)	11	Door Is Still Open To My Heart
12/12/64	1 (1 week)	9	You're Nobody 'Til Somebody Loves You
12/26/64	13	4	You'll Always Be The One I Love
			(B-side of above)
2/20/65	5	9	Send Me The Pillow You Dream On
5/22/65	7	8	(Remember Me) I'm The One Who Loves You
8/7/65	2 (1 week)	9	Houston
10/30/65	3	12	I Will
2/12/66	2 (2 weeks)	13	Somewhere There's A Someone

5/7/66	4	11	Come Running Back
7/23/66	4	11	A Million And One
10/8/66	6	10	Nobody's Baby Again
12/10/66	7	9	(Open Up The Door) Let The Good Times In
4/29/67	6	10	Lay Some Happiness On Me
7/15/67	1 (3 weeks)	11	In The Chapel In The Moonlight
8/26/67	5	9	Little Ole Wine Drinker, Me
12/9/67	1 (2 weeks)	11	In The Misty Moonlight
3/23/68	7	12	You've Still Got A Place In My Heart
8/17/68	9	10	April Again
8/24/68	19	6	That Old Time Feeling (B-side of above)
11/2/68	4	10	Not Enough Indians
2/22/69	9	8	Gentle On My Mind
8/9/69	15	10	I Take A Lot Of Pride In What I Am
10/11/69	15	7	One Cup Of Happiness
10/31/70	36	2	Detroit City
5/8/71	36	2	She's A Little Bit Country
8/18/73	50	2	Get On With Your Livin'

Country Singles

7/9/83	35	12	My First Country Song (With Conway Twitty)

Albums

5/12/62	73	16	*ITALIAN LOVE SONGS*
1/26/63	99	5	*DINO LATINO*
3/30/63	109	4	*DEAN TEX MARTIN COUNTRY STYLE*
8/15/64	2 (2 weeks)	49	*EVERYBODY LOVES SOMEBODY*
8/29/64	15	31	*DREAM WITH DEAN*
11/14/64	9	30	*DOOR IS STILL OPEN TO MY HEART*
2/13/65	13	29	*DEAN MARTIN HITS AGAIN*
8/28/65	13	39	*(REMEMBER ME) I'M THE ONE WHO LOVES YOU*
11/20/65	11	34	*HOUSTON*
3/12/66	40	27	*SOMEWHERE THERE'S A SOMEONE*
7/2/66	108	3	*SILENCERS*
8/27/66	50	25	*HIT SOUND OF DEAN MARTIN*
12/3/66	34	31	*DEAN MARTIN T.V. SHOW*
12/17/66	95	13	*BEST OF DEAN MARTIN*
5/13/67	46	25	*HAPPINESS IS DEAN MARTIN*
9/2/67	20	48	*WELCOME TO MY WORLD*
6/1/68	26	38	*GREATEST HITS, VOL. 1*
9/7/68	83	21	*GREATEST HITS, VOL. 2*
1/4/69	14	25	*GENTLE ON MY MIND*
2/22/69	145	7	*BEST OF DEAN MARTIN, VOL. 2*
10/4/69	90	17	*I TAKE A LOT OF PRIDE IN WHAT I AM*

237

9/12/70	97	12	*MY WOMAN, MY WOMAN, MY WIFE*
2/27/71	113	15	*FOR THE GOOD TIMES*
2/5/72	117	4	*DINO*

Christmas Album

DEAN MARTIN CHRISTMAS ALBUM
(Note: This LP peaked at number one on
Billboard's special Christmas album chart in
1966. It also recharted during the next three
holiday seasons.)

Country Albums

3/20/71	41	2	*FOR THE GOOD TIMES*
7/23/83	49	10	*NASHVILLE SESSIONS*

CASHBOX CHARTS

Singles

12/12/53	2	15	That's Amore
12/24/55	1 (2 weeks)	14	Memories Are Made Of This
3/29/58	3	22	Return To Me
6/28/58	38	8	Angel Baby
8/16/58	1 (6 weeks)	17	Volare
11/8/58	94	2	Once Upon A Time
1/31/59	80	3	It Takes So Long To Say Goodnight
7/4/59	36	15	On An Evening In Roma
2/25/61	98	2	Sparklin' Eyes
1/5/63	93	6	From The Bottom Of My Heart
6/27/64	1 (1 week)	16	Everybody Loves Somebody
10/3/64	8	11	Door Is Still Open To My Heart
12/19/64	26	8	You're Nobody 'Til Somebody Loves You
12/19/64	79	7	You'll Always Be The One I Love
			(B-side of above)
2/20/65	20	8	Send Me The Pillow You Dream On
5/22/65	35	6	(Remember Me) I'm The One Who Loves You
8/7/65	24	9	Houston
10/30/65	11	12	I Will
2/12/66	34	7	Somewhere There's A Someone
5/7/66	40	7	Come Running Back
7/23/66	45	5	A Million And One
10/1/66	52	8	Nobody's Baby Again
12/10/66	55	6	(Open Up The Door) Let The Good Times In
4/22/67	55	6	Lay Some Happiness On Me
7/1/67	30	8	In The Chapel In The Moonlight
8/19/67	48	6	Little Ole Wine Drinker, Me

12/2/67	62	7	In The Misty Moonlight
3/23/68	44	6	You've Still Got A Place In My Heart
8/10/68	67	4	April Again
10/26/68	44	7	Not Enough Indians
3/1/69	93	3	Gentle On My Mind
8/9/69	71	5	I Take A Lot Of Pride In What I Am
10/11/69	82	3	One Cup Of Happiness
8/15/70	97	1	My Woman, My Woman, My Wife
10/24/70	99	2	Detroit City

Albums

(Note: Through the end of 1964, *Cashbox* published separate album charts for both stereo and mono releases. The peak positions for the stereo albums are listed first.)

8/15/64	1 (6 weeks)	35	*EVERYBODY LOVES SOMEBODY*
	1 (5 weeks)	35	
9/5/64	25	17	*DREAM WITH DEAN*
	32	21	
11/7/64	7	21	*DOOR IS STILL OPEN TO MY HEART*
	11	21	
2/20/65	18	18	*DEAN MARTIN HITS AGAIN*
8/21/65	25	26	*(REMEMBER ME) I'M THE ONE WHO LOVES YOU*
11/20/65	12	30	*HOUSTON*
3/12/66	34	17	*SOMEWHERE THERE'S A SOMEONE*
4/23/66	71	4	*SILENCERS*
9/3/66	31	13	*HIT SOUND OF DEAN MARTIN*
12/3/66	18	15	*DEAN MARTIN T.V. SHOW*
5/13/67	25	16	*HAPPINESS IS DEAN MARTIN*
8/19/67	27	20	*WELCOME TO MY WORLD*
5/25/68	19	21	*GREATEST HITS, VOL. 1*
9/28/68	81	7	*GREATEST HITS, VOL. 2*
12/28/68	22	21	*GENTLE ON MY MIND*
10/4/69	62	7	*I TAKE A LOT OF PRIDE IN WHAT I AM*
9/19/70	61	6	*MY WOMAN, MY WOMAN, MY WIFE*

Country Album

8/6/83	57	13	*NASHVILLE SESSIONS*

R.I.A.A. GOLD RECORD AWARDS

8/19/64	Everybody Loves Somebody (Single)
1/29/65	*EVERYBODY LOVES SOMEBODY*
12/2/65	*DOOR IS STILL OPEN TO MY HEART*
4/25/66	*(REMEMBER ME) I'M THE ONE WHO LOVES YOU*
11/7/66	*DEAN MARTIN HITS AGAIN*
2/2/68	*DREAM WITH DEAN*
3/19/68	*HOUSTON*
3/19/68	*WELCOME TO MY WORLD*
5/2/68	*SOMEWHERE THERE'S A SOMEONE*
11/27/68	*DEAN MARTIN CHRISTMAS ALBUM*
2/3/69	*GREATEST HITS, VOL. 1*
8/30/69	*GENTLE ON MY MIND*
12/23/70	*GREATEST HITS, VOL. 2*

QUIGLEY AWARDS

1950	BEST COMEDY SHOW - Colgate Comedy Show
1953	BEST COMEDY SHOW - Colgate Comedy Hour
1967	BEST TELEVISION PERFORMER
1967	BEST MUSICAL SHOW (POPULAR) - Dean Martin Show
1968	BEST TELEVISION PERFORMER
1968	BEST VARIETY PROGRAM - Dean Martin Show
1968	BEST MALE VOCALIST
1969	BEST VARIETY PROGRAM - Dean Martin Show
1972	BEST MALE VOCALIST

MOTION PICTURE HERALD AWARDS

1951	#2 BOX OFFICE ATTRACTION (Martin and Lewis)
1952	#1 BOX OFFICE ATTRACTION (Martin and Lewis)
1953	#2 BOX OFFICE ATTRACTION (Martin and Lewis)
1954	#2 BOX OFFICE ATTRACTION (Martin and Lewis)
1955	#7 BOX OFFICE ATTRACTION (Martin and Lewis)
1956	#6 BOX OFFICE ATTRACTION (Martin and Lewis)
1967	#4 BOX OFFICE ATTRACTION (Dean Martin)
1968	#6 BOX OFFICE ATTRACTION (Dean Martin)

MISC. AWARDS and HONORS

1964	FOOTPRINTS IN CEMENT AT GRAUMAN'S CHINESE THEATRE (March 23)
1966	NARM (National Academy of Recorded Music) BEST-SELLING MALE VOCALIST

1966	GOLDEN GLOBE - MOST POPULAR TELEVISION PERSONALITY (MALE)

1984   FRIARS CLUB - MAN OF THE YEAR

Dean has three stars on the Hollywood Walk Of Fame: for his work on television, in movies and on record.

Between 1973 and 1985, over one million people saw Dean perform at the MGM Grand in Las Vegas.

Chapter 6

Alphabetical Listing of Sheet Music

Ain't That A Kick In The Head
All In A Night's Work (Not performed by Dean in the movie)
All For One And One For All ** *(Robin and the 7 Hoods)*
All The Livelong Day ** *(Kiss Me, Stupid)*
Angel Baby
Any Man Who Loves His Mother
Artists And Models *

Baby-O
Baby Obey Me
Ballin' The Jack *
Bamboozled
Bang Bang ** *(Robin and the 7 Hoods)*
Bat Lady ** *(Artists and Models)*
The 'Be Careful' Song **(Money From Home)
Belle From Barcelona
Bells Are Ringing ** *(Bells Are Ringing)*
Better Than A Dream
Big Blue Sky *
Buckskin Beauty ** *(Pardners)*
Bumming Around

Career (Not performed by Dean in the movie)
Cha Cha Cha D'Amour
Champagne And Wedding Cake ** *(Living It Up)*
Charlotte Couldn't Charleston ** *(Robin and the 7 Hoods)*
Christmas Blues
Come Running Back

Day In The Country
Detroit City
Devil Rides In Jericho ** *(Rough Night In Jericho)*
Do It Yourself
Don't Be A Do-Badder
Door Is Still Open To My Heart (2 Versions)
Drop That Name ** *(Bells Are Ringing)*

Ee-O-Eleven ** *(Ocean's 11)*
Enchilada Man *
Everybody Loves Somebody (2 Versions)
Every Minute, Every Hour
Ev'ry Street's A Boulevard In Old New York (2 Versions)

Face The Music
Fiddle And Guitar Band *
5 Card Stud
Forgetting You
For The Love Of A Woman
Four For Texas ** *(Four For Texas)*
From The Bottom Of My Heart

Gay Continental ** *(Caddy)*
Gentle On My Mind
Girl Named Mary And A Boy Named Bill (2 Versions)
Giuggiola
Give Praise, Give Praise, Give Praise ** *(Robin and the 7 Hoods)*
Good Mornin', Life
Grazie, Prego, Scusi

Happy Feet
Hello Hello There ** *(Bells Are Ringing)*
Here We Go Again
Here's To Love *
Hey, Brother, Pour The Wine
Hey Punchinello *
Hold Me Now And Forever ** *(Rough Night In Jericho)*
Hollywood Or Bust
Houston

I Ain't Gonna Lead This Life No More
I Can't Help Remembering You
I Can't Resist A Boy In Uniform ** *(Jumping Jacks)*
I Know A Dream When I See One
I Know Your Mother Loves You *

I Like Them All
I Like To Hike *
I Like To Lead When I Dance ** *(Robin and the Seven Hoods)*
I Met A Girl
I Ran All The Way Home
I Take A Lot Of Pride In What I Am
I Will (2 Versions)
I Wonder Who's Kissing Her Now
If You're Thinking What I'm Thinking ** *(Murderers' Row)*
I'll Always Love You (2 Versions)
I'm A Poached Egg ** *(Kiss Me, Stupid)*
I'm Gonna Steal You Away
I'm In The Mood For Love *
I'm Not The Marrying Kind
Independent ** *(Bells Are Ringing)*
In The Misty Moonlight (2 Versions)
Innamorata
It Just Happened That Way
It Looks Like Love
It's A Whistle-In Kinda Morning *

Just For Fun
Just In Time
Just One More Chance

Keep A Little Dream Handy *

Lady With The Big Umbrella
Lay Some Happiness On Me
Let's Be Friendly
Little Lovely On
Little Ole Wine Drinker, Me
Long Before I Knew You ** *(Bells Are Ringing)*
Long, Long Ago
Louisa's Theme ** *(What A Way To Go!)*
Love Is All That Matters
Lovey Kravezit ** *(Silencers)*
Lucky Song

Magician
Man Who Plays The Mandolino
Memories Are Made Of This (3 Versions)
Me 'N' You 'N' The Moon
Merci Beaucoup ** *(Sailor Beware)*
Mine To Love ** *(Caddy)*

Mississippi Dreamboat
Mister Booze
Moments Like This *
Money Burns A Hole In My Pocket
Money Is A Problem
Mu-Cha-Cha ** *(Bells Are Ringing)*
My Friend Irma ** *(My Friend Irma)*
My Kind Of Town ** *(Robin and the Seven Hoods)*
My Own, My Only, My All

Navy Gets The Gravy But The Army Gets The Beans ** *(At War With The Army)*
Never Before

Old Calliope *
On An Evening In Roma
One Big Love *
Once Upon A Time
Only Trust Your Heart
Open Up The Doghouse

Parachute Jump *
Pardners
Party's Over ** *(Bells Are Ringing)*
Promise Her Anything

Rainbows Are Back In Style
Relax-Ay-Voo
Return To Me (2 Versions)
Rio Bravo

Sailor's Polka
San Domingo *
Santiago ** *(Silencers)*
Send Me The Pillow You Dream On
Shades (2 Versions)
She's A Little Bit Country
Shutters And Boards
Silencers ** *(Silencers)*
Simpatico
Solitaire
Something Big ** *(something big)*
Sons Of Katie Elder ** *(Sons of Katie Elder)*
Sophia
Story Of Life
Street Of Love

Strictly For The Birds** (Jerry Lewis solo song)
Style
Sway

Ten Thousand Bedrooms
Test Of Time
Texas Across The River ** *(Texas Across the River)*
That Old Clock On The Wall
That's Amore
That's What I Like
There's Got To Be A Better Way ** *(Bandolero!)*
Three Ring Circus ** *(Three Ring Circus)*
To Love And Be Loved ** *(Some Came Running)*
Today, Tomorrow, Forever *
Tonda Wanda Hoy
Toys In The Attic ** *(Toys In The Attic)*
Try Again

Under The Bridges Of Paris

Volare

Watching The World Go By
Welcome To My World
What Have You Done For Me Lately *
What Wouldcha Do Without Me *
When It's Sleepy Time Down South
When Someone Wonderful Thinks You're Wonderful *
When You Pretend
Where Can I Go Without You
Who Was That Lady? (2 Versions)
Who's Been Sleeping In My Bed ** *(Who's Been Sleeping In My Bed)*
Who's Got The Action
Wild And Woolly West *
The Wind, The Wind
Won't You Surrender
Write To Me From Naples

You And Your Beautiful Eyes (2 Versions)
You I Love
You Look So Familiar
You'll Always Be The One I Love
You're Gonna Dance With Me, Baby ** *(Living It Up)*
You're Never Too Young ** *(You're Never Too Young)*
You're The Right One

You've Still Got A Place In My Heart

* DEAN RECORDED, BUT SONG WASN'T COMMERCIALLY RELEASED
** DEAN NEVER RECORDED, BUT IS PICTURED ON THE COVER

SONGBOOKS

Bells Are Ringing Vocal Selections
(Stratford Music Corp.)

Bells Are Ringing **
Better Than A Dream
Do It Yourself
Drop That Name **
I Met A Girl
Just In Time
Mu-Cha-Cha **
The Party's Over **

Dean Martin Sings, Book One
(Sands Music Corp.)

Abbracciami **
Baby-O
Belle From Barcelona
Bridge Of Sighs **
Everybody Loves Somebody
Forgetting You
I'll Bring You A Rainbow **
Look To Your Heart **
Once Upon A Time
Outta My Mind
Talk To Me **
Your Love For Me **

Dean Martin Sings, Book Two
(Sands Music Corp.)

Ain't That A Kick In The Head
All My Tomorrows **
Don't Call Me, I'll Call You **
Every Minute, Every Hour
How Sweet It Is
Just Close Your Eyes

Mala Femmena **
Nice 'N' Easy **
Sleep Warm
Sogni D'Oro
Tell Her You Love Her **
You'll Always Be The One I Love

Dean Martin's Recorded Hits
(Hansen Publications)

Always Together
Besame Mucho
Come Running Back
Door Is Still Open To My Heart
I Can't Help Remembering You
I'm Not The Marrying Kind
In A Little Spanish Town
Little Ole Wine Drinker, Me
Memories Are Made Of This
Mimi
My Heart Cries For You
Tangerine
Tell Her You Love Her **
That's Amore
Things
We'll Sing In The Sunshine
You're Nobody 'Til Somebody Loves You

Songs From The Silencers
(Shapiro, Bernstein, and Co.)

Anniversary Song **
Empty Saddles
Glory Of Love
If You Knew Susie
Last Round Up
Lord, You Made The Night Too Long **
On The Sunny Side Of The Street
Red Sails In The Sunset
Side By Side

** SONG NEVER RECORDED BY DEAN

(Capitol Records publicity photo)

Chapter 7

Radio Shows/Appearances

THE MARTIN and LEWIS SHOW

Producer/Director	Robert L. Redd
Producer/Director (1951-53)	Dick Mack
Writers	Ray Allen
	Dick McKnight
	Chet Castellaw
	Norman Sullivan
	Charley Isaacs
	Leon Fry
	Jack Douglas
Writers (1951-53)	Norman Lear
	Ed Simmons
Sponsors (1951-53)	Chesterfield
	Anacin
	Dentyne/Chicklets
Announcers	Ed Herlihy
	Mike Roy
	Jimmy Wallington
	Charles Mountain
	George Fenneman
	Ben Alexander
	Wayne Howell
Guest Cast (in various episodes)	Flo McMichael
	Sheldon Leonard
	Shirley Mitchell
	Jane Morgan

Dean, Jerry Lewis and bandleader Dick Stabile
(NBC publicity photo)

                                        Geraldine Kay
                                        Carol Richards
                                        Mary Costa
                                        Bonnie Bishop
Orchestra   Dick Stabile

12/22/48   LUCILLE BALL
(Pilot Show)   You Won't Be Satisfied
                You Was (With Ilene Woods)
                Money Song (With Jerry and Lucille)
                        (Note: This song is included on the Radiola LP version of
                        this show, but not on the Radio Spirits release which
                        comes directly from Jerry Lewis' collection.)

2/1/49   (Unaired Preview Show)
                Powder Your Face With Sunshine
                My Darling (With Mary Hatcher)

Sundays, 6:30-7:00 pm

4/3/49   BOB HOPE
                Bye Bye Blackbird
                Tarra Ta-Larra Ta-Lar

4/4/49   (Unaired Preview Show with HAL WALLIS)
                Cruising Down The River
                Galway Bay
                Money Song (With Jerry)

4/10/49   WILLIAM BENDIX
                Bye Bye Blackbird
                My Darling (With Mary Hatcher)
                        Note: The above songs are included on the Radiola LP
                        version of this show. The following two tracks are con-
                        tained on the Radio Spirits release of this program:
                                You Won't Be Satisfied
                                Faraway Places
                        The entire show differs in sections on the two releases.)

4/17/49   GEORGE MARSHALL
                        Cruising Down The River
                        Galway Bay
                        Money Song (With Jerry)

4/24/49   DICK POWELL
You Broke Your Promise
My Melancholy Bay
Ragtime Cowboy Joe (With Jerry and Dick)

5/1/49   MADELINE CARROLL
She's A Sunflower
Dreamer With A Penny

5/8/49   PETER LORRE
Someone Like You
Again
Drop Dead Little Darling (With Jerry and Peter)

5/15/49   BURL IVES
How It Lies
I Don't See Me In Your Eyes Anymore

5/22/49   ARTHUR TREACHER
Candy Kisses
3 Wishes

5/29/49   JOHN GARFIELD
I Can't Give You Anything But Love

6/5/49   HENRY FONDA
I Can't Give You Anything But Love
'A' You're Adorable
Drop Dead Little Darling (With Jerry and Henry)

6/12/49   MARILYN MAXWELL
Toot Toot Tootsie
Sioux St. Marie
Baby It's Cold Outside (With Marilyn)

Tuesdays, 9:00-9:30 pm

6/21/49   TONY MARTIN
Take Your Girlie To The Movies
Some Enchanted Evening
Oh Marie (Excerpt)
Anything You Can Do, I Can Do Better (With Tony)

6/28/49   JOHN CARRADINE
Candy Kisses
You're So Understanding

7/5/49	RALPH BELLAMY
	Swanee
	Ghost Riders In The Sky
	Parody song in skit

7/12/49   CHARLES RUGGLES
How It Lies
Sweet Kentucky Babe

7/19/49   VINCENT PRICE
Cruising Down The River
You're So Understanding

7/26/49   FRANCES LANGFORD
Someday
September Song
Parody song in skit

8/2/49   WILLIAM BOYD (HOPALONG CASSIDY)
Five Foot Two, Eyes Of Blue
Again

8/9/49   BURT LANCASTER
Darktown Strutter's Ball
I Don't See Me In Your Eyes Anymore

8/16/49   VICTOR MOORE
Where Are You
Just For Fun

8/23/49   BILLIE BURKE
Let's Take An Old-Fashioned Walk

8/30/49   JANE RUSSELL
There's 'Yes Yes' In Your Eyes
Room Full Of Roses

9/6/49   CESAR ROMERO
Laurabell Lee
You're Breaking My Heart

Fridays, 8:30-9:00 pm

10/7/49   Someday
Vieni Su
(No guest star)

10/14/49	DOROTHY KIRSTEN
	Toot Toot Tootsie
	Let's Take An Old-Fashion Walk (With Dorothy)

10/21/49	GEORGE JESSEL
	Darktown Strutter's Ball
	Just For Fun
	Oh You Beautiful Doll (With Jerry and George)

10/28/49	I Can't Give You Anything But Love
	Dreamer's Holiday
	(No guest star)

Mondays, 10:00-10:30 pm

(Note: There were no guest stars during the 11/7/49 to 1/30/50 Monday night run.)

11/7/49	Everywhere You Go
	Georgia On My Mind

11/14/49	Ain't She Sweet
	Younger Than Springtime

11/21/49	Be Goody Good Good To Me
	A Man Wrote A Song

11/28/49	Just One Of Those Things
	There's No Tomorrow

12/5/49	Jingle Bells
	Don't Cry Joe

12/12/49	(Dean's songs unknown)

12/19/49	Santa Claus Is Coming To Town
	White Christmas
	Silent Night (In English and Italian)

12/26/49	(Dean's songs unknown)

1/2/50	Sometimes I'm Happy
	Rockabye Your Baby With A Dixie Melody

1/9/50	I Found A Million Dollar Baby
	I Can Dream, Can't I

1/16/50	Someday
	There's No Tomorrow

1/23/50	My Blue Heaven
	You're Wonderful To Love

1/30/50	Bibbidy Bobbidy Boo
	Marta

Fridays, 8:30-9:00 pm

10/5/51	DINAH SHORE
	(Ma Come Bali) Bella Bimba
	I Wanna Be With You Tonight
	Trolley Song (Parody with Dinah and Jerry)
	If You Were The Only Girl

10/12/51	GEORGE RAFT
	Meanderin'
	I Ran All The Way Home
	Give Me The Old Soft Shoe (With Carol Richards)
	I Don't Know Why

10/19/51	BING CROSBY
	I Wish I Was
	Little Man (With Jerry)
	Sam's Song (With Bing)
	We're Three Crosby Brothers (With Jerry and Bing)
	I'll String Along With You

10/26/51	ARLENE DAHL
	(Dean's songs unknown)

11/2/51	DENISE DARCEL
	Walking My Baby Back Home
	Hangin' Around With You
	You Gotta Be A Football Hero (With Denise and Jerry)
	Just One More Chance
	Fere Jacques (With Denise and Jerry)

11/9/51	DANNY THOMAS
	Whispering
	It's The Talk Of The Town (Parody with Jerry)
	While You Danced (With Bonnie Bishop)
	Game Show Song Parody (With Danny and Jerry)
	What'll I Do

11/16/51 SHELLEY WINTERS
      Night Train To Memphis
      Blue Smoke
      Parody song with Shelley and Jerry
      If I Could Be With You

11/23/51 DENNIS MORGAN
      I Wonder Who's Kissing Her Now
      I Won't Cry Anymore
      Bye Bye Blackbird (Parody with Jerry and Dennis)
      Pennies From Heaven

11/30/51 JANE WYMAN
      My Blue Heaven
      How Ya Gonna Keep 'Em Down On The Farm
      Rockabye Your Baby With A Dixie Melody

12/7/51   JOAN DAVIS
      Who's Sorry Now
      Never Before
      Parody from the opera Carmen
      You've Got Me Crying Again

12/14/51 JANE RUSSELL
      In The Cool, Cool, Cool Of The Evening
      A Kiss To Build A Dream On
      If I Knew Then What I Know Now

12/21/51 HELEN O'CONNELL
      Jingle Bells
      White Christmas
      How D'Ya Like Your Eggs In The Morning? (With Helen)
      Let's Put Out The Lights And Go To Sleep
          (Parody with Jerry and Helen)
      It's Easy To Remember

12/28/51 DALE EVANS
      Sailor's Polka
      Blue Smoke
      Parody song with Jerry and Dale
      With My Eyes Wide Open I'm Dreaming

1/4/52   MONA FREEMAN
      I'll String Along With You
      Meanderin'
      Never Before

1/11/52   MARION MARSHALL/HANS CONREID
      Oh Boy, Oh Boy, Oh Boy, Oh Boy, Oh Boy
      As You Are
      June In January

1/18/52   FRANK SINATRA
      (Ma Come Bali) Bella Bimba
      These Foolish Things (Parody with Jerry)
      School Days (With Jerry and Frank)
      Little White Cloud That Cried

1/25/52   ALEXIS SMITH
      Aw C'mon
      Anytime
      That Old Feeling

2/1/52   GORDON MacRAE
      I Love The Way You Say Goodnight (With Carol Richards)
      It Might As Well Be Spring

2/8/52   RHONDA FLEMING
      Bye Bye Blackbird
      Close To You
      Out Of Nowhere

2/15/52   WILLIAM HOLDEN
      Down Yonder
      Little Man (Parody with Jerry)
      Cry
      I Surrender Dear

2/22/52   LINDA DARNELL
      There's A Rainbow 'Round My Shoulder
      Until
      When You're Smiling

2/29/52   TONY CURTIS
      San Fernando Valley
      Never Before

3/7/52   CORINNE CALVET
Oh Boy, Oh Boy, Oh Boy, Oh Boy, Oh Boy
My Heart Has Found A Home Now
We Just Couldn't Say Goodbye

3/14/52   LIZABETH SCOTT
I Wonder Who's Kissing Her Now
A Kiss To Build A Dream On
Night Train To Memphis
That Old Gang Of Mine

3/21/52   MARLENE DIETRICH
When You're Smiling
Maybe
Hands Across The Table

3/28/52   ANN SOTHERN
When The Red, Red Robin Comes Bob, Bob, Bobbin' Along
Please Mr. Sun
Only Forever

4/4/52   CLAIRE TREVOR
About A Quarter To Nine
Pretty As A Picture
I Kiss Your Hand, Madam

4/11/52   VIRGINIA MAYO
For Me And My Gal
All I Have To Give You Is My Love
Trolley Song Parody (With Jerry and Virginia)
Mighty Like A Rose

4/18/52   BORIS KARLOFF
You Must Have Been A Beautiful Baby
Little White Cloud That Cried
School Days Parody (With Jerry and Boris)
Empty Saddles In The Old Corral

4/25/52   ANN SHERIDAN
The Object Of My Affection
Anytime
Never In A Million Years

Tuesdays, 9:00-9:30 pm

9/16/52   ROSEMARY CLOONEY
              Hominy Grits
              You Belong To Me
              Once In A While

9/23/52   JEFF CHANDLER
              Pretty Baby
              Wish You Were Here
              Riding Down The Canyon

9/30/52   JIMMY STEWART
              Walking My Baby Back Home
              You Belong To Me

10/7/52   JANE WYMAN
              My Baby Just Cares For Me
              Second Chance
              I Found A Million Dollar Baby

10/14/52   HOAGY CARMICHAEL
              Sometimes I'm Happy
              Half As Much
              Two Sleepy People

10/21/52   ANN SHERIDAN
              I'm An Old Cowhand
              Here I'll Stay
              I Only Have Eyes For You

10/28/52   JOAN DAVIS
              I Wonder Who's Kissing Her Now
              I'll Always Love You
              Oh Marie

11/11/52   DOROTHY LAMOUR
              About A Quarter To Nine
              Somewhere Along The Way
              June In January

11/18/52   WILLIAM HOLDEN
              For Me And My Gal
              I Know A Dream When I See One
              If You Were The Only Girl

11/25/52   GEORGE JESSEL
Glow Worm
Because You're Mine
One Bright & Shining Light (Brief part in sketch)
Deep Purple

12/2/52   ANN BLYTHE
My Lady Loves To Dance
It Takes Two To Tango
Bye Bye Blackbird (Parody with Jerry and Ann)
I'm Yours

12/9/52   LINDA DARNELL
Louise
Why Don't You Believe Me
It's Beginning To Look A Lot Like Christmas

12/16/52   GINGER ROGERS
I Feel Like A Feather In The Breeze
To See You Is To Love You
Silver Bells

12/23/52   TONY MARTIN
Who's Your Little Who-Zis
It's Nothing (With Tony)
Silent Night

12/30/52   ESTHER WILLIAMS
Don't Let The Stars Get In Your Eyes
Kiss
Heart And Soul

1/6/53   VICTOR MATURE
If I Could Be With You
What Could Be More Beautiful
You Were Meant For Me

1/13/53   JACK WEBB
Is You Is Or Is You Ain't My Baby
Everything Happens To Me
I Went To Your Wedding

1/20/53 JANET LEIGH
      Just One Of Those Things
      Keep It A Secret
      There Must Be A Way

1/27/53 TONY CURTIS
      Sweet Georgia Brown
      Kiss
      Can't We Talk It Over

2/3/53   TERRY MOORE
      Do You Ever Think Of Me
      Congratulations
      The Very Thought Of You

2/10/53 GEORGE JESSEL
      Bye Bye Blues
      I Miss You So
      Toot Toot Tootsie (Parody with Jerry and George)
      The One In My Arms

2/17/53 DONNA REED
      I Want To Be Happy
      Because You're Mine
      I'm Yours

2/24/53 MARILYN MONROE
      You'd Be Surprised
      There's My Lover
      How Deep Is The Ocean

3/3/53   GEORGE RAFT
      No Deposit, No Return
      'Til I Waltz Again With You
      Blue Moon

3/10/53 ZSA ZSA GABOR
      My Jealous Eyes
      Little Did We Know
      Let Me Love You Tonight

3/17/53 GLORIA SWANSON
      It's Only A Paper Moon
      How Do You Speak To An Angel
      It's A Sin To Tell A Lie

3/24/53   PHIL HARRIS
When My Sugar Walks Down The Street
I Confess
Twilight On The Trail

3/31/53   JACK WEBB
(Dean's songs unknown)

4/7/53   MITZI GAYNOR
(Dean's songs unknown)

4/14/53   LINDA DARNELL
(Dean's songs unknown)

4/21/53   VIC DAMONE
In The Shade Of The Old Apple Tree
The Second Star To The Right
Alone
Sheik Of Araby (Parody with Jerry and Vic)

4/28/53   LORAINE DAY
Thumbelina
Have You Heard
You Always Hurt The One You Love

5/5/53   ANNE BAXTER
The Breeze
Your Cheating Heart
Moments Like This

5/12/53   JOANNE DRU
Wild Horses
The Time Is Now
High Noon

5/19/53   FRED MacMURRAY
Side By Side
Ohio
I Could Write A Book

5/26/53   DEBBIE REYNOLDS
Looka My See
A Fool Such As I
I Only Have Eyes For You

6/2/53   JEFF CHANDLER
                What Can I Say After I Say I'm Sorry
                Down Hearted
                Long Ago And Far Away

6/9/53   PHYLLIS THAXTER
                Twice As Much
                A Girl Named Mary And A Boy Named Bill
                The Nearness Of You

6/16/53   JOSEPH COTTON
                About A Quarter To Nine
                The Second Star To The Right
                Say It Isn't So

6/23/53   VERA ELLEN
                I'm Sitting On Top Of The World
                Outside Of Heaven
                I'll Be With You In Apple Blossom Time

6/30/53   IDA LUPINO
                Please Don't Talk About Me When I'm Gone
                I Miss You So
                I'll Get By As Long As I Have You

7/7/53   MARLENE DIETRICH
                (Dean's songs unknown)

7/14/53   GLORIA GRAHAM
                If I Could Sing Like Bing
                Love Me, Love Me
                I Won't Cry Anymore

MISC. APPEARANCES

7/5/42   FITCH BANDWAGON (WTAM; Cleveland, OH)
                What'll I Do
                Sweet Leilani
                A Boy In Khaki, A Girl In Lace
                So Long, Until Victory
                        (Note: This was Dean's network radio debut.)

12/2/43   HOMEFRONT MATINEE (WCBS)

1943   FULL SPEED AHEAD (WOR; NY)

Note: From August to December 1944, Dean had his own fifteen minute radio show on WMCA in New York. A transcription from 8/30/44 survives. Dean sings a brief excerpt of Melancholy Baby at the beginning and end of the show. Till Then, If I Knew Then What I Know Now and There'll Be A Hot Time In The Town Of Berlin are heard in their entirety.

9/46   PAUL BRENNER SHOW (WAAT; Newark, NJ)
                     Interview

11/25/46   WIP LINE (WIP; Philadelphia, PA)
                     Sonny Boy (Parody with Jerry)
                     Someday

8/5/47   BARRY GRAY SHOW - SCOUT ABOUT TOWN
                     Peg O' My Heart

1/13/48   OLD GOLD SHOW (WJJD; Chicago, IL)
                     Interview

10/26/48   BOB HOPE
                     Everybody Loves Somebody
                     I'm Looking Over A Four Leaf Clover (With Bob)

11/23/48   BOB HOPE
                     Money Song (With Jerry and Bob)
                     On A Slow Boat To China

11/25/48   ELGIN SHOW
                     That Certain Party (With Jerry)
                     Ramblin' Rose Of Mine

1/31/49   MARCH OF DIMES
                     Here I'll Stay

2/10/49   CHESTERFIELD SUPPER CLUB
                     Money Song (With Jerry)
                     You Was (With Peggy Lee)

2/17/49   SEALTEST VARIETY THEATER
                     Tarra Ta-Larra Ta-Lar

3/29/49   BOB HOPE
                     Johnny Get Your Girl

4/4/49   HOLLYWOOD PREMIERE

4/12/49	BOB HOPE Have A Little Sympathy
5/9/49	TEX AND JINX SHOW Interview
	JACK EIGEN SHOW (WMGM; NY) Dean and Jerry were interviewed several times during their 6-week engagement at the Copa (May 4-June 15, 1950.)
4/11/50	NEXT WITH DAVE GARROWAY
6/28/50	MAKE BELIEVE BALLROOM (WNEW; NY) Interview from Las Vegas regarding *My Friend Irma Goes West*
6/29/50	STARGAZING WITH FRANCIS SCULLY Interview from Las Vegas regarding *My Friend Irma Goes West*
7/1/50	STARS ON BROADWAY Interview at premiere of *My Friend Irma Goes West* (From the Flamingo Hotel, Las Vegas)
9/2/50	CEREBRAL PALSY ALL-STAR BENEFIT (Dean only)
11/11/50	WAYNE HOWELL SHOW
12/17/50	BIG SHOW La Vie En Rose
2/11/51	BIG SHOW Tonda Wanda Hoy I Love You Truly May The Good Lord Bless And Keep You (Dean and Jerry sing one line.)
11/7/51	BING CROSBY In The Cool, Cool, Cool Of The Evening (Parody with Bing) Sweet Leilani (Parody with Bing) Hawaiian War Chant (Parody with Bing and Jerry) Sound Off For Chesterfield (With Bing and Jerry)
1/18/52	BUICK
4/2/52	CARDIAC TELETHON

12/29/52   PREMIERE
            Interview from Hollywood regarding *The Stooge*

3/29/53   PHIL HARRIS/ALICE FAYE SHOW

11/16/54   AMOS AND ANDY MUSIC HALL
            Interview regarding *Three Ring Circus*

2/3/55   MARCH OF DIMES
            Almost Like Being In Love
            There's No Tomorrow (With Tony Martin)
                        (From the Sands Hotel, Las Vegas; Martin Block's
                        20th Anniversary show.)

6/24/56   MONITOR
            Interview

7/18/56   MAKE BELIEVE BALLROOM (WNEW; NY)
            Interview regarding *Pardners*

9/21/57   MONITOR
            (Interview; Dean only)

1960   PETE EPSTEEN'S PONTIAC
            Dean sings special lyrics to "Ain't That A Kick In The Head" to
            promote this Chicago, IL car dealership.

Chapter 8

Television Appearances

COLGATE COMEDY HOUR

Sundays, 8:00-9:00 pm
1950-1955

Executive Producer/NBC Production Supervisor	Sam Fuller
Director	Robert S. Finkel
Stage Manager	Bud Yorkin
Writers	Arthur Phillips
	Harry Crane
	Danny Arnold
	Austin Kalish
	Norman Lear
	Jerry Lewis
	Ed Simmons
	George Axelrod
	Arnold Horwitt
	Snag Werris
Musical Director/Conductor/Arranger	Dick Stabile
Vocal Arrangements	Norman Luboff
Art Director	Bill Martin
Art Director/Production Design	Furth Ullman
Technical Directors	Joe Conn
	Ross Miller
	William Waterbury
Audio	Bob Jensen
Special Lyrics	Sammy Cahn
Wardrobe	Sy Devore

Costumes	Kate Drain Larson
	Frank Thompson
Furs	Teitelbaum
Unit Manager	Kaslon K. Zoller
Producer/Director	Ernest D. Glucksman
Directors	Kingman Moore
	Bud Yorkin
Choreography	Nick Castle
	Lee Sherman
Gowns	Beaumelle
Casting Director	Howard Ross
Production Supervisor	Edward Sobol
Television Director	Alan Yorkin
Settings	Theodore Cooper
Associate NBC Supervisor	Robert B. Masson
Associate Producer	Bob Henry
Executive Producer	Pete Barnum

9/17/50   I'm Gonna Sit Right Down And Write Myself A Letter
           It's The Talk Of The Town (With Jerry)
           La Vie En Rose
           Frankie And Johnny (With Jerry and Marilyn Maxwell)

10/15/50   I'll Always Love You
           C'est Si Bon (With the Skylarks)
           Once In A While (With Jerry)
           Oh Marie

11/12/50   Glory Of Love
           Be Honest With Me
           San Fernando Valley (With Jerry)

2/4/51   Tonda Wanda Hoy
           You And Your Beautiful Eyes (With Polly Bergen)
           It's Magic (With Jerry)

4/29/51   Would I Love You
           I Wonder Who's Kissing Her Now
           Luna Mezzo Mare (With Jerry)

5/20/51   With My Eyes Wide Open I'm Dreaming
           Ever True, Ever More
           There's No Tomorrow (With Jerry)

You're Just In Love (With Jerry)
My Heart Cries For You (With Jerry)

6/3/51   Too Young

6/24/51   Pennies From Heaven
                Walking My Baby Back Home
                That Old Gang Of Mine (With Jerry)

11/4/51   Solitaire
                Oh Marie (With Jerry)

12/30/51   Kentucky Babe
                Night Train To Memphis
                A Good Man Nowadays Is Hard To Find (With Jerry)

2/10/52   When You're Smiling

3/23/52   You Made Me Love You
                There's A Rainbow 'Round My Shoulder

4/27/52   One For My Baby
                3 Blind Mice (With Jerry and Kitty Kalen)
                Oh Marie

9/21/52   You Belong To Me
                Hominy Grits

11/30/52   There Goes My Heart
                Louise
                You'll Never Get Away (With Jerry)

1/25/53   I'll String Along With You
                I Don't Care If The Sun Don't Shine
                You'll Never Get Away (With Jerry)

5/3/53   Your Cheatin' Heart
                When The Red, Red Robin Comes Bob, Bob, Bobbin' Along

5/31/53   Love Me, Love Me
                I Don't Care If The Sun Don't Shine
                You'll Never Get Away

10/4/53   Great To Be Home (With Jerry)
                You're The Right One

That's Amore
There's No Tomorrow (Jerry "conducts" the orchestra.)

1/10/54   Pretty Baby
It's Easy To Remember
That's Amore (Jerry disrupts Dean's performance.)

5/2/54   If You Were The Only Girl
We Belong Together (With Jerry)
Almost Like Being In Love
Rockin' Is Our Business (With Jerry and the Treniers)
        Dean and Jerry also perform a song celebrating their
        eighth anniversary as a team.

5/30/54   That's Entertainment (With Jerry)
Money Burns A Hole In My Pocket
That's What I Like
Ev'ry Street's A Boulevard In Old New York (With Jerry)

12/19/54   Longface (With Jerry)
Without A Word Of Warning
Mambo Italiano
Ev'ry Street's A Boulevard In Old New York (With Jerry)

2/13/55   Belle From Barcelona
Melancholy Baby
We Belong Together (With Jerry)
Young And Foolish

5/8/55   For You
Is It True What They Say About Dixie

6/5/55   Kentucky Babe (With Ebonaires)
You've Gotta Have Heart (With Jerry)
Carolina In The Morning

COLGATE VARIETY HOUR

9/18/55   Nevertheless
Side By Side (With Jerry)
I Like Them All
Shake A Hand (With Jerry and Freddy Bell and the Bellhops)

11/13/55   It Must Be True
Two Lost Souls (With Jerry)

Memories Are Made Of This
Sometimes I'm Happy (With Norman Luboff Choir)

THE DEAN MARTIN SHOW

Thursdays, 10:00-11:00 pm
Season One: 1965-66

Producer	Bill Colleran (9/16-10/21)
Producer/Director	Greg Garrison (10/28-on)
Writer/Co-Producer	Paul W. Keyes
Associate Producer	Norman Hopps
Musical Arrangements	J. Hill
	Les Brown
Choreography	Kevin Carlisle
Unit Manager	P. Dean Reed
Associate Director	Tom Foulkes
Music Coordinator	Mack Gray
Music Consultant	Ken Lane
Art Director	Spencer Davies
Costumes	Campbel
Music Routines	Hal Hidey
	Lee Hale
Assistant to the Producer	Jan Buchanan
Production Assistant	Janet Tigue
Assistant to the Choreographer	Drusilla Davis
Makeup	Claude Thompson
Technical Director	Karl Messerschmidt
Lighting Directors	John Freschi
	Lon Stuckey
Audio	Bill Levitsky
Video	Jerry Smith
Tape Editor	Stan Chlebek
Executive Producer	Harold Kemp

9/16/65   FRANK SINATRA; DIAHANN CARROLL; BOB NEWHART;
JAN & DEAN; JOEY HEATHERTON
      (Cameos by DANNY THOMAS; EDDIE FISHER;
      STEVE ALLEN; JACK JONES)
Houston
The Oldest Established Permanent Floating Crap Game
      In New York (With Frank)
Witchcraft (With Frank and Diahann)

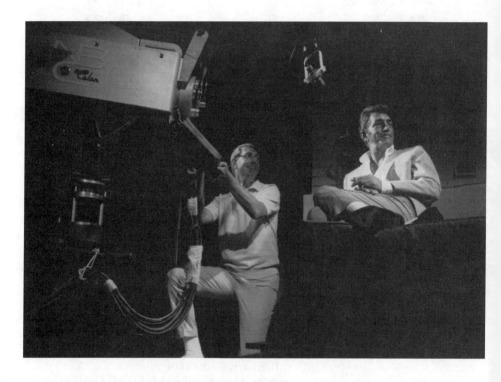

Dean rehearsing his weekly "couch song."
(NBC publicity photo)

9/23/65
JOHN WAYNE; PEGGY LEE; JACK JONES; SHARI LEWIS;
         RUDY CARDENAS; WALTER DARE WAHL
Send Me The Pillow You Dream On
Don't Fence Me In (With John)
I Can't Give You Anything But Love (With Peggy and Jack)
Tweedle Dee (With Krofft Puppet)

9/30/65
EDDIE FISHER; ABBE LANE; DAVE CLARK FIVE;
         PHYLLIS DILLER; JOHN BUBBLES; YONELY
Here Comes My Baby
Lady Be Good; When My Baby Smiles At Me; We Three
         (With Eddie and John)
C'est Magnifique (With Krofft Puppet)

10/7/65
VIC DAMONE; GORDON AND SHEILA MacRAE;
         ALLAN SHERMAN; SHANI WALLIS;
         FERRANTE AND TEICHER; CURTIS BROTHERS;
         HARDY FAMILY
Born To Lose
Medley with Vic and Allan

10/14/65
PEARL BAILEY; GRETCHEN WYLER; GEORGE GOBEL;
         DINO, DESI AND BILLY; DUKES OF DIXIELAND;
         SERENDIPITY SINGERS; RUDELLS
Take These Chains From My Heart
In A Little Spanish Town; It Happened In Monterey
         (With Pearl and George)

10/21/65
LOUIS ARMSTRONG; ROBERT GOULET; LAINIE KAZAN;
         KIRBY STONE FOUR; BRASCIA AND TYBEE;
         HELENE AND HOWARD; TRIO LEEMA
King Of The Road
My Kind Of Girl; Sweet Sue; Sweet Georgia Brown; Hello Dolly
         (With Louis)
C'est Si Bon (With Krofft Puppet)

10/28/65
JONATHAN WINTERS; JANE POWELL; JOHN GARY; LOUIS
         JORDAN; DAVIS AND REESE; SEVEN STANEKS
I Will
Rosalie; Rose Marie (With Jane)
Gimme A Little Kiss (With Krofft Puppet)
Medley with Jonathan and Jane

11/4/65   ETHEL MERMAN; LESLIE UGGAMS; JACK CARTER; JOEY
HEATHERTON; NEW CHRISTY MINSTRELS;
LEONARD BARR; CARLSSONS
Where Or When
Clinging Vine
I Get A Kick Out Of You; Small World; I Got Rhythm;
You're Just In Love; Together (With Ethel)

11/11/65   MICKEY ROONEY; KATE SMITH; TAMMY GRIMES; ELAINE
DUNN; CORBETT MONICA; AMIN BROTHERS
Birds And The Bees
You're Nobody 'Til Somebody Loves You
Embraceable You (With Krofft Puppet)
That's Amore; I'll Be Seeing You; Last Time I Saw Paris;
King Of The Road; When The Moon Comes Over The
Mountain (With Kate)
The Girl That I Marry; Once In A While; The Girl Next Door;
Nevertheless; Lady Be Good (With Mickey)

11/25/65   MILTON BERLE; LISA KIRK; PHIL FORD AND MIMI HINES;
XAVIER CUGAT; CHARO AND COMPANY;
WINDSOR BOYS CHORAL GROUP; RONNIE
DeMARCO
Things
Nevertheless
Happy Talk; I Want To Be Happy; Sometimes I'm Happy;
C'mon Get Happy; Put On A Happy Face (With
Milton and Lisa)
Swinging On A Star (With Windsor Boys Choral Group)

12/2/65   TONY BENNETT; BARBARA McNAIR; NANETTE FABRAY;
GUY MARKS; DUNHILLS; YONELY
Blue, Blue Day
Hands Across The Table
If You Were The Only Girl
Best Things In Life Are Free (With Barbara)
Darktown Strutter's Ball (With Krofft Puppet)
Come Fly With Me; Chicago; Houston; I'll Take Manhattan;
I Love Paris; A Foggy Day In London Town;
Way Down Yonder In New Orleans (With Tony)
Gimme A Little Kiss; Mean To Me (With Nanette)

12/9/65   LOUIS ARMSTRONG; CAROL LAWRENCE;
ANDREWS SISTERS; RICH LITTLE; GENE BAYLOS;
LINE RENAUD
Singing The Blues
I've Grown Accustomed To Her Face

That's Amore; Don't Fence Me In; In Apple Blossom Time
    (With Andrews Sisters)
Side By Side (With Line)
When It's Sleepy Time Down South; Swanee; Mississippi Mud;
    Won't You Come Home Bill Bailey; Gotta Travel On;
    Rockabye Your Baby With A Dixie Melody; Down By
    The Riverside; When The Saints Go Marching In (With
    Louis)
Baby Face (With Carol)

12/16/65   ELLA FITZGERALD; GORDON AND SHEILA MacRAE;
    GEORGE GOBEL; BARRIE CHASE; VAGABONDS;
    GUS AUGSPURG'S MONKEY ACT
Bumming Around
I'm Confessin'
Thank Heaven For Little Girls
Take These Chains From My Heart (With George)
Anytime; Bouquet Of Roses; Bury Me Not On The Lone Prairie;
    Red River Valley; Tumbling Tumbleweeds; You Are My
    Sunshine (With Ella and Gordon)

12/30/65   STANLEY HOLLOWAY; JANIS PAIGE; JOANIE SUMMERS;
    LOUIS PRIMA; HOMER AND JETHRO; RICHARD
    HEARNE
Everybody But Me
Blue Moon
She'll Be Comin' 'Round The Mountain; Everybody Loves
    Somebody (With Homer and Jethro)
Girl I Marry; Love And Marriage; Aba-Dabba Honeymoon (With
    Louis and Stanley)
Medley with Joanie and Janis

1/6/66   PEGGY LEE; FRANKIE AVALON; ALLAN SHERMAN; GUY
    MARKS; ROSE MARIE; KELLY SISTERS
Bye Bye Blackbird
I Wonder Who's Kissing Her Now
I Love Being Here With You; Manana; It's A Good Day (With
    Peggy)
Makin' Whoopee (With Frankie)
Smile (With Rose Marie)
Good Advice (With Allan and Guy)

1/13/66   KAY STARR; MAHALIA JACKSON; VIC DANA; SWINGLE
    SISTERS; SOUPY SALES; JOHN BYNER; DAVIS AND
    REESE; YONELY
I'm Gonna Sit Right Down And Write Myself A Letter
S'posin

Silver Dollar; Money Burns A Hole In My Pocket; Wheel Of
        Fortune (With Kay)
Medley with Soupy

1/20/66   GISELE MacKENZIE; TOMMY SANDS; McGUIRE SISTERS;
        JACK CARTER; SHARI LEWIS; TRENIERS
I Could Write A Book
Always
The Party's Over
Life Is Just A Bowl Of Cherries (With Gisele)
All I Do Is Dream Of You; Little Girls; I Don't Want To Walk
        Without You; Say It Isn't Joe (So); Guys And Dolls (With
        McGuire Sisters)
When The Saints Go Marching In (With Shari)
I Don't Care If The Sun Don't Shine (With Tommy)
Rockabye Your Baby With A Dixie Melody (With Treniers)

1/27/66   POLLY BERGEN; BUDDY GRECO; STANLEY HOLLOWAY;
        BILL DANA; ROWAN AND MARTIN
On A Slow Boat To China
Pennies From Heaven
Bumming Around (With Polly)
My Kind Of Girl; Lady Is A Tramp (With Buddy)
South Of The Border; Arrivederci, Roma; We Open In Venice (With
        Bill and Stanley)

2/3/66   BOB HOPE; JULIET PROWSE; PETE FOUNTAIN; JOEL GREY;
        DONNA BUTTERWORTH; LIVELY SET; JOSE GRECO
        AND NINA LORCA
C'est Si Bon
Home
Real Live Girl
Medley with Juliet
Medley with Donna
Medley with Bob and Juliet
Get Happy (With Lively Set)

2/10/66   LUCILLE BALL; BILL COSBY; KATE SMITH; ROWAN AND
        MARTIN; BIG TINY LITTLE
Where Or When
Melancholy Baby
Look For The Silver Lining
You've Got To Be A Football Hero (With Bill)
Medley with Kate and Lucille includes Give My Regards To
        Broadway;
          In The Shade Of The Old Apple Tree;
          Wait 'Til The Sun Shines, Nellie; Bird In A Gilded Cage;

Yankee Doodle Dandy
Tavern In The Town; Roll Out The Barrel (With Big Tiny Little)

2/17/66   EDDIE ALBERT; MAHALIA JACKSON; JULIE LONDON;
                PHYLLIS DILLER; GUY MARKS; SWINGLE SISTERS
           I Will
           True Love
           Look For The Silver Lining
           Two Sleepy People (With Julie)
           I Hate Men; You Must Have Been A Beautiful Baby (With Phyllis)
           Style (With Eddie and Guy)

2/24/66   EDDIE FISHER; KATE SMITH; DON ADAMS; RICH LITTLE;
                PIERO BROTHERS
           Here Comes My Baby
           You Made Me Love You
           Back In Your Own Backyard; My Baby Just Cares For Me
                (With Eddie)
           Shine On Harvest Moon; Moonlight And Roses;
                Alexander's Ragtime Band (With Kate)
           Paper Doll (With Don)

3/3/66   SID CAESAR; GEORGE GOBEL; MARGUERITE PIAZZA;
                ABBE LANE; LETTERMEN; DAVID AND GOLIATH
           Birds And The Bees
           Hands Across The Table
           There Is Nothing Like A Dame; Standing On The Corner;
                A Fellow Needs A Girl (With George and Sid)
           Santa Lucia (With Marguerite)
           Real Live Girl (With Abbe and Sid)

3/10/66   ELLA FITZGERALD; JOHNNY MATHIS; SHELLEY BERMAN;
                YOUNG AMERICANS; GENE SHELDON
           My Kind Of Girl
           What Can I Say After I Say I'm Sorry
           Lollipop Tree (With Young Americans)
           S'Wonderful; Let's Call The Whole Thing Off; They Can't Take
                That Away From Me; Nice Work If You Can Get It;
                They All Laughed (With Ella)
           Put Your Arms Around Me, Honey (With Shelley)
           Take Me Out To The Ballgame (With Johnny)

3/17/66   KEELY SMITH; FRANKIE RANDALL;
                GODFREY CAMBRIDGE; ALLEN AND ROSSI; JOEY
                HEATHERTON; HAL LeROY; TANGIERS
           They Didn't Believe Me

It's Easy To Remember
I'm An Old Cowhand; Ragtime Cowboy Joe; Across The Alley
From The Alamo; Buttons And Bows (With Keely)
In The Cool, Cool, Cool Of The Evening (With Frankie)

3/24/66   IMOGENE COCA; JANE MORGAN; SUPREMES; JACKIE
MASON; HERB ALPERT; STEP BROTHERS
I'm Gonna Change Everything
I Don't Know Why
When You're Smiling (With Imogene)
Side By Side (With Krofft Puppet)
Love Makes The World Go 'Round; I'm In The Mood For Love;
Love Is The Reason (With Imogene, Jane, and the
Supremes)

3/31/66   SID CAESAR; BOB NEWHART; MORGANA KING; PAT SUZUKI
PAUL ANKA
Somewhere There's A Someone
It's The Talk Of The Town
Pretty Baby
Red Roses For A Blue Lady (With Paul)
Sole, Sole, Sole (With Pat)
Loch Lomond; Goodnight Irene (With Morgana)
Medley with Sid and Bob includes Let's All Sing Like The
Birdies Sing; Learn To Croon; Sweet Adeline;
Singing In The Rain

4/7/66   JONATHAN WINTERS; GEORGE JESSEL; LAINIE KAZAN;
RIGHTEOUS BROTHERS; SWINGING LADS; GUS
AUGSPURG'S MONKEY ACT
Born To Lose
You Ought To Be In Pictures
Imagination
I Can't Give You Anything But Love;
Why Don't We Do This More Often; Ain't We Got Fun;
How About You (With Lainie)
Carolina In The Morning (With George)

4/21/66   PATTI PAGE; GORDON AND SHEILA MacRAE; JACK JONES;
ROGER MILLER; CHITA RIVERA; GENE BAYLOS
Second Hand Rose
You'll Never Know
This Could Be The Start Of Something Big; You; 'Deed I Do
(With Patti, Chita and Jack)
King Of The Road (With Roger)
Would You Like To Take A Walk (With Patti)

Personality (With Gordon)
Donkey Serenade (With Jack)

5/5/66   LIBERACE; BILL COSBY; GUY MARKS; DOROTHY
          LOUDON; TANYA THE ELEPHANT
          That Old Clock On The Wall
          Last Time I Saw Paris (Couch song; Liberace plays piano)
          Everybody Loves Somebody
          I Love Paris (With Liberace)
          End Of Season Medley (With Liberace; parodies sung to the tunes
              of: After The Ball Is Over; The Band Played On; Pretty
              Baby; Makin' Whoopee; Ain't We Got Fun)
          Teamwork (With Liberace and Bill)

Season Two: 1966-67

Producer/Director	Greg Garrison
Writers	Paul W. Keyes
	Harry Crane
	Rich Eustis
	Al Rogers
Associate Producers	Paul W. Keyes
	Norman Hopps
Choreography	Robert Sidney
Art Director	Spencer Davies
Special Musical Material	Lee Hale
Musical Arrangements	J. Hill
	Les Brown
Unit Manager	P. Dean Reed
Associate Producer	Tom Foulkes
Music Coordinator	Mack Gray
Music Consultant	Ken Lane
Assistant To The Producer	Janice Buchanan
Production Assistant	Janet Tighe
Production Coordinator	Craig Martin
Costumes	Campbel
	Ed Wassall
Music Routines	Robert B. Bailey
	Geoffrey Clarkson
Assistant To The Choreographer	Wisa D'Orso
	Bob Street
Makeup	Claude Thompson
Technical Director	Karl Messerschmidt
Lighting Directors	Lon Stuckey
	John Freschi
Audio	Bill Levitsky

Video   Jerry Smith
Tape Editor   Stan Chlebek
Stage Managers   George Fulton
                                         Bob Graner
Executive Producer   Harold Kemp

9/15/66   BUDDY HACKETT; PEGGY LEE; GUY MARKS; DOROTHY
                PROVINE; ROWAN AND MARTIN
            Don't Let The Blues Make You Bad
            You're Nobody 'Til Somebody Loves You
            All Alone; Call Me; I Couldn't Sleep A Wink Last Night; Good
                Morning (With Peggy Lee)
            Oldest Established Permanent Floating Crap Game In New York;
                Guys And Dolls (With entire cast)

9/22/66   CAROL LAWRENCE; LIBERACE; BOB NEWHART; GENE
                KRUPA; DOM DeLUISE
            Somewhere There's A Someone
            That Old Feeling
            That's Amore (With Dom)
            Somebody Loves Me (With Carol)
            It's Better With A Union Man (With Liberace, Dom and Bob)
            Crazy Rhythm; We've Got Rhythm (With entire cast)

9/29/66   DUKE ELLINGTON; ANDREWS SISTERS; FRANK GORSHIN;
                TIM CONWAY; LAINIE KAZAN
            My Heart Cries For You
            I'm Forever Blowing Bubbles
            You've Got Possibilities; Teach Me Tonight; Glory Of Love (With
                Lainie)
            Memories Are Made Of This; Manana; South America, Take It
                Away; Rum And Coca Cola (With Andrews Sisters)
            Swing Medley (With entire cast)

10/6/66   GEORGE GOBEL; PHIL HARRIS; VIKKI CARR; BRASCIA
                AND TYBEE
            Today Is Not The Day
            Stars Fell On Alabama
            Them There Eyes (With Vikki)
            Hole In The Bucket (With George)
            Mr. Gallagher, Mr. Shean (With Phil)

10/13/66   DINAH SHORE; GEORGE BURNS; PAIR EXTRAORDINAIRE;
                WISA D'ORSO
            If You Knew Susie
            I'm In The Mood For Love

I Ain't Got Nobody (With George)
They Say It's Wonderful; Take It Easy; Anything You Can Do, I
        Can Do Better (With Dinah)
Yankee Doodle Dandy (With entire cast)

10/20/66   KATE SMITH; FLORENCE HENDERSON; BILL DANA;
                FRANK FONTAINE
Bye Bye Blackbird
It Had To Be You
Play A Simple Melody (With Kate)
Just In Time; Makin' Whoopee (With Florence)
Old MacDonald (Comedy with Frank)
I've Grown Accustomed To Her Face; I Remember It Well (With
        Kate)

10/27/66   BILL COSBY; JOHN WAYNE; JOEY HEATHERTON; GAIL
                MARTIN; ROWAN AND MARTIN
Shoe Goes On The Other Foot Tonight
Red Sails In The Sunset
Honey; Bye Bye Blackbird; When The Red, Red Robin Comes
        Bob, Bob, Bobbin' Along; Back In Your Own Backyard
        (With Gail)
Everybody Loves Somebody (With John who lip-synchs to Frank
        Sinatra's recording)
Crying medley with entire cast includes I Cried For You; Boo-Hoo;
        I've Got Tears In My Ears; Cry

11/3/66   LOUIS ARMSTRONG; RAY BOLGER; NANETTE FABRAY;
                LAINIE KAZAN; ALLAN DRAKE
I'm Living In Two Worlds
If I Had You
We Three; Tea For Two; No Two People; Indian Love Call; Two
        Sleepy People; Together (With Nanette and Lainie)
Georgia On My Mind; Sweet Georgia Brown; Hard Hearted
        Hannah (With Louis)
Object Of My Affection (With Ray)

11/10/66   SID CAESAR; PHYLLIS DILLER; DIAHANN CARROLL; STEP
                BROTHERS
One Lonely Boy
A Million And One
What Can I Say After I Say I'm Sorry
A Hundred Years From Today (With Diahann)
One For My Baby (Excerpt Only)
Applause (With Sid and Phyllis)

283

11/17/66   TONY MARTIN; CATERINA VALENTE; ALLEN AND ROSSI;
        RUSS LEWIS
Nobody But A Fool
It Just Happened That Way
The One I Love Belongs To Somebody Else
There Is Nothing Like A Dame; I Could Write A Book; I've Got
        You Under My Skin (With Tony)
Hit The Road To Dreamland; All I Do Is Dream Of You; Goodnight
        My Love (With Caterina)

11/24/66   EDDIE ALBERT; PHIL HARRIS AND ALICE FAYE; JAN
        MURRAY
Wallpaper Roses
Baby, Won't You Please Come Home
Smile
Beautiful Brown Eyes (With Eddie)
You're A Sweetheart (With Alice)
South Rampart Street Parade (With Phil)
Slumming On Park Avenue; We're A Bunch Of Swells
        (With entire cast)

12/1/66   ARTHUR GODFREY; EDDY ARNOLD; DOM DeLUISE;
        ELAINE DUNN; FRANK SINATRA (as "surprise" guest
        at end of show)
I'm Gonna Change Everything
Just Friends
Tiny Bubbles (With Arthur)
You're Nobody 'Til Somebody Loves You (With Elaine)
Singing The Blues; Blue, Blue Day; Anytime (With Eddy)

12/8/66   ROBERT GOULET; GISELE MacKENZIE; JONATHAN
        WINTERS; ROWAN AND MARTIN; DEANA MARTIN
Cold, Cold Heart
Things We Did Last Summer
Breezing Along With The Breeze (With Robert)
Walking My Baby Back Home; I Can't Give You Anything But
        Love (With Gisele)
You Are My Lucky Star; Side By Side (With Deana)

12/15/66   SID CAESAR; GEORGE KIRBY; VIC DAMONE; CATERINA
        VALENTE; DON CHERRY
Nobody's Baby Again
Home
Ciao Compare (With Vic)
One Note Samba (With Caterina)
Glory Of Love; Gotta Travel On (With Don)
Medley of popular foreign songs (With entire cast)

Dean with his longtime accompanist, Ken Lane.
(NBC publicity photo)

12/22/66   LIBERACE; TENNESSEE ERNIE FORD; BARBARA McNAIR;
JANE POWELL; HAL LeROY
Clinging Vine
Nearness Of You
On The Sunny Side Of The Street (With Barbara)
Empty Saddles (With Liberace)
Where Were You When The Ship Hit The Sand (With Tennessee)
Medley of hillbilly songs (With entire cast)

12/29/66   SERGIO FRANCHI; STANLEY HOLLOWAY; BOB NEWHART;
LAINIE KAZAN
I'm Not The Marrying Kind
April Showers
America; Chicago; Houston; San Francisco;
California, Here I Come (With Sergio)
Gimme A Little Kiss; Cuddle Up A Little Closer;
Put Your Arms Around Me, Honey (With Lainie)
Medley of tavern songs (With Stanley)

1/5/67   DOM DeLUISE; FLORENCE HENDERSON; JACK JONES;
KAYE STEVENS; BOB MELVIN
(Open Up The Door) Let The Good Times In
Young At Heart
Ain't We Got Fun; Put On A Happy Face (With Florence)
Detour (With Jack)
Please Don't Talk About Me When I'm Gone (With Kaye)
Gilbert and Sullivan medley (With entire cast)

1/12/67   LESLIE UGGAMS; EDDIE FOY, JR.; JACKIE MASON; ALLEN
AND ROSSI
Closet Guest: PAT BOONE
Marshmallow World
I've Grown Accustomed To Her Face
Snap Your Fingers; Accentuate The Positive (With Leslie)
Heart Of My Heart; Toot Toot Tootsie; When You Wore A Tulip
(With entire cast)

1/19/67   KATE SMITH; SHIRLEY BASSEY; ROWAN AND MARTIN;
BAJA MARIMBA BAND
Come Running Back
Blue Moon
In The Cool, Cool, Cool Of The Evening; Are You Having Any Fun;
It's A Grand Night For Singing; Beer Barrel Polka
(With Kate)
Pennies From Heaven; April Showers (With Shirley)
Let's Take An Old-Fashioned Walk; I'll Walk Alone
(With entire cast)

1/26/67   PETULA CLARK; JACK JONES; PHYLLIS DILLER;
                   JACKIE VERNON; DINO, DESI AND BILLY
           If You Knew Susie
           All By Myself
           Get Happy; Aren't You Glad You're You; (Open Up The Door) Let
                 The Good Times In (With Petula)
           South Of The Border; It Happened In Monterey; In A Little Spanish
                 Town (With Jack)

2/9/67   JANE MORGAN; MYRON COHEN; ROSE MARIE;
                   FRANK GORSHIN; KIM SISTERS
           My Blue Heaven
           Ma Blushin' Rosie
           It Had To Be You
           It's Only A Paper Moon (With Jane)
           Happiness Is (With Rose)
           Getting To Know You (With Kim Sisters)
           Lovely To Look At (Jane and Rose)
           Honey (With Jane and Frank)

2/16/67   SID CAESAR; PATRICE MUNSEL; ADAM WEST;
                   TRINI LOPEZ
           Back In Your Own Backyard
           I Can't Believe That You're In Love With Me
           Nobody (With Adam)
           It's Nice To Go Traveling; Come Fly With Me; On A Slow Boat To
                 China; Tijuana Taxi; Chattanooga Choo Choo
                 (With Patrice)
           Bye, Bye Love; Oh, Lonesome Me; Down By The Riverside
                 (With Trini)

2/23/67   CONNIE FRANCIS; DON CHERRY; PHIL HARRIS;
                   DOM DeLUISE
           Is It True What They Say About Dixie
           Welcome To My World
           Yankee Doodle Boy; My Old Kentucky Home; Indiana; Way Down
                 Yonder In New Orleans; California, Here I Come
                 (With Connie)
           San Antonio Rose (With Phil and Don)
           Saloon Medley (With Phil and Don)

3/2/67   VINCENT EDWARDS; KEELY SMITH; MARILYN MICHAELS;
                   ROWAN AND MARTIN
           Love, Love, Love
           Rockabye Your Baby With A Dixie Melody
           Smiles; When My Baby Smiles At Me; When You're Smiling
                 (With Keely)
           Cecilia; That's My Weakness Now; That Certain Party;
                 My Time Is Your Time (With Vincent)

'A' You're Adorable; Harrigan; Mississippi; Constantinople; L-O-V-E
    (With Marilyn)
There's No Business Like Show Business (With entire cast)

3/9/67   ARTHUR GODFREY; SID CAESAR; PEGGY LEE;
                JOEY HEATHERTON; BOB MELVIN;
                CLAUDIA MARTIN; GUY MARKS
In The Cool, Cool, Cool Of The Evening
Please
Just You, Just Me; Exactly Like You; For You;
        The Very Thought Of You; You're Driving Me Crazy;
        Then I'll Be Happy (With Peggy)
Baby Face; You Must Have Been A Beautiful Baby (With Joey)
Keep Your Eyes On The Hands (With Arthur)
Three Little Fishes (With Peggy and Joey)
Boo-Hoo (With Arthur and Guy)

3/16/67   ELLA FITZGERALD; EDIE ADAMS; RED BUTTONS;
                DOM DeLUISE
You're Nobody 'Til Somebody Loves You
Born To Lose
Thank Heaven For Little Girls (With Red)
For You; I'd Climb The Highest Mountain (With Ella)
By The Light Of The Silvery Moon (With Edie)
On The Good Ship Lollipop; I Don't Want To Play In Your Yard;
        Playmates (With Edie, Red and Dom)

3/23/67   BUDDY GRECO; JANET BLAIR; LOUIS PRIMA;
                BOB NEWHART; McGUIRE SISTERS
Easter Parade
Ol' Man River
Hey, Good Lookin'; Just A Little Lovin' (With Buddy)
Darktown Strutters' Ball; Ma, He's Makin' Eyes At Me;
        This Is My Lucky Day (With Janet)
I'll Never Smile Again; Witchcraft; My Kind Of Town;
        All The Way; It Was A Very Good Year; Night And Day;
        Strangers In The Night; High Hopes; Love And Marriage
        (With McGuire Sisters)

3/30/67   EDDIE FISHER; ABBE LANE; GENE BARRY;
                HERMAN'S HERMITS; CORBETT MONICA
                    Closet Guest: JOHNNY CARSON
Baby Face
Paper Doll
Look For The Silver Lining

C'est Magnifique; C'est Si Bon (With Abbe)
Mairzy Doats (With Herman's Hermits)
It's Nice To Go Traveling (With Gene)
Baseball Medley (With entire cast; Dean wears the baseball cap
    pictured on the *Dino* LP cover.)

4/6/67   PHIL HARRIS; SALLY ANN HOWES; PAUL WINCHELL;
                BOB MELVIN; KESSLER TWINS
            L-O-V-E
            It's The Talk Of The Town
            Let's Call The Whole Thing Off (With Sally)
            If I Knew You Were Comin', I'd Have Baked A Cake (With Phil)
            Lovely Conversation (With Kessler Twins)
            I've Got Sixpence; Maybe It's Because I'm A Londoner;
                I've Got A Lovely Bunch Of Cocoanuts
                (With Phil and Sally)

4/13/67   BING CROSBY; POLLY BERGEN; DON CHERRY;
                ROWAN AND MARTIN
            Second Hand Rose
            It's Easy To Remember
            Everybody Loves Somebody
            Style (With Bing and Don)
            Let's Do It; Let's Fall In Love (With Polly)
            Hicktown (With Don)
            Learn To Croon; Thanks; Please; Empty Saddles;
                I'm An Old Cowhand; Pocketful Of Dreams;
                Pennies From Heaven; Swinging On A Star;
                Accentuate The Positive;
                In The Cool, Cool, Cool Of The Evening; Personality;
                Love Thy Neighbor; True Love;
                Love Is Just Around The Corner; But Beautiful;
                Second Time Around (With Bing)

Season Three: 1967-68

Producer/Director	Greg Garrison
Writers	Paul W. Keyes
	Harry Crane
	Rich Eustis
	Al Rogers
	Bob Ellison
	Davis Panich
	Robert Sidney
Associate Producer	Norman Hopps
Choreography	Robert Sidney
Special Musical Material	Lee Hale
Art Director	Spencer Davies

Musical Arrangements	J. Hill
	Bob Florence
	Gus Donahue
Choral Director	Jack Halloran
Unit Manager	P. Dean Reed
Associate Directors	John Kittleson
	Clay Daniel
	Tom Foulkes
Music Coordinator	Mack Gray
Music Consultant	Ken Lane
Assistant To The Producer	Janice Buchanan
Production Assistant	Janet Tighe
Production Coordinator	Craig Martin
Costumes	Ed Wassall
Makeup	Claude Thompson
Assistant To The Choreographer	Wisa D'Orso
Stage Managers	George Fulton
	Al Melino
	Robert Graner
Technical Director	Karl Messerschmidt
Lighting Directors	Richard Pickens
	Lon Stuckey
Audio	Bill Levitsky
Video	Jerry Smith
Tape Editors	John Teele
	Steve Orland
	Stan Chlebek
Talent Coordinator	Henry Frankel
Music Routines	Robert B. Bailey
	Geoffrey Clarkson

9/14/67   ORSON WELLES; JIMMY STEWART; JULIET PROWSE
Birds And The Bees
Welcome To My World
Real Live Girl (Voice Over)
Ragtime Cowboy Joe (With Jimmy)
Personality (With Jimmy and Orson)
Cheek To Cheek (With Juliet)
Brush Up Your Shakespeare (With Orson)

9/21/67   BUDDY HACKETT; ROSEMARY CLOONEY; MINNIE PEARL;
            DAVID STEINBERG
                Closet Guest: DICK MARTIN
Things
Born To Lose

[handwritten in left margin:] ✓ 129 / end missing / 49.35 (56)

290

Wait 'Til The Sun Shines, Nellie; Ma Blushin' Rosie; Mary; Billy;
    Mame; If You Knew Susie (With Rosemary)
Truckload Of Starvin' Kangaroos (With Minnie)

9/28/67   ROY ROGERS AND DALE EVANS; PETULA CLARK;
    DON RICKLES
Nobody But A Fool
Nearness Of You
Until The Real Thing Comes Along; If This Isn't Love; True Love;
    Love, Love, Love (With Petula)

10/5/67   PHIL SILVERS; EDDY ARNOLD; JANET LEIGH;
    MILLS BROTHERS; JEREMY VERNON
Little Ole Wine Drinker, Me
Green, Green Grass Of Home
I Never Knew Anyone Like You (With Janet)
Paper Doll (With Mills Brothers)
My Buddy (With Phil)
Lay Some Happiness On Me; Sometimes I'm Happy; Just A Little
    Lovin'; (Open Up The Door) Let The Good Times In
    (With Eddy)

10/12/67   GEORGE GOBEL; STANLEY HOLLOWAY; JACK GILFORD;
    GAIL MARTIN
Blue, Blue Day
It's The Talk Of The Town
High Hopes
Too Marvelous For Words (With Gail)
It Ain't Gonna Rain No More; With A Little Bit Of Luck
    (With Stanley)
Thank Heaven For Little Girls (With George)

10/19/67   BING CROSBY; LENA HORNE; DOM DeLUISE
On A Slow Boat To China
You Made Me Love You
Bumming Around (With Lena)
There Will Never Be Another You;
        They Can't Take That Away From Me;
        Life Is Just A Bowl Of Cherries; Together;
        I Get A Kick Out Of You; You Do Something To Me;
        Surrey With The Fringe On Top; Exactly Like You;
        Wrap Your Troubles In Dreams; I Want To Be Happy;
        Why Don't We Do This More Often (With Lena and Bing)
Waiting For The Robert E. Lee; Alexander's Ragtime Band;
        Back In Your Own Backyard; Avalon;
        Carolina In The Morning;
        Is It True What They Say About Dixie; Toot Toot Tootsie;
        Alabamy Bound; Swanee; April Showers (With Bing)

10/26/67   DONALD O'CONNOR; JONATHAN WINTERS;
                       NANCY AMES; FLIP WILSON
I'm Gonna Change Everything
I'm Confessin'
Lady's In Love With You; They Didn't Believe Me;
             My Buddy (With Donald)
Nice Work If You Can Get It; Cuddle Up A Little Closer;
             Will You Still Be Mine;
             Let The Rest Of The World Go By;
             I'm Sitting On Top Of The World (With Nancy)

11/2/67   VAN JOHNSON; PEGGY LEE; HOMER AND JETHRO;
                       JOHN BARBOUR
Pride
Release Me
Button Up Your Overcoat (With Van)
I've Got Tears In My Ears (With Homer and Jethro)
Basin St. Blues; Blues In The Night;
             I Gotta Right To Sing The Blues;
             I Get The Blues When It Rains; Bye Bye Blues;
             St. Louis Blues (With Peggy)

11/9/67   PHIL HARRIS; JOEL GREY; LAINIE KAZAN; DON CHERRY;
                       PAT HENRY
I'm Gonna Sit Right Down And Write Myself A Letter
I Can't Help Remembering You
Way Back Home (With Joel)
Pass That Peace Pipe (With Phil and Don)
King Of The Road (Comedy with Phil)
Games That Lovers Play; Temptation; I've Got You Under My Skin;
             Nice 'N' Easy (With Lainie)

11/16/67   CYD CHARISSE; BUDDY EBSEN; BARBARA McNAIR;
                       DOM DeLUISE; ALBERT BERRY
                         Closet Guest: PHIL HARRIS
Turn To Me
Nevertheless
I Won't Dance (With Cyd)
Sam's Song (With Buddy)
Devil And The Deep Blue Sea (With Barbara)

11/23/67   WOODY ALLEN; KATE SMITH; KAYE STEVENS; JANIE GEE
(Open Up The Door) Let The Good Times In
Home
I Wish I Were In Love Again (With Kaye)
Let Me Call You Sweetheart (With Kate)

Little Girl; You're An Old Smoothie; You Make Me Feel So Young
    (With Janie)
Traveling Medley (With Kate)
May The Good Lord Bless And Keep You (With entire cast)

11/30/67   LENA HORNE; DON RICKLES; ANDREWS SISTERS
        (Cameos by PAT BOONE; RICARDO MONTALBAN;
        DANNY THOMAS; DON ADAMS; ROSS MARTIN;
        ERNEST BORGNINE; ROSE MARIE; BOB NEWHART;
        MacDONALD CAREY; DOM DeLUISE; BOB HOPE)
If You Knew Susie
I've Grown Accustomed To Her Face
Pistol Packin' Mama; Don't Sit Under The Apple Tree;
    Boogie Woogie Bugle Boy; Beat Me Daddy, Eight To The
    Bar (With Andrews Sisters)
I've Heard That Song Before; Honeysuckle Rose; Paper Moon;
    As Long As I Live; I Can't Give You Anything But Love;
    On A Slow Boat To China;
    On The Sunny Side Of The Street (With Lena)
When The Idle Rich Become The Idle Poor
    (With the Andrews Sisters and Lena)

12/7/67   VAN JOHNSON; PATRICE MUNSEL; SUSAN BARRETT;
        JOHN BARBOUR
L-O-V-E
Rockabye Your Baby With A Dixie Melody
Something's Gotta Give; Getting To Know You (With Susan)
Making Whoopee (With Patrice)
Too Marvelous For Words; Ain't She Sweet (With Van)

12/14/67   CATERINA VALENTE; BOB NEWHART; DOM DeLUISE;
        GUY MARKS
Where Or When
Oh, You Beautiful Doll
Walking On New Grass (With girl chorus)
Rain; I Don't Care If The Sun Don't Shine; Sunny Side Up;
    Look For The Silver Lining;
    There's A Rainbow 'Round My Shoulder (With Caterina)

12/21/67   FRANK SINATRA; NANCY SINATRA; TINA SINATRA;
        FRANK SINATRA, JR.; CRAIG MARTIN;
        CLAUDIA MARTIN; GAIL MARTIN; DEANA MARTIN;
        DINO MARTIN; RICCI MARTIN; GINA MARTIN;
        JEANNE MARTIN
        Closet Guest: SAMMY DAVIS, JR.

Dean and Frank Sinatra extol the virtues of a "Marshmallow World" (12/21/67)
(NBC publicity photo)

Marshmallow World (With Frank)
I'll Be Home For Christmas
Do Re Mi (With Frank, Tina, and Deana)
We Wish You The Merriest; More I Cannot Wish You; Ding Dong;
    It's A Most Unusual Day (With Frank, Nancy, and Gail)
How Do You Talk To Your Son/Dad (With Frank, Dino, and Frank Jr.)
White Christmas; O Little Town Of Bethlehem; Joy To The World;
    We Wish You A Merry Christmas; Silent Night
    (Medley with entire cast)
I Can't Give You Anything But Love; Too Marvelous For Words;
    Pennies From Heaven; A Foggy Day In London Town;
    Embraceable You; Lady Is A Tramp; Where Or When;
    I've Got The World On A String; Oh Marie; All Of Me;
    When You're Smiling (With Frank)

12/28/67   POLLY BERGEN; MILLS BROTHERS; JACKIE VERNON;
        PAT COOPER
            Closet Guest: BUDDY HACKETT
Almost Like Being In Love
Blue Moon
Tumbling Tumbleweeds; Crawdad Song (With Polly)
Lazy River (With Mills Brothers)
Cabaret; Ach Du Lieber; Blue Danube Waltz (With entire cast)

1/4/68   PHIL SILVERS; HELEN GRAYCO; MORGANA KING;
        HENNY YOUNGMAN
Is It True What They Say About Dixie
I Love You Much Too Much
Walking My Baby Back Home; Would You Like To Take A Walk
    (With Helen)
So Long; Now Is The Hour; Auld Lang Syne (With Morgana)

1/11/68   BUDDY HACKETT; ROWAN AND MARTIN; SUSAN BARRETT;
        BARBARA HELLER; BRASCIA AND TYBEE
            Closet Guest: DON ADAMS
I Will
Young At Heart
Gypsy In My Soul; King Of The Road; Bumming Around;
    Breezin' Along With The Breeze (With Susan)

1/18/68   GEORGE BURNS; EDDIE ALBERT; FLORENCE HENDERSON;
        JANIE GEE
Singing The Blues
S'posin
Sleepy Time Gal (With Janie)

It's A Well Known Fact (With George)
Let's Have Another Cup Of Coffee; Buddy, Can You Spare A Dime;
   Best Things In Life Are Free;
   Now's The Time To Fall In Love;
   Happy Days Are Here Again (With Florence)
Mighty Like A Rose (With Eddie)

1/25/68 ORSON WELLES; JOEY HEATHERTON; BOB MELVIN;
     PROFESSOR BACKWARDS; BUCK OWENS
Things
Welcome To My World
Just In Time (With Joey)
I've Got A Tiger By The Tail; Love's Gonna Live Here (With Buck)

2/1/68 PHIL HARRIS AND ALICE FAYE; JULIUS LA ROSA;
     NORM CROSBY; YONELY; KIDS NEXT DOOR
Don't Let The Blues Make You Bad
What Can I Say After I Say I'm Sorry
Ma Blushin' Rosie; You'll Never Know (With Alice)
Vino Or Cappuccino (With Julius)
Pop Goes The Weasel (With Kids Next Door)
Eh Cumpari (With Julius)

2/8/68 LORNE GREENE; RED BUTTONS; JANE MORGAN;
     SKILES AND HENDERSON
Blue, Blue Day
I Don't Know Why
Don't Fence Me In; I'm An Old Cowhand; Home On The Range;
   Bury Me Not On The Lone Prairie (With Lorne)
We Could Make Such Beautiful Music;
   I Don't Know Enough About You;
   You're The Cream In My Coffee; How About You;
   I Can't Believe That You're In Love With Me (With Jane)

2/15/68 ETHEL MERMAN; ROGER MILLER; LAINIE KAZAN;
     JOHN BARBOUR; CARL BALLANTINE
Clinging Vine
That Old Feeling
Gimme A Little Kiss; Cuddle Up A Little Closer;
   Put Your Arms Around Me, Honey (With Lainie)
Dang Me; Chug A Lug; England Swings;
   You Can't Rollerskate In A Buffalo Herd (With Roger)
Let Me Sing And I'm Happy; Everything's Coming Up Roses;
   Great Day; Whispering; Friendship;
   Love Is Sweeping The Country; Swanee
   (With Ethel and Lainie)

2/22/68   MICKEY ROONEY; KEELY SMITH; MINNIE PEARL;
                 DON CHERRY; LEONARD BARR
          They Didn't Believe Me
          I Left My Heart In San Francisco
          Eyes Of Texas; Yellow Rose Of Texas; Houston; San Antonio Rose;
                 Deep In The Heart Of Texas (With Don)
          Make 'Em Laugh (With Mickey)
          It All Depends On You; Sometimes I'm Happy;
                 I Want To Be Happy (With Keely)
          May The Bird Of Paradise Fly Up Your Nose (With Minnie)

2/29/68   JONATHAN WINTERS; ARTHUR GODFREY;
                 SANDLER AND YOUNG; GRECCO AND WILLARD
          Houston
          Red Sails In The Sunset
          Five Foot Two; Ain't She Sweet; Sweet Georgia Brown; Sweet Sue;
                 Singing In The Rain (With Arthur)

3/7/68   GEORGE GOBEL; PEGGY LEE; EDDIE FOY, JR.; GUY MARKS
          That Old Clock On The Wall
          I'm In The Mood For Love
          Ode To Billy Joe (With George)
          Doodling Song; Zip-A-Dee Dooh Dah; Hoop De Doo (With Peggy)
          I Murdered Them In Chicago (With Eddie)
          Come Back To Me (With entire cast)

3/14/68   LIBERACE; GEORGE JESSEL; CATERINA VALENTE;
                 PAT BUTTRUM; PAT HENRY
                          Closet Guest: JACK BENNY
          Little Ole Wine Drinker, Me
          A Hundred Years From Today
          It Had To Be You (With Caterina on guitar)
          Toot Toot Tootsie (With George)
          Parody medley with Liberace includes The Band Played On;
                 Pretty Baby; Makin' Whoopee; Ain't We Got Fun
          Ev'ry Street's A Boulevard In Old New York; I'll Take Manhattan;
                 Bowery; Sidewalks Of New York; Lullaby Of Broadway;
                 Forty-Second Street; Easter Parade (With Caterina)

3/21/68   TONY BENNETT; BOB NEWHART;
                 FLORENCE HENDERSON; DINO, DESI AND BILLY
          Here Comes My Baby
          Pennies From Heaven
          Small Fry (With Dino)
          Nothing Like A Dame; Dolores; Sweet Lorraine; Mimi; Sweet Sue;

297

If You Knew Susie; Mame (With Tony)
Steppin' Out With My Baby; Hernando's Hideaway; Sway;
    Cheek To Cheek; Arthur Murray Had Me Dancing In A
    Hurry; Poppa, Won't You Dance With Me (With Florence)

3/28/68   VINCE EDWARDS; BILLY De WOLFE; MORGANA KING;
        LINDA BENNETT; COLVIN AND WILDER;
        KIDS NEXT DOOR
Second Hand Rose
Always
Honeymoon Is Over (With Vince)
So Long; Now Is The Hour; Auld Lang Syne (With Morgana)
I've Got A Pocketful Of Dreams; All I Do Is Dream Of You;
    Dream; Wrap Your Troubles In Dreams (With Linda)
Medley of children's songs (With Kids Next Door)

4/4/68   JIMMY STEWART; GEORGE GOBEL; SHECKY GREENE;
        WISA D'ORSO
        Closet Guest: ROBERT MITCHUM
Nobody's Baby Again
It's Easy To Remember
Look For The Silver Lining
Everybody Loves Somebody
For Me And My Gal (With Wisa)

Season Four: 1968-69

Producer/Director	Greg Garrison
Writers	Harry Crane
	Rich Eustis
	Al Rogers
	Stan Daniels
	Arnie Kogan
	Ed Weinberger
Associate Producer	Norman Hopps
Choreography	Robert Sidney
Special Musical Material	Lee Hale
Art Director	Spencer Davies
Musical Arrangements	Van Alexander
	Gus Donahue
Choral Director	Jack Halloran
Unit Manager	P. Dean Reed
Associate Directors	Clay Daniel
	Tom Foulkes
Music Coordinator	Mack Gray
Music Consultant	Ken Lane

Assistants To The Producer	Janice Buchanan
	Janet Tighe
Production Assistants	Lynne Voeth
	Robert Chic
Production Supervisor	Craig Martin
Costumes	Ed Wassall
Makeup	Harry Blake
Assistant To The Choreographer	Ed Kerrigan
Stage Managers	George Fulton
	Ted Baker
	Robert Graner
Technical Director	Karl Messerschmidt
Lighting Director	Lon Stuckey
Audio	Bill Levitsky
Video	Jerry Smith
	Harry Glyer
Video Tape Editor	Steve Orland
Talent Coordinator	Henry Frankel
Music Routines	Robert B. Bailey
	Geoffrey Clarkson

9/19/68   LENA HORNE; ZERO MOSTEL; BUDDY EBSEN;
                      SHECKY GREENE
             Gentle On My Mind
             By The Time I Get To Phoenix
             If I Was A Millionaire
             Two Of Us (With Lena)
             A Couple Of Swells (With Zero)
             Mr. Gallagher, Mr. Shean (With Buddy)

9/26/68   ORSON WELLES; EDGAR BERGEN; PAT CROWLEY;
                      JACK GILFORD; STANLEY MYRON HANDELMAN
             Rainbows Are Back In Style
             That Old Time Feeling
             Everybody Ought To Have A Maid (With Pat, Orson, and Jack)
             Baby It's Cold Outside (With Pat)

10/3/68   LORNE GREENE; JULIET PROWSE; DOM DeLUISE;
                      SAMMY SHORE; BARBARA HELLER
             Not Enough Indians
             It Just Happened That Way
             Bosom Buddies (With Lorne)
             I Still Get Jealous (With Juliet)
             Some Enchanted Evening (With Barbara)

10/10/68   VINCE EDWARDS; ROGER MILLER; PHIL HARRIS;
         GLORIA LORING; STANLEY MYRON HANDELMAN
Bye Bye Blackbird
Real Live Girl
Girls Names Medley (With Vince)
Tea For Two (With Gloria)
Old Master Painter (With Phil)

10/17/68   CYD CHARISSE; BEN BLUE; DON CHERRY; LINDA BENNETT;
         STANLEY MYRON HANDELMAN
Almost Like Being In Love
Green, Green Grass Of Home
I Got Rhythm (With Cyd)
Oh, Lonesome Me (With Don)
Romantic Medley (With Linda)

10/24/68   VAN JOHNSON; ALICE FAYE; JACKIE MASON; SUE RANEY;
         HENDRA AND ULLETT
L-O-V-E
Honey
The Soft Shoe Song (With Van)
Glory Of Love (With Sue)
By The Light Of The Silvery Moon; You're A Sweetheart;
         Blue Skies; Ma Blushin' Rosie; Alexander's Ragtime
         Band (With Alice and Van)

10/31/68   TONY BENNETT; ELKE SOMMER; DAVID FRYE;
         SKILES AND HENDERSON; GOLDDIGGERS
Somebody Stole My Gal
I'm Confessin'
You've Got To Be A Football Hero;
         Ramblin' Wreck From Georgia Tech (With Golddiggers)
Blue Moon; Sometimes I'm Happy; Lady's In Love;
         My Baby Just Cares For Me; Guys And Dolls (With Tony)
Side By Side; Gimme A Little Kiss; It's Been A Long, Long Time
         (With Elke)

11/7/68   FLORENCE HENDERSON; DOM DeLUISE; SHECKY GREENE;
         AVERY SCHREIBER; MORGANA KING
            Closet Guest: FESS PARKER
If You Knew Susie
I've Grown Accustomed To Her Face
My Old Kentucky Home; Beautiful Dreamer; Oh Susannah;
         Camptown Races; Swanee River (With Morgana)

11/14/68   DAVID JANSSEN; MINNIE PEARL; LAINIE KAZAN;
                            STU GILLIAM; STANLEY MYRON HANDELMAN
Do You Believe This Town
Oh, You Beautiful Doll
Love Is Just Around The Corner; Dream A Little Dream Of Me;
                     Show Me The Way To Go Home (With Lainie)

11/21/68   GORDON MacRAE; BOB NEWHART; ABBE LANE;
                            PAUL LYNDE
Nobody But A Fool
Welcome To My World
I Could Have Danced All Night (With Abbe)
What's In A Name Medley (With Gordon)
The Game (With Gordon and Paul)

11/28/68   LENA HORNE; GEORGE GOBEL; SKILES AND HENDERSON;
                            GOLDDIGGERS
                                    Closet Guest: ROY ROGERS
Blue, Blue Day
Home
May The Good Lord Bless And Keep You (With entire cast)
Crazy Rhythm; I'm Old Fashioned; Nice 'N' Easy (With Lena)
Louise; Toot Toot Tootsie; Now's The Time To Fall In Love
                     (With entire cast)
Happiness Medley and College Medley (With Golddiggers)

12/5/68   JIMMY STEWART; CATERINA VALENTE; DOM DeLUISE;
                            STANLEY MYRON HANDELMAN
Someday
Born To Lose
Mimi; That's What I Like About The South;
                     When The Blue Of The Night; Top Hat, White Tie, And
                     Tails; Inka Dinka Doo; Hello Dolly (With Caterina)
I'm Always Chasing Rainbows (With Caterina)

12/12/68   GEORGE BURNS; PHIL HARRIS; SUSAN BARRETT;
                            BARBARA HELLER
Little Ole Wine Drinker, Me
Let The Rest Of The World Go By
King Of The Road; Last Night On The Back Porch (With George)
Mountain Greenery; You'd Be So Nice To Come Home To;
                     Home On The Range (With Susan)
It Must Be Him (With Barbara)
Cigarettes, Whiskey and Wild, Wild Women (With Phil)

12/19/68 DENNIS WEAVER; BOB NEWHART; DOM DeLUISE;
    GOLDDIGGERS
    Closet Guest: BOB HOPE
  (Cameos by ELKE SOMMER; TONY BENNETT;
  VINCE EDWARDS; PHIL HARRIS; GORDON MacRAE;
  GEORGE GOBEL; LENA HORNE; JIMMY STEWART;
  GEORGE BURNS; FRANK SINATRA, JR.;
  STANLEY MYRON HANDELMAN; DAVID JANSSEN;
  PHYLLIS DILLER; VICTOR BORGE; GREG MORRIS;
  PETER GRAVES; JOSEPH COTTON; DON RICKLES;
  DON ADAMS; JOEY BISHOP; JIM NABORS; RED SKELTON;
  DIAHANN CARROLL; KATE SMITH; ROWAN AND MARTIN;
  JACK BENNY; TENNESSEE ERNIE FORD; NANCY SINATRA;
  DAN BLOCKER; JOHNNY CARSON; ROY ROGERS;
  BARBARA EDEN)
  Marshmallow World
  I'll Be Home For Christmas
  Silent Night; Christmas Is For Kids (With Golddiggers)
  Daddy; True Love; We Wish You The Merriest (With Golddiggers)

1/2/69 GEORGE GOBEL; FRANK SINATRA, JR.; FRAN JEFFRIES;
    DOM DeLUISE; GENE BAYLOS
  Where Or When
  Red Sails In The Sunset
  I Could Write A Book; They Can't Take That Away From Me;
    I've Got You Under My Skin; Too Marvelous For Words;
    I Get A Kick Out Of You; You Make Me Feel So Young
    (With Frank Jr.)
  Bleep Medley (With Dom)
  Harper Valley P. T. A. (With George)

1/9/69 ORSON WELLES; BEN BLUE; NANCY AMES;
    HENDRA AND ULLETT; JERRY SHAYNE
  Things
  April Showers
  Cinderella Rockefella (With Nancy)

1/23/69 DAN DAILEY; GLORIA LORING; PAUL LYNDE; DON RICE
  Bumming Around
  Honey
  When My Baby Smiles At Me (With Dan)
  How About You (With Gloria)

1/30/69   LENA HORNE; VICTOR BORGE; SID CAESAR;
           TIMES SQUARE TWO
                     Closet Guest: ARTE JOHNSON
           (Open Up The Door) Let The Good Times In
           What Can I Say After I Say I'm Sorry
           Welcome To My World; Gentle On My Mind; By The Time I Get
                     To Phoenix; Honey; Up Up And Away (With Lena)
           Punctuation medley with Victor includes Remember;
                     Fly Me To The Moon; Wunderbar; Do Re Mi

V 128 + 129
14·27 (20) +
31·20 (93)

2/6/69   LOU RAWLS; LAINIE KAZAN; SHECKY GREENE;
           STANLEY MYRON HANDELMAN
           Is It True What They Say About Dixie
           Release Me
           Chattanooga Choo Choo (With Lou)
           It's Easy To Remember (With Lainie)

2/13/69   GINA LOLLOBRIGIDA; PHIL SILVERS; MILBURN STONE;
           NORM CROSBY
                     Closet Guest: LAWRENCE WELK
           Lay Some Happiness On Me
           S'posin
           Top Banana (With Phil)
           Volare; Say Si Si (With Gina)
           When You And I Were Young, Maggie (With Milburn)

V 129
end missing
44·17 (89

2/20/69   BOBBY DARIN; PHYLLIS DILLER; BOB NEWHART;
           MILLS BROTHERS; DON RICE
           Don't Let The Blues Make You Bad
           Green, Green Grass Of Home
           Little Green Apples
           Glow Worm; Paper Doll (With Mills Brothers)
           Gimme A Little Kiss; Cuddle Up A Little Closer (With Phyllis)
           I'm Sitting On Top Of The World;
                     There's A Rainbow 'Round My Shoulder;
                     Toot Toot Tootsie (With Bobby)

2/27/69   PAT BOONE; GEORGE GOBEL; ANGIE DICKINSON;
           PAUL GILBERT; BOBBI MARTIN
                     Closet Guest: BARBARA EDEN
           On A Slow Boat To China
           I Don't Know Why

Laughing it up with guest Phyllis Diller (2/20/69)
(NBC publicity photo)

Style (With Pat)
Surrey With The Fringe On Top; Hit The Road To Dreamland
      (With Angie)
Hey, Good Lookin'; Just A Little Lovin' (With Bobbi)

3/6/69   PETER GRAVES; PEGGY LEE; MINNIE PEARL;
              STANLEY MYRON HANDELMAN;
              DINO, DESI AND BILLY
                    Closet Guest: TED MACK
I Will
That Old Feeling
Smiles; Little Girl; The Man I Love; A Good Man Is Hard To Find;
      My Kind Of Girl (With Peggy)
Melancholy Baby (With Peter on clarinet)

3/13/69   EDDIE ALBERT; LINDA BENNETT; DOM DeLUISE;
              GEORGIE KANE
                    Closet Guest: CHARLEY WEAVER
Do You Believe This Town
Stars Fell On Alabama
John Henry (With Eddie)
Nevertheless (With Linda)

3/20/69   MICKEY ROONEY; KATE SMITH; BARBARA EDEN;
              NORM CROSBY; TIMES SQUARE TWO
Not Enough Indians
Young At Heart
Stumblin'; At Sundown (With Barbara)
School Days; Farmer In The Dell; Mary Had A Little Lamb;
      Baa Baa Black Sheep; A Tisket, A Tasket (With Kate)

3/27/69   SHIRLEY JONES; PAUL LYNDE; SHECKY GREENE;
              DON CHERRY; KAREN WYMAN
I'm Sitting On Top Of The World
Always
Gotta Travel On (With Don)
Oh, You Beautiful Doll; Someone To Watch Over Me;
      Lovely To Look At (With Shirley)
I Could Write A Book; Just Friends; Friendship;
      I Am Woman, You Are Man; Let's Be Buddies
      (With Karen)

4/3/69   MICHAEL LANDON; DOM DeLUISE; STU GILLIAM;
              WILL JORDAN; BOBBI MARTIN; KIDS NEXT DOOR
                    Closet Guests: DON RICKLES and DON ADAMS
Birds And The Bees

True Love
Sound Off; I've Got A Lovely Bunch Of Coconuts
    (With the Kids Next Door)
Is It True What They Say About Dixie; Way Down Yonder In New
    Orleans; Sweet Georgia Brown; Hard Hearted Hannah
    (With Michael)
Jambalaya (With Bobbi)

4/10/69   SID CAESAR; LOU RAWLS; GAIL MARTIN; RAY STEVENS;
                STANLEY MYRON HANDELMAN
                L-O-V-E
                It's The Talk Of The Town
                Your Cheatin' Heart; Bye Bye Love (With Lou)
                We Got Us (With Gail)

4/17/69   ORSON WELLES; CATERINA VALENTE; JACK GILFORD;
                LEONARD BARR
                      Closet Guest: JIMMY STEWART
                Back In Your Own Backyard
                A Hundred Years From Today
                I'm Always Chasing Rainbows (With Caterina)

4/24/69   JIMMY STEWART; RAQUEL WELCH; VICTOR BORGE;
                GOLDDIGGERS
                      Closet Guest: LEO DUROCHER
                Gentle On My Mind
                By The Time I Get To Phoenix
                Everybody Loves Somebody
                Little Green Apples

Season Five: 1969-70

Producer/Director	Greg Garrison
Writers	Harry Crane
	Rich Eustis
	Al Rogers
	Stan Daniels
	Ray Jessel
	George Bloom
	Norm Liebmann
	Tom Tenowich
	Ed Scharlach
Associate Producer	Norman Hopps
Choreography	Robert Sidney
	Jonathan Lucas
Special Musical Material	Lee Hale

Art Director	Spencer Davies
Musical Arrangements	Van Alexander
	Joe Lipman
Choral Director	Jack Halloran
Unit Manager	P. Dean Reed
Associate Directors	Clay Daniel
	Bill Wyse
Music Coordinator	Mack Gray
Music Consultant	Ken Lane
Assistants To The Producer	Janice Buchanan
	Janet Tighe
Production Assistants	Lynne Voeth
	Robert Chic
Production Supervisor	Craig Martin
Costumes	Ed Wassall
Makeup	Harry Blake
Assistant To The Choreographer	Ed Kerrigan
	Tommy Tune
Stage Managers	George Fulton
	Ted Baker
	Bill Wyse
Technical Director	Karl Messerschmidt
Lighting Directors	Lon Stuckey
	Carl Gibson
Audio	Bill Levitsky
Video	Jerry Smith
Video Tape Editor	Steve Orland
	Peter Groom
Talent Coordinator	Henry Frankel
Music Routines	Robert B. Bailey
	Geoffrey Clarkson

9/18/69   DENNIS WEAVER; GOLDIE HAWN; DOM DeLUISE
Do You Believe This Town
Little Green Apples
A Word A Day (With Goldie)

9/25/69   DAVID JANSSEN; ELKE SOMMER;
         CHARLES NELSON REILLY; DON RICE III
            Closet Guest: RALPH EDWARDS
Here Comes My Baby
By The Time I Get To Phoenix
Stranger In Paradise; Jeepers Creepers; My Heart Stood Still;
    There's A Small Hotel; Thank Heaven For Little Girls;
    Getting To Know You (With Elke)

10/2/69 BOB NEWHART; SEBASTIAN CABOT; CATERINA VALENTE;
    STANLEY MYRON HANDELMAN;
    CORBETT MONICA; GOLDDIGGERS
Rainbows Are Back In Style
That Old Time Feeling
Medley with Caterina
Love, Love, Love; Things; Best Things In Life Are Free
    (With Golddiggers)

10/9/69 FESS PARKER; BARBARA FELDON; JENNIFER;
    CHARLES NELSON REILLY; DINO, DESI AND BILLY
Nobody But A Fool
Born To Lose
Medley with Charles
I Walk The Line (With Jennifer)

10/16/69 ORSON BEAN; JACK GILFORD; GEORGE BURNS;
    JOEY HEATHERTON; MILLS BROTHERS
Singing The Blues
Where The Blue And Lonely Go
You're Nobody 'Til Somebody Loves You (With Mills Brothers)
Mother Goose Medley (With Joey)

10/23/69 CAROL CHANNING; WALTER BRENNAN; VICTOR BORGE;
    DOM DeLUISE
      Closet Guest: DEBBIE REYNOLDS
Sun Is Shining
Crying Time
Inflation Medley (With Victor)
I'm Glad I'm Not Young Anymore (With Walter)
I Am Curious Yellow (With Carol)

10/30/69 TONY BENNETT; SID CAESAR; CHARLES NELSON REILLY;
    PAT HENRY
L-O-V-E
It Just Happened That Way
Medley with Tony

11/6/69 BING CROSBY; EVA GABOR; JACK GILFORD; DOM DeLUISE
Somebody Stole My Gal
It's The Talk Of The Town
Then I'll Be Happy; Mississippi Mud; I'm A Ding Dong Daddy;
    Got A Date With An Angel; Dig You Later;
    Let Me Sing And I'm Happy (With Bing)

11/13/69 PEGGY LEE; DALE ROBERTSON; PAULA KELLY;
      PAUL LYNDE; MORTY GUNDY
         Closet Guest: GINA LOLLOBRIGIDA
     Little Ole Wine Drinker, Me
     S'posin
     Would You Like To Take A Walk (With Paula)
     Zip A Dee Doo Dah; I Got Rhythm; Beer Barrel Polka (With Peggy)

11/20/69 GORDON MacRAE; GAIL MARTIN; DOM DeLUISE;
      TOMMY TUNE; STANLEY MYRON HANDELMAN
     Gentle On My Mind
     Release Me
     Paris (With Gail)

11/27/69 VICTOR BORGE; JOEY HEATHERTON; DON RICE III;
      SUSAN COWSILL; BOBBI MARTIN
         Closet Guest: BING CROSBY
     Back In Your Own Backyard
     Home
     May The Good Lord Bless And Keep You
     Detour (With Bobbi)
     Shine On Harvest Moon (With Susan)
     No, No, A Thousand Times, No (With Joey)

12/4/69 NANCY WILSON; ROMY SCHNEIDER; MILBURN STONE;
      CHARLES NELSON REILLY
         Closet Guest: ANN-MARGRET
     Not Enough Indians
     Welcome To My World
     K-K-K-Katy; Ma Blushin' Rosie; Ida, Sweet As Apple Cider;
       Someone's In The Kitchen With Dinah;
       Serenade To An Old Fashioned Girl (With Milburn)
     Television Medley with Nancy includes parodies of I Love Paris;
       I'm Just Wild About Harry;
       You're Getting To Be A Habit With Me;
       Thank Heaven For Little Girls; Whispering

12/11/69 VAN JOHNSON; BARBARA FELDON; IRENE RYAN;
      PAUL LYNDE; JACKIE GAYLE
         Closet Guest: FLIP WILSON
     Make It Rain
     I'm Confessin'
     Standing On The Corner (With Van)
     You're Just In Love (With Irene)
     Think Pink (With Paul)

12/18/69   ORSON WELLES; GINA LOLLOBRIGIDA; GEORGE GOBEL;
                CHARLES NELSON REILLY; GOLDDIGGERS
                      Closet Guest: IRENE RYAN
Almost Like Being In Love
Red Sails In The Sunset
Here's To You (With Orson)
Here Come The Seventies; I'll Never Fall In Love Again;
         Everybody's Talkin'; Love's Been Good To Me
         (With Golddiggers)

1/8/70   PETULA CLARK; PETER GRAVES; GALE GORDON;
                DON RICE III
                      Closet Guest: GENE KELLY
Birds And The Bees
Green, Green Grass Of Home
You Are My Sunshine; We'll Sing In The Sunshine; Sunny Side Up;
         Look For The Silver Lining (With Petula)

1/15/70   SAMMY DAVIS, JR.; ANDY GRIFFITH; PAUL LYNDE;
                GLENN ASH
                      Closet Guest: DICK MARTIN
(Open Up The Door) Let The Good Times In
I Don't Know Why
Sam's Song; What Kind Of Fool Am I; I've Gotta Be Me;
         Pennies From Heaven; Birth Of The Blues (With Sammy)

1/22/70   ORSON WELLES; VIRNA LISI; LOU RAWLS;
                ROCKY GRAZIANO; DON RICE III
Don't Let The Blues Make You Bad
Stars Fell On Alabama
Give Me The Simple Life (With Orson)
Body And Soul; I'm Old Fashioned; Spinning Wheel; Hurts So Bad
         (With Lou)

1/29/70   MICHAEL LANDON; PAT CROWLEY; SHECKY GREENE;
                CHARLES NELSON REILLY
                      Closet Guest: BARBARA FELDON
Where Or When
A Hundred Years From Today
Gotta Travel On (With Michael)
Let's Do It (With Pat)

2/5/70   DAME MARGOT FONTEYN AND RUDOLPH NUREYEV;
                CATERINA VALENTE; CORBETT MONICA;
                LEONARD BARR; ALBERT BROOKS; GOLDDIGGERS

Someday
Honey
South American Way; Orchids In The Moonlight; Brazil; Manana
    (With Caterina)

2/12/70   KATE SMITH; PAUL LYNDE; ROSS MARTIN; GREG MORRIS
Blue, Blue Day
Nearness Of You
Medley with Ross
I'll Be Seeing You; Volare; Last Time I Saw Paris; King Of The Road;
    When The Moon Comes Over The Mountain (With Kate)

2/19/70   LEE J. COBB; BUDDY EBSEN; CHARLES NELSON REILLY;
    CLINGER SISTERS
Is It True What They Say About Dixie
What Can I Say After I Say I'm Sorry
Getting To Know You (With Clinger Sisters)
Real Live Girl; Together (With Debbie Clinger)

2/26/70   ANN-MARGRET; BOB NEWHART
    Closet Guest: RUTH BUZZI
Second Hand Rose
Welcome To My World
Hey, Good Lookin'; Sittin' On The Dock Of The Bay;
    That Old Feeling; I Take A Lot Of Pride In What I Am
    (With Ann-Margret)
It's Better With A Union Man (With Ann-Margret and Bob)

3/5/70   SID CAESAR; BARBARA ANDERSON; MARTY ROBBINS;
    GALE GORDON; ALICE GHOSTLEY
    Closet Guest: HENRY GIBSON
I'm Sitting On Top Of The World
By The Time I Get To Phoenix
Young At Heart
Nashville Medley (With Marty)
Fitness Medley (With Barbara)

3/12/70   SHIRLEY BOOTH; VIKKI CARR; PAUL LYNDE
Things
Always
Exactly Like You; I Wanna Be Loved By You; Very Thought Of You
    (With Vikki)

3/19/70   DEANA MARTIN; ELKE SOMMER; FRANK SINATRA, JR.;
    CHARLES NELSON REILLY; DON RICE III
They Didn't Believe Me

I've Grown Accustomed To Her Face
Glory Of Love (With Deana and Frank Jr.)
Spelling Medley (With Elke)

3/26/70   PEGGY LEE; TOMMY TUNE; DOM DeLUISE;
          ALBERT BROOKS; ART METRANO
I'm Gonna Sit Right Down And Write Myself A Letter
Green, Green Grass Of Home
Two Medleys with Peggy

4/2/70   FORREST TUCKER; GAIL MARTIN; JANICE HARPER;
          GENE BAYLOS; NORM CROSBY;
          CHARLES NELSON REILLY
I Take A Lot Of Pride In What I Am
Blue Moon
You Can't Love 'Em All (With Forrest)
I Wish I Were In Love Again (With Janice)
Make Your Own Kind Of Music (With Gail)

4/9/70   PHIL HARRIS; ARTE JOHNSON; LOU RAWLS; NANCY KWAN
          Closet Guest: GEORGE RAFT
Bye Bye Blackbird
If I Had You
There Is Nothing Like A Dame; Girls; I Can Always Find A Little
          Sunshine (With Arte and Phil)
Al Jolson Medley (With Lou)
Mr. Gallagher, Mr. Shean (With Phil)

4/16/70   NINO BENVENUTI; GLORIA LORING; PATTI AUSTIN;
          PAUL GILBERT; CHARLES NELSON REILLY;
          GOLDDIGGERS
             Closet Guest: KIRK DOUGLAS
If You Knew Susie
It's Easy To Remember
That's Amore (With Nino)
Embraceable You (With Gloria)
Lady's In Love With You; My Baby Just Cares For Me;
          Guys And Dolls (With Golddiggers)

4/23/70   DOM DeLUISE; JIMMY STEWART; LESLIE UGGAMS;
          ALBERT BROOKS; DANNY LOCKIN; JAN DALEY
             Closet Guest: JACK HALLORAN
I Will
Hands Across The Table
Basin Street Blues; Way Down Yonder In New Orleans; Mississippi Mud;

Waiting For The Robert E. Lee; Swanee (With Leslie)

Season Six: 1970-71

Producer/Director	Greg Garrison
Writers	Harry Crane
	Rod Parker
	Bernie Rothman
	Jay Burton
	Jack Wohl
	Stan Daniels
	George Bloom
	Norm Liebmann
	Tom Tenowich
	Ed Scharlach
Associate Producer	Norman Hopps
Musical Conductor	Les Brown
Choreography	Jonathan Lucas
Special Musical Material	Lee Hale
Art Director	Spencer Davies
Musical Arrangements	Van Alexander
Choral Director For The Golddiggers	Jack Halloran
Unit Manager	P. Dean Reed
Associate Directors	Clay Daniel
	Bill Wyse
	John Kittleson
Music Coordinator	Mack Gray
Music Consultant	Ken Lane
Assistants To The Producer	Janice Buchanan
	Janet Tighe
Production Assistant	Lynne Voeth
Production Supervisor	Craig Martin
Costumes	Ed Wassall
Makeup	Harry Blake
Assistant To The Choreographer	Tommy Tune
Stage Managers	George Fulton
	Ted Baker
	Bob Chic
Technical Director	Karl Messerschmidt
Lighting Directors	Lon Stuckey
	Carl Gibson
Audio	Bill Levitsky
Video	Jerry Smith
Video Tape Editor	Peter Groom
Talent Coordinator	Henry Frankel
Music Routines	Geoffrey Clarkson

9/17/70   ORSON WELLES; PETULA CLARK; JOEY BISHOP;
                     KAY MEDFORD; LAURIE ICHINO
                          Closet Guest: RED SKELTON
(Cameos by THE SMOTHERS BROTHERS; EVA GABOR;
DIONNE WARWICK; LEE MARVIN; DAN BLOCKER;
JOEY HEATHERTON; ALAN SUES; SUGAR RAY ROBINSON;
GLEN CAMPBELL; PAT CROWLEY; DICK CAVETT;
MERV GRIFFIN; JOHNNY CARSON; FLIP WILSON;
LLOYD NOLAN; VINCE EDWARDS; PAUL LYNDE;
RAYMOND BURR; MIKE CONNORS; CAROL BURNETT;
ERNEST BORGNINE; ARTE JOHNSON; DANNY THOMAS;
ROWAN AND MARTIN; LUCILLE BALL; BOB HOPE)
Way Down Yonder In New Orleans
Here We Go Again
I'd Like To Get To Know You; Getting To Know You (With Laurie)
I Want To Be Happy; Put On A Happy Face; Lay Some Happiness
         On Me; You've Made Me So Very Happy (With Petula)
I Will Wait For You; Houston; By The Time I Get To Phoenix
         (With Golddiggers)

9/24/70   JOE NAMATH; SHIRLEY JONES; PETER FALK; PAUL LYNDE;
                     KENNY ROGERS AND THE FIRST EDITION
                          Closet Guest: BURL IVES
Heart Over Mind
Turn The World Around
Bidin' My Time (With Shirley)
Hey, Good Lookin' (With Kenny/First Edition)
Everything Is Beautiful; Gentle On My Mind; Little Green Apples
         (With Golddiggers)

10/1/70   GODFREY CAMBRIDGE; BRITT EKLAND; RUTH BUZZI;
                     DOM DeLUISE; CHARLES NELSON REILLY
                        Closet Guest: DAN BLOCKER
Detroit City
I'm Confessin'
Somebody Loves Me (With Ruth, Dom, Charles, Ken Lane)
Little Tin Box (With Charles and Dom)
More; I Will; Honey (With Golddiggers)

10/8/70   DIONNE WARWICK; VINCE EDWARDS; ROCKY GRAZIANO;
                     MARTY FELDMAN
                        Closet Guest: VAN HEFLIN
Once A Day
Say It Isn't So
Accentuate The Positive (With Dionne)

I'll Never Fall In Love Again; I'm Through With Love;
 I Wonder Who's Kissing Her Now;
 I Get Along Without You Very Well;
 I Wish I Were In Love Again (With Dionne)
Born Free; I Take A Lot Of Pride In What I Am; Release Me
 (With Golddiggers)

10/15/70 JOEY HEATHERTON; EVA GABOR; NORM CROSBY;
  PAUL LYNDE; JOE FRAZIER
   Closet Guest: LEE MARVIN
When The Red, Red Robin Comes Bob, Bob, Bobbin' Along
Try A Little Tenderness
Wanting You (With Eva, Paul and Joey)
Makin' Whoopee (With Joe)
What The World Needs Now Is Love; Love, Love, Love; True Love
 (With Golddiggers)

10/22/70 ENGELBERT HUMPERDINCK; DOM DeLUISE; PAT CROWLEY;
  CHARLES NELSON REILLY
   Closet Guest: MIKE CONNORS
Walking My Baby Back Home
I Cried For You
Crosby, Sinatra And Me (With Engelbert)
Accentuate The Positive (With Pat)
On A Clear Day; Blue, Blue Day; Look For The Silver Lining
 (With Golddiggers)

10/29/70 DAVID FROST; BARBARA FELDON; JIM BROWN;
  CHARLES NELSON REILLY
   Closet Guest: PETER MARSHALL
L-O-V-E
My Woman, My Woman, My Wife
If You Hadn't, But You Did (With Barbara)
Stormy Weather (Comedy with Joey Faye)
Somewhere There's A Someone; People; Once In A While
 (With Golddiggers)

11/5/70 ERNEST BORGNINE; EVERLY BROTHERS;
  SUGAR RAY ROBINSON; ALAN SUES
   Closet Guest: BOB HOPE
A Little Bit South Of North Carolina
Crying Time
Bye, Bye Love; Your Cheatin' Heart (With Everly Brothers)
A Couple Of Song And Dance Men; Singing In The Rain;
  Just One Of Those Things (With Sugar Ray)

When You're Smiling; Rainbows Are Back In Style; Smile
(With Golddiggers)

11/12/70 ZERO MOSTEL; TONY BENNETT; GLORIA LORING
     Closet Guest: JACK BENNY
Is It True What They Say About Dixie
Make The World Go Away
You Are My Lucky Star; I'll String Along With You;
   You Were Meant For Me (With Gloria)
Fascinating Rhythm; Crazy Rhythm; Lullaby Of Broadway
   (With Tony)
Strangers In The Night; In The Misty Moonlight; Blue Moon
   (With Golddiggers)

11/19/70 VIKKI CARR; TEMPTATIONS; BILLY BAXTER;
     CHARLES NELSON REILLY
       Closet Guest: DENNIS WEAVER
Where Or When
It Had To Be You
I Left My Heart In San Francisco
We Got Us; Tea For Two; Just You, Just Me (With Vikki)
Get Happy; (Open Up The Door) Let The Good Times In
   (With Temptations)
You're Nobody 'Til Somebody Loves You; Taking A Chance On Love;
   I'll Get By As Long As I Have You (With Golddiggers)

11/26/70 MIKE CONNORS; DOM DeLUISE; RUTH BUZZI;
     LAURIE ICHINO
       Closet Guest: LEE HALE
I Take A Lot Of Pride In What I Am
Home
I Got Rhythm (With Laurie)
Style (With Dom and Mike)
I Wish I Were A Kid Again (With Ruth and Mike)
Dream; The Sun Is Shining; I'm Always Chasing Rainbows
   (With Golddiggers)
May The Good Lord Bless And Keep You (With Golddiggers)

12/3/70 PETER GRAVES; JILL ST. JOHN; RONNIE BARKER;
     RON CORBETT; PAUL LYNDE; KATHLEEN FREEMAN
       Closet Guest: PHYLLIS DILLER
I'm Gonna Sit Right Down And Write Myself A Letter
S'posin'
Just One Of Those Songs (With Jill)
Love Is A Many Splendored Thing; Glory Of Love; But Beautiful
   (With Golddiggers)

12/10/70   GLENN FORD; BARBARA FELDON; CHARLES
NELSON REILLY; LANCELOT LINK AND THE
EVOLUTION REVOLUTION
         Closet Guest: LOUIS ARMSTRONG
Invisible Tears
Don't Blame Me
Elegance (With Glenn and Charles)
Life Is Just A Bowl Of Cherries; Don't Let The Blues Make You Bad;
     For The Good Times (With Golddiggers)

12/17/70   GLEN CAMPBELL; GALE GORDON; DOM DeLUISE
         Closet Guest: WILLIAM HOLDEN
She's A Little Bit Country
Raindrops Keep Falling On My Head
Jingle Bells
Blue, Blue Day; Singing The Blues; We'll Sing In The Sunshine;
     You Are My Sunshine (With Glen)
You're My Everything; Things; Best Things In Life Are Free
     (With Golddiggers)

12/24/70   Repeat of 12/19/68, but with new finale.
         (Cameos by GEORGE BURNS; WILLIAM HOLDEN;
         TONY BENNETT; VINCE EDWARDS; GALE GORDON;
         PHIL HARRIS; CHARLES NELSON REILLY;
         NANCY SINATRA; JOHNNY CARSON; GLENN FORD;
         GLEN CAMPBELL; GREG MORRIS; RAYMOND BURR;
         KAY MEDFORD; PETER GRAVES; DON RICKLES;
         LORNE GREENE; PETULA CLARK;
         BARBARA FELDON; DAN ROWAN; DAN BLOCKER;
         ROY ROGERS; JOEY BISHOP; MICHAEL LANDON;
         JIM NABORS; DIAHANN CARROLL;
         ANDY GRIFFITH; FRANK SINATRA; RED SKELTON;
         PAUL LYNDE; KATE SMITH;
         TENNESSEE ERNIE FORD; JIMMY STEWART;
         JACK BENNY; BOB HOPE; LUCILLE BALL)

12/31/70   FRANK SINATRA; RUTH BUZZI; KAY MEDFORD;
         BARBARA HELLER; INGA NEILSON;
         CHARLES NELSON REILLY
         Closet Guest: JIMMY DURANTE
Love Is Just Around The Corner; My Kind Of Girl; But Beautiful;
     L-O-V-E; I Get A Kick Out Of You; Goody Goody;
     Guys And Dolls (With Frank)
Young At Heart
Now Is The Hour; So Long; Auld Lang Syne
     (With Frank and Golddiggers)

1/7/71   DENNIS WEAVER; BOB NEWHART; BOBBI MARTIN
        Closet Guest: CHARLEY WEAVER
    Georgia Sunshine
    How Deep Is The Ocean
    Don't Fence Me In (With Dennis)
    We're A Little Bit Country; Anytime;
        I Can't Help It If I'm Still In Love With You;
        Just A Little Lovin' (With Bobbi)
    You Always Hurt The Ones You Love;
        (Remember Me) I'm The One Who Loves You;
        The One I Love Belongs To Somebody Else
        (With Golddiggers)

1/14/71   ORSON WELLES; CHARLES NELSON REILLY; DON RICE III
        Closet Guest: MILBURN STONE
    Second Hand Rose
    April Showers
    Three Coins In The Fountain; I Love Paris;
        A Foggy Day In London Town (With Golddiggers)

1/21/71   RAYMOND BURR; DIAHANN CARROLL;
        CHARLES NELSON REILLY; PAT HENRY;
        KAY MEDFORD
          Closet Guest: BARBARA FELDON
    For Once In My Life
    Raining In My Heart
    A Pretty Girl Is Like A Melody
    Gypsy In My Soul; King Of The Road; Bumming Around;
        Breezin' Along With The Breeze (With Diahann)
    On The Street Where You Live; Back In Your Own Backyard;
        I'll Be Seeing You (With Golddiggers)

1/28/71   BOB NEWHART; FRANK SINATRA, JR.;
        DEANA, GAIL AND DINO MARTIN;
        LUCIE AND DESI ARNAZ, JR.; MAUREEN REAGAN;
        MEREDITH MacRAE; BILLY HINSCHE
          Closet Guests: ROY ROGERS/DALE EVANS
    On A Slow Boat To China
    Mean To Me
    What Is This Thing Called Love; Love Is The Reason
        (With entire cast)
    Street Of Dreams; Memories Are Made Of This;
        Very Thought Of You (With Golddiggers)

2/4/71   ZERO MOSTEL; RUTH BUZZI; PAUL LYNDE
        Closet Guest: JOANNE WORLEY
    I'm Sitting On Top Of The World

Tips Of My Fingers
Side By Side; Gimme A Little Kiss; It's Been A Long, Long Time
    (With Ding-A-Lings)
Invisible Tears; Pennies From Heaven (With Golddiggers)

2/11/71   DEBBIE REYNOLDS; PAUL LYNDE; MARTY FELDMAN
              Closet Guest: LLOYD NOLAN
Somebody Stole My Gal
Together Again
Couple Of Swells (With Debbie)
It Happened In Monterey; South Of The Border;
    Red Sails In The Sunset (With Golddiggers)

2/18/71   DIAHANN CARROLL; CHARLES NELSON REILLY;
              RONNIE BARKER; RONNIE CORBETT
              Closet Guest: VAN JOHNSON
Someday
For The Good Times
Nice Work If You Can Get It; Cuddle Up A Little Closer;
    Will You Still Be Mine; Let The Rest Of The World Go By;
    I'm Sitting On Top Of The World (With Diahann)
It's Magic; Until The Real Thing Comes Along; Where Or When
    (With Golddiggers)

2/25/71   ZERO MOSTEL; FRED SMOOT; JACKIE VERNON
              Closet Guest: ROBERT WAGNER
There's A Rainbow 'Round My Shoulder
It's The Talk Of The Town
Brush Up Your Shakespeare (With Zero)
Me And My Shadow (With Zero and Tommy Tune)
I Could Write A Book; Just Friends; It's Easy To Remember
    (With Golddiggers)

3/4/71   MARTY FELDMAN; RONNIE CORBETT; RONNIE BARKER;
              ODIA COATES
              Closet Guest: RAYMOND BURR
Sweetheart
A Hundred Years From Today
It's The Talk Of The Town (Comedy with Joey Faye)
Pennies From Heaven; April Showers (With Odia)
It All Depends On You; I'm Gonna Sit Right Down And Write
    Myself A Letter; Imagination (With Golddiggers)

319

3/11/71   ORSON WELLES; PETULA CLARK; NORM CROSBY;
       LEONARD BARR; EUBIE BLAKE
         Closet Guest: JOSE FERRER
Swanee
Stars Fell On Alabama
I'm Just Wild About Harry (With Eubie)
Until The Real Thing Comes Along; If This Isn't Love; True Love;
    Love, Love, Love (With Petula)
Raindrops Keep Falling On My Head;
      I Don't Care If The Sun Don't Shine;
      Come Rain Or Come Shine (With Golddiggers)

3/25/71   MARTY FELDMAN; NORM CROSBY; MILT KAMEN;
       LAURIE ICHINO
         Closet Guest: FLIP WILSON
Almost Like Being In Love
P. S. I Love You
Cheek To Cheek; Put Your Little Foot Right Out (With Laurie)
Sittin' On The Dock Of The Bay; Lazy Bones; Bumming Around
    (With Golddiggers)

4/1/71   ERNEST BORGNINE; PEGGY LEE; DOM DeLUISE
         Closet Guest: DONALD O'CONNOR
Bye Bye Blackbird
Imagination
Together Again; For The Good Times;
      Raindrops Keep Falling On My Head (With Peggy)
Turn The World Around; Just Say I Love Her; Say It Isn't So
    (With Golddiggers)

4/8/71   JIMMY STEWART; DOM DeLUISE; LAURIE ICHINO
         Closet Guest: MICKEY ROONEY
Back In Your Own Backyard
For The Good Times
Everybody Loves Somebody
Sentimental Journey; Home; America The Beautiful
    (With Golddiggers)

Season Seven: 1971-72

Producer/Director	Greg Garrison
Writers	Harry Crane
	Rod Parker
	Charles Isaacs
	Jay Burton
	Stan Daniels
	George Bloom

	Norm Liebmann
	Tom Tenowich
	Robert Hilliard
Associate Producer	Norman Hopps
Musical Conductor	Les Brown
Choreography	Jaime Rogers
Special Musical Material	Lee Hale
Art Director	Gene McAvoy
Musical Arranger	Van Alexander
Choral Director For The Ding-A-Lings	Jack Halloran
Unit Manager	P. Dean Reed
Associate Director	Clay Daniel
Music Coordinator	Mack Gray
Assistants To The Producer	Janice Buchanan
	Janet Tighe
Production Assistant	Lynne Voeth
Production Supervisor	Craig Martin
Costume Designer	Bob Fletcher
Makeup	Harry Blake
Stage Managers	George Fulton
	Ted Baker
	Bob Chic
Technical Director	Karl Messerschmidt
Lighting Director	Carl Gibson
Audio	Bill Levitsky
	Joe Ralston
Video	Jerry Smith
	Bob Pattison
Video Tape Editors	Peter Groom
	Stan Jenkins
Talent Coordinator	Henry Frankel
Music Routines	Geoffrey Clarkson
Sketch Supervisor	Jonathan Lucas

9/16/71   ART CARNEY; PETULA CLARK; LIBERACE;
                  RICHARD CASTELLANO
                          Closet Guest: RONALD REAGAN
             Non Dimenticar
             I Get A Kick Out Of You (With Ding-A-Lings)
             For Once In My Life; We've Only Just Begun (With Petula)
             I've Got A Pocketful Of Dreams; All I Do Is Dream Of You;
                  Dream; Wrap Your Troubles In Dreams (With Petula)
             Steppin' Out With My Baby; Hernando's Hideaway; Sway;
                  Cheek To Cheek;
                  Arthur Murray Got Me Dancing In A Hurry;
                  Poppa Won't You Dance With Me (With Ding-A-Lings)

321

9/23/71   CARROLL O'CONNOR; RUTH BUZZI; VIKKI CARR
                        Closet Guest: LUCILLE BALL
              Detroit City
              Proud Mary; Way Down Yonder In New Orleans (With Vikki)
              Real Live Girl; Thank Heaven For Little Girls (With Ding-A-Lings)
              Rainbows Are Back In Style (With Vikki)

9/30/71   LESLIE UGGAMS; DICK MARTIN; DENNIS WEAVER
                        Closet Guest: MAYOR SAM YORTY
              C'est Magnifique
              L-O-V-E; Isn't It Romantic (With Ding-A-Lings)
              You're Nobody 'Til Somebody Loves You (With Leslie)
              I've Got Tears In My Ears; Nobody's Business (With entire cast)
              (Open Up The Door) Let The Good Times In; Joy To The World
                    (With Leslie)

10/7/71   BING CROSBY; RIP TAYLOR; RICHARD CASTELLANO;
                        CLAIR AND McMAHON
                              Closet Guest: RAYMOND BURR
              On An Evening In Roma
              I Don't Know Enough About You; How About You
                    (With Ding-A-Lings)
              Put Your Hand In The Hand; Lay Some Happiness On Me
                    (With Bing)
              I'm An Old Cowhand; Pocketful Of Dreams; Swinging On A Star;
                    Accentuate The Positive;
                    In The Cool, Cool, Cool Of The Evening; Personality;
                    Love Thy Neighbor; True Love;
                    Love Is Just Around The Corner; But Beautiful;
                    Second Time Around; Learn To Croon
                    (With Bing and Ding-A-Lings)

10/14/71   ART CARNEY; RUTH BUZZI; LYNN KELLOGG;
                        LONNIE SHORR; CLAIR AND McMAHON
              Young At Heart
              On A Slow Boat To China; Rose Garden (With Ruth)
              Cuddle Up A Little Closer; Close To You (With Ding-A-Lings)
              Goodnight Irene; Loch Lomand (With Lynn)

10/21/71   WAYNE NEWTON; PAUL LYNDE; RIP TAYLOR; DON RICE III
                        Closet Guest: ED McMAHON
              Arrivederci, Roma
              Gigi
              I'm Sitting On Top Of The World; Danke Schoen (With Wayne)
              They Didn't Believe Me; You'd Be Surprised (With Ding-A-Lings)
              Swanee; Carolina In The Morning; Is It True What They Say About
                    Dixie; Alabamy Bound; April Showers; Toot Toot Tootsie
                    (With Wayne)

10/28/71 ERNEST BORGNINE; ELAINE STRITCH; NORM CROSBY;
     LEONARD BARR
        Closet Guest: GENE KELLY
    La Vie En Rose
    Embraceable You; You Took Advantage Of Me (With Ding-A-Lings)
    Almost Like Being In Love; Sooner Or Later (With Ding-A-Lings)

11/4/71 EDDIE ALBERT; JONATHAN WINTERS; LYNN KELLOGG;
     LONNIE SHORR
    River Seine
    Nearness Of You; I Am Woman, You Are Man (With Ding-A-Lings)
    Georgia Sunshine; Take Me Home Country Roads (With Eddie)

11/11/71 MIKE CONNORS; RUTH BUZZI; BOBBI MARTIN;
     CLAIR AND McMAHON; DR. JOYCE BROTHERS
    Darling, Je Vous Aime Beaucoup
    All The Way
    It's Easy To Remember; A Fine Romance (With Ding-A-Lings)
    Taking A Chance On Love; When You're Hot, You're Hot (With Mike)
    Singing The Blues; Blue, Blue Day (With Bobbi)

11/18/71 JOEY BISHOP; JO ANN PFLUG
        Closet Guest: LEONARD BARR
    C'est Si Bon
    Until The Real Thing Comes Along; Show Me
      (With Ding-A-Lings)
    She's A Little Bit Country; Born To Lose; Your Cheatin' Heart
      (With Joey)
    Tea For Three; No Three People Have Ever Been So In Love;
      Indian Love Call; Side By Side; Three Sleepy People;
      Together (With Joey and Jo Ann)
    Almost Like Being In Love (Comedy with Joey)

11/25/71 CAROL CHANNING; DAN BLOCKER; JACK KRUSCHEN;
     DAN JOHNSON; BILLY BAXTER; JOE CAPPO
    Home
    Tea For Two; I Want To Be Happy (With Carol)
    Style (With Carol and Dan)
    She's Funny That Way; I Believe In You (With Ding-A-Lings)
    Great Day; Whispering; Friendship (With Carol)
    Swanee; Let Me Sing And I'm Happy (With Carol)

12/2/71 PETER GRAVES; RIP TAYLOR; KELLY GARRETT;
     JEANNINE BURNIER; ALICE GHOSTLEY
        Closet Guest: ARTE JOHNSON
    For The Good Times

Together Again; I've Grown Accustomed To Her Face
        (With Ding-A-Lings)
Lady's In Love With You; Guys And Dolls (With Peter)
Nevertheless (With Kelly)
Class (With Peter and Ding-A-Lings)

12/9/71   JULIET PROWSE; RUTH BUZZI; CHARLES NELSON REILLY;
                      JERRY COLLINS
              Return To Me
              I Can't Give You Anything But Love; I've Got Your Number
                      (With Ding-A-Lings)
              America medley with Juliet includes Yankee Doodle Dandy;
                      Deep In The Heart Of Texas;
                      Way Down Yonder In New Orleans; San Francisco;
                      Hurrah For Hollywood; Give My Regards To Broadway;
                      America
              Love Is A Good Foundation; L-O-V-E (With Juliet)

12/16/71   GINGER ROGERS; ARTE JOHNSON; DON MEREDITH;
                      NORM CROSBY
              Tips Of My Fingers
              I Only Have Eyes For You; You Do Something To Me
                      (With Ding-A-Lings)
              Bewitched; Too Marvelous For Words; Cheek To Cheek; Dancing
                      (With Carol)

12/23/71   JONATHAN WINTERS; DAN ROWAN; LONNIE SHORR
                      Closet Guest: JOEY BISHOP
              Marshmallow World
              That Old Feeling; Too Close For Comfort (With Ding-A-Lings)
              Walking My Baby Back Home; My Baby Just Cares For Me
                      (With Jonathan)

12/30/71   ART CARNEY; HOWARD COSELL; LONNIE SHORR
                      Closet Guest: DON MEREDITH
              Make The World Go Away
              Anniversary Song; I Love You Truly;
                      Get Me To The Church On Time;
                      Love And Marriage (With Art)
              Try A Little Tenderness; Everything I Have Belongs To You
                      (With Ding-A-Lings)

1/6/72   ART CARNEY; CATERINA VALENTE; JEANNINE BURNIER
                      Closet Guest: DICK CAVETT
              What's Yesterday
              You Were Meant For Me
              Time And Love; Where Or When; My Melancholy Baby
                      (With Caterina)

I'm Confessin'; I've Got My Eyes On You (With Ding-A-Lings)

1/13/72   PETULA CLARK; BILLY BAXTER; JEANNINE BURNIER
          Closet Guest: BING CROSBY
P. S. I Love You
Put A Little Love In Your Heart; When You're Smiling (With Petula)
I'll Get By As Long As I Have You; There'll Never Be Another You
      (With Ding-A-Lings)
Let's Call The Whole Thing Off; For The Good Times;
          Raindrops Keep Falling On My Head; Joy To The World;
          (Open Up The Door) Let The Good Times In;
          Sign Of The Times (With Petula)
There'll Be Some Changes Made; I'm Just Wild About Harry;
          She's Funny That Way; I Enjoy Being A Girl;
          They Didn't Believe Me; Tea For Two
          (Comedy skit with Petula)

1/20/72   JONATHAN WINTERS; FRANK SINATRA, JR.; NORM CROSBY
          Closet Guest: GINGER ROGERS
What's Yesterday
If I Had You; What A Man (With Ding-A-Lings)
It Was A Very Good Year; My Kind Of Town; Witchcraft;
          Night And Day; High Hopes; Strangers In The Night;
          I'll Never Smile Again; Love And Marriage; All The Way
          (With Frank Jr. and Ding-A-Lings)
I've Gotta Be Me; I Take A Lot Of Pride In What I Am
          (With Frank Jr.)

1/27/72   RAYMOND BURR; ELAINE STRITCH; BOB NEWHART
It's The Talk Of The Town
I Can't Believe That You're In Love With Me (With Ding-A-Lings)
What The World Needs Now Is Love; Glory Of Love
          (With Ding-A-Lings)

2/17/72   LESLIE UGGAMS; PAUL LYNDE; NORM CROSBY;
          LONNIE SHORR
I've Grown Accustomed To Her Face
All Of Me (With Ding-A-Lings)
I Love You So Much It Hurts; Body And Soul; Spinning Wheel;
          I'm Old Fashioned; Hurts So Bad;
          Back In Your Own Backyard;
          When The Red, Red Robin Comes Bob, Bob, Bobbin'
          Along (With Leslie)

2/24/72   EVA GABOR; CHARLES NELSON REILLY; LONNIE SHORR;
          JEANNINE BURNIER
              Closet Guest: DENNIS WEAVER
Party Dolls And Wine

Oh, You Beautiful Doll; Lady Is A Tramp (With Eva)
Just Friends (With Ding-A-Lings)

3/2/72   JONATHAN WINTERS
By The Time I Get To Phoenix
Somebody Stole My Gal (With Ding-A-Lings)
Don't Blame Me (With Ding-A-Lings)
Embraceable You (Comedy with Jonathan)

3/9/72   PHIL SILVERS; DOM DeLUISE; NORM CROSBY;
         LEONARD BARR
            Closet Guest: MIKE CONNORS
Release Me
Red Sails In The Sunset
Imagination; Something's Gotta Give (With Ding-A-Lings)
Make 'Em Laugh; Comedy Tonight (With Phil)
Everybody Ought To Have A Maid (With Phil and Dom)

3/16/72   ART CARNEY; BARBARA McNAIR; JACKIE MASON
I Don't Know What I'm Doing
Pardon
Bumming Around (With Barbara)
Here Comes That Rainy Day Feeling Again; Pennies From Heaven
       (With Barbara)
Mean To Me (With Ding-A-Lings)

3/30/72   JONATHAN WINTERS; PAUL LYNDE; NORM CROSBY;
         LONNIE SHORR
Small Exception Of Me
Is It True What They Say About Dixie; Dixieland
       (With Ding-A-Lings)
Them There Eyes; Witchcraft (With Ding-A-Lings)

4/6/72   JOEY BISHOP; BILLY BAXTER
Turn The World Around
Birth Of The Blues; Bye Bye Blues (With Joey)
If I Could Be With You; What Do You Think I Am
       (With Ding-A-Lings)

4/13/72   BUDDY HACKETT; LAURIE ICHINO; KENDREW LASCELLES;
         JEANNINE BURNIER; DON RICE III
            Closet Guest: HOWARD COSELL
Green, Green Grass Of Home
Love Is A Simple Thing (With Laurie)
I'll Never Fall In Love Again; Someday (With Ding-A-Lings)
All I Do Is Dream Of You (With Ding-A-Lings)

Season Eight: 1972-73

Producer/Director	Greg Garrison
Writers	Harry Crane
	Stan Daniels
	Norm Liebmann
	Tom Tenowich
	Larry Markes
	Hal Goldman
	Al Gordon
	Mickey Rose
Associate Producer	Craig Martin
Musical Conductor	Les Brown
Choreography	Ed Kerrigan
Special Musical Material	Lee Hale
Art Director	Gene McAvoy
Musical Arranger	Van Alexander
Choral Director For The Ding-A-Lings	Jack Halloran
Unit Manager	P. Dean Reed
Associate Director	Clay Daniel
Music Coordinator	Mack Gray
Music Consultant	Ken Lane
Assistants To The Producer	Janice Buchanan
	Janet Tighe
Production Assistant	Lynne Voeth
Production Coordinator	Roger Warnix
Costumes	Bob Fletcher
Makeup	Harry Blake
Stage Managers	Ted Baker
	Bob Chic
Technical Director	Karl Messerschmidt
Lighting Director	Lon Stuckey
Audio	Joe Ralston
Video	Jerry Smith
Video Tape Editors	Peter Groom
	Stan Jenkins
Talent Coordinator	Henry Frankel
Music Routines	Geoffrey Clarkson
Sketch Supervisor	Jonathan Lucas

9/14/72   GENE KELLY; GILBERT O'SULLIVAN
Raindrops Keep Falling On My Head
Give Me Something To Remember You By (Comedy)
L-O-V-E (With Ding-A-Lings)
Gentle On My Mind (With Gilbert)
When You're Smiling; I Want To Be Happy (With Gene)

You'd Be So Nice To Come Home To (With Kitty)
S'Wonderful (With Gene)
Our Love Is Here To Stay

9/21/72   ANNA MOFFO; LLOYD BRIDGES; BARBARA FELDON
Small Exception Of Me
Gigi
If I Could Be With You (With Ding-A-Lings)
Let's Do It (With Kitty)
I'm Gonna Sit Right Down And Write Myself A Letter;
        I Cried For You (With Ding-A-Lings)
In a parody medley with Anna and Lloyd, Dean "sings" excerpts of
        By The Time I Get To Phoenix, Proud Mary and
        Close To You

9/28/72   EVE ARDEN; FESS PARKER; LYNN ANDERSON
All Of Me
Turn The World Around
Cuddle Up A Little Closer (With Kitty)
Bidin' My Time (With Fess, Eve and Lynn)
Almost Like Being In Love (With Eve)
Memories Are Made Of This; It's Easy To Remember
        (With Ding-A-Lings)

10/5/72   JOEY BISHOP; KAREN BLACK; WILLIAM CONRAD
Way Down Yonder In New Orleans
Once In A While (With Ding-A-Lings)
Three Little Words Finale (With entire cast)

10/12/72   HUGH O'BRIEN; ANNE MURRAY; MONTY HALL
What's Yesterday
My Baby Just Cares For Me
Mean To Me
Just In Time; If I Had You (With Ding-A-Lings)
Lady's In Love; Guys And Dolls (With Hugh and Monty)
It All Depends On You (With Hugh and Monty)
Ten Cents A Dance (With Monty and Dom DeLuise)

10/26/72   WILLIAM CONRAD; OLIVIA NEWTON-JOHN
You Made Me Love You
Crying Time
Is It True What They Say About Dixie (With Ding-A-Lings)
Just A Little Lovin'; True Love (With Olivia)
Mountain Greenery; Home On The Range (With Ding-A-Lings)
Rose Marie Finale (With entire cast)

11/2/72   DANNY THOMAS; CHARO
As Time Goes By
Dancing In The Dark
A Little Bit South Of North Carolina (With Ding-A-Lings)
'A' You're Adorable; Hernando's Hideaway; Rain In Spain;
        Toot Toot Tootsie (With Danny and Charo)
Somebody Loves You (With Ding-A-Lings)
By Myself (With Danny, Dom DeLuise and Nipsey Russell)
That's Entertainment (With Danny, Lou Jacobi and Kay Medford)

11/9/72   DENNIS HOPPER; CHARLEY PRIDE;
        CHARLES NELSON REILLY; LEONARD BARR
Try A Little Tenderness
Singing In The Rain
Bye Bye Blackbird (With Ding-A-Lings)
Hey, Good Lookin'; I Can't Help It If I'm Still In Love With You
        (With Charley)
Broadway Rhythm (With Charles)
Wrap Your Troubles In Dreams; Dream A Little Dream Of Me
        (With Ding-A-Lings)

11/23/72   JACK BENNY; LYNN ANDERSON
Non Dimenticar
Blue Room
Then I'll Be Happy (With Ding-A-Lings)
Wouldn't It Be Loverly (With Kitty)
Lady Is A Tramp (With Nipsey Russell; Kay Medford; Lou Jacobi)
Love Is Just Around The Corner; My Ideal (With Ding-A-Lings)
April Showers; Tiptoe Through The Tulips; Sweet Violets;
        Sweet And Lovely (With Lynn)

11/30/72   STEVE LAWRENCE; CHARLES NELSON REILLY
Arrivederci, Roma
I'm Sitting On Top Of The World (With Ding-A-Lings)
Buttons And Bows; Red River Valley (With Ding-A-Lings)
Swingin' Down The Lane; Way Down Yonder In New Orleans;
        Birth Of The Blues; It's A Good Day (With Steve)
Here's To The Beautiful Girls (With Steve)

12/7/72   CAROL CHANNING; MIKE CONNORS
On An Evening In Roma
Ol' Man River
Almost Like Being In Love (With Ding-A-Lings)
Sun Is Shining; I'm Always Chasing Rainbows
        (With Ding-A-Lings)
Make Believe (With Mike)

12/14/72   GLEN CAMPBELL
Always
Ev'ry Street's A Boulevard In Old New York
      (With Glen, Dom DeLuise and Nipsey Russell)
(Open Up The Door) Let The Good Times In (With Glen)
Ain't Misbehavin'; Nice 'N' Easy (With Ding-A-Lings)
Breezing Along With The Breeze; King Of The Road;
      Bumming Around; Wahoo (With Glen)

12/21/72   GLENN FORD; LYNN ANDERSON; GOLDDIGGERS
Marshmallow World
They Didn't Believe Me
Ol' Man River
I'll Be Home For Christmas
Fine Romance (With Lynn)
This Old House; You'd Be So Nice To Come Home To (With Lynn)

12/28/72   ERNEST BORGNINE; O. C. SMITH; GOLDDIGGERS
Born To Lose
I Get A Kick Out Of You (With Golddiggers)
After You've Gone (With Ernest and Dom DeLuise)
By The Sea (With entire cast)
I'd Like To Teach The World To Sing (With Golddiggers)
For Once In My Life; Little Green Apples; That's Life (With O. C.)

1/4/73   GENE KELLY; STEVE LANDESBERG; GOLDDIGGERS
Welcome To My World
All Of A Sudden My Heart Sings
There's A Rainbow 'Round My Shoulder (With Gene)
Girl Medley (With Gene)

1/11/73   BOB NEWHART; STEVE LANDESBERG
It Just Happened That Way
Swanee; I'm Sitting On Top Of The World;
      Rockabye Your Baby With A Dixie Melody;
      Waiting For The Robert E. Lee; April Showers;
      Pennies From Heaven (Excerpts in *Jazz Singer* salute)
My Kind Of Girl (With Ding-A-Lings)

1/18/73   STEVE LAWRENCE; DICK MARTIN
Young At Heart
Wrap Your Troubles In Dreams (With Steve and Dick)
Take Me Out To The Ball Game (With entire cast)
Nice Work If You Can Get It; These Foolish Things
      (With Ding-A-Lings)

You're Nobody 'Til Somebody Loves You;
    Almost Like Being In Love;
    Taking A Chance On Love (With Steve)

1/25/73   JOEY BISHOP; PETULA CLARK
Tips Of My Fingers
Exactly Like You (With Petula)
All The Way; Always True To You In My Fashion
    (With Ding-A-Lings)
Together; You Were Meant For Me; It Had To Be You;
    I Can't Give You Anything But Love; If This Isn't Love
    (With Petula)
Girl That I Marry; Anything You Can Do (With Petula)

2/1/73   RUTH BUZZI; LONNIE SHORR; LAURIE ICHINO
I've Grown Accustomed To Her Face
L-O-V-E (With Ding-A-Lings)
You'll Never Know; If This Isn't Love (With Ding-A-Lings)
Just One Of Those Things (With Ruth)
Tramp, Tramp, Tramp (With Dom DeLuise and Nipsey Russell)

2/15/73   RICHARD ROUNDTREE; BOBBY GOLDSBORO;
    JACKIE VERNON; STEVE LANDESBERG
For The Good Times
When The Red, Red Robin Comes Bob, Bob, Bobbin' Along
    (With Ding-A-Lings)
Good News; Pass That Peace Pipe; Varsity Drag (With entire cast)
Straight Life; Little Green Apples (With Bobby)

2/22/73   WILLIAM CONRAD; LONNIE SHORR
Return To Me
Stranger In Paradise (With Ding-A-Lings)
Where Or When (With William)
It Was A Very Good Year; Thank Heaven For Little Girls;
    A Fella Needs A Girl;
    Why Can't A Woman Be More Like A Man
    (With William)

3/1/73   GINGER ROGERS; NORM CROSBY; LEONARD BARR
Just In Time
L-O-V-E (With Ding-A-Lings)
Stout-Hearted Men (With Dom DeLuise and Nipsey Russell)
Your Land And My Land (With entire cast)
It's Only A Paper Moon (With Ding-A-Lings)
Beautiful Dreamer; Dream Along With Me;
    Wrap Your Troubles In Dreams;
    I'll See You In My Dreams (With Ginger)

3/8/73   JONATHAN WINTERS; LISA KIRK
C'est Magnifique
I Love The Look Of You
Taking A Chance On Love (With Dom DeLuise and Nipsey Russell)
I Wish I Were In Love Again (With Lisa)
Don't Fence Me In; I Wish I Was (With Ding-A-Lings)
Stereophonic Sound; In Cheery Siberia (With Dom and Nipsey)

3/15/73   JOSEPH CAMPANELLA; RUTH BUZZI; GAIL MARTIN
Pardon
It's Easy To Remember; A Fine Romance (With Ding-A-Lings)
Too Marvelous For Words; Cheek To Cheek (With Joseph and Ruth)
Buckle Down Winsocki (With entire cast)

3/22/73   JIMMY STEWART; FRANK SINATRA, JR.
Glory Of Love
I Could Write A Book
Embraceable You (With Ding-A-Lings)
Alexander's Ragtime Band (With Jimmy)
Lady Is A Tramp (With Frank Jr. and Jimmy)
Parodies of Cecilia; Mame; Mona Lisa; Ida, Sweet As Apple Cider;
    Dolores; Dinah; Mimi; Hello Dolly (With Frank Jr.)

3/29/73   MARTIN MILNER; ANNA MOFFO; LONNIE SHORR
She's A Little Bit Country
Back In Your Own Backyard (With Kay Medford)
I Don't Know Enough About You; How About You
    (With Ding-A-Lings)
Volare; Funniculi, Funnicula (With Anna)
Lovely To Look At (With Anna and Martin)
Story Of Sorrento (With Anna)
I Won't Dance (With Kay and Martin)

4/5/73   PETER SELLERS; PHYLLIS McGUIRE
Just Say I Love Her
Girl Next Door
This Could Be The Start Of Something Big;
    I Get A Kick Out Of You; Deed I Do (With Phyllis)
I Can't Give You Anything But Love (With Ding-A-Lings)
Trolley Song (With Peter, Dom DeLuise, Kay Medford and
    Nipsey Russell)

4/12/73   WILLIAM CONRAD; NANCY SINATRA
There's No Tomorrow
Somebody Stole My Gal (With Dom DeLuise and Nipsey Russell)

Sometimes I'm Happy; I Want To Be Happy; Smile;
    Lay Some Happiness On Me (With Nancy)
Where Or When (With Nancy)
There's Nothing Like A Dame; I Could Write A Book;
    They Can't Take That Away From Me;
    I've Got You Under My Skin; Too Marvelous For Words;
    I Get A Kick Out Of You; You Make Me Feel So Young
    (With William)
I Love A Piano (With William, Dom DeLuise and Nipsey Russell)
Steppin' Out With My Baby (With Ding-A-Lings)
Couple Of Swells (With William)
Easter Parade (With William, Dom DeLuise and Nipsey Russell)

THE DEAN MARTIN COMEDY HOUR

Fridays, 10:00-11:00 pm
Season Nine: 1973-74

Producer/Director	Greg Garrison
Writers	Harry Crane
	Stan Daniels
	Tom Tenowich
	Larry Markes
	Mike Barrie
	Jim Mulholland
Associate Producer	Craig Martin
Musical Conductor	Les Brown
Choreography	Ed Kerrigan
Special Musical Material	Lee Hale
Art Director	Gene McAvoy
Musical Arranger	Van Alexander
Choral Director	Jack Halloran
Unit Manager	P. Dean Reed
Associate Director	Clay Daniel
Music Coordinator	Mack Gray
Music Consultant	Ken Lane
Assistants To The Producer	Janice Buchanan
	Lynne Voeth
Production Coordinator	Roger Warnix
Production Supervisor	Janet Tighe
Costumes	Bob Fletcher
Makeup	Harry Blake
Stage Managers	Bob Chic
	Doug Quick
Man Of The Week Coordinator	Kendis Rochlen
Technical Director	Karl Messerschmidt

Lighting Director	Lon Stuckey
Audio	Joe Ralston
Video	Jerry Smith
Video Tape Editors	Stan Jenkins
	Gustavo Aguilera
Talent Coordinator	Henry Frankel
Music Routines	Geoffrey Clarkson
Sketch Supervisor	Jonathan Lucas
Man Of The Week Creative Consultant	Buddy Arnold

9/14/73   AUDREY MEADOWS; KRIS KRISTOFFERSON;
               RITA COOLIDGE; DON RICKLES; JONATHAN
               WINTERS
             Man of the Week Roast: RONALD REAGAN
             Roasters: Jackie Vernon; Phyllis Diller; Dom DeLuise; Pat Henry;
                 Mark Spitz; Jack Benny; Jonathan Winters; Nipsey Russell;
                 Nancy Reagan; Don Rickles
             Smile
             Gotta Travel On; Just The Other Side Of Nowhere (With Kris)
             Toot Toot Tootsie (With bar patrons)

9/21/73   HOWARD COSELL; JOEY BISHOP; DICK MARTIN;
               AUDREY MEADOWS; LORETTA LYNN; TOM T. HALL
             Man of the Week Roast: HUGH HEFNER
             Roasters: Billy Baxter; Howard Cosell; Audrey Meadows;
                 Jackie Gayle; Dick Martin; Joey Bishop
             There's A Rainbow 'Round My Shoulder
             Glory Of Love
             Little Tin Box (With Joey and Dick)
             Hey, Good Lookin'; Blue, Blue Day; Just A Little Lovin'
                 (With Loretta and Tom)
             Rockabye Your Baby With A Dixie Melody (With bar patrons)

9/28/73   ERNEST BORGNINE; DOM DeLUISE; DIONNE WARWICK;
               CHARLIE RICH; CHARO
             Man of the Week Roast: ED McMAHON
             Roasters: Pat Buttrum; Jackie Vernon; Dionne Warwick;
                 Steve Landesberg; Charo; Jack Carter
             Return To Me
             Anytime; Behind Closed Doors; Singing The Blues
                 (With Charlie and Dionne)
             If You Knew Susie (With bar patrons)

10/5/73   PETULA CLARK; BOB NEWHART; NIPSEY RUSSELL;
                MAC WISEMAN
           Man of the Week Roast: WILLIAM CONRAD
           Roasters: Phyllis Diller; Nipsey Russell; Petula Clark;
                Bob Newhart; Jackie Gayle
           C'est Magnifique
           Sometimes I'm Happy (With Petula)
           She's A Little Bit Country; For The Good Times
                (With Petula and Mac)
           Heart Of My Heart (With bar patrons)

10/12/73   BURNS AND SCHREIBER; TED KNIGHT; LYNN ANDERSON;
                RAY PRICE; TIM CONWAY
           Man of the Week Roast: KIRK DOUGLAS
           Roasters: Ted Knight; Norm Crosby; Burns and Schreiber;
                Rich Little; Lynn Anderson; Jackie Gayle; Don Rickles
           It Just Happened That Way
           Sun Is Shining; Sing About Love; Make It Rain (With Lynn and Ray)
           California, Here I Come (With bar patrons)

10/19/73   KAY MEDFORD; HOWARD COSELL; JEANNIE C. RILEY;
                TOM T. HALL; VINCENT PRICE
           Woman of the Week Roast: BETTE DAVIS
           Roasters: Pat Buttrum; Kay Medford; Nipsey Russell; Joyce Haver;
                Vincent Price; Army Archard; Barbara Heller; Henry Fonda;
                Howard Cosell
           Non Dimenticar
           This Old House; Release Me; Do You Believe This Town
                (With Tom and Jeannie)
           Bye Bye Blackbird (With bar patrons)

10/26/73   DAN ROWAN; WILLIAM CONRAD; WILLIAM HOLDEN;
                RAY STEVENS
           Man of the Week Roast: BARRY GOLDWATER
           Roasters: William Conrad; Norm Crosby; Steve Landesberg;
                Carroll O'Connor; William Holden; Mark Russell;
                Zsa Zsa Gabor; Don Rice III; Dan Rowan
           Free To Carry On
           Y'all Come; Bumming Around; Things (With Ray)

11/2/73   ROAST OF JOHNNY CARSON
           Roasters: George Burns; Truman Capote; Doc Severinsen;
                Joey Bishop; Ruth Buzzi; Dom DeLuise; Bob Newhart;
                Fred De Cordova; Jonathan Winters; Foster Brooks;
                Dionne Warwick; Rich Little; Barry Goldwater;
                Bette Davis; Martin Milner; Kent McCord; Redd Foxx;
                Jack Benny; Mrs. Johnny Carson

11/9/73   AUDREY MEADOWS; GEORGE KENNEDY; FERLIN HUSKY;
       KEN BERRY
      Man of the Week Roast: WILT CHAMBERLAIN
      Roasters: Norm Crosby; Audrey Meadows; Ken Berry;
        Nipsey Russell; Bill Shoemaker; Vernon Scott;
        George Kennedy; Jackie Gayle
      Young At Heart
      Down By The Riverside; Houston; Ramblin' Rose (With Ferlin)
      Ev'ry Street's A Boulevard In Old New York; I'll Take Manhattan;
        Sidewalks Of New York; Lullaby Of Broadway;
        Easter Parade (With Ken)

11/23/73 ROAST OF HUBERT HUMPHREY
      Roasters: Pat Henry; Nipsey Russell; Gene Kelly; Leo Durocher;
        Audrey Meadows; Mort Sahl; Ted Knight; Mark Russell;
        Rich Little; Don Rice III; Foster Brooks

12/7/73   ROAST OF CARROLL O' CONNOR
      Roasters: Rowan and Martin; Marty Allen; Mike Connors;
        Norm Crosby; John Lindsay; Nipsey Russell; Gene Kelly;
        Joey Bishop; Robert Wood; William Conrad;
        William Holden; Donald O'Connor;
        Charles Nelson Reilly; Zsa Zsa Gabor; Ruth Buzzi;
        Barry Goldwater; Cass Elliott; Redd Foxx; Don Rickles;
        Foster Brooks

12/14/73 FOSTER BROOKS; GENE KELLY; DOUG DILLARD;
       TED KNIGHT; AUDREY MEADOWS
      Man of the Week Roast: MONTY HALL
      Roasters: Bert Parks; Audrey Meadows; Rocky Graziano; Donald
        O' Connor; Gene Kelly; Art Linkletter; Jack Carter
      Just Say I Love Her
      Nevertheless (With bar patrons)
      You Are My Sunshine; Honey; Born To Lose (With Gene)
      Birth Of The Blues; Singing The Blues; Blue Skies; Bye Bye Blues
        (With Gene)

12/21/73 RUTH BUZZI; DOUG KERSHAW; LORETTA LYNN;
       GARY BURGHOFF; MIKE CONNORS
      Men of the Week Roast: TONY RANDALL AND JACK KLUGMAN
      Roasters: Mike Connors; Loretta Lynn; Soupy Sales; Leonard Barr;
        Gary Burghoff; Ruth Buzzi; Jack Carter
      As Time Goes By
      Birth Of The Blues (With bar patrons)
      Detour; Turn The World Around (With Loretta and Doug)
      Standing On The Corner; Brush Up Your Shakespeare
        (With Gary and Mike)

1/11/74   FOSTER BROOKS; DONALD O' CONNOR;
                         CHARLES NELSON REILLY; BUDDY HACKETT;
                         MEL TILLIS; DONNA FARGO
Woman of the Week Roast: ZSA ZSA GABOR
Roasters: Donald O' Connor; Charles Nelson Reilly; Sue Cameron;
        Corbett Monica; Donna Fargo; Lonnie Shorr; Ruth Buzzi;
        Buddy Hackett
I've Grown Accustomed To Her Face
Is It True What They Say About Dixie;
        Way Down Yonder In New Orleans;
        Carolina In The Morning; Swanee (With Donald)
Along Came Jones (With Buddy, Charles and Donald)
Rainbows Are Back In Style; Make The World Go Away
        (With Donna and Mel)

1/18/74   CHUCK CONNORS; GLADYS KNIGHT AND THE PIPS;
                         ANDY AND DAVID WILLIAMS
Man of the Week Roast: LEO DUROCHER
Roasters: Maury Wills; Bobby Riggs; Dizzy Dean; Chuck Connors;
        Alex Karras; Jack Carter; Foster Brooks
I'm Sitting On Top Of The World
Small Exception Of Me
Take Me Home Country Roads; I Walk The Line
        (With Golddiggers)
Georgia Sunshine
You're Nobody 'Til Somebody Loves You (With Gladys)

1/25/74   JOHNNY RUSSELL; TED KNIGHT; ANNA MOFFO
Man of the Week Roast: TRUMAN CAPOTE
Roasters: Ted Knight; Audrey Meadows; Donald O' Connor;
        Rich Little; Joseph Wambaugh; Rocky Graziano;
        Jean Simmons; Foster Brooks
What's Yesterday
I Believe In Music; Tie A Yellow Ribbon (With Johnny)
It's Nice To Go Traveling; Say Si Si; I Love Paris;
        Lovely Conversation; On An Evening In Roma;
        Mad Dogs And Englishmen (With Anna)

2/8/74   ROAST OF DON RICKLES
Roasters: Joey Bishop; Phyllis Diller; Lorne Greene;
        Rowan and Martin; Casey Kasem; Bob Newhart;
        Carol Channing; Nipsey Russell; Cliff Robertson;
        Jack Klugman; Pat Henry; Kirk Douglas; Rich Little;
        Telly Savalas; Charlie Callas; Foster Brooks

2/15/74   STATLER BROTHERS; DONNA FARGO; JACK KLUGMAN;
RUTH BUZZI
Man of the Week Roast: RALPH NADER
Roasters: Jack Klugman; Jane Withers; Steve Landesberg;
       Mort Sahl; Donna Fargo; Rich Little; Ruth Buzzi;
       Jackie Gayle; Foster Brooks
C'est Si Bon
Happy Days Are Here Again (With bar patrons)
Cottonfields; Green, Green Grass Of Home;
       When You're Hot, You're Hot
       (With Donna and Statler Brothers)

2/22/74   ROAST OF JACK BENNY
Roasters: Joey Bishop; Florence Henderson; George Burns;
       Jimmy Stewart; Norm Crosby; Zuban Metah;
       Pearl Bailey; Dick Martin; Mark Spitz; Wayne Newton;
       Rich Little; Demond Wilson; Jack Carter; Foster Brooks

3/1/74   FOSTER BROOKS; JIM BAILEY; MICHELLE DELLA FAVE
Man of the Week Roast: REDD FOXX
Roasters: Norm Crosby; Slappy White; Audrey Meadows;
       Joey Bishop; John Barbour; Nipsey Russell;
       Jeannine Bernier; Rich Little; Demond Wilson;
       Jackie Gayle
It's The Talk Of The Town
Oh, You Beautiful Doll (With bar patrons)
(Open Up The Door) Let The Good Times In; Crying Time;
       Party Dolls And Wine (With Michelle)

3/6/74   FOSTER BROOKS; WAYNE NEWTON; LYNN ANDERSON;
VINCENT PRICE
Man of the Week Roast: BOBBY RIGGS
Roasters: Vincent Price; Leo Durocher; Lynn Anderson;
       Wayne Newton; Alex Karras; Don Rice III;
       Chuck Connors; Jack Carter
Turn The World Around
Get On With Your Livin'; Detroit City; Not Enough Indians
       (With Wayne and Lynn)
Alexander's Ragtime Band (With bar patrons)
Lazy River (With Wayne)
       (Note: Shown on Wednesday instead of Friday)

3/15/74   CONWAY TWITTY; LORETTA LYNN; DOUG KERSHAW;
MAC DAVIS
Man of the Week Roast: "GEORGE WASHINGTON"
       (Portrayed by Jan Leighton)
Roasters: Dick Martin; Audrey Meadows; Leonard Barr;
       Steve Lawrence; Corbett Monica; Nipsey Russell;
       Euell Gibbons; Henny Youngman; Jack Carter;
       Foster Brooks

For The Good Times
Lay Some Happiness On Me; Tips Of My Fingers
    (With Loretta and Conway)
I Believe In Music; Hey, Good Lookin'; Crying Time;
    King Of The Road; I Walk The Line; Blue, Blue Day;
    For The Good Times (With Mac)

3/22/74   STEVE LAWRENCE; BUCK OWENS; DORSEY BURNETTE
    Men of the Week Roast: ROWAN AND MARTIN
    Roasters: Joey Bishop; Audrey Meadows; Arte Johnson;
        Richard Dawson; Nipsey Russell; Steve Lawrence;
        Bob Newhart; Ruth Buzzi; Foster Brooks
    We've Got A Lot In Common; We Three; My Kind Of Town;
        L-O-V-E; Style; Act Naturally;
        She's A Little Bit Country (With Steve and Buck)
    I'd Like To Teach The World To Sing;
        By The Time I Get To Phoenix;
        We'll Sing In The Sunshine (With Dorsey)

3/29/74   JOEY BISHOP; LOU RAWLS; LYNN ANDERSON
    Man of the Week Roast: HANK AARON
    Roasters: Joey Bishop; Eddie Matthews; Audrey Meadows;
        Lou Rawls; Norm Crosby; Lynn Anderson;
        Nipsey Russell; Dizzy Dean; Jeannine Burnier;
        Rodney Allen Rippy; Foster Brooks
    It Had To Be You
    April Showers (With bar patrons)
    Bye Bye Love; That Old Time Feeling; One Cup Of Happiness
    (With Lou)

4/5/74   ROAST OF JOE NAMATH
    Roasters: Joey Bishop; Bear Bryant; Slappy White; Dick Butkus;
        Corbett Monica; Angie Dickinson; Charlie Callas;
        David Janssen; Nipsey Russell; Jim Plunkett;
        Audrey Meadows; Don Meredith; Rich Little;
        Bishop Fulton J. Sheen; Jack Carter; Foster Brooks;
        Weeb Eubank

MISC. TELEVISION APPEARANCES

6/20/48   TOAST OF THE TOWN

8/3/48   TEXACO STAR THEATER

10/3/48   WELCOME ABOARD

10/10/48   WELCOME ABOARD

10/17/48   WELCOME ABOARD
            You Won't Be Satisfied
            San Fernando Valley (Comedy with Jerry on drums)
                    (Earliest surviving television appearance)

6/25/49   TV SCREEN MAGAZINE
                    (Dean only)

10/18/49   TEXACO STAR THEATER
            Darktown Strutter's Ball
            Shine On Harvest Moon
                    (Comedy as Jerry and Milton Berle "conduct" the orchestra)

4/15/50   SATURDAY NIGHT REVIEW WITH JACK CARTER

5/23/50   TEXACO STAR THEATER
            I Don't Care If The Sun Don't Shine

5/30/50   BROADWAY OPEN HOUSE

6/10/50   SHOW OF THE YEAR (CEREBRAL PALSY)

6/13/50   TEXACO STAR THEATER
            I Wonder Who's Kissing Her Now
            Too Ra Loo Ra Loo Ra (Crosby and Fitzgerald routine with Jerry)

12/12/50   TEXACO STAR THEATER
                    Dean (in a solo outing) appears in a sketch with
                    Milton Berle.

5/6/51   COLGATE COMEDY SHOW
            Someday
            Oh Marie (Comedy)

6/8/51   WE THE PEOPLE
                    Cameo

6/9/51   DAMON RUNYON MEMORIAL FUND TELETHON WITH
                    MILTON BERLE

3/14-15/52 NEW YORK CARDIAC HOSPITAL TELETHON FOR
                    MUSCULAR DYSTROPHY
            My Heart Has Found A Home Now

6/21/52   HOPE/CROSBY TELETHON FOR OLYMPIC COMMITTEE
            When You're Smiling

340

3/22/53	COLGATE COMEDY SHOW Alone
11/1/53	COLGATE COMEDY SHOW I Love Paris You're Just In Love; My Heart Cries For You (Parody with Jerry)
11/25/53	THANKSGIVING PARTY FOR MUSCULAR DYSTROPHY That's Amore You Alone Once In A While (Comedy) Christmas Blues (with Sammy Cahn on piano) I Don't Care If The Sun Don't Shine It's The Talk Of The Town (Comedy) There's No Tomorrow
1/17/54	COLGATE COMEDY SHOW (Remote from Bing Crosby's Pebble Beach Golf Tournament) Dean duets with Phil Harris
1/24/54	WHAT'S MY LINE Dean and Jerry as "mystery" guests
3/25/54	ACADEMY AWARDS That's Amore
5/23/54	JACK BENNY Cameo
7/2/54	PERSON TO PERSON Interview
7/15/54	TODAY SHOW Telecast from Atlantic City, NJ
9/29/54	*A STAR IS BORN* PREMIERE Dean is interviewed at the opening of this Judy Garland flick.
11/21/54	COLGATE COMEDY HOUR Cameo (MDA appeal)
12/17/54	TODAY SHOW My Blue Heaven White Christmas (With entire cast)

3/30/55   ACADEMY AWARDS
              Three Coins In The Fountain

4/4-8/55   SHEILAH GRAHAM SHOW
                    Week-long interview segments

6/12/55   MONITOR
                    Film clip of *You're Never Too Young* is shown

9/27/55   MILTON BERLE
                    Cameo
                         (Note: This was Dean and Jerry's first color
                         television appearance.)

10/16/55   COLGATE COMEDY SHOW
              Some Enchanted Evening

11/11/55   TONIGHT SHOW
              Almost Like Being In Love

12/20/55   MILTON BERLE
              Memories Are Made Of This
                         (Jerry presents Dean with the gold record award for
                              Memories Are Made Of This.)

3/21/56   ACADEMY AWARDS
              Tender Trap

4/10/56   DINAH SHORE CHEVY SHOW
                         (Note: This was a solo appearance by Dean.)
              Innamorata
              Let's Call the Whole Thing Off (Parody with Dinah)
              You Made Me Love You (With Dinah)
              Makin' Whoopee (Parody with Goward Champion)

6/6/56   THIS IS YOUR LIFE - MILTON BERLE
                    Guest

6/26/56   TODAY SHOW
              Embraceable You

6/29-30/56   21-HOUR MUSCULAR DYSTROPHY TELETHON FROM
                    CARNEGIE HALL (WABD-TV; Dumont Network)
                         Hosts

11/2/56   JUKEBOX JURY
       Panelist

1/28/57   TONIGHT! AMERICA AFTER DARK
       Interview

4/19/57   DINAH SHORE
       Only Trust Your Heart
       Yes Sir, That's My Baby (With Dinah)
       Let's Take The Long Way Home (With Dinah)
       When Rock and Roll Came To Trinidad
          (With Dinah, Joey Bishop, Hugh O'Brien and Sally Forrest)

5/21/57   TONIGHT! AMERICA AFTER DARK
       Dean assists in interviews.

5/25/57   PERRY COMO
       Cameo

5/25-26/57 CITY OF HOPE TELETHON (WABD-TV)
       Host

5/26/57   STEVE ALLEN

6/30/57   STEVE ALLEN
       Beau James (Lip-Synch)

10/5/57   DEAN MARTIN SHOW
       Guests: JAMES MASON; LOUIS PRIMA; KEELY SMITH;
          JOEL GREY
       Promise Her Anything
       Just In Time
       When You're Smiling
       It's Easy To Remember
       Medley: Once In A While; I Don't Know Why; Embraceable You
       Oh Marie (With Louis Prima)
       Baby Won't You Please Come Home (With Keely Smith)

11/9/57   PERRY COMO
       Oh Marie (With Perry)
          Split-screen effect with Dean in Hollywood and Perry in
          New York.

11/9/57   CLUB OASIS
       Guests: GISELE MacKENZIE; EDGAR BERGEN
       Makin' Love Ukelele Style

All The Way

Medley: I'm Gonna Sit Right Down And Write Myself A Letter; It's Alright With Me; Walking My Baby Back Home (With Gisele)

11/17/57   GENERAL MOTORS 50TH ANNIVERSARY
Dean was scheduled to perform a medley with Doretta Morrow and Howard Keel but canceled due to minor surgery.

11/29/57   FRANK SINATRA
They Didn't Believe Me
In a medley with Frank, Dean sings parts of the following: On A Slow Boat To China; Memories Are Made Of This; Innamorata; Oh Marie; and Don't Cry Joe

1/4/58   CLUB OASIS
Guests: EDIE ADAMS; COLLINS KIDS; BARBARA HELLER

1/12/58   BING CROSBY AND HIS FRIENDS
Cameo

2/1/58   DEAN MARTIN SHOW
Guests: FRANK SINATRA; DANNY THOMAS; BARBARA PERRY
It Was Much Better Last Week (With Frank and Danny)
I Love To Love (With Frank)
Forgetting You
When You're Smiling (Excerpt)
All Alone (Excerpt)
In a medley of Academy Award-nominated songs with Frank and Danny, Dean sings excerpts of That's Amore; April Love; Tammy (With Danny); Jailhouse Rock (Parody with Frank and Danny)

2/7/58   PERSON TO PERSON
Interview

2/24/58   MAKE ROOM FOR DADDY - "TERRY'S CRUSH"
I Don't Know Why

3/15/58   CLUB OASIS
Guests: PHIL HARRIS; SAMMY CAHN; JIMMY VAN HEUSEN
Return To Me
I Can't Give You Anything But Love
I Remember It Well (With Kathy Barr)
St. Patrick's Day Salute
Well, Did'Ya Ever (With Phil)

344

3/26/58	30TH ANNUAL ACADEMY AWARDS All The Way
4/12/58	CLUB OASIS Guest: EDDIE FISHER
5/24/58	PERRY COMO Return To Me (With Perry)

5/24-25/58	PARADE OF STARS (WABD-TV)
	DEAN MARTIN BLOOD DISEASE RESEARCH CENTER AT
	    THE CITY OF HOPE 19-HOUR TELETHON
	        Host

9/30/58	EDDIE FISHER Dean surprises Eddie's guest, Jerry Lewis.

10/1/58   BING CROSBY
Well Did'Ya Ever (With Bing and Patti Page)
True Love (With Bing and Patti Page)
Once Upon A Time
Medley With Bing: Come Back To Sorrento; Oh Marie; O Solo Mio
Medley With Bing: In A Little Spanish Town; Swinging On A Star;
        I Only Have Eyes For You; Life Is Just A Bowl Of Cherries
        (With Bing and Patti)
Grace and Swing Parodies
My Good Fortune (With Bing and Patti)
When The Saints Go Marching In (With Bing and Mahalia Jackson)

11/22/58   DEAN MARTIN SHOW
Guests: BING CROSBY; PHIL HARRIS; TRENIERS
Volare (Parody with Bing and Phil)
Guys and Dolls (With Phil)
Just In Time
Medley: What'll I Do; All By Myself; All Alone
Medley with Bing: Songs include I Surrender Dear;
        Just One More Chance; May I; Learn To Croon; Please;
        Thanks; June In January; Love In Bloom; Love Is Just
        Around The Corner; Love Thy Neighbor; Soon; It's Easy
        To Remember, etc.
I'm Gonna Sit Right Down And Write Myself A Letter
        (With Treniers)
Now You Has Jazz (With Bing)
They Didn't Believe Me (With Treniers)

12/12/58   PHIL SILVERS SHOW - "BILKO'S SECRET MISSION"
        Cameo

12/19/58	JUKEBOX JURY
	Panelist (Dean's son Craig is also a panelist.)

2/6/59 PHIL HARRIS
I Could Have Danced All Night
Blues Were Born In New Orleans (With Phil)
Medley with Phil, Alice Faye and Betty Hutton

3/2/59 BING CROSBY
It's Easy To Remember (With Bing)

3/19/59 DEAN MARTIN SHOW
Guests: DONALD O' CONNOR; GISELE MACKENZIE
Pennies From Heaven
I Won't Dance
Let's Do It (With Gisele)
You're The Top (With Donald)

4/6/59 ACADEMY AWARDS
Dean presents the "Best Song" award with Sophia Loren.

5/3/59 DEAN MARTIN SHOW
Guests: BOB HOPE; MAE WEST
I Can't Give You Anything But Love (With Mae)
Personality (With Mae and Bob)
Medley of Hope movie songs (With Bob and Mae)
Sleep Warm
Protection (With Bob)
Almost Like Being In Love

10/8/59 BOB HOPE
On An Evening In Roma
Together (With Bob, Natalie Wood and the Crosby Brothers)
Life Is Just A Bowl Of Pizza (Parody with Bob)

10/19/59 FRANK SINATRA
High Hopes (Parody lyrics with Bing Crosby and Mitzi Gaynor)
Together (With Frank and Bing)
Cheek To Cheek (With Bing and Mitzi)
Wrap Your Troubles In Dreams
In a medley with Frank and Bing, Dean sings excerpts of the
following: Those Good Old Songs;
In the Shade Of The Old Apple Tree; Rocking Chair;
You're An Old Smoothie; Ol' Man River;
Start Off Each Day With A Song; Inka Dinka Doo

Won't You Come Home Bill Bailey
     (With Frank, Bing, Mitzi and Jimmy Durante)

11/3/59   DEAN MARTIN SHOW
     Guests: FRANK SINATRA; MICKEY ROONEY
     Mack The Knife
     Dream
     Rodgers and Hart Medley includes: Lover; Where Or When;
                I Didn't Know What Time It Was; This Can't Be Love;
                There's A Small Hotel; Blue Moon;
                The Most Beautiful Girl In The World;
                It's Easy To Remember; Mountain Greenery;
                Lady Is A Tramp; We'll Take Manhattan (With Frank)
     It's Jubilee Time and excerpts of Hallelujah;
                It's Gonna Be A Great Day; September Song;
                Sunny Side Up; Fine and Dandy; I'll Never Smile Again;
                There's No Business Like Show Business;
                When You're Smiling (With Frank and Mickey)
     How About You (With Frank and Mickey)

1/12/60   DEAN MARTIN SHOW
     Guests: FABIAN; ANDRE PREVIN; NANETTE FABRAY
     Dino's Back In Town
     June In January
     Who Was That Lady (With Andre Previn)
     But Yours (With Nanette Fabray)
     I Love To Love (With Fabian)
     Question and Answer Medley (With Nanette and Fabian)

11/1/60   DEAN MARTIN SHOW
     Guests: FRANK SINATRA; DOROTHY PROVINE;
                DON KNOTTS; DAVID ROSE
     I Get A Kick Out Of You
     Where Or When
     All Or Nothing At All
     In The Cool, Cool, Cool Of The Evening (With Dorothy Provine)
     Medley With Frank: Three Coins In The Fountain; Young At Heart;
                I Love Paris; South Of The Border; Learning The Blues;
                Nice 'N' Easy; I've Got You Under My Skin;
                Love And Marriage; Makin' Whoopee;
                I've Got The World On A String; Well Did'Ya Ever

1960   CELEBRITY GOLF
     Dean plays nine holes with golfing legend Sam Snead at
     the Lakeside Country Club. Martin, playing with an "8"
     handicap, loses to Snead by one stroke.

347

2/15/61   BOB HOPE SPORTS AWARD SHOW
              Dean presents golf award to Arnold Palmer

4/25/61   DEAN MARTIN SHOW
              Guests: ANDY GRIFFITH; TONY MARTIN; TINA LOUISE
              You Can't Love 'Em All
              Just In Time
              Rockabye Your Baby With A Dixie Melody
              They Didn't Believe Me
              I Know Someone (With Tina)
              Lazy River (With Andy and Tony)

9/17/61   DUPONT SHOW OF THE WEEK - LAUGHTER U.S.A.
              Clip

11/3/61   DINAH SHORE
              My Kind Of Girl
              I've Grown Accustomed To Her Face
              Two Sleepy People; Why Don't We Do This More Often
                     (With Dinah and Donald O'Connor)
              Smile; Happy Medley (With Dinah)

2/25/62   JUDY GARLAND
              You Do Something To Me (With Frank Sinatra and Judy Garland)
              You Must Have Been A Beautiful Baby
              The One I Love Belongs To Somebody Else (With Frank Sinatra)
              Let There Be Love; You're Nobody 'Til Somebody Loves You
                     (With Frank Sinatra and Judy Garland)

11/11/62   DINAH SHORE
              Just In Time
              From The Bottom Of My Heart
              I Left My Heart In San Francisco
              I'll Remember You; Them There Eyes; Ain't We Got Fun
                     (Comedy with Dinah)
              When I Take My Sugar To Tea (With Stephen Boyd)
              Cuddle Up A Little Closer (Brief; with Stephen)
              Who Takes Care Of The Caretaker's Daughter (With Stephen)
              Consider Yourself (With Dinah and Stephen)

Late 1962   HOLLYWOOD FILM REPORT
              Dean is shown on the set of *Toys In The Attic*

1/4/63	ONCE UPON A DIME: 25TH ANNIVERSARY OF THE MARCH OF DIMES

        (Dean appears with Bing Crosby in this show which originated from KTTV in Los Angeles. It was syndicated throughout the week. Local airdates may vary.)

2/23/63   DICK POWELL THEATER - "TISSUE OF HATE"
        Guest host

4/14/63   BOB HOPE
        Face In A Crowd

9/27/63   BOB HOPE
        Via Venetto

12/8/63   BEST ON RECORD
        Dean introduces Connie Francis

12/16/63   HOLLYWOOD AND THE STARS - "THE FUNNY MEN"
        It's Magic
        (1951 Martin and Lewis clip from Photoplay Awards)

2/13/64   PERRY COMO
        Hello Dolly (With Perry and Lena Horne)
        That's Amore; When You Were Sweet 16; Love Is The Reason; Guys and Dolls (With Perry and Lena)
        They Didn't Believe Me
        On A Slow Boat To China
        Melancholy Baby
        Why Did I Leave Ohio; Sentimental Journey (With Perry)

2/15/64   BING CROSBY
        Oldest Established Permanent Floating Crap Game In New York (With Frank Sinatra and Bing Crosby)

2/16/64   CBS SPORTS SPECTACULAR
        Celebrity tennis matches taped in the spring of 1963 at Dean's Beverly Hills home; they were charity events to benefit handicapped children. Dean and Pancho Gonzalez opposed Pancho Segura and Rod Taylor. Phil Silvers refereed the tournament.

3/7/64   HOLLYWOOD PALACE
        Volare; On An Evening In Roma
        Nevertheless; It Had To Be You; You Made Me Love You
        That's Amore (With Piccolo Pupa)

3/20/64   INSIDE THE MOVIE KINGDOM

6/13/64   HOLLYWOOD PALACE
               Everybody Loves Somebody
               Smile
               Take These Chains From My Heart

9/25/64   BOB HOPE
               Door Is Still Open To My Heart
               Everybody Loves Somebody
                       (Note: Bob presents Dean with the gold record for
                       Everybody Loves Somebody)

10/30/64   RAWHIDE - "CANLISS"
                       Dean has the lead dramatic role in this episode.

11/26/64   YOUR ALL-TIME FAVORITE SONGS
               Dean sings excerpts of the following:
               Ol' Man River
               Some Enchanted Evening
               Moon River
               Blue Moon
               That's Amore
               Begin The Beguine
               I Left My Heart In San Francisco
               Sentimental Journey
               Tonight
               Night and Day
               Tea For Two
               Always
               As Time Goes By

1/7/65   PERRY COMO
               Lullaby Medley (With Perry and Carol Lawrence)
                       Dean sings Moonshine Lullaby; Hit The Road To
                       Dreamland; Peace and Quiet
               That's Amore
               You're Nobody 'Til Somebody Loves You
               Everybody Loves Somebody (With Perry and Carol)

3/14/65   DANNY THOMAS' WONDERFUL WORLD OF BURLESQUE
                       Cameo

5/18/65   BEST ON RECORD
                       Host

350

6/20/65	FRANK SINATRA SPECTACULAR

(Closed-circuit broadcast from the Kiel Opera House in St. Louis, Missouri. With FRANK SINATRA; SAMMY DAVIS, JR.; TRINI LOPEZ; KAYE STEVENS; THE STEP BROTHERS; COUNT BASIE & HIS ORCHESTRA. Master of Ceremonies: JOHNNY CARSON)
Send Me The Pillow You Dream On
King Of The Road
Everybody Loves Somebody
Volare/On An Evening In Roma
You're Nobody 'Til Somebody Loves You
Birth Of The Blues (With Frank, Sammy, Johnny)

10/4/65	TONIGHT SHOW

(With Frank Sinatra; Joey Bishop is the guest host)

11/16/65	SINATRA-AN AMERICAN ORIGINAL

Clips from the Dismas House concert are shown.

1/7/66	SAMMY DAVIS, JR. SHOW

Cameo

1/31/66	GOLDEN GLOBE AWARDS

Dean presents Cecil B. DeMille Award to John Wayne

2/14/66	LUCY SHOW - "LUCY DATES DEAN MARTIN"

Everybody Loves Somebody

6/16/66	DEAN MARTIN SUMMER SHOW

Introduces premiere show

12/2/66	PAT BOONE

12/11/66	WONDERFUL WORLD OF BURLESQUE II

Cameo

1/18/67	BARRUMP BUMP SHOW

Cameo

2/15/67	GOLDEN GLOBE AWARDS

Receives award for "Most Popular Male TV Personality"

4/10/67	ACADEMY AWARDS

Dean presents the award for "Best Song" and mispronounces "Georgy Girl" as "GREGORY Girl."

12/11/67   MOVIN' WITH NANCY
Bumming Around (Lip-Synch without the backing vocal choir)
Things (Lip-Synch with Nancy)

3/20/68   JACK BENNY'S CARNIVAL NIGHTS
Cameo

9/25/68   BOB HOPE
Cameo

2/21/69   TONIGHT SHOW
Classic appearance with Bob Hope and George Gobel

2/23/69   HERE COME THE STARS
Dean appears on this George Jessel-hosted roast of
Sid Caesar.

8/19/69   TONIGHT SHOW
Guest

10/1/69   TONIGHT SHOW 7TH ANNIVERSARY
Clip from 2/21/69

11/24/69   TONIGHT SHOW
Cameo

12/6/69   ANN-MARGRET - "FROM HOLLYWOOD WITH LOVE"
Medley: Let It Be Me; It Just Happened That Way;
Little Green Apples; I Really Don't Want To Know;
Sleep In the Grass (Voice Over) (With Ann-Margret)

12/18/69   BOB HOPE
Cameo

1970   TELEVISION AD FOR 'DINO' BRAND GOLF BALLS

1/14/70   ROWAN AND MARTIN BITE THE HAND THAT FEEDS THEM
Cameo

2/3/70   DEBBIE REYNOLDS - "NOTHING BUT THE TRUTH"
Cameo

4/13/70   BING CROSBY - "COOLIN' IT"
Medley: Breezin' Along With The Breeze; Bidin' My Time;
Lazy River; Enjoy Yourself (With Bing)

9/21/70	**RED SKELTON** Dean "introduced" the show.
11/5/70	**FLIP WILSON** Cameo
11/15/70	**GLEN CAMPBELL** (Open Up The Door) Let The Good Times In; Lay Some Happiness On Me; Things; Old Yellow Line; I Walk The Line (With Glen)
11/16/70	**JACK BENNY** Cameo
11/29/70	**JOHN WAYNE - SWING OUT SWEET LAND** Dean appears as Eli Whitney
12/9/70	**PETULA CLARK** I Don't Know Why (With Petula) Medley: Hey, Good Lookin'; Detour; Things; I Walk The Line; Just A Little Lovin' (With Petula)
12/12/70	**CAROL BURNETT** Dean made a cameo appearance in a skit satirizing "Sesame Street" as an "adult" program.
2/11/71	**TONIGHT SHOW** Guest
5/31/71	**MERV GRIFFIN** Guest on a program saluting filmmaker Andrew V. McLaglen
8/17/71	**TONIGHT SHOW** Cameo
8/26/71	**DEAN MARTIN PRESENTS SNEAK PREVIEW** Dean introduces two half-hour pilots that didn't sell. "Powder Room" stars Jack Cassidy, Joey Heatherton, Jeannine Burnier and Elaine Stritch. "What's Up" was hosted by Jackie Cooper and featured Tom Bosley, Phil Leeds and Marian Mercer.
10/5/71	**GLEN CAMPBELL** Cameo

1/22-23/72   DEAN MARTIN TUCSON GOLF

10/2/72   TONIGHT SHOW 10TH ANNIVERSARY
        Pre-taped appearance.

1/18/73   JACK BENNY'S FIRST FAREWELL SPECIAL
        S'posin

1/20-21/73   DEAN MARTIN TUCSON GOLF

9/6/73   DEAN MARTIN MUSIC COUNTRY
        Cameo

10/2/73   TONIGHT SHOW
        Guest

1/19-20/74   DEAN MARTIN TUCSON GOLF

1/21/74   JACK BENNY'S SECOND FAREWELL SPECIAL
        Cameo

2/7/74   MUSIC COUNTRY U. S. A.
        Turn The World Around

2/14/74   MUSIC COUNTRY U. S. A.
        For The Good Times

10/1/74   TONIGHT SHOW 12TH ANNIVERSARY

10/21/74   ROAST OF BOB HOPE
        Roasters: Flip Wilson; Ronald Reagan; John Wayne; Foster Brooks;
              Jimmy Stewart; Milton Berle; Billy Graham; Rich Little;
              Howard Cosell; Jack Benny; Zsa Zsa Gabor;
              Nipsey Russell; General Omar Bradley; Phyllis Diller;
              Neil Armstrong; Henry Kissinger; Don Rickles;
              Dolores Hope

11/15/74   ROAST OF TELLY SAVALAS
        Roasters: Phyllis Diller; Howard Cosell; George Kennedy;
              Dom DeLuise; Peter Graves; Shelley Winters;
              Ernest Borgnine; Rowan and Martin; Foster Brooks;
              Richard Roundtree; Robert Stack; Nipsey Russell;
              Rich Little; Angie Dickinson; Don Rickles

12/15/74   BOB HOPE
        Marshmallow World

1/18-19/75   DEAN MARTIN TUCSON GOLF

1/19/75   DON RICKLES
              Dean appears in "roast" skit.

2/7/75   ROAST OF LUCILLE BALL
              Roasters: Phyllis Diller; Rowan and Martin; Ruth Buzzi;
                  Bob Hope; Milton Berle; Gary Morton; Gale Gordon;
                  Totie Fields; Rich Little; Henry Fonda; Ginger Rogers;
                  Foster Brooks; Nipsey Russell; Jack Benny; Vivian Vance;
                  Don Rickles

2/8/75   BOB HOPE DESERT CLASSIC GOLF TOURNAMENT

2/27/75   ROAST OF JACKIE GLEASON
              Roasters: Phyllis Diller; Milton Berle; Danny Thomas;
                  Audrey Meadows; Gene Kelly; Nipsey Russell;
                  Sid Caesar; Sheila MacRae; Art Carney; Frank Gorshin;
                  Foster Brooks

3/1/75   LUCILLE BALL
              Everybody Loves Somebody
              Tie A Yellow Ribbon

4/8/75   CAVALCADE OF CHAMPIONS AWARDS
              Dean presents the golf award.

4/24/75   ROAST OF SAMMY DAVIS JR.
              Roasters: Milton Berle; Wilt Chamberlain; Freddie Prinze;
                  Norm Crosby; Dionne Warwick; Joey Bishop;
                  Nipsey Russell; Phyllis Diller; Jan Murray;
                  Frank Gorshin; Foster Brooks; Don Rickles;
                  Altovise Davis

5/15/75   ROAST OF MICHAEL LANDON
              Roasters: Phyllis Diller; Ernest Borgnine; Joey Bishop;
                  Norm Crosby; Euell Gibbons; Guy Marks; Jan Murray;
                  Cliff Robertson; Lorne Greene;Sid Caesar; Amanda Blake;
                  Victor Sen-Yung; Don Rickles

9/6/75   DEAN'S PLACE
              Guests: FOSTER BROOKS; JACK CASSIDY;
                  RONALD AND NANCY REAGAN; GEORGIA ENGEL;
                  SHERMAN HEMSLEY; ISABEL SANFORD;
                  ROBERT MITCHUM; VINCENT GARDENIA;
                  JESSI COLTER; ANGIE DICKINSON;
                  KELLY MONTEITH; THE UNTOUCHABLES
              Bad, Bad Leroy Brown

I've Grown Accustomed To Her Face
A Couple of Song and Dance Men; Lullaby of Broadway;
>Just One Of Those Things (With Sherman Hemsley)

10/1/75 JOHNNY CARSON
>Johnny's thirteenth anniversary show. The classic clip
>with Dean, Bob Hope and George Gobel was shown.

10/24/75 HIGHLIGHTS OF A QUARTER CENTURY OF
>BOB HOPE SPECIALS
>Clip

11/10/75 ROAST OF EVEL KNIEVEL
>Roasters: Gabe Kaplan; Isabel Sanford; Ernest Borgnine;
>Milton Berle; William Conrad; Barry Goldwater;
>Glen Campbell; Georgia Engel; Jackie Cooper;
>Nipsey Russell; Dr. Joyce Brothers; Charlie Callas;
>Cliff Robertson; McLean Stevenson; Ruth Buzzi;
>Don Rickles

11/12/75 DINAH!
>Pre-taped tribute to Bing Crosby (Recorded 10/14/75)

11/20/75 ROAST OF VALERIE HARPER
>Roasters: Rich Little; Isabel Sanford; David Groh; Red Buttons;
>Phyllis Diller; Jack Albertson; Shelley Winters;
>Milton Berle; Ed Asner; Jamie Farr; Eva Gabor;
>Chad Everett; Julie Kavner; Nipsey Russell;
>Georgia Engel; Foster Brooks; Jack Carter

12/12/75 TONIGHT SHOW
>Interview regarding Dean's Christmas special.

12/14/75 CHRISTMAS IN CALIFORNIA
>Guests: DIONNE WARWICK; MICHAEL LEARNED;
>FREDDY FENDER; STATLER BROTHERS;
>GEORGIA ENGEL
It's A Bicycle Morning (With Golddiggers)
I'm Sitting On Top Of The World
How About You (With Dionne)
Welcome To My World
Marshmallow World
Sound of Music (With All)
Raindrops Keep Falling On My Head (Voice Over)
I'm Old Fashioned (With Michael Learned)
Bumming Around
A Word A Day (With Georgia Engel)
White Christmas

1/13/76 DEAN'S PLACE
    Guests: THE UNTOUCHABLES; FOSTER BROOKS;
       ED BLUESTONE; PETER AND CLAUDIA GRAVES;
       VINCENT GARDENIA; JACK CASSIDY;
       FREDDY FENDER; KELLY MONTEITH;
       THE COMMITTEE; JESSI COLTER;
       MIKE PREMINGER
    Tie A Yellow Ribbon
    Young At Heart
    South of the Border; It Happened In Monterey;
       In A Little Spanish Town (With Freddy Fender)

2/19/76 ROAST OF MUHAMMAD ALI
    Roasters: Freddie Prinze; Gabe Kaplan; Red Buttons;
       Tony Orlando; Charlie Callas; Wilt Chamberlain;
       Georgia Engel; Billy Crystal; Floyd Patterson;
       Howard Cosell; Ruth Buzzi; Gene Kelly; Isabel Sanford;
       Sherman Hemsley; Rocky Graziano; Foster Brooks;
       Orson Welles; Nipsey Russell

2/27/76 ROAST OF DEAN MARTIN
    Roasters: Don Rickles; Orson Welles; Paul Lynde; Joe Namath;
       Barry Goldwater; Angie Dickinson; Muhammad Ali;
       Jimmy Stewart; Gabe Kaplan; Gene Kelly;
       Hubert Humphrey; Charlie Callas; John Wayne;
       Freddie Prinze; Milton Berle; Phyllis Diller; Peter Graves;
       Dom DeLuise; Monty Hall; Ernest Borgnine;
       Jack Klugman; Tony Randall; Bob Hope; Michael Landon;
       Jan Murray; Totie Fields; William Conrad; Evel Knievel;
       Jackie Gleason; Danny Thomas; Art Carney; Joey Bishop;
       Rich Little; Ruth Buzzi; Tony Orlando; Georgia Engel;
       Nipsey Russell; Foster Brooks; Howard Cosell;
       Rowan and Martin

3/5/76 BOB HOPE SPECIAL - "JOYS"
    Cameo

3/18/76 MAC DAVIS
    Medley With Mac: Yankee Doodle; You're A Grand Old Flag;
       That's America To Me; This Land Is Your Land;
       That's Amore; Everybody Loves Somebody

4/27/76 ROAST OF DENNIS WEAVER
    Roasters: William Conrad; Shelley Winters; Steve Forrest;
       Red Buttons; Rich Little; Mike Connors; Milburn Stone;
       Ruth Buzzi; Nipsey Russell; Zsa Zsa Gabor;
       Georgia Engel; Amanda Blake; Peter Graves;
       Foster Brooks; Milton Berle

5/25/76   ROAST OF JOE GARAGIOLA
Roasters: Jack Carter; Mickey Mantle; Orson Welles;
        Charlie Callas; Pat Henry; Hank Aaron; Yogi Berra;
        Shirley Jones; Charlie Finley; Norm Crosby; Luis Tiant;
        Jackie Gayle; Stan Musial; Nipsey Russell; Willie Mays;
        Foster Brooks; Red Buttons; Maury Wills; Gabe Kaplan

9/6/76   MDA TELETHON
Medley with Frank Sinatra: I Can't Give You Anything But Love;
        Too Marvelous For Words; Pennies From Heaven;
        A Foggy Day; Embraceable You; Lady Is A Tramp;
        Where Or When; All Of Me; When You're Smiling

10/29/76   BOB HOPE'S WORLD OF COMEDY
        Clip

11/8/76   RED-HOT SCANDALS OF 1926
Guests: JONATHAN WINTERS; DOM DeLUISE; ABE VIGODA;
        HERMIONE BADDELEY; GEORGIA ENGEL;
        CHARLENE RYAN
It Had To Be You
I'm Sitting On Top Of The World
There's A Rainbow 'Round My Shoulder
Toot Toot Tootsie (With Golddiggers)
April Showers (With entire cast)
All I Do Is Dream Of You
He's A Ladies Man

11/21/76   NBC - THE FIRST 50 YEARS
        Dean introduces two segments on musical and comedy
        performers.

11/26/76   ROAST OF REDD FOXX
Roasters: Slappy White; Steve Allen; Milton Berle; LaWanda Page;
        George Kirby; Liz Torres; Abe Vigoda;
        Jimmie Walker; Orson Welles; Marty Allen;
        Isabel Sanford; Joe Garagiola; Nipsey Russell;
        Isaac Hayes; Don Rickles

11/28/76   CBS SALUTES LUCY - THE FIRST 25 YEARS
        Dean introduces clip of his appearance on the 2/14/66
        Lucy Show.

12/15/76   ROAST OF DANNY THOMAS
Roasters: Jimmie Walker; Charo; Red Buttons; Harvey Korman;
        Charlie Callas; Gene Kelly; Ruth Buzzi; Nipsey Russell;
        Dena Dietrich; Howard Cosell; Jan Murray; Don Knotts;
        Orson Welles; Lucille Ball; Milton Berle

Dean and producer/director Greg Garrison on the set of *NBC: The First 50 Years* (1976)
(NBC publicity photo)

1/21/77 BOB HOPE
      I've Grown Accustomed To Her Face
      Road To Lake Tahoe (Parody with Bob)

2/8/77   ROAST OF ANGIE DICKINSON
      Roasters: Jimmie Walker; Cindy Williams; Earl Holliman;
         Red Buttons; Jackie Mason; Jimmy Stewart; Joey Bishop;
         Scatman Crothers; LaWanda Page; Ruth Buzzi;
         Charlie Callas; Orson Welles; Foster Brooks; Rex Reed

2/21/77 ROAST OF GABE KAPLAN
      Roasters: Nipsey Russell; Liz Torres; Billy Crystal; Charo;
         Red Buttons; Jimmie Walker; Orson Welles;
         Howard Cosell; Johnny Bench; Ed Bluestone;
         Alice Ghostley; Joe Garagiola; Charlie Callas;
         Abe Vigoda; George Kirby; Milton Berle

3/2/77   ROAST OF TED KNIGHT
      Roasters: Jimmie Walker; Harvey Korman; Jackie Mason;
         Red Buttons; LaWanda Page; Paul Williams; Ed Asner;
         Foster Brooks; Jimmy Stewart; Scatman Crothers;
         Gavin MacLeod; Georgia Engel; Kelly Monteith;
         Orson Welles; Willie Tyler and Lester; Jack Carter;
         Julia McWhirter; Dr. Renee Richards

3/12/77 SHIRLEY MacLAINE - "WHERE DO WE GO FROM HERE"
      Cameo

4/4/77   RED-HOT SCANDALS OF 1926 PART II
      Guests: JONATHAN WINTERS; GEORGIA ENGEL;
         DOM DeLUISE; CHARLENE RYAN; ABE VIGODA;
         HERMIONE BADDELEY
      Ain't We Got Fun
      I Can't Give You Anything But Love
      Best Things In Life Are Free
      Now's The Time To Fall In Love
      Happy Days Are Here Again

4/21/77 SINATRA AND FRIENDS
      Oldest Established Permanent Floating Crap Game In New York
         (With Frank Sinatra and Robert Merrill)

4/25/77 PAUL ANKA - "MUSIC MY WAY"
      Parody of My Way with other celebrities.

5/2/77   ROAST OF PETER MARSHALL
Roasters: Joey Bishop; Rose Marie; Red Buttons; Zsa Zsa Gabor;
     Orson Welles; Rip Taylor; Vincent Price; Karen Valentine;
     Ed Bluestone; Foster Brooks; Jimmie Walker;
     Jackie Gayle; Wayland Flowers and Madam; Paul Lynde;
     Jack Carter

5/15/77   BILLION DOLLAR MOVIES
Clip

5/23/77   NEW YORK STATE LOTTERY DRAWING
Dean and Frank Sinatra select the winner.

10/23/77   NBC THE FIRST 50 YEARS - A CLOSER LOOK
Clip

10/28/77   BOB HOPE ON THE ROAD WITH BING
Clip

11/2/77   ROAST OF DAN HAGGERTY
Roasters: Rich Little; Ruth Buzzi; Orson Welles; Red Buttons;
     Jimmie Walker; Denver Pyle; Charlie Callas; Abe Vigoda;
     LaWanda Page; Foster Brooks; Marilyn Michaels;
     Jackie Gayle; Tom Dreesen

12/18/77   CHRISTMAS IN CALIFORNIA
Guests: LINDA LAVIN; CRYSTAL GAYLE; GABRIEL MELGAR;
     MIREILLE MATHIEU; JONATHAN WINTERS;
     GOLDDIGGERS
I'll Be Home For Christmas
Back In Your Own Backyard
Thank God I'm A Country Boy (With Linda and Crystal)
We Three; Tea For Three;
     No Three People Have Ever Been So In Love;
     Indian Love Call; Together (With Linda and Crystal)
She's A Little Bit Country
Don't Fence Me In (With Mireille Mathieu)
Funiculi, Funicula; Love Makes The World Go 'Round
     (With Linda, Crystal, Mireille, and Gabriel)
Almost Like Being In Love

2/7/78   ROAST OF FRANK SINATRA
Roasters: George Burns; Ronald Reagan; Dom DeLuise; Peter Falk;
     Jimmy Stewart; Flip Wilson; Ruth Buzzi; Milton Berle;
     Charlie Callas; Redd Foxx; Gene Kelly; Telly Savalas;
     LaWanda Page; Ernest Borgnine; Orson Welles;

Red Buttons; Jack Klugman; Jonathan Winters; Rich
Little; Jilly Rizzo; Don Rickles

3/17/78   ROAST OF JACK KLUGMAN
             Roasters: Milton Berle; Katherine Helmond; Dick Martin;
                        Red Buttons; Joey Bishop; LaWanda Page; Ruth Buzzi;
                        Robert Guillume; Kay Medford; Connie Stevens;
                        Tony Randall; Foster Brooks; Don Rickles

3/26/78   A TRIBUTE TO MR. TELEVISION, MILTON BERLE
                        Clip

5/8/78   STARS SALUTE ISRAEL AT 30

5/10/78   ROAST OF JIMMY STEWART
             Roasters: Milton Berle; Lucille Ball; Barry Goldwater; Ruth Buzzi;
                       June Allyson; Mickey Rooney; LaWanda Page;
                       Janet Leigh; Henry Fonda; George Burns; Greer Garson;
                       Foster Brooks; Eddie Albert; Red Buttons; Tony Randall;
                       Rich Little; Jessie White; Don Rickles; Orson Welles

5/17/78   ROAST OF GEORGE BURNS
             Roasters: Milton Berle; Abe Vigoda; Gene Kelly; Ruth Buzzi;
                       Jimmy Stewart; Dom DeLuise; LaWanda Page;
                       Phyllis Diller; Red Buttons; Orson Welles; Jack Carter;
                       Ronald Reagan; Charlie Callas; Connie Stevens;
                       Don Rickles; Tom Dreesen; Frank Welker

5/25/78   BING CROSBY - HIS LIFE AND LEGEND
                       Dean discusses Bing's influence on his career.

5/31/78   ROAST OF BETTY WHITE
             Roasters: Peter Marshall; Jimmie Walker; Bonnie Franklin;
                       Red Buttons; Orson Welles; Charlie Callas;
                       LaWanda Page; Phyllis Diller; Rich Little;
                       John Hillerman; Georgia Engel; Foster Brooks;
                       Dan Haggerty; Milton Berle; Allen Ludden

8/9/78   TONIGHT SHOW
                       Guest

9/7/78   NBC WELCOMES JOE NAMATH
                       AND THE "WAVERLY WONDERS"
                       Cameo

9/13/78   CHARLIE'S ANGELS - "ANGELS IN VEGAS"
          Dean stars as the owner of a Las Vegas casino in this
          third-season opener.

11/21/78 ROAST OF SUZANNE SOMMERS
          Roasters: Milton Berle; Lorne Greene; Dr. Joyce Brothers;
                    Norman Fell; Norm Crosby; Lee Meriwether;
                    Charlie Callas; Bernie Kopell; Red Buttons;
                    LaWanda Page; Paul Anka; Ruth Buzzi; Tom Bosley;
                    Audra Lindley; Rich Little; Jackie Gayle

12/9/78   CHRISTMAS IN CALIFORNIA
          Guests: LEE MERIWETHER; CONNIE STEVENS; MEL TILLIS;
                  JONATHAN WINTERS; GOLDDIGGERS
          Winter Wonderland
          Surrey With A Fringe On Top; Hit The Road To Dreamland
                  (With Connie Stevens)
          Real Live Girl (Voice Over)
          School Days; Farmer In The Dell; Mary Had A Little Lamb;
                  Baa Baa Black Sheep; A Tisket A Tasket (With Lee)
          Love Thy Neighbor
          My Kind Of Girl
          Bumming Around (With Mel Tillis)
          San Fernando Valley (With Mel Tillis)
          White Christmas

1/19/79   ROAST OF JOE NAMATH
          Roasters: Mel Tillis; Bruce Jenner; Milton Berle; Lee Meriwether;
                    Dick Butkus; Red Buttons; Norm Crosby; Bernie Kopell;
                    Joey Bishop; Orson Welles; Jackie Gayle;
                    Angie Dickinson; Ruth Buzzi; Jimmie Walker;
                    Charlie Callas; George Blanda; Rich Little

1/20/79   SUPERBOWL SATURDAY NIGHT
          Cameo

1/22/79   GEORGE BURNS' 100TH BIRTHDAY PARTY
          Cameo

4/9/79   ACADEMY AWARDS
          Dean presents the "Best Original Score" and
          "Best Adaptation Score" awards with Raquel Welch.

5/11/79   BEST OF DEAN
               Guests: Newly-taped segments from ORSON WELLES;
                     BOB NEWHART; DOM DeLUISE; GENE KELLY;
                     JIMMY STEWART; DON RICKLES and
                     DEAN MARTIN

9/25/79   MISADVENTURES OF SHERIFF LOBO -
                   "DEAN MARTIN AND THE MOONSHINERS"
                         Dean stars as himself in this episode.

9/26/79   VEGA$ - "USURPERS"
               Cameo

10/1/79   TONIGHT SHOW 17TH ANNIVERSARY
                     The classic clip with George Gobel is shown.

11/3/79   NBC NEWS
                     Reagan rally clip shown.

12/13/79   CHRISTMAS IN CALIFORNIA
               Guests: SHIRLEY JONES; DOM DeLUISE; RUTH BUZZI;
                     GOLDDIGGERS
               It's A Good Day
               Let It Snow, Let It Snow, Let It Snow (With Shirley Jones)
               Young At Heart (Voice Over)
               Love Makes The World Go 'Round (With Shirley Jones)
               Birds And The Bees
               White Christmas

1/3/80   SINATRA - THE FIRST 40 YEARS
                     Dean presents Sinatra with an honorary high school
                     diploma. They also waltz with each other!

1/13/80   CEREBRAL PALSY TELETHON
                     Dean and Paul Anka perform My Way with special
                     "telethon" lyrics.

1/31/80   20/20
                     Another Reagan rally clip is shown.

2/4/80   TODAY SHOW
                     Yet another Reagan rally clip is shown.

2/11/80   AMERICAN MOVIE AWARDS
                     Presenter

2/22/80   **TONIGHT SHOW**
                Guest

2/26/80   **HIGHLIGHTS OF THE DEAN MARTIN ROASTS**
                Features segments of the Bob Hope, Johnny Carson,
                Muhammad Ali, Jackie Gleason, Jack Benny,
                Michael Landon, Lucille Ball and Dean Martin roasts.
                Dean recorded new intros for the segments.

3/18/80   **BIG SHOW**
            I Could Write A Book; How About You (With Mariette Hartley)
            I Will (With Tanya Tucker)
            When You're Caught, You're Caught
                (With Mariette Hartley and Joe Namath)

5/1/80   **15TH ANNUAL ACADEMY OF COUNTRY MUSIC AWARDS**
                Clip

5/20/80   **MAC DAVIS**
                Clip from 1976 special

5/22/80   **SHIRLEY MacLAINE - "EVERY LITTLE MOVEMENT"**
            Ain't We Got Fun (With Shirley)

5/80   **DINAH AND FRIENDS**
                Interview

8/19/80   **MIKE DOUGLAS**
                Interview with Dean and Sammy Davis, Jr. on the set of
                Cannonball Run.

8/26/80   **NEWS REPORT ON DEAN AND FRANK SINATRA'S**
                SOFTBALL GAME (For the Lions Club of Absecon, PA)

9/30/80   **PRELUDE TO VICTORY**
            Where Or When
                Dean hosted this closed-circuit fund-raising dinner for
                Ronald Reagan.

10/7/80   **MEN WHO RATE A "10"**
                Clip

12/16/80   **CHRISTMAS SPECIAL**
            Guests: ERIK ESTRADA; ANDY GIBB; MEL TILLIS;
                BEVERLY SILLS
            It's a Most Unusual Day (With All)

Marshmallow World (With Beverly)
Como, Sinatra And Me (With Andy)
Country Medley (Dean sings excerpts of the following:)
       Hey, Good Lookin'; She's A Little Bit Country;
       Just A Little Lovin'; For The Good Times;
       Make The World Go Away;
       Take Me Home Country Roads
Raindrops Keep Falling On My Head (Voice Over)

1/5/81   LOVE LETTER TO JACK BENNY
              Clip

1/17-18/81   CEREBRAL PALSY TELETHON
              Dean "plugs" the telethon from his home and a repeat of
              last year's My Way duet with Paul Anka is shown.

1/18/81   BOB HOPE'S 30TH ANNIVERSARY SPECIAL
              Clip

2/26/81   THIS IS YOUR LIFE 30TH ANNIVERSARY SPECIAL
              Clip

5/12/81   COMEDY CLASSICS
              Guests: Newly-taped segments from: ORSON WELLES;
              FRANK SINATRA; DOM DeLUISE; BOB NEWHART
              and DEAN MARTIN

5/14/81   LADIES AND GENTLEMEN, BOB NEWHART PART II
              Dean appears in a skit.

5/15/81   TV'S CENSORED BLOOPERS
              Clip

9/13/81   33RD ANNUAL EMMY AWARDS
              Clip

1981   PORTRAIT OF A LEGEND (Interview taped 6/1/81)
              Syndicated half-hour retrospective of Dean's career hosted
              by James Darren.

12/10/81   CHRISTMAS AT SEA WORLD
              Guests: BUCK OWENS; LYNN ANDERSON;
                    CHARLIE CALLAS; T. G. SHEPPARD; SYLVIA
              I'm Forever Blowing Bubbles (Lip Synch)
              I Take A Lot Of Pride In What I Am (Lip Synch)
              Raindrops Keep Falling On My Head (Voice Over)

Bumming Around (Lip-Synch)
Singing The Blues; Blue, Blue Day; Together Again
    (With Buck Owens and Lynn Anderson)
White Christmas (Lip-Synch)

1981   A. T. & T. COMMERCIALS
           At least two are known to exist.

2/8/82   3RD ANNUAL T.V. GUIDE SPECIAL
           Clip

4/18/82   WILD ANIMAL PARK
           Guests: JERRY REED; BARBI BENTON; DOM DeLUISE
           Lay Some Happiness On Me (Lip Synch)
           Things (With Barbi Benton)
           Little Ole Wine Drinker, Me (With Jerry Reed)
           I'm Sitting On Top Of The World (Lip Synch)
           When The Red, Red Robin Comes Bob, Bob, Bobbin' Along
               (Lip Synch)
           I've Grown Accustomed To Her Face (Voice Over)

8/5/82   NEWS COVERAGE OF DEAN'S ARREST

11/21/82   BOB HOPE - PINK PANTHER TRIBUTE
           Bumming Around
           We're All Waiting In The Wings
               (Parody with Bob Hope, Robert Preston, and
               Robert Wagner)

2/14/83   ENTERTAINMENT TONIGHT
           Dean is seen performing "New York, New York" with
           Frank Sinatra and Sammy Davis, Jr.

2/15/83   ENTERTAINMENT TONIGHT
           Interview about filming his long-running television series.

2/16/83   DOM DeLUISE AND FRIENDS
           Dean appears in comedy skits.

4/19/83   ENTERTAINMENT TONIGHT
           S.H.A.R.E. benefit rehearsals

4/28/83   ENTERTAINMENT TONIGHT
           About the making of Dean's *NASHVILLE SESSIONS*
           album.

5/22/83   HOLLYWOOD'S PRIVATE HOME MOVIES
           Home movies from the 1950s of Dean and his family are
           shown.

10/3/83   JOHNNY CARSON
> The Tonight Show's 21st anniversary special. Once again, the classic clip of Dean, George Gobel and Bob Hope is shown.

10/19/83   ENTERTAINMENT TONIGHT
> Dean and his son Ricci are interviewed regarding Dean's "Since I Met You Baby" music video.

11/8/83   DEAN MARTIN IN LONDON (SHOWTIME NETWORK)
When You're Drinking; Bourbon From Heaven (Parody)
L-O-V-E
Everybody Loves Somebody
Where Or When
Welcome To My World
Drinking Champagne
That's Amore
Bad, Bad Leroy Brown
For The Good Times
Here Comes My Baby
Little Ole Wine Drinker, Me
Bumming Around

12/19/83   ENTERTAINMENT TONIGHT
> Dean and Frank Sinatra perform at the grand opening of the University of Nevada's new arena.

1983   GOLDEN NUGGET COMMERCIAL
> Dean and Frank Sinatra are seen "auditioning" "New York, New York" for owner Stephen Wynn.

2/20/84   T.V.'S BLOOPERS AND PRACTICAL JOKES
> Out-takes from the Joan Collins roast are shown.

2/21/84   FOUL UPS, BLEEPS AND BLUNDERS
> Out-takes from "Dom DeLuise and Friends Part II" are shown.

2/23/84   DOM DeLUISE AND FRIENDS PART II
> Dean appears in comedy skits.

2/23/84   ROAST OF JOAN COLLINS
Roasters: Gavin MacLeod; Beatrice Arthur; Red Buttons;
     Phyllis Diller; Angie Dickinson; Charlie Callas;
     Rich Little; Anne Baxter; Don Rickles; Zsa Zsa Gabor;
     John Forsythe; Aaron Spelling; Dom DeLuise;
     Milton Berle

3/14/84   ROAST OF MR. T.
Roasters: Gary Coleman; Ann Jillian; Red Buttons; Rich Little;
        Ricky Schroeder; Bob Hope; Gavin MacLeod;
        Slappy White; Dick Shawn; George Peppard;
        Howard Cosell; Maureen Murphy; Don Rickles

4/4/84   BOB HOPE - WHO MAKES THE WORLD LAUGH PART II
Clip

4/4/84   ON-STAGE AMERICA
Where Or When
Bumming Around
    Dean was also interviewed on this syndicated program.

5/10/84   FUNNIEST GAME SHOW MOMENTS
    1954 clip of Martin and Lewis on "What's My Line."

9/14/84   ENTERTAINMENT TONIGHT
    Interview regarding Friar's Club "Man Of The Year"
    award

9/28/84   BOB HOPE - UNREHEARSED ANTICS OF THE STARS
    1974 clip

9/28/84   ON T.V. - VIOLENCE FACTOR
Clip

10/4/84   ENTERTAINMENT TONIGHT
    Interview at the dedication of the Cary Grant Theater.

11/13/84   GOOD MORNING AMERICA
    Part I of a 2-part interview with David Hartman.

11/14/84   GOOD MORNING AMERICA
    Conclusion of a 2-part interview with David Hartman.

12/7/84   ROAST OF MICHAEL LANDON
Roasters: Rich Little; Pat Harrington; Dick Butkus; Bubba Smith;
        Dick Shawn; Merlin Olsen; Lorne Greene; Norm Crosby;
        Melissa Gilbert; Vic Tayback; Maureen Murphy;
        Orson Welles; Slappy White; Brian Keith; Don Rickles

12/9/84   ALL-STAR PARTY FOR LUCILLE BALL
When You're Lucy (Parody)

1/18/85	ENTERTAINMENT TONIGHT Interview regarding Reagan's inauguration.
1/19/85	REAGAN INAUGURATION Where Or When
1/21/85	ENTERTAINMENT TONIGHT Another interview regarding Reagan's inauguration.
3/24/85	HALF NELSON - TWO HOUR PILOT MOVIE Dean played himself in the pilot and the following six episodes of this Joe Pesci television show.
3/29/85	HALF NELSON - "DEADLY VASE"
4/5/85	HALF NELSON - "UPPERS AND DOWNERS"
4/12/85	HALF NELSON - "DIPLOMATIC IMMUNITY"
4/19/85	ENTERTAINMENT TONIGHT Interview on the set of "Half Nelson"
4/19/85	HALF NELSON - "NOSE JOB"
5/3/85	HALF NELSON - "MALIBU COLONY"
5/10/85	HALF NELSON - "BEVERLY HILLS PRINCESS"
5/28/85	MUSEUM OF BROADCASTING TRIBUTE - MILTON BERLE Clip
8/23/85	MOTOWN REVIEW For Once In My Life (With Smokey Robinson) Nowhere To Run (With Smokey, Ashford and Simpson and Kim Carnes)
12/8/85	ALL-STAR PARTY FOR "DUTCH" REAGAN Mr. Wonderful (Parody)
5/17/86	DOM DeLUISE AND FRIENDS PART IV Dean appears in comedy skit.
11/29/87	LAS VEGAS 75TH Dean hosted this program.

12/1/87 CHASEN'S PRESS CONFERENCE
      Dean, Frank Sinatra and Sammy Davis, Jr. announce the
      "Together Again" tour.

1987   DOM DeLUISE
      Dean appeared in various sketches on this syndicated
      show.

3/11/88 ENTERTAINMENT TONIGHT
      Dean is seen singing a portion of "Oldest Established
      Permanent Floating Crap Game In New York" in
      preparation for the "Together Again" tour.

3/14/88 ENTERTAINMENT TONIGHT
      Segment on the "Together Again" tour.

3/14/88 PEOPLE'S CHOICE AWARDS
      Pre-taped segment with Frank and Sammy; they present
      Barbra Streisand with an award.

3/14/88 SHOWBIZ TODAY
      Segment on the "Together Again" tour.

3/21/88 ENTERTAINMENT TONIGHT
      Announcement of Dean's withdrawal from the
      "Together Again" tour. A clip of him singing
      "Side By Side" is shown.

6/4/88   CHILDREN'S MIRACLE NETWORK TELETHON
      Where Or When
      That's Amore

6/8/89   ENTERTAINMENT TONIGHT
      Clip of Jerry Lewis surprising Dean on stage at Bally's in
      Las Vegas for Dean's 72nd birthday.

8/4/89   ENTERTAINMENT TONIGHT
      Clip with Jerry regarding "Hollywood Feuds."

11/89   CURRENT AFFAIR
      Re: Will Dean and Jeanne reconcile? Interviews with
      JOEY BISHOP and GREG GARRISON

11/20/89 ENTERTAINMENT TONIGHT
      Interview regarding tribute to Sammy Davis, Jr.

2/4/90   SAMMY DAVIS, JR.
              Dean reads "celebrity telegrams" to Sammy.

12/16/90   SINATRA 75 - "THE BEST IS YET TO COME"
              Pre-taped segment has Dean wishing Frank a happy 75th
              birthday followed by clips of Frank and Dean on each
              other's variety shows.

1990   MARILYN MONROE: SOMETHING'S GOT TO GIVE
              Fox-TV Documentary on the making of the aborted
              Marilyn Monroe film.

3/9/91   SINATRA - VOICE OF OUR TIME
              Clip

1992-1994   DISNEY CHANNEL 5-PART SPECIAL -
              "MARTIN AND LEWIS-KINGS OF COMEDY"
                  Features rare footage of the Colgate Comedy
                  Shows, Jerry's private films and home movies.

1/28/92   ENTERTAINMENT TONIGHT
              Dean is shown signing a contract to appear at the Desert
              Inn, Las Vegas along with Frank Sinatra; Steve and Eydie;
              Paul Anka and Shirley MacLaine. Unfortunately, Dean
              never performed at the hotel.

11/25/92   BEST OF THE HOLLYWOOD PALACE
              Clip of Dean introducing the Rolling Stones.

1994   RAGU SPAGHETTI SAUCE COMMERCIAL
              Dean's Capitol recording of I Don't Know Why plays in
              the background.

5/14/94   BOB HOPE
              Clip from 1974 appearance.

11/25/94   SINATRA DUETS
              Clip

11/25/94   GERALDO
              Dean's final interview via telephone.

1994   FUN AND FEEL OF THE FIFTIES
              Clip

1994	BIOGRAPHY (A&E NETWORK) Biography of Sammy Davis, Jr. Dean is seen in several "Rat Pack" clips.
1994	CURRENT AFFAIR Dean falls outside of Da Vinci's restaurant.
1995	HARD COPY Report on Dean's ailing health
1/19/95	AMERICAN JOURNAL Interview with Dean's son Ricci regarding Dean's health.
9/4/95	BIOGRAPHY (A&E NETWORK) Biography of Dean. New interviews with JERRY LEWIS; JOEY BISHOP; GREG GARRISON; DOM DeLUISE; ALAN KING; BOB NEWHART; JIMMY BOWEN; JEANNE MARTIN; RICCI MARTIN; BUD YORKIN; MIKE WEINBLATT
12/14/95	SINATRA: 80 YEARS MY WAY Clip
12/95	Upon Dean's passing, retrospective segments on his career were aired on "Good Morning America," "CBS This Morning," "Today Show," "Showbiz Today" and "Entertainment Tonight" as well as many local news shows.
2/12/96	AMERICAN JOURNAL Conversation with Edy Williams, Dean's last "girlfriend."
8/18/96	BIOGRAPHY (A&E NETWORK) Biography of Jerry Lewis with clips of Dean.
11/23/96	BOB HOPE Clip
12/1/96	LAS VEGAS PART 1 (A&E NETWORK) Clip
12/1/96	SHIRLEY MacLAINE (LIFETIME NETWORK) Clip
12/2/96	LAS VEGAS PART 2 (A&E NETWORK) Clip

373

1996   BIOGRAPHY (A&E NETWORK)
Biography of Marilyn Monroe shows clips of Dean on the set of *Something's Gotta Give.*

4/18/97   ENTERTAINMENT TONIGHT
Coverage of the "Dismas House" premiere.

4/29/97   DEAN MARTIN SHOW (NICK AT NITE'S TV LAND)
A half-hour edited version of Dean's 12/31/70 television show.

6/13/97   NBC DATELINE
Segment on "The Rat Pack"

1997   MICROSOFT COMPUTERS
Dean and Line Renaud's version of Relax-Ay-Voo plays in the background.

1997   INTIMATE PORTRAITS (LIFETIME NETWORK)
Biography of Janet Leigh. Clip of Janet on Dean's television show.

4/17/98   ENTERTAINMENT TONIGHT
Report on TV Land's broadcast of the "Dismas House" concert.

4/17/98   HARD COPY
Report on TV Land's broadcast of the "Dismas House" concert.

4/20/98   FRANK, DEAN, SAMMY: AN EVENING WITH THE RAT PACK (NICK AT NITE'S TV LAND)
"Dismas House" concert from 6/20/65 formerly titled "FRANK SINATRA SPECTACULAR"

4/21/98   EXTRA
Report on TV Land's broadcast of the "Dismas House" concert.

4/28/98   HARD COPY
Interview with Dean's daughter Deana.

Chapter 9

Motion Pictures

MY FRIEND IRMA (1949)

Credits: Produced by Hal B. Wallis; Directed by George Marshall; Screenplay by Cy Howard and Parke Levy; Based on the CBS radio program created by Cy Howard; Director of photography: Leo Tover; Art Direction: Hans Dreier and Henry Bumstead; Special photographic effects: Gordon Jennings; Process photography: Farciot Edouart; Set decoration: Sam Comer and Grace Gregory; Associate producer: Cy Howard; Music score: Roy Webb; New songs by Jay Livingston and Ray Evans; Costumes by Edith Head; Editor: Leroy Stone; Makeup Supervision: Wally Westmore; Sound Recording: Gene Merritt and Walter Oberst; Assistant director: Oscar Rudolph

Cast: John Lund (Al); Diana Lynn (Jane Stacey); Don DeFore (Richard Rhinelander); Marie Wilson (Irma Peterson); Dean Martin (Steve Laird); Jerry Lewis (Seymour); Hans Conreid (Professor Kropotkin); Kathryn Givney (Mrs. Rhinelander); Percy Helton (Mr. Clyde); Gloria Gordon (Mrs. O'Reilly); Erno Verebese (Mr. Ubang); Margaret Field (Alice); Charles Coleman (butler); Douglas Spencer (interior decorator); Ken Niles (announcer); Francis Pierlot (income-tax agent); Chief Yowlachie (Native American); Jimmy Dundee (wallpaper man); Tony Merrill (newspaper man); Jack Mulhall (photographer); Nick Cravat (Mushie); Leonard B. Ingoldest (orchestra leader); Chester Conklin (waiter)

Dean's Songs: Donkey Serenade (With Jerry); Here's To Love; Just For Fun; My Own, My Only, My All

Reviews:

VARIETY	8/17/49
NEW YORK TIMES	9/29/49
NEWSWEEK	10/3/49
COMMONWEAL	10/7/49
TIME	10/24/49

Clowning around with *My Friend Irma*
(Left to right: Don DeFore, Diana Lynn, Jerry Lewis, Marie Wilson, Dean and
John Lund)
(Paramount Pictures Corp. publicity photo)

Released by Paramount in August 1949; black and white; 102 minutes

Movie Gross: $2,800,000

MY FRIEND IRMA GOES WEST (1950)

Credits: Produced by Hal B. Wallis; Directed by Hal Walker; Screenplay by Cy Howard and Parke Levy; Based on the CBS radio program created by Cy Howard; Director of photography: Art Direction: Hans Dreier and Henry Bumstead; Special photographic effects: Gordon Jennings; Process photography: Farciot Edouart; Set decoration: Sam Comer and Emile Kuri; Associate producer: Cy Howard; Music score: Leigh Harline; New songs by Jay Livingston and Ray Evans; Costumes by Edith Head; Editorial supervision: Warren Low; Dialogue director: Joan Hathaway; Sound recording: Gene Merritt and Walter Oberst; Makeup supervision: Wally Westmore; Assistant director: Francisco Day

Cast: John Lund (Al); Marie Wilson (Irma Peterson); Dean Martin (Steve Laird); Jerry Lewis (Seymour); Corinne Calvet (Yvonne Yvonne); Diana Lynn (Jane Stacey); Lloyd Corrigan (Sharpie); Donald Porter (Mr. Brent); Harold Huber (Pete); Jose Vitale (Slim); Charles Evans (Mr. C. Y. Sanford); Kenneth Tobey (pilot); James Humbert (chef); Roy Gordon (Jensen); Link Clayton (Henry); Mike Mahoney (cigarette gag man); Bob Johnson (Red Cap); Al Ferguson (news vendor); Napoleon Whiting (waiter); Paul Lees (unemployment clerk); Stan Johnson, Charles Dayton, Jasper D. Weldon, Ivan H. Browning (reporters); Julia Montoya and Rose Higgins (Native American women); Maxie Thrower (bartender); Chief Yowlachie (Native American chief); Joe Hecht, Gil Herman, Gregg Palmer (attendants); Jimmy Dundee and David Clark (deputies); James Flavin (sheriff); Pierre the Monkey

Dean's Songs: Baby Obey Me (With Corrine Calvet and Jerry); I'll Always Love You; Singing A Vagabond Song (With Jerry); Santa Lucia/Fiddle And Guitar Band (With Jerry)

Reviews:

VARIETY	5/31/50
NEW YORK TIMES	8/3/50
NEWSWEEK	8/14/50

Released by Paramount in May 1950; black and white; 90 minutes

Movie Gross: $2,400,000

AT WAR WITH THE ARMY (1950)

Credits: Executive producer: Abner J. Greshler; Producer/screenwriter: Fred F. Finklehoffe; Directed by Hal Walker; Based on a play by James B. Allardice; Presented on the stage by Henry May and Jerome E. Rosenfeld in association with Charles Ray MacCallum; Musical director: Joseph Lilley; Songs by Mack David and Jerry Livingston; Director of photography: Stuart Thompson; Assistant director: Alvin Granzer; Assistant to the producer: Vern Alves; Art director: George Jenkins; Dialogue director: Joan Hathaway; Makeup: Lee

377

Greenway; Wardrobe: Jack Dowsing; Sound: Frank McWhorter; Production manager: Norman Cook; Film editor: Paul Weatherwax

Cast: Dean Martin (Vic Puccinelli); Jerry Lewis (Alvin Korwin); Mike Kellin (Sgt. McVey); Jimmie Dundee (Eddie); Dick Stabile (Pokey); Tommy Farrell (Cpl. Clark); Frank Hyers (Cpl. Shaughnessy); Danny Dayton (Sgt. Miller); William Mendrek (Capt. Caldwell); Kenneth Forbes (Lt. Davenport); Paul Livermore (Pvt. Evans); Ty Perry (Lt. Terray); Jean Ruth (Millie); Angela Greene (Mrs. Caldwell); Polly Bergen (Helen); Douglas Evans (colonel); Steve Roberts (doctor); Al Neglo (orderly); Dewey Robinson (bartender)

Dean's Songs: You And Your Beautiful Eyes (With Polly Bergen); Tonda Wanda Hoy; Too Ra Loo Ra Loo Ra

Reviews:

VARIETY	12/13/50
NEW YORK TIMES	1/25/51
TIME	1/29/51
NEWSWEEK	2/5/51
CHRISTIAN CENTURY	2/14/51
COMMONWEAL	3/9/51

Released by Paramount in December 1950; black and white; 93 minutes

Movie Gross: $3,350,000

THAT'S MY BOY (1951)

Credits: Produced by Hal B. Wallis; Directed by Hal Walker; Story and screenplay by Cy Howard; Director of photography: Lee Garmes; Art direction: Hal Pereira and Franz Bachelin; Second unit director: C. C. Coleman; Process photography: Farciot Edouart; Technical advisor for football sequences: Mickey McCardle; Set decoration: Sam Comer and Ray Moyer; Associate producer: Cy Howard; Music score: Leigh Harline; Editorial supervision: Warren Low; Costumes by Edith Head; Dialogue director: Rudy McKool; Makeup supervision: Wally Westmore; Sound recording: Hugo Grenzback and Walter Oberst

Cast: Dean Martin (Bill Baker); Jerry Lewis (Junior Jackson); Ruth Hussey (Ann Jackson); Eddie Mayehoff ("Jarring" Jack Jackson); Marion Marshall (Terry Howard); Polly Bergen (Betty Hunter); Hugh Sanders (Coach Wheeler); John McIntire (Benjamin Green); Francis Pierlot (Henry Baker); Lillian Randolph (May); Selmar Jackson (Doc Hunter); Tom Harmon (sports announcer); Torben Meyer (photographer); Mickey Kuhn, Leon Tyler, Gregg Palmer, Robert Board, Lynn Thomas, Barbara Logan, Drew Cahill (students); Don Haggerty (Hazel "Sonny" Boyne)

Dean's Songs: Ballin' The Jack (With Polly Bergen); I'm In The Mood For Love

Reviews: *VARIETY*   6/13/51
                      NEWSWEEK   7/23/51
                      SATURDAY REVIEW   7/25/51
                      NEW YORK TIMES   8/2/51
                      COMMONWEAL   8/24/51
                      TIME   8/27/51
                      NATION   9/1/51
                      CHRISTIAN CENTURY   9/19/51

Released by Paramount in May 1951; black and white; 98 minutes

Movie Gross: $3,800,000

SAILOR BEWARE (1952)

Credits: Produced by Hal B. Wallis; Directed by Hal Walker; Screenplay by James Allardice and Martin Rackin; Additional dialogue by John Grant; Adapted by Elwood Ullman; Based on the play by Kenyon Nicholson and Charles Robinson; Director of photography: Daniel L. Fapp; Art direction: Hal Pereira and Henry Bumstead; Special photographic effects: Gordon Jennings; Process photography: Farciot Edouart; Set decoration: Sam Comer and Bertram Granger; Editorial supervision: Warren Low; Costumes by Edith Head; Makeup supervision: Wally Westmore; Sound recording: Harry Mills and Walter Oberst; Music direction: Joseph J. Lilley; New songs by Mack David and Jerry Livingston

Cast: Dean Martin (Al Crowthers); Jerry Lewis (Melvin Jones); Corinne Calvet (herself); Marion Marshall (Hilda Jones); Robert Strauss (Lardoski); Leif Erickson (Commander Lane); Don Wilson (Mr. Chubby); Vincent Edwards (Blayden); Skip Homeier (Mac); Dan Barton ('Bama); Mike Mahoney (Tiger); Mary Treen (Ginger); Danny Arnold (Turk); Louis Jean Heydt (Navy doctor); Donald MacBride (Chief Bos'n Mate); Elaine Stewart (Lt. Saunders); Drew Cahill (Bull); James Flavin (petty officer); Don Haggerty (Lt. Connors); Mary Murphy (girl); Jerry Hausner (corpsman); Darr Smith (Jeff Spencer); Bobby and Eddie Mayo (Mayo Brothers); Richard Karlan (guard); Eddie Samms (Killer Jackson); Stephen Gregory (McDurk); Robert Carson (Navy captain); Richard Emory (petty officer); Marshall Reed and John V. Close (hospital corpsmen); Elaine Riley (female commentator); Larry McGrath (referee); Duke Mitchell (Melvin's boxing second); James Dean (opponent's boxing second); Dick Stabile (bandleader); Marimba Merry Makers (themselves); Betty Hutton (Hetty Button)

Dean's Songs: Never Before; Sailor's Polka; Today, Tomorrow, Forever; Old Calliope (With Jerry)

Reviews: *VARIETY*   12/5/51
                      HOLIDAY   2/51
                      NEW YORK TIMES   2/1/52
                      TIME   2/18/52

Dean and Jerry "salute" their highest-grossing film, *Sailor Beware*
(Paramount Pictures Corp. publicity photo)

NEWSWEEK   3/10/52
CHRISTIAN CENTURY   4/9/52
Released by Paramount in February 1952; black and white; 108 minutes

Movie Gross: $4,300,000

JUMPING JACKS (1952)

Credits: Produced by Hal B. Wallis; Directed by Norman Taurog; Screenplay by Robert Lees, Fred Rinaldo and Herbert Baker; Additional dialogue by James Allardice and Richard Weil; Based on a story by Brian Marlow; Director of photography: Daniel L. Fapp; Art direction: Hal Pereira and Henry Bumstead; Special photographic effects: Gordon Jennings; Process photography: Farciot Edouart; Set decoration: Sam Comer and Emile Kuri; Editorial supervision: Warren Low; Editor: Stanley Johnson; Costumes by Edith Head; Makeup supervision: Wally Westmore; Sound recording: Don McKay and Gene Garvin; Music direction: Joseph J. Lilley; Songs by Mack David and Jerry Livingston; Musical numbers staged by Robert Sidney

Cast: Dean Martin (Chip Allen); Jerry Lewis (Hap Smith); Mona Freeman (Betty Carter); Don DeFore (Kelsey); Robert Strauss (Sgt. McCluskey); Dick Erdman (Dogface Dolan); Ray Teal (General Timmons); Marcy McGuire (Julia Loring); Danny Arnold (Evans); Ed Max (Sam Gilmore); Alex Garry (Earl White); Charles Evans (Bond); James Flavin (Sterling); Russell Conway (colonel); Robert A. Karnes (officer); Drew Cahill (soldier at bar); Arthur Space (doctor); Ray Paige (MP); Monty O'Grady, Joseph Keane, Walter Kelly, Robert Einer, Don and Tommy Rockland (soldiers)

Dean's Songs: Parachute Jump; Big Blue Sky Is The Place For Me; I Know A Dream When I See One; Keep A Little Dream Handy (With Jerry)

Reviews:
VARIETY	6/4/52
NEWSWEEK	6/30/52
COMMONWEAL	7/18/52
NEW YORK TIMES	7/29/52
TIME	8/4/52
SATURDAY REVIEW	8/9/52

Released by Paramount in June 1952; black and white; 96 minutes

Movie Gross: $4,000,000

THE STOOGE (1953)

Credits: Produced by Hal B. Wallis; Directed by Norman Taurog; Screenplay by Fred F. Finklehoffe and Martin Rackin; Additional dialogue: Elwood Ullman; From a story by Fred F. Finklehoffe and Sid Silvers; Director of photography: Daniel L. Fapp; Art direction: Hal Pereira and Franz Bachelin; Special photographic effects: Gordon Jennings; Process photography: Farciot Edouart; Set decoration: Sam Comer and Bertram Granger; Editorial supervision:

Warren Low; Costumes by Edith Head; Makeup supervision: Wally Westmore; Sound recording: Don McKay and Walter Oberst; Music direction: Joseph J. Lilley; "A Girl Named Mary And A Boy Named Bill" written by Mack David and Jerry Livingston

Cast: Dean Martin (Bill Miller); Jerry Lewis (Ted Rogers); Polly Bergen (Mary Turner); Marion Marshall (Frecklehead Tait); Eddie Mayehoff (Leo Lyman); Richard Erdman (Ben Bailey); Frances Bavier (Mrs. Rogers); Jerry Hausner (Al Borden); Percy Helton (Mr. Robertson); Mary Treen (Miss Reagan); Donald MacBride (waiter); Harry Hines (bitman); Eddie Parks (janitor); Freeman Lusk (Frank Darling); Charles Smith (soda jerk); Don Haggerty, Charles Evans, Tommy Farrell, Oliver Blake (bit parts)

Dean's Songs: A Girl Named Mary And A Boy Named Bill (With Polly Bergen); I Feel A Song Coming On (With Jerry); I Feel Like A Feather In The Breeze; I'm Yours; Just One More Chance (With Jerry); Who's Your Little Who-Zis (With Jerry); With My Eyes Wide Open I'm Dreaming

Reviews:

VARIETY	10/8/52
TIME	1/26/53
CATHOLIC WORLD	2/53
NEW YORK TIMES	2/5/53
SATURDAY REVIEW	2/7/53
NEWSWEEK	2/23/53

Released by Paramount in February 1953; black and white; 100 minutes

Movie Gross: $3,500,000

SCARED STIFF (1953)

Credits: Produced by Hal B. Wallis; Directed by George Marshall; Screenplay by Herbert Baker and Walter Deleon; Additional dialogue by Ed Simmons and Norman Lear; Based on the play by Paul Dickey and Charles W. Goddard; Director of photography: Ernest Laszlo; Art direction: Hal Pereira and Franz Bachelin; Special photographic effects: Gordon Jennings and Paul Lerpae; Process photography: Farciot Edouart; Set decoration: Sam Comer and Ross Dowd; Editorial supervision: Warren Low; Costumes by Edith Head; Dialogue coach: Rudy McKool; Assistant director: C. C. Coleman, Jr.; Makeup supervision: Wally Westmore; Sound recording: Hugo Grenzbach and Walter Oberst; Music direction: Joseph J. Lilley; Music score: Leith Stevens; New songs by Mack David and Jerry Livingston; Musical numbers staged by Billy Daniels

Cast: Dean Martin (Larry Todd); Jerry Lewis (Myron Myron Mertz); Lizabeth Scott (Mary Caroll); Carmen Miranda (Carmelita Castina); George Dolenz (Mr. Cortega); Dorothy Malone (Rosie); William Ching (Tony Warren); Paul Marion (Carriso Twins); Jack Lambert (zombie); Tom Powers (police lieutenant); Anthony Barr (Trigger); Leonard Strong (Shorty); Henry Brandon (Pierre); Hugh Sanders (cop on pier); Frank Fontaine (drunk); Dick Stabile (band leader); Earl Holliman (elevator operator); Chester Clute (man with spaghetti); Bing Crosby and Bob Hope (themselves)

Dean's Songs: I Don't Care If The Sun Don't Shine; What Have You Done For Me Lately (With Jerry); Enchilada Man (With Jerry and Carmen Miranda); When Someone Wonderful Thinks You're Wonderful; San Domingo/Bongo Bingo (With Jerry and Carmen Miranda); You Hit The Spot

Reviews:

VARIETY	4/15/53
NATIONAL PARENT/TEACHER	6/53
SATURDAY REVIEW	6/20/53
TIME	6/29/53
CATHOLIC WORLD	7/53
NEW YORK TIMES	7/3/53
AMERICA	7/18/53
NEWSWEEK	7/20/53

Released by Paramount in April 1953; black and white; 108 minutes

Movie Gross: $3,500,000

THE CADDY (1953)

Credits: Produced by Paul Jones; Directed by Norman Taurog; Screenplay by Edmund Hartmann and Danny Arnold; Additional dialogue: Ken Englund; Story by Danny Arnold; Director of photography: Daniel L. Fapp; Art direction: Hal Pereira and Franz Bachelin; Special photographic effects: John P. Fulton and Paul Lerpae; Process photography: Farciot Edouart; Set decoration: Sam Comer and Ray Moyer; Editor: Warren Low; Makeup supervisor: Wally Westmore; Assistant director: Michael Moore; Technical advisor: "Lighthorse" Harry Cooper; Sound recording: Gene Merritt and Gene Garvin; Music direction: Joseph J. Lilley; Costumes by Edith Head; Dances staged by Jack Baker; New songs written by Harry Warren (music) and Jack Brooks (lyrics)

Cast: Dean Martin (Joe Anthony); Jerry Lewis (Harvey Miller); Donna Reed (Kathy Taylor); Barbara Bates (Lisa Anthony); Joseph Calleia (Papa Anthony); Fred Clark (Mr. Baxter); Clinton Sundberg (Charles the Butler); Howard Smith (golf official); Marshall Thompson (Bruce Reeber); Marjorie Gateson (Mrs. Taylor); Frank Puglia (Mr. Spezzato); Lewis Martin (Mr. Taylor); Romo Vincent (Eddie Lear); Argentina Brunetti (Mama Anthony); Housely Stevenson, Jr. (officer); John Gallaudet (Mr. Bell); William Edmunds (Caminello); Charles Irwin (golf starter); Freeman Lusk (official); Keith McConnell (Mr. Benthall); Henry Brandon (Mr. Preen); Maurice Marsac (Mr. Leron); Donald Randolph (Harvey Miller, Sr.); Stephen Chase (George Garrison, Sr.); Tom Harmon (announcer); Dick Wessel (big bully); King Donovan (Emma's husband); Nancy Kulp (Emma); Ned Glass (stage manager); Bess Flowers (party guest); Al Thompson (Mr. Phillips); Mario Siletti, Mary Treen, Mike Mahoney, Hank Mann, Joe Stabile, Dorothy Abbott, Wendell Niles (bit parts); Ben Hogan, Sam Snead, Byron Nelson, Julius Boros, Jimmy Thomson, "Lighthorse" Harry Cooper (themselves)

Dean's Songs: That's Amore (With Jerry); What Wouldcha Do Without Me (With Jerry); You're The Right One; It's A Whistle-In Kinda Morning; One Big Love (With Jerry)

Reviews:

VARIETY	8/5/53
NEW YORK TIMES	9/18/53
TIME	9/28/53
McCALL'S	10/53
NATIONAL PARENT/TEACHER	10/53
NEWSWEEK	10/5/53
FARM JOURNAL	11/53
HOLIDAY	11/53

Released by Paramount in August 1953; black and white; 95 minutes

Movie Gross: $3,500,000

MONEY FROM HOME (1954)

Credits: Produced by Hal B. Wallis; Directed by George Marshall; Screenplay by Hal Kanter; Adapted by James Allardice and Hal Kanter from a story by Damon Runyon; Director of photography: Daniel L. Fapp; Technicolor color consultant: Richard Mueller; Art direction: Hal Pereira and Henry Bumstead; Special photographic effects: John P. Fulton and Paul K. Lerpae; Process photography: Farciot Edouart; Set decoration: Sam Comer and Ross Dowd; Assistant director: Michael D. Moore; Editorial supervision: Warren Low; Costumes by Edith Head; Makeup supervision: Wally Westmore; Sound recording: Harry Lindgren and Gene Garvin; Songs arranged and conducted by Joseph J. Lilley; Music score: Leigh Harline; "The 'Be Careful' Song" and "Love Is The Same All Over The World" written by Jack Brooks and Joseph J. Lilley; Special material in song numbers staged by Jerry Lewis; Technicolor

Cast: Dean Martin (Herman "Honey Talk" Nelson); Jerry Lewis (Virgil Yokum); Marjie Millar (Phyllis Leigh); Pat Crowley (Autumn Claypool); Richard Haydn (Bertie Searles); Robert Strauss (Seldom Seen Kid); Gerald Mohr (Marshall Preston); Sheldon Leonard (Jumbo Schneider); Romo Vincent (Poojah); Jack Kruschen (Short Boy); Mara Corday (Mary); Charles Frank Horvath and Richard J. Reeves (henchmen); Lou Lubin (Sam); Frank Richards (driver); Harry Hayden (first judge); Henry McLemore (second judge); Mortie Dutra (third judge); Wendell Niles (announcer); Sam "Society Kid" Hogan (himself); Joe McTurk (Hard Top Harry); Frank Mitchell (Lead Pipe Louie); Phil Arnold (Fat Phil); Louis Nicoletti (Hot Horse Herbie); Edward Clark (Dr. Capulet); Grace Hayle (Mrs. Cheshire); Al Hill (first reporter); Ben Astar (manservant); Robin Hughes (bankfair); Sidney Marion (Gorgan the Growler); Carolyn Phillips (Poojah's wife); Maidie Norman (Mattie);

Rex Lease (man with hairpiece); Bess Flowers (party guest); Frank Nelson (radio voice); Joe Stabile (bandleader)

Dean's Songs: Moments Like This; Love Is The Same All Over The World; I Only Have Eyes For You

Reviews:

VARIETY	12/2/53
NEWSWEEK	12/7/53
NATIONAL PARENT/TEACHER	1/54
AMERICAN MAGAZINE	2/54
FARM JOURNAL	2/54
LIBRARY JOURNAL	2/1/54
NEW YORK TIMES	2/27/54
AMERICA	3/6/54
TIME	3/15/54

Released by Paramount in February 1954; color; originally released in 3-D; 99 minutes

Movie Gross: $3,500,000

LIVING IT UP (1954)

Credits: Produced by Paul Jones; Directed by Norman Taurog; Screenplay by Jack Rose and Melville Shavelson; From the musical comedy "Hazel Flagg"; Book by Ben Hecht; Music by Jule Styne; Lyrics by Bob Hilliard; Based on a story by James Street; Director of photography: Daniel Fapp; Technicolor color consultant: Richard Mueller; Art direction: Hal Pereira and Albert Nozaki; Special photographic effects: John P. Fulton; Process photography: Farciot Edouart; Set decoration: Sam Comer and Emile Kuri; Assistant director: Michael D. Moore; Editor: Archie Marshek; Gowns: Edith Head; Second unit director: Arthur Rosson; Second unit photography: Wallace Kelley; Sound recording: Gene Merritt and Gene Garvin; Music arranged and conducted by Walter Scharf; Choreography: Nick Castle; Vocal arrangements: Charles Henderson; Dialogue coach: Rudy Makoul;

Assistant to the producer: Jack Mintz; Technicolor

Cast: Dean Martin (Dr. Steve Harris); Jerry Lewis (Homer Flagg); Janet Leigh (Wally Cook); Edward Arnold (New York mayor); Fred Clark (Oliver Stone); Sheree North (dancer); Sammy White (waiter); Sid Tomack (master of ceremonies); Sig Ruman (Dr. Egelhofer); Richard Loo (Dr. Chung Lee See); Raymond Greenleaf (conductor); Walter Baldwin (Isaiah Jackson); Fay Roope (Dr. Nasseau); Marla English and Kathryn Grandstaff (manicurists); Emmett Lynn (station attendant); Dabbs Greer (head ranger); Clancy Cooper (slugger); John Alderson (baseball catcher); Booth Colman (Fernandez); Stanley Blystone (engineer); Fritz Feld (barber); Torben Meyer (chef); Art Baker (radio announcer); Grady Sutton (gift shop owner); Norman Leavitt (photographer); Frankie Darro (bellboy captain); Jean Del Val (French chef); Lane Chandler (cop); Gino Corrado (shoe specialist); Donald Kerr (Martin); Al Hill (slugger); Hank Menn (busboy); Gretchen Houser (dancer); Bobby Barber, Snub Pollard and Philo McCollugh (bit parts)

Dean's Songs: Ev'ry Street's A Boulevard In Old New York (With Jerry); How Do You Speak To An Angel; Money Burns A Hole In My Pocket; That's What I Like; Hallelujah Train (With Jerry; cut from final print)

Reviews:

VARIETY	5/5/54
FARM JOURNAL	7/54
TIME	7/19/54
NEW YORK TIMES	7/24/54
SATURDAY REVIEW	7/31/54
CATHOLIC WORLD	8/54
NATIONAL PARENT/TEACHER	10/54

Released by Paramount in July 1954; color; 94 minutes

Movie Gross: $4,250,000

THREE RING CIRCUS (1954)

Credits: Produced by Hal B. Wallis; Directed by Joseph Pevney; Story and screenplay by Danny Arnold; Director of photography: Loyal Griggs; Technicolor color consultant: Richard Mueller; Art direction: Hal Pereira and Tambi Larsen; Special photographic effects: John P. Fulton; Process photography: Farciot Edouart; Set decoration: Sam Comer and Ray Moyer; Dialogue coach: Rudy Makoul; Assistant directors: C. C. Coleman, Jr. and Daniel McCauley; Editorial supervision: Warren Low; Costumes: Edith Head; Makeup supervision: Wally Westmore; Sound recording: Harold Lewis and John Cope; Music score: Walter Scharf; "Hey Punchinello" written by Jay Livingston and Ray Evans; Choreography: Nick Castle; Technicolor

Cast: Dean Martin (Pete Nelson); Jerry Lewis (Jerry Hotchkiss); Joanne Dru (Jill Brent); Zsa Zsa Gabor (Saadia); Wallace Ford (Sam Morley); Sig Ruman (Fritz Shlitz); Gene Sheldon (Puffo); Nick Cravat (Timmy); Elsa Lanchester (bearded lady); Douglas Fowley (payroll official); Sue Casey (snake charmer); Mary L. Orosco (fat lady); Frederick E. Wolfe (giant); Phil Van Zandt (shell game con artist); Ralph Peters (chef); Chick Chandler (dunk tank pitchman); Kathleen Freeman (custard customer); Sandy Descher (handicapped girl); Robert McKibbon, Neil Levitt, Al Hill, Robert LeRoy Diamond, George E. Stone, Lester Dorr, Donald Kerr, James Davies, Louis Michael Lettieri, Billy Curtis, Harry Monty, Milton A. Dickinson, Bobby Kay, Sonny Vallie, Robert Lock Lorraine, John Minshull, Joe Evans, George Boyce (bit parts)

Dean's Songs: It's A Big Wide Wonderful World; Hey Punchinello (With Jerry); It's A Good Day (With Jerry; cut from final print)

Reviews:

VARIETY	10/27/54
NATIONAL PARENT/TEACHER	12/54

NEW YORK TIMES 12/25/54
FARM JOURNAL 1/55
NEWSWEEK 1/3/55
TIME 1/17/55

Released by Paramount in December 1954; color; 103 minutes

Movie Gross: $4,000,000

YOU'RE NEVER TOO YOUNG (1955)

Credits: Produced by Paul Jones; Directed by Norman Taurog; Screenplay by Sidney Sheldon; Suggested by the Edward Childs Carpenter play; From a story by Frannie Kilbourne; Director of photography: Daniel L. Fapp; Technicolor color consultant: Richard Mueller; Art direction: Hal Pereira and Earl Hedrick; Special photographic effects: John P. Fulton; Process photography: Farciot Edouart; Set decoration: Sam Comer and Frank McKelvy; Assistant director: Michael D. Moore; Editor: Archie Marshek; Costumes: Edith Head; Makeup supervision: Wally Westmore; Sound recording: Gene Merritt and Gene Garvin; Music: Arthur Schwartz; Lyrics: Sammy Cahn; Music arranged and conducted by Walter Scharf; Choreography: Nick Castle; Vocal arrangements: Norman Luboff; Assistant to the producer: Jack Mintz; Technicolor

Cast: Dean Martin (Bob Miles); Jerry Lewis (Wilbur Hoolick); Diana Lynn (Nancy Collins); Nina Foch (Gretchen Brendan); Raymond Burr (Noonan); Mitzi McCall (Skeets); Veda Ann Borg (Mrs. Noonan); Margery Maude (Mrs. Brendan); Romo Vincent (ticket agent); Nancy Kulp (Marty's mother); Milton Frome (Lt. O' Mally); Whitey Haupt (Mike Brendan); Tommy Ivo (Marty); James Burke (pullman conductor); Emory Parnell (conductor); Mickey Finn (Sgt. Brown); Peggy Moffitt (Agnes); Hans Conreid (Francois); Donna Percy (girl); Johnstone White and Richard Simmons (professors); Louise Lorimer, Isabel Randolph, Marty Newton (faculty members); Stanley Blystone (passenger); Bobby Barber (newsboy); Donna Jo Gribble, Irene Walpole, Gloria Penny Moore (schoolgirls); Bob Morgan (Texan); Dick Cutting (hotel guard); Hank Mann (bit part)

Dean's Songs: I Like To Hike; Face The Music; I Know Your Mother Loves You; Love Is All That Matters; Simpatico; Relax-Ay-Voo (With Jerry; cut from final print)

Reviews:
VARIETY 6/15/55
TIME 8/8/55
NEW YORK TIMES 8/26/55
NEW YORKER 9/3/55
NATIONAL PARENT/TEACHER 10/55

Released by Paramount in August 1955; color; 102 minutes

Movie Gross: $3,400,000

387

ARTISTS AND MODELS (1955)

Credits: Produced by Hal B. Wallis; Directed by Frank Tashlin; Screenplay by
Frank Tashlin, Hal Kanter and Herbert Baker; Adapted by Don
McGuire; Based on a play by Michael Davidson and Norman
Lessing; Director of photography: Daniel L. Fapp; Technicolor
color consultant: Richard Mueller; Art direction: Hal Pereira and
Tambi Larsen; Special photographic effects: John P. Fulton; Process
photography: Farciot Edouart; Set decoration: Sam Comer and
Arthur Krams; Dialogue coach: Rudy Makoul; Assistant director: C.
C. Coleman, Jr.; Editorial supervision: Warren Low; Costumes:
Edith Head; Makeup supervision: Wally Westmore; Sound
recording: Hugo Grenzbach and Gene Garvin; Associate producer:
Paul Nathan; Musical numbers created and staged by Charles O'
Curran; Music arranged and conducted by Walter Scharf; Vocal
arrangements: Norman Luboff; Music: Harry Warren; Lyrics: Jack
Brooks; Technicolor

Cast: Dean Martin (Rick Todd); Jerry Lewis (Eugene Fullstack); Shirley
MacLaine (Bessie Sparrowbush); Dorothy Malone (Abigail Parker);
Eddie Mayehoff (Mr. Murdock); Eva Gabor (Sonia); Anita Ekberg
(Anita); George "Foghorn" Winslow (Richard Stilton); Jack Elam
(Ivan); Herbert Rudley (Chief Samuels); Richard Shannon (Agent
Rogers); Richard Webb (Agent Peters); Alan Lee (Otto); Otto
Waldis (Kurt); Art Baker (himself); Nick Castle (dancer); Kathleen
Freeman (Mrs. Muldoon); Emory Parnell (Kelly); Carleton Young
(Col. Drury); Martha Wentworth (fat lady); Sara Berner (Mrs.
Stilton); Patti Ross (masseuse); Frank Jenks, Mike Ross, Glen
Walters, Sharon Baird, Eve Meyer, Mickey Little, Tommy
Summers, Max Power (bit parts)

Dean's Songs: Artists And Models (With Jerry); Innamorata; Lucky Song;
When You Pretend (With Jerry, Shirley MacLaine and Dorothy
Malone); You Look So Familiar

Reviews: VARIETY 11/9/55
NEW YORK TIMES 12/22/55
NATIONAL PARENT/TEACHER 1/56
TIME 1/9/56

Released by Paramount in December 1955; color; 109 minutes

Movie Gross: $3,800,000

PARDNERS (1956)

Credits: Produced by Nick Castle; Directed by Paul Jones and Norman Taurog;
Screenplay by Sidney Sheldon; Screenstory by Jerry Davis; Based
on a story by Mervin J. Houser; Director of photography: Daniel
Fapp; Technicolor color consultant: Richard Mueller; Art direction:
Hal Pereira and Roland Anderson; Second unit photography:
Wallace Kelley; Special photographic effects: John P. Fulton;
Process photography: Farciot Edouart; Set decoration: Sam Comer

and Ray Moyer; Assistant director: Michael D. Moore; Costumes: Edith Head; Editor: Archie Marsher; Makeup supervision: Wally Westmore; Technical advisor: Rodd Redwing; Sound recording: Gene Merritt and Gene Garvin; Songs by Sammy Cahn and James Van Heusen; Music arranged and conducted by Frank De Vol; Vocal arrangements: Norman Luboff; Assistant to the producer: Jack Mintz; Choreography: Nick Castle; Technicolor

Cast: Dean Martin (Slim Mosely); Jerry Lewis (Wade Kingsley); Lori Nelson (Carol Kingsley); Jeff Morrow (Pete Rio); Jackie Loughery (Dolly Riley); John Baragrey (Dan Hollis); Agnes Moorehead (Mrs. Kingsley); Lon Chaney (Whitey); Milton Frome (Hawkins the butler); Richard Aherne (chauffeur); Lee Van Cleef (Gus); Stuart Randall (Carol's cowhand); Scott Douglas (Salvin); Jack Elam (Pete); Bob Steele (Shorty); Mickey Finn (Masked Raider Red); Douglas Spencer (Smith); Philip Tonge (Footman); Emory Parnell (Col. Hart); Frances Mercer (Sally); William Forrest (Hocker); James Parnell (bank teller); Mary Newton (Laura); Len Hendry (cowboy); Charles Stevens (Indian); Gavin Gordon, Robert Brubaker, Tony Michael, Johnstone White (businessmen); Valerie Allen, Elaine Riley, Ann McCrae (dance hall girls); Bobby Barber (short man in bank); Stanley Blystone, Hank Mann, Don House, Frank Cordell, Robert Garvey, Keith Wilson, Emily Belser (townspeople); Dorothy Abbott, Claudia Martin, Gail Martin, Deana Martin (bit parts)

Dean's Songs: Pardners (With Jerry); Me 'N' You 'N' The Moon; The Wind, The Wind; The Test Of Time (Cut from final print)

Reviews:

VARIETY	6/27/56
NEW YORK TIMES	7/26/56
SATURDAY REVIEW	7/28/56
AMERICA	8/11/56
TIME	8/13/56
NEWSWEEK	8/20/56
NATIONAL PARENT/TEACHER	9/56

Released by Paramount in July 1956; color; 85 minutes

Movie Gross: $3,600,000

HOLLYWOOD OR BUST (1956)

Credits: Produced by Hal B. Wallis; Directed by Frank Tashlin; Written by Erna Lazarus; Director of photography: Daniel Fapp; Technicolor consultant: Richard Mueller; Art direction: Hal Pereira and Henry Bumstead; Special photographic effects: John P. Fulton; Process photography: Farciot Edouart; Set decoration: Sam Comer and Faye Babcock; Dialogue coach: Rudy Makoul; Assistant director: James Rosenberger; Editor: Howard Smith; Costumes: Edith Head; Makeup supervision: Wally Westmore; Sound recording: Hugo Grenzbach and Gene Garvin; Associate producer: Paul Nathan; Second unit director: William Watson; Second unit photography: Wallace Kelley; Music arranged and conducted: Walter Scharf;

Dean, Jerry Lewis, Pat Crowley and "Mr. Bascom" en route to *Hollywood Or Bust*
(Paramount Pictures Corp. publicity photo)

Musical numbers created and staged by Charles O' Curran; Vocal arrangements by Norman Luboff; New songs written by Sammy Fain and Paul Francis Webster; Technicolor; VistaVision

Cast: Dean Martin (Steve Wiley); Jerry Lewis (Malcolm Smith); Pat Crowley (Terry Roberts); Maxie Rosenbloom (Bookie Benay); Anita Ekberg (herself); Willard Waterman (Neville); Bcn Welden (boss); Jack McElroy (Stupid Sam); Mike Ross (guard); Wendell Miles (master of ceremonies); Frank Wilcox (director); Kathryn Card (old lady); Richard Karlan (Sammy Ross); Tracy Roberts (redhead); Ralph Peters (cab driver); Chief Yowlachie (Indian); Ross Westlake (sheep woman); Gretchen Houser (dancer); Sandra White, Adele August, Valerie Allen, Claudia Martin, Gail Martin, Deana Martin, Frank Farnum, Major Sam Harris (bit parts); Baron (Mr. Bascom)

Dean's Songs: Hollywood Or Bust (With Jerry; Voice Over); A Day In The Country (With Jerry); It Looks Like Love (With Pat Crowley); Let's Be Friendly; Wild And Woolly West (With Jerry and Pat Crowley)

Reviews:

VARIETY	12/5/56
NEW YORK TIMES	12/24/56
TIME	1/21/57
NATIONAL PARENT/TEACHER	2/57

Released by Paramount in December 1956; color; 95 minutes

Movie Gross: $3,300,000

10,000 BEDROOMS (1957)

Credits: Produced by Joe Pasternak; Directed by Richard Thorpe; Written by Laslo Vadnay and Art Cohn and William Ludwig and Leonard Spiegelgass; New songs: music by Nicholas Brodszky, lyrics by Sammy Cahn; Music composed and conducted by George Stoll; Orchestrations: Skip Martin and Robert Van Eps; Vocal supervision: Robert Tucker; "Money Is A Problem" staged by Jack Baker; Music coordinator: Irving Aaronson; Director of photography: Robert Bronner; Art directors: William A. Horning and Randall Duell; Set decorations: Edwin B. Willis and Richard Pefferle; Costumes: Helen Rose; Film editor: John McSweeney, Jr.; Special effects: A. Arnold Gillespie; Color consultant: Charles K. Hagedon; Recording supervisor: Dr. Wesley C. Miller; Assistant director: Robert Saunders; Hairstyles: Sydney Guilaroff; Makeup: William Tuttle; Cinemascope; Metrocolor

Cast: Dean Martin (Ray Hunter); Anna Maria Alberghetti (Nina Martelli); Eva Bartok (Marla Martelli); Dewey Martin (Mike Clark); Walter Slezak (Vittorio Martelli); Paul Henreid (Anton); Jules Munshin (Arthur); Evelyn Varden (Countess Alzoni); Marcel Dalio (Vittorio Gisini); Lisa Montell (Diana Martelli); Lisa Gaye (Anna Martelli); John Archer (Bob Dudley); Steve Dunne (Tom Crandall); Dean Jones (Dam); Monique Van Vooren (girl on main title)

Dean's Songs: 10,000 Bedrooms (Voice Over); You I Love (With Anna Maria
Alberghetti); Only Trust Your Heart (With Anna Maria Alberghetti
and Walter Slezak); Money Is A Problem (With Jules Munshin)

Reviews:

VARIETY	2/20/57
COMMONWEAL	3/22/57
NEWSWEEK	4/1/57
NEW YORK TIMES	4/4/57
SENIOR SCHOLASTIC	4/4/57
NEW YORKER	4/13/57
AMERICA	4/20/57
NATIONAL PARENT/TEACHER	5/57

Released by MGM in April 1957; color; 113 minutes

Movie Gross: $1,000,000

THE YOUNG LIONS (1958)

Credits: Produced by Al Lichtman; Directed by Edward Dmytryk; Screenplay by
Edward Anhalt; Based on a novel by Irwin Shaw; Music: Hugo
Friedhofer; Conducted by Lionel Newman; Director of
photography: Joe MacDonald; Art direction: Lyle R. Wheeler and
Addison Hehr; Set decoration: Walter M. Scott and Stuart A. Reiss;
Special photographic effects: L. B. Abbott; Film editor: Dorothy
Spencer; Executive wardrobe design: Charles LeMaire; Costume
designer: Adele Balkan; Orchestration: Edward B. Powell; Assistant
director: Ad Schaumer; Technical advisor: Lt. Col. Allison A.
Conrad; Makeup: Ben Nye; Hairstyles: Helen Turpin; Sound:
Alfred Bruzlin and Warren B. Delaplain; Cinemascope lenses by
Bausch and Lomb

Cast: Marlon Brando (Christian Diesti); Montgomery Clift (Noah Ackerman);
Dean Martin (Michael Whiteacre); Hope Lange (Hope Plowman);
Barbara Rush (Margaret Freemantle); May Britt (Gretchen
Hardenberg); Maximilian Schell (Capt. Hardenberg); Dora Doll
(Simone); Lee Van Cleef (Sgt. Rickett); Liliane Montevecchi
(Franciose); Parley Baer (Brandt); Arthur Franz (Lt. Green); Hal
Baylor (Pvt. Burnecker); Richard Gardner (Pvt. Cowley); Herbert
Rudley (Capt. Colclough); Sam Gilman (Pvt. Faber); L. Q. Jones
(Pvt. Donnelly); Julian Burton (Pvt. Brailsford); John Alderson
(Col. Kraus); John Banner (Burgermeister); Stephen Bekassy
(German major); Robert Burton (Col. Mead); Ann Codee (French
lady); Paul Comi (Pvt. Abbott); Ashley Cowan (Maier); Robert
Ellenstein (rabbi); Harry Ellerbe (draft board chairman); Milton
Frome (physician); John Gabriel (Burn); Stan Kamber (Acaro);
Kurt Katch (camp commandant); George Meader (milkman); Clive
Morgan (British colonel); Alberto Morin (bartender); Michael
Pataki (Pvt. Hagstrom); Voltaire Perkins (druggist); Otto Reichow
(Bavarian); Gene Roth (cafe manager); Henry Rowland (sergeant);
Jeffrey Sayre (drunk); Norbert Schiller (civilian); Michael G. Smith
(draft board member); Harvey Stephens (Gen. Rockland); Vaughan

Dean's critically-acclaimed role as Michael Whiteacre in *The Young Lions*
(20th Century Fox publicity photo)

Taylor (John Plowman); Alfred Tonkel (German waiter); Ivan Triesault (German colonel)

Dean's Songs: Blue Moon; How About You

Reviews:		
	VARIETY	3/19/58
	LIBRARY JOURNAL	4/1/58
	NEW YORK TIMES	4/3/58
	NEWSWEEK	4/7/58
	NEW YORKER	4/12/58
	SATURDAY REVIEW	4/12/58
	LIFE	4/14/58
	TIME	4/14/58
	LOOK	4/15/58
	COMMONWEAL	4/18/58
	AMERICA	4/19/58
	NATION	4/19/58
	NEW REPUBLIC	4/28/58
	CATHOLIC WORLD	6/58

Released by 20th Century Fox in April 1958; black and white; 167 minutes

Movie Gross: $5,000,000

SOME CAME RUNNING (1959)

Credits: Produced by Sol C. Siegel; Directed by Vincente Minnelli; Screenplay by John Patrick and Arthur Sheekman; Based on the novel by James Jones; Music score: Elmer Bernstein; Orchestrations: Leo Shuken and Jack Hayes; Director of photography: William H. Daniels; Art directors: William A. Horning and Urie McCleary; Set decorations: Henry Grace and Robert Priestley; Color consultant: Charles K. Hagedon; "To Love And Be Loved" written by Sammy Cahn and James Van Heusen; Film editor: Adrienne Fazan; Assistant director: William McGarry; Recording supervisor: Franklin Milton; Costumes: Walter Plunkett; Makeup: William Tuttle; Cinemascope; Metrocolor

Cast: Frank Sinatra (Dave Hirsh); Dean Martin (Bama Dillert); Shirley MacLaine (Ginny Moorehead); Martha Hyer (Gwen French); Arthur Kennedy (Frank Hirsh); Nancy Gates (Edith Barclay); Leora Dana (Agnes Hirsh); Betty Lou Keim (Dawn Hirsh); Larry Gates (Robert Haven French); Steven Peck (Raymond Lanchak); Connie Gilchrist (Jane Barclay); Ned Weaver (Smitty); Carmen Phillips (Rosalie); John Brennan (Wally Dennis); Denny Miller (Dewey Cole); Don Haggerty (Ted Harperspoon); William Schallert (Al); Geraldine Wall (Mrs. Stevens); Janelle Richards (Virginia Stevens); George E. Stone (Slim); Anthony Jochim (Judge Baskin); Marion Ross (Sister Mary Joseph); Ric Roman (Joe); Roy Engel (sheriff); Elmer Peterson (radio announcer)

Reviews:	*VARIETY*	12/24/58

With John Wayne and Ricky Nelson in the classic western *Rio Bravo*
(Warner Bros. publicity photo)

NEWSWEEK	12/29/58
SATURDAY REPUBLIC	1/3/59
NEW REPUBLIC	1/12/59
TIME	1/12/59
LIBRARY JOURNAL	1/15/59
COMMONWEAL	1/23/59
NEW YORK TIMES	1/23/59
NEW YORKER	1/31/59

Released by MGM in January 1959; color; 127 minutes

Movie Gross: $4,200,000

RIO BRAVO (1959)

Credits: Produced and directed by Howard Hawks; Screenplay by Jules Furthman and Leigh Brackett; From a short story by B. H. McCampbell; Title song: Music by Dimitri Tiomkin, Lyrics by Paul Frances Webster; Director of photography: Russell Harlan; Art director: Leo K. Kuter; Film editor: Folmar Blangsted; Sound: Robert B. Lee; Set decorator: Ralph S. Hurst; Costume designer: Marjorie Best; Makeup supervisor: Gordon Bau; Assistant director: Paul Hemlick; Music composed and conducted by Dimitri Tiomkin; Technicolor; An Armada Production

Cast: John Wayne (John T. Chance); Dean Martin (Dude); Ricky Nelson (Colorado Ryan); Angie Dickinson (Feathers); Walter Brennan (Stumpy); Ward Bond (Pat Wheeler); John Russell (Nathan Burdette); Pedro Gonzalez-Gonzalez (Carlos Remonte); Estelita Rodriguez (Consuela); Claude Akins (Joe Burdette); Malcolm Atterbury (Jake); Harry Carey, Jr. (Harold); Nesdon Booth (Clark); Bob Steele (Matt Harris); George Bruggeman (Clem); Fred Graham (gunman); Myron Healey (barfly); Riley Hill (Messenger); Eugene Iglesias (first Burdette man in shootout); Tom Monroe (henchman); Bing Russell (cowboy killed in saloon); Bob Terhune (Charlie the bartender); Ted White (Bart)

Dean's Songs: Rio Bravo (Voice Over); My Rifle, My Pony And Me (With Ricky Nelson); Cindy (With Ricky Nelson and Walter Brennan)

Reviews:

VARIETY	2/18/59
SATURDAY REVIEW	3/14/59
NEW YORK TIMES	3/19/59
COMMONWEAL	3/27/59
AMERICA	3/28/59
NEWSWEEK	3/30/59
CATHOLIC WORLD	4/59
TIME	4/6/59

Released by Warner Brothers in March 1959; color; 140 minutes

Movie Gross: $5,100,000

CAREER (1959)

Credits: Produced by Hal B. Wallis; Directed by Joseph Anthony; Screenplay based on a play by James Lee; Director of photography: Joseph La Shelle; Art direction: Hal Pereira and Walter Tyler; Special photographic effects: John P. Fulton; Process photography: Farciout Edouart; Editorial supervision: Warren Low; Costumes: Edith Head; "Love Is A Career" written by Sammy Cahn and James Van Heusen; Set decoration: Sam Comer and Arthur Krans; Makeup supervision: Wally Westmore; Assistant director: D. Michael Moore; Hair style supervisor: Nellie Manley; Jewels by Ruser; Sound recording: Gene Merritt and Winston Leverett; Associate producer: Paul Nathan; Music: Franz Waxman

Cast: Dean Martin (Maury Novack); Anthony Franciosa (Sam Lawson); Shirley MacLaine (Sharon Kensington); Carolyn Jones (Shirley Drake); Joan Blackman (Barbara); Robert Middleton (Robert Kensington); Frank McHugh (Charley Gallagher); Donna Douglas (Marjorie Burkel); Jerry Paris (Allan Burke); Chuck Wassil (Eric Peters); Mary Treen (Shirley's secretary); Alan Hewitt (Matt Helmsley); Marjorie Bennett (columnist)

Reviews:

VARIETY	9/30/59
NEW YORK TIMES	10/9/59
SATURDAY REVIEW	10/10/59
AMERICA	10/17/59
NEW YORKER	10/17/59
NEWSWEEK	10/19/59
TIME	10/19/59
COMMONWEAL	11/6/59

Released by Paramount in November 1959; black and white; 105 minutes

Movie Gross: $1,100,000

WHO WAS THAT LADY (1960)

Credits: Produced and written by Norman Krasna; Directed by George Sidney; Title song by Sammy Cahn and James Van Heusen; Based on the play "Who Was That Lady I Saw You With" by Norman Krasna as produced on the New York stage by Leland Hayward; Gowns: Jean Louis; Music: Andre Previn; Director of photography: Harry Stradling; Art director: Edward Haworth; Film editor: Viola Lawrence; Set decorator: James M. Crowe; Assistant director: David Silver; Makeup supervision: Ben Lane; Hairstyles: Helen Hunt; Miss Leigh's hair styles by Larry Germain; Recording supervisor: Charles J. Rice; Sound: James Flaster; An Ansark-George Sidney Production

Cast: Tony Curtis (David Wilson); Dean Martin (Michael Haney); Janet Leigh (Ann Wilson); James Whitmore (Harry Powell); John McIntire (Bob Doyle); Barbara Nichols (Gloria Coogle); Larry Keating (Parker); Larry Storch (Orenov); Simon Oakland (Belka); Joi

Lansing (Florence Coogle); Barbara Hines (girl); Marion Javits (Miss Mellish); Michael Lane (Glinka); Kam Tong (Lee Wong); William Newell (Schultz); Harry Jackson (Joe Bendix); Snub Pollard (tattoo artist)

Dean's Song: Who Was That Lady

Reviews:	*VARIETY*	1/13/60
	COMMONWEAL	1/22/60
	McCALL'S	3/60
	TIME	3/14/60
	NEW YORK TIMES	4/16/60
	AMERICA	4/23/60

Released by Columbia pictures in April 1960; black and white; 116 minutes

Movie Gross: $3,000,000

BELLS ARE RINGING (1960)

Credits: Produced by Arthur Freed; Directed by Vincente Minnelli; Screenplay and lyrics by Betty Comden and Adolph Green; Music: Jule Styne; Based on the musical play "Bells Are Ringing"; book and lyrics by Betty Comden and Adolph Green; music by Jule Styne; As presented on the stage by the Theatre Guild; Music adapted and conducted by Andre Previn; Orchestrations: Alexander Courage and Pete King; Choreography: Charles O' Curran; Director of photography: Milton Krasner; Art directors: George W. Davis and Preston Ames; Set decorations: Henry Grace and Keogh Gleason; Color consultant: Charles K. Hagedon; Film editor: Adrienne Tuzar; Special effects: A. Arnold Gillespie and Leo LeBlanc; Assistant director: William McGarry; Hairstyles: Sydney Guilaroff; Makeup creator: William Tuttle; Costume designer: Walter Plunkett; Recording supervisor: Franklin Milton; Photographic lenses by Panavision; Cinemascope; Metrocolor

Cast: Judy Holliday (Ella Peterson); Dean Martin (Jeffrey Moss); Fred Clark (Larry Hastings); Eddie Foy, Jr. (J. Otto Prantz); Jean Stapleton (Sue); Ruth Storey (Gwynee); Dort Clark (Inspector Barnes); Frank Gorshin (Blake Barton); Ralph Roberts (Francis); Valerie Allen (Olga); Bernie West (Dr. Joe Kitchell); Steven Peck (gangster); Gerry Mulligan (Ella's blind date)

Dean's Songs: Better Than A Dream (With Judy Holliday); I Met A Girl; Just In Time (With Judy Holliday); Do It Yourself

Reviews:	*VARIETY*	6/8/60
	TIME	6/20/60
	NEW YORK TIMES	6/24/60
	NEW REPUBLIC	6/27/60
	NEWSWEEK	6/27/60
	COMMONWEAL	7/8/60
	NEW YORKER	7/9/60
	SATURDAY REVIEW	7/9/60

Jack Entratter's dream becomes a reality: "The Rat Pack" create their own
"place in the sun" at the Sands Hotel in Las Vegas, 1960.
(Left to right: Peter Lawford, Frank Sinatra, Dean, Sammy Davis, Jr., and Joey Bishop)
(Las Vegas News Bureau)

AMERICA   7/16/60
Released by MGM in June 1960; color; 126 minutes

Movie Gross: $2,700,000

OCEAN'S 11 (1960)

Credits: Produced and directed by Lewis Milestone; Screenplay by Harry Brown and Charles Lederer; Based on a story by George Clayton Johnson and Jack Golden Russell; Director of photography: William H. Daniels; Art director: Nicolai Remisoff; Film editor: Philip W. Anderson; Sound: M. A. Merrick; Set decorator: Howard Bristol; Assistant to the director: Dick Benedict; Production manager: Jack R. Berne; Costume designer: Howard Shoup; Makeup supervisor: Gordon Bau; Assistant director: Ray Gosnell, Jr.; Photographic lenses: Panavision; Title design: Saul Bass; Orchestration: Arthur Morton; Music composed and conducted by Nelson Riddle; Songs: "Ain't That A Kick In The Head" (Sung by Dean Martin) and "Eee-o-eleven" (Sung by Sammy Davis, Jr.) written by Sammy Cahn and James Van Heusen; Technicolor; A Dorchester Production

Cast: Frank Sinatra (Danny Ocean); Dean Martin (Sam Harmon); Sammy Davis, Jr. (Josh Howard); Peter Lawford (Jimmy Foster); Angie Dickinson (Beatrice Ocean); Richard Conte (Tony Bergdorf); Cesar Romero (Duke Santos); Patrice Wymore (Adele Ekstrom); Joey Bishop (Mushy O' Conners); Akim Tamiroff (Spyros Acebos); Henry Silva (Roger Corneal); Ilka Chase (Mrs. Restes); Buddy Lester (Vince Massler); Richard Benedict (George "Curly" Steffens); Jean Wiles (Grace Bergdorf); Norman Fell (Peter Rheimer); Clem Harvey (Louis Jackson); Hank Henry (Mr. Kelly); Lew Gallo (young man); Robert Foulk (Sheriff Wimmer); Charles Meredith (Mr. Cohen); Ronnie Dapo (Timmy Bergdorf); George E. Stone (store owner); Louis Quinn (DeWolfe); John Indrisano (Texan); Carmen Phillips (hungry girl); Murray Alper (deputy); Hoot Gibson (road block deputy); Gregory Gay (Freeman); Don "Red" Barry (McCoy); Red Skelton (client at casino); George Raft (Jack Strager); Shirley MacLaine (drunk lady); Red Norvo (himself)

Dean's Song: Ain't That A Kick In The Head (With Red Norvo)

Reviews:

VARIETY	8/10/60
NEW YORK TIMES	8/11/60
AMERICA	8/20/60
NEW YORKER	8/20/60
NEWSWEEK	8/22/60
TIME	8/22/60

Released by Warner Brothers in August 1960; color; 127 minutes

Movie Gross: $4,900,000

ALL IN A NIGHT'S WORK (1961)

Credits: Produced by Hal B. Wallis; Directed by Joseph Anthony; Screenplay by Edmund Beloin and Maurice Richlin and Sidney Sheldon; Based on a story by Margit Veszi and a play by Oven Elford; Director of photography: Joseph Lashelle; Technicolor color consultant: Richard Mueller; Art direction: Hal Pereira and Walter Tyler; Special photographic effects: John P. Fulton; Process photography: Farciot Edouart; Set decoration: Sam Comer and Arthur Krams; Editorial supervision: Warren Low; Editor: Howard Smith; Assistant director: Daniel J. McCauley; Associate producer: Paul Nathan; Costumes: Edith Head; Makeup supervision: Wally Westmore; Hair style supervision: Nellie Manley; Sound recording: Gene Merritt and Charles Grenzbach; Music: Andre Previn; Technicolor

Cast: Dean Martin (Tony Ryder); Shirley MacLaine (Katie Robbins); Cliff Robertson (Warren Kingsley, Jr.); Charlie Ruggles (Warren Kingsley, Sr.); Norma Crane (Marge Coombs); Jack Weston (Lasker); John Hudson (Harry Lane); Jerome Cowan (Sam Weaver); Gale Gordon (Oliver Dunning); Ralph Dumke (Baker); Mabel Albertson (Mrs. Kingsley); Rex Evans (Carter); Mary Treen (Miss Schuster); Roy Gordon (Albright); Ian Wolfe (O' Hara); Charles Evans (Colonel Ryder); Gertrude Astor (customer)

Reviews:

VARIETY	3/22/61
NEW YORK TIMES	3/23/61
NEW YORKER	3/25/61
McCALL'S	4/61
TIME	4/7/61
COMMONWEAL	4/21/61
AMERICA	4/29/61

Released by Paramount in March 1961; color; 94 minutes

Movie Gross: $2,200,000

ADA (1961)

Credits: Produced by Lawrence Weingarten; Directed by Daniel Mann; Screenplay by Arthur Sheekman and William Driskill; Based on the novel "Ada Dallas" by Wirt Williams; Music score: Bronislau Kaper; Orchestra conductor: Robert Armbruster; Director of photography: Joseph Ruttenberg; Art direction: George W. Davis and Edward Carfagno; Set decoration: Henry Grace and Jack Mills; Color consultant: Charles K. Hagedon; Special visual effects: Lee LeBlanc; Film editor: Ralph E. Winters; Costume designer: Helen Rose; Assistant director: Al Jennings; Hairstyles: Mary Keats; Makeup: William Tuttle; Recording supervisor: Franklin Milton; Photographic lenses by Panavision; "May The Lord Bless You Real Good" by Warren Roberts and Wally Fowler; Cinemascope; Metrocolor; An Avon Productions, Inc., Chalmar Picture

Cast: Susan Hayward (Ada Dallas); Dean Martin (Bo Gillis); Wilfrid Hyde Whit

(Sylvester Marin); Ralph Meeker (Col. Yancy); Martin Balsam (Steve Jackson); Frank Maxwell (Ronnie Hallerton); Connie Sawyer (Alice Sweet); Ford Rainey (speaker); Charles Watts (Al Winslow); Larry Gates (Joe Adams); Robert S. Simon (Warren Natfield); William Zuckert (Harry Davers); Mary Treen (clubwoman)

Dean's Song: May The Lord Bless You Real Good

Reviews:

VARIETY	7/26/61
NEW YORK TIMES	8/26/61
TIME	9/8/61

Released by MGM in August 1961; color; 109 minutes

Movie Gross: $1,000,000

SERGEANT'S 3 (1962)

Credits: Produced by Frank Sinatra; Directed by John Sturges; Executive producer: Howard W. Koch; Written by W. R. Burnett; Music: Billy May; Director of photography: Winton Hoch; "And The Night Wind Sang" written by Johnny Rotella and Franz Steininger; Art director: Frank Hotaling; Film editor: Ferris Webster; Assistant director: Jack Reddish; Set director: Victor Gangelin; Wardrobe: Wesley Jefferies and Angela Alexander; Makeup: Bernard Ponedel; Hairstylist: Mary Westmoreland; Sound recorder: Harold Lewis; Second unit director: Al Wyatt; Second unit photography: Carl Guthrie; Special effects: Paul Pollard; Technicolor; Panavision; An Essex-Claude Production

Cast: Frank Sinatra (Mike Merry); Dean Martin (Chip Deal); Sammy Davis, Jr. (Jonah Williams); Peter Lawford (Larry Barrett); Joey Bishop (Roger Boswell); Henry Silva (Mountain Hawk); Ruta Lee (Amelia Parent); Buddy Lester (Willie Sharpknife); Philip Crosby (Ellis); Dennis Crosby (Page); Lindsay Crosby (Wills); Hank Henry (blacksmith); Richard Simmons (William Collingwood); Michael Pate (Watanka); Armand Alzamora (Caleb); Richard Hale (White Eagle); Mickey Finn (Morton); Sonny King (corporal); Eddie Littlesky (ghost dancer); Ceffie (herself); Rodd Redwing (Irregular); James Waters (colonel's aide); Madge Blake (Mrs. Parent); Dorothy Abbott (Mrs. Collingwood); Walter Merrill (telegrapher)

Reviews:

VARIETY	1/24/62
TIME	2/9/62
NEW YORK TIMES	2/12/62
COMMONWEAL	3/16/62

Released by Warner Brothers in February 1962; color; 112 minutes

Movie Gross: $3,955,000

WHO'S GOT THE ACTION (1962)

Credits: Produced by Jack Rose; Directed by Daniel Mann; Screenplay by Jack Rose; Based on the novel "Four Horse Players Are Missing" by Alexander Rose; Director of photography: Joseph Ruttenberg;

Art direction: Hal Pereira and Arthur Lonergan; Process photography: Farciot Edouart; Assistant director: Arthur Jacobson; Set decoration: Sam Comer and Darrell Silvera; Technicolor color consultant: Richard Mueller; Orchestration: Arthur Morton; Editor: Howard Smith; Makeup supervision: Wally Westmore; Hairstyle supervision: Nellie Manley; Miss Turner's hairstyles by Helen Young; Sound recording: Hugo and Charles Grenzbach; Costumes: Edith Head; Music scored and conducted by George Duning; Title song written by Jack Brooks and George Duning; Technicolor; Panavision; An Amro-Claude-Mea Production

Cast: Dean Martin (Steve Flood); Lana Turner (Melanie Flood); Eddie Albert (Clint Morgan); Walter Matthau (Tony Gagoots); Paul Ford (Judge Boatwright); Nita Talbot (Saturday Knight); Lewis Charles (Clutch); John McGiver (Judge Fogel); Margo (Roza); Jack Albertson (Officer Hodges); Alexander Rose (Mr. Goody); Ned Glass (Baldy); Dan Tobin (Mr. Sanford); John Indrisano (hood); George Dee (waiter); Wilbur Mack (groom/octogenarian); Alphonse Martell (maitre d'); Ralph Montgomery (street cleaner); House Peters, Jr. (cop in elevator); Eddie Quillan (Dingo the phone repairman); Joe Vitale (bartender); June Wilkinson (bride)

Dean's Song: Who's Got The Action (Voice Over)

Reviews:

VARIETY	12/12/62
NEW YORK TIMES	12/26/62
NEWSWEEK	1/7/63
TIME	2/9/63

Released by Paramount in December 1962; color; 93 minutes

Movie Gross: $1,400,000

TOYS IN THE ATTIC (1963)

Credits: Produced by Walter Mirisch; Directed by George Roy Hill; Screenplay by James Poe; Based upon the stage play by Lillian Hellman; Produced on the Broadway stage by Kermit Bloomgarden; Music: George Duning; Director of photography: Joseph F. Biroc; Art director: Cary Odell; Film editor: Stuart Gilmore; Set decorator: Victor Gilmore; Property: Ross C. Burke; Costume designer: Bill Thomas; Production manager: Allen K. Wood; Assistant director: Emmett Emerson; Script supervisor: Dixie McCoy; Music editor: Richard Carruth; Sound effects editor: Gilbert D. Marchant; Assistant film editor: Marshall M. Borden; Wardrobe: Mick James and Angela Alexander; Makeup: Frank Prehoda and Loren Cosand; Hairstylist: Mary Westmoreland; Casting: Talmaster-Lister, Co.; Panavision

Cast: Dean Martin (Julian Berniers); Geraldine Page (Carrie); Yvette Mimieux (Lilly Prine); Wendy Hiller (Anna); Gene Tierney (Albertine Prine); Frank Silvera (Henry); Larry Gates (Cyrus Warkins); Nan Martin (Charlotte Warkins); Charles Lampkin (Gus)

Reviews: *SATURDAY REVIEW*   7/20/63

VARIETY	7/26/63
NEW YORK TIMES	8/1/63
TIME	8/9/63
NEW YORKER	8/10/63
NEWSWEEK	8/12/63
NEW REPUBLIC	8/17/63

Released by United Artists in August 1963; black and white; 88 minutes
Movie Gross Unavailable

WHO'S BEEN SLEEPING IN MY BED (1963)

Credits: Produced and written by Jack Rose; Directed by Daniel Mann; Director
of photography: Joseph Ruttenberg; Art direction: Hal Pereira and
Arthur Lonergan; Set decoration: Sam Comer and Arthur Krams;
Sculpture: Delia Salvi; Dances staged by Steven Peck; Makeup
supervisor: Wally Westmore; Hairstyle supervisor: Nellie Manley;
Editor: George Tomasini; Assistant director: Arthur Jacobson;
Orchestration: Arthur Morton; "Tangerine" written by Johnny
Mercer and Dorothy Fields; "I'm In The Mood For Love" written
by Jimmy McHugh and Dorothy Fields; Special photographic
effects: Paul K. Lerpae; Process photography: Farciot Edouart;
Sound recording: Harry Lindgren and Charles Grenzbach;
Technicolor color consultant: Richard Mueller; Costumes: Edith
Head; Music score: George Duning; Technicolor; Panavision;
An Amro-Claude Production

Cast: Dean Martin (Jason Steel); Elizabeth Montgomery (Melissa Morris); Martin
Balsam (Sanford Kaufman); Jill St. John (Toby Tobler); Richard
Conte (Leonard Ashley); Macha Meril (Jacqueline Edwards); Louis
Nye (Harry Tobler); Yoko Tani (Isami Hiroti); Jack Soo (Yoshimi
Hiroti); Dianne Foster (Mona Kaufman); Elliott Reed (Tom
Edwards); Johnny Silver (Charley); Elisabeth Fraser (Dora Ashley);
Steve Clinton (Sam Jones); Daniel Ocko (lawyer); Allison Hayes
(Mrs. Grayson); James O' Rear (policeman); Carol Burnett (Stella)

Released by Paramount in December 1963; color; 103 minutes
Movie Gross Unavailable

4 FOR TEXAS (1963)

Credits: Produced and directed by Robert Aldrich; Executive producer: Howard
W. Koch; Written by Teddi Sherman and Robert Aldrich; Stunt
supervisor: John Indrisano; Assistant directors: Tom Connors and
Dave Salven; Script supervisor: Robert Cary; Script apprentice:
Adell Aldrich; Property master: John Orlando; Sound mixer: Jack
Solomon; Dialogue supervisor: Robert Sherman; Set decorator:
Raphael Bretton; Makeup: Robert Schiffer; Orchestration: Gil Grau;
Director of photography: Ernest Laszlo; Second unit director: Oscar
Rudolph; Second unit photography: Joseph Biroc, Carl Guthrie and
Burnett Guffey; Associate producer: Walter Blake; Costume

designer: Norma Koch; Production supervisor: Jack R. Berne;
Music: Nelson Riddle; Art direction: William Glasgow; Film editor:
Michael Luciano; Technicolor

Cast: Frank Sinatra (Zack Thomas); Dean Martin (Joe Jarrett); Anita Ekberg
(Elya Carlson); Ursula Andress (Maxine Richter); Charles Bronson
(Matson); Victor Buono (Harvey Burden); Edric Connor (Prince
George); Nick Dennis (Angel); Richard Jaeckel (Mancini); Mike
Mazurki (Chad); Wesley Addy (Trowbridge); Marjorie Bennett
(Miss Ermaline); Virginia Christine (Brunhilde); Ellen Corby
(widow); Jack Elam (Dobie); Jesslyn Fak (widow); Fritz Field
(maitre d'); Percy Helton (Ansel); Jonathan Hole (Renee); Jack
Lambert (monk); Paul Langton (Beauregard); Keith McConnell
(Sweeney); Teddy Buckner and His All-Stars (themselves); Michel
Montau (Helaine); Maidie Norman (maid); Bob Steele (customer);
Mario Siletti (Bedoni); Eva Six (Mrs. Burden); Abraham Sofaer
(Pulaski); Michael St. Angel (Williams); Grady Sutton (secretary);
Ralph Volkie (bartender); Max Wagner (bartender); William
Washington (doorman); Dave Willock (Alfred); Arthur Godfrey
(croupier); The Three Stooges (themselves)

Reviews: *VARIETY*   12/25/63
 NEW YORK TIMES   12/26/63
 TIME   1/10/64

Released by Warner Brothers in December 1963; color; 124 minutes
Movie Gross Unavailable

WHAT A WAY TO GO! (1964)

Credits: Produced by Arthur P. Jacobs; Directed by J. Lee Thompson;
Screenplay: Betty Comden and Adolph Green; Based on a story by
Gwen Davis; Art direction: Jack Martin Smith and Ted Haworth;
Miss MacLaine's gowns designed by Edith Head; "I Think That
You And I Should Get Acquainted" and "Musical Extravaganza" -
lyrics by Betty Comden and Adolph Green; music by Jule Styne;
Choreography: Gene Kelly; Music: Nelson Riddle; Directors of
photography: Leon Shamrov and Ted Haworth; Set decoration:
Walter M. Scott and Stuart A. Reiss; Special photographic effects:
L. B. Abbott and Emil Kosa, Jr.; Unit production manager: William
Eckhardt; Assistant director: Fred R. Simpson; Mens' wardrobe:
Moss Mabry; Film editor: Marjorie Fowler; Assistant to Mr. Kelly:
Richard Humphrey; Dialogue coach: Leon Charles; Sound: Bernard
Freericks and Elmer Raguse; Orchestration: Arthur Morton;
Makeup: Ben Nye; Supervising hairstylist: Margaret Donovan; Miss
MacLaine's hairstyles created by Sidney Guilaroff; Precious stones
by Harry Winston; Gloves by Kislav; Color: DeLuxe; Produced by
Apjac-Orchard Productions, Inc.; Released through 20th Century
Fox Film Corporation

Cast: Shirley MacLaine (Louisa); Paul Newman (Larry Flint); Robert Mitchum
(Rod Anderson); Dean Martin (Leonard Crawley); Gene Kelly

With Frank Sinatra and Sammy Davis, Jr. in *Robin and the 7 Hoods*
(Warner Bros. publicity photo)

(Jerry Benson); Bob Cummings (Dr. Steffanson); Dick Van Dyke (Edgar Hopper); Reginald Gardiner (painter); Margaret Dumont (Mrs. Foster); Lou Nova (Trentino); Fifi Dorsay (baroness); Maurice Marsac (Rene); Wally Vernon (agent); Jane Wald (Polly); Lenny Kent (Hollywood lawyer)

Reviews:

VARIETY	4/1/64
COMMONWEAL	5/1/64
LIFE	5/8/64
NEW YORK TIMES	5/15/64
NEW YORKER	5/16/64
NEWSWEEK	5/18/64
TIME	5/22/64
NEW REPUBLIC	5/30/64

Released by 20th Century Fox in May 1964; color; 111 minutes

Movie Gross: $5,000,000

ROBIN AND THE SEVEN HOODS (1964)

Credits: Produced by Frank Sinatra; Directed by Gordon Douglas; Executive producer: Howard W. Koch; Written by David R. Schwartz; Musical numbers staged by Jack Baker; Songs by Sammy Cahn and James Van Heusen; Music scored and conducted by Nelson Riddle; Director of photography and associate producer: William H. Daniels; Art director: LeRoy Deane; Film editor: Sam O' Steen; Sound: Everett Hughes and Vinton Vernon; Dialogue supervisor: Thom Conroy; Assistant directors: David Salven and Lee White; Costume supervisor: Don Feld; Makeup supervisor: Gordon Bau; Supervising hair stylist: Jean Burt Reilly; Set decorator: Raphael Bretton; Orchestration: Gilbert C. Grau; Choreographer: Jack Baker; Technicolor; Panavision; A P-C Productions Picture

Cast: Frank Sinatra (Robbo); Dean Martin (John); Sammy Davis, Jr. (Will); Peter Falk (Guy Gisborne); Barbara Rush (Marian); Victor Buono (Sheriff Potts); Bing Crosby (Allen A. Dale); Hank Henry (Six Seconds); Allen Jenkins (Vermin); Jack LaRue (Tomatoes); Robert Foulk (Sheriff Glick); Phil Crosby (Robbo's hood); Robert Carricart (Blue Jaw); Phil Arnold (Hatrack); Sonny King (Robbo's hood); Richard Simmons (prosecutor); Harry Swoger (Soupmeat); Harry Wilson (Gisborne's hood); Richard Bakalyan (Robbo's hood); Bernard Fein (Charlie Bananas); Joseph Ruskin (Twitch); Al Silvani (Robbo's hood); Carol Lee Hill (cocktail waitress); Mickey Finn (bartender); Sig Ruman (Hammacher); Barry Kelley (police chief); Hans Conreid (Mr. Ricks); Edward G. Robinson (Big Jim)

Dean's Songs: Any Man Who Loves His Mother; Style (With Frank Sinatra and Bing Crosby); Mister Booze (With Frank Sinatra, Bing Crosby and Sammy Davis, Jr.); Don't Be A Do-Badder (With Frank Sinatra and Sammy Davis, Jr.)

Reviews:

SATURDAY REVIEW	5/16/64
EBONY	6/64

COMMONWEAL	6/19/64
VARIETY	6/24/64
NEWSWEEK	7/6/64
TIME	7/17/64
LIFE	7/24/64
NEW YORK TIMES	8/6/64

Released by Warner Brothers in August 1964; color; 123 minutes

Movie Gross: $1,000,000

KISS ME, STUPID (1964)

Credits: Produced and directed by Billy Wilder; Screenplay by Billy Wilder and I. A. L. Diamond; Based on "L'oro Della Fantasia" by Anna Bonacci; Costume designer: Bill Thomas; Songs by George and Ira Gershwin; Music score: Andre Previn; Production designer: Alexander Trauner; Director of photography: Joseph LaShelle; Associate producers: I. A. L. Diamond and Doane Harrison; Art director: Robert Luthardt; Set decoration: Edward G. Boyle; Film editor: Daniel Mandell; Sound: Robert Martin; Music editor: Richard Carruth; Re-recording: Clem Portman; Sound effects editor: Wayne Fury; Production manager: Allen K. Wood; Unit manager: Ray Gosnell; Assistant director: C. C. Coleman, Jr.; Properties: Frank Agnone; Script supervisor: Marshall Wolins; Special effects: Milton Rice; Wardrobe: Wea Jefferies and Irene Cain; Makeup: Emile La Vigne and Loren Cosand; Hairdressers: Alice Monte and Maudlee McDougall; Casting: Lynn Stalmaster; Choreographer: Wally Green; Panavision; A Phalanx Production; Distributed by Lopert Picture Corporation

Cast: Dean Martin (Dino); Kim Novak (Polly the Pistol); Ray Walston (Orville J. Spooner); Felicia Farr (Zelda Spooner); Cliff Osmond (Barney Milsap); Barbara Pepper (Big Bertha); James Ward (milkman); Dora Merande (Mrs. Pettibone); Bobo Lewis (waitress); Tommy Nolan (Johnnie Mulligan); Alice Pearce (Mrs. Mulligan); John Fiedler (Rev. Carruthers); Arlen Stuart (Rosalie Schultz); Howard McNear (Mr. Pettibone); Cliff Norton (Mack Gray); Mel Blanc (Dr, Sheldrake); Eileen O' Neil and Susan Wedell (showgirls); Bern Hoffman (bartender); Henry Gibson (Smith); Alan Dexter (Wesson); Henry Beckman (truck driver); Gene Dartler (Nevada state trooper); Sam the Parrot

Dean's Songs: S'Wonderful; Sophia

Reviews:

VARIETY	12/16/64
COMMONWEAL	12/18/64
NEW YORK TIMES	12/23/64
NEWSWEEK	12/28/64
TIME	1/1/65
SATURDAY REVIEW	1/2/65
NEW REPUBLIC	1/9/65
CHRISTIAN CENTURY	2/3/65

On the set of *The Sons of Katie Elder* with John Wayne
(Paramount Pictures Corp. publicity photo)

VOGUE   3/1/65
Released by Lopert in December 1964; black and white; 126 minutes
Movie Gross: $1,420,000

THE SONS OF KATIE ELDER (1965)

Credits: Produced by Hal B. Wallis; Directed by Henry Hathaway; Screenplay
by William H. Wright, Allan Weiss and Harry Essex; Based on a
story by Talbot Jennings; Director of photography: Lucien Ballard;
Art direction: Hal Pereira and Walter Tyler; Set decoration: Sam
Comer and Ray Moyer; Makeup artists: Loren Cossand and Webb
Overlander; Hairstylist: Dorothy White; Sound recording: Harold
Lewis and Charles Grenzbach; Editorial supervision: Warren Low;
Costumes: Edith Head; Assistant director: D. Michael Moore; Unit
production manager: William W. Gray; Associate producer: Paul
Nathan; Music: Elmer Bernstein; Technicolor; Panavision

Cast: John Wayne (John Elder); Dean Martin (Tom Elder); Martha Hyer (Mary
Gordon); Michael Anderson, Jr. (Bud Elder); Earl Holliman (Matt
Elder); Jeremy Slate (Ben Latta); James Gregory (Morgan
Hastings); Paul Fix (Sheriff Billy Wilson); George Kennedy
(Curley); Dennis Hopper (Dave Hastings); Sheldon Allman (Harry
Evers); John Litel (minister); John Doucette (Hyselman); James
Westerfield (Mr. Vennar); Rhys Williams (Charlie Striker); John
Qualen (Charlie Biller); Rodolfo Acosta (Bondie Adams); Strother
Martin (Jeb Ross); Percy Helton (Mr. Peevey); Karl Swenson (Doc
Isdell and bartender); Jerry Gatlin (Amboy); Harvey Grant (Jeb);
Loren Janes (Ned Reese); Boyd "Red" Morgan (Burr Sandeman);
Chuck Roberson (townsman); Ralph Volkie (bit man); J. Williams
(Andy Sharp); Henry Wills (Gus Dolly); Joe Yrigoyen (Buck
Mason)

Reviews: *VARIETY*   6/30/65
NEW YORK TIMES   8/26/65
TIME   9/3/65
SATURDAY REVIEW   9/4/65
NEWSWEEK   9/6/65
AMERICA   9/18/65

Released by Paramount in August 1965; color; 120 minutes
Movie Gross: $5,000,000

MARRIAGE ON THE ROCKS (1965)

Credits: Producer and director of photography: William H. Daniels; Directed by
Jack Donohue; Written by Cy Howard; Art director: LeRoy Deane;
Film editor: Sam O' Steen; Set decorators: Arthur A. Krams and
William L. Kuehl; Dialogue supervisor: Thom Conroy; Sound:
Francis E. Stahl; Assistant director: Richard Lang; Women's
costumes designed by Walter Plunkett; Mr. Sinatra's wardrobe by
Carroll and Company; Makeup supervisor: Gordon Bau;
Supervising hairstylist: Jean Burt Reilly; Jewelry by Ruser of

Beverly Hills; "Sinner Man" - music by Trini Lopez, lyrics by Bobby Weinstein, Bobby Hart, Billy Barberis and Teddy Randazzo; Production: Joseph C. Behm; Choreography: Jonathan Lucas; Music composed and conducted by Nelson Riddle; Technicolor; Panavision; A Sinatra Enterprise; An A-C Production

Cast: Frank Sinatra (Dan Edwards); Deborah Kerr (Valerie Edwards); Dean Martin (Ernie Brewer); Cesar Romero (Miguel Santos); Hermione Baddeley (Jeannie MacPherson); Tony Bill (Jim Blake); John McGiver (Shad Nathan); Nancy Sinatra (Tracy Edwards); Davey Davidson (Lisa Sterling); Michael Petit (David Edwards); Trini Lopez (himself); Joi Lansing (Lola); Tara Ashton (Bunny); Kathleen Freeman (Miss Blight); Flip Mark (Rollo); DeForest Kelley (Mr. Turner); Sigrid Valdis (Kitty); Byron Foulger (Mr. Bruno); Parley Baer (Dr. Newman); Reta Shaw (Saks' saleslady); Nacho Galindo (mayor); Hedley Mattingly (Mr. Smythe)

Reviews: *NEW YORK TIMES* 9/16/65
  VARIETY 9/22/65

Released by Warner Brothers n September 1965; color; 109 minutes

Movie Gross: $2,500,000

THE SILENCERS (1966)

Credits: Produced by Irving Allen; Directed by Phil Karlson; Screenplay by Oscar Saul; Based on the books "The Silencers" and "Death Of A Citizen" by Donald Hamilton; Music by Elmer Bernstein; Original songs by Elmer Bernstein and Mack David; Choreography: Robert Sidney; Director of photography: Burnett Guffey; Art director: Joe Wright; Associate producer: Jim Schmerer; Parodies written by Herbert Baker; Film editor: Charles Nelson; Set decorator: George R. Nelson; Costume designer: Moss Mabry; Makeup supervision: Ben Lane; Hairstyles by Virginia Jones; Dean Martin's wardrobe coordinator: Sy Devore; Unit production managers: Sergei Petchnikorf and Ralph Black; Assistant director: Clark Paylow; Second assistant director: James Havens; Sound supervisor: Charles J. Rice; Sound: Lambert Day; Title by Pacific Title; Color by Pathe; Vocals by Dean Martin and Vikki Carr

Cast: Dean Martin (Matt Helm); Stella Stevens (Gail); Daliah Lavi (Tina Batori); Victor Buono (Tung-Tze); Arthur O' Connell (Wigman); Robert Webber (Sam Gunther); James Gregory (MacDonald); Nancy Kovack (Barbara); Roger C. Carmel (Andrevev); Cyd Charisse (Sarita); Beverly Adams (Lovey Kravezit); Richard Devon (Domino); David Bond (Dr. Naldi); John Reach (Traynor); Robert Phillips (first armed man); John Willis (master of ceremonies); Frank Gerstle (Frazer); Grant Woods (radio man); Patrick Waltz (hotel clerk); Amedee Chabot (girl); Carol Cole (waitress); Sol Gorss (pilot); Frank S. Hagney (drunk); Harry Holcombe (Agent X); Gary Lasdun (armed man); Ray Montgomery (Agent C); Inga Neilsen (statue); Guy Wilkerson (farmer); Barbara Burgess,

411

Mary Jane Mangler, Margie Nelson, Margaret Teele, Marilyn Tindall, Jann Watson (Slaygirls)

Dean's Songs: Anniversary Song; Empty Saddles In The Old Corral; Glory Of Love; Red Sails In The Sunset; If You Knew Susie; On The Sunny Side Of The Street; Last Roundup; Side By Side; South Of The Border; Everybody Loves Somebody (All songs are Voice Overs; Everybody Loves Somebody is a newly recorded version)

Reviews:

VARIETY	2/9/66
TIME	3/4/66
NEW YORK TIMES	3/17/66
SATURDAY REVIEW	4/9/66

Released by Columbia in March 1966; color; 103 minutes

Movie Gross: $7,000,000

TEXAS ACROSS THE RIVER (1966)

Credits: Produced by Harry Keller; Directed by Michael Gordon; Written by Wells Root, Harold Greene and Ben Starr; Director of photography: Russell Metty; Art directors: Alexander Golitzen and William D. Decinces; Set directors: John McCarthy and James S. Redd; Sound: Waldon O' Watson and David H. Moriarty; Post production manager: Wallace Worsley; Assistant director: Terry Morse, Jr.; Film editor: Gene Milford; Makeup: Bud Westmore; Hairstylist: Larry Germain; Ladies' costumes: Rosemary Odell; Mens' costumes: Helen Coluig; Dialogue coach: Walter Kelley; Stunt coordinator: Robert Buzz Henry; Cosmetics by Cinematique; Fees by National Screen Service; Title song written by Sammy Cahn and James Van Heusen, sung by The Kingston Trio; Music by DeVol; Music supervision: Joseph Gershenson; Technicolor; Techniscope

Cast: Dean Martin (Sam Hollis); Alain Delon (Don Andrea Baldasar); Rosemary Forsyth (Phoebe Ann Taylor); Joey Bishop (Kronk); Tina Marquand (Lonetta); Peter Graves (Capt. Simpson); Michael Ansara (Chief Iron Jacket); Linden Chiles (Yellow Knife); Andrew Prine (Lt. Sibley); Stuart Anderson (Yancy); Roy Barcroft (Cy Morton); George Wallace (Floyd Willet); Don Beddoe (Mr. Naylor); Kelly Thordsen (turkey shoot boss); Nora Marlowe (Emma); John Harmon (Gabe Hutchins); Dick Farnsworth (medicine man)

Reviews:

VARIETY	9/14/66
SATURDAY REVIEW	11/5/66
SENIOR SCHOLASTIC	11/18/66
NEW YORK TIMES	11/24/66
NEW YORKER	12/4/66
NEWSWEEK	12/5/66
TIME	12/9/66

Released by Universal in November 1966; color; 100 minutes

Movie Gross: $4,500,000

About to make a big splash with Corinne Cole in *Murderers' Row*
(Columbia Pictures Corp. publicity photo)

MURDERERS' ROW (1966)

Credits: Produced by Irving Allen; Directed by Henry Levin; Screenplay by Herbert Baker; Based on the book "Murderers' Row" by Donald Hamilton; Makeup: Loren Cosand; Director of photography: Sam Leavitt; Music: Lalo Schifrin; "If You're Thinkin' What I'm Thinkin'" written by Tommy Boyce and Bobby Hart; "I'm Not The Marrying Kind" written by Lalo Schifrin and Howard Greenfield; Associate producer: Evan Lloyd; Second unit director: James Havens; Production supervision: Ivan Volkman; Special effects: Danny Lee and Howard Jensen; Art director: Joe Wright; Film editor: Walter Thompson; Choreographer: Miriam Nelson; Costume designer: Moss Mabry; Set director: George R. Nelson; Assistant director: Ray Gosnell; Second unit photography: Mark Davis; Ann-Margret's hairstyles: Cherie; Makeup supervision: Ben Lane; Sound supervisor: Charles J. Rice; Sound: Lambert Day and Jack Haynes; Technicolor; A Meadway-Claude Production

Cast: Dean Martin (Matt Helm); Ann-Margret (Suzie Solaris); Karl Malden (Jullian Wall); Camilla Sparv (Coco Duquette); James Gregory (MacDonald); Beverly Adams (Lovey Kravezit); Richard Eastham (Dr. Norman Solaris); Tom Reese (Ironhead); Duke Howard (Billy Orcutt); Ted Hartley (guard); Marcel Hillaire (Capt. Deveraux); Corinne Cole (Miss January); Robert Terry (Dr. Rogas); Dino, Desi and Billy (themselves); Jacqueline Fontaine (singer at funeral); Dale Brown, Barbara Burgess, Amedee Chabot, Lucy Anne Cook, Dee Duffy, Dee Gardner, Lynn Hartoch, Mary Hughes, Karen Joy, Mary Jane Mangler, Marilyn Tindall, Jann Watson (Slaygirls)

Dean's Songs: I'm Not The Marrying Kind (Without the backing vocals found on the Reprise version); Old Spinning Wheel (Both songs are Voice Overs)

Reviews:

VARIETY	12/14/66
NEW YORK TIMES	12/22/66
TIME	12/23/66
NEWSWEEK	1/16/67

Released by Columbia in December 1966; color; 108 minutes

Movie Gross: $6,240,000

ROUGH NIGHT IN JERICHO (1967)

Credits: Produced by Martin Rackin; Directed by Arnold Laven; Screenplay by Sydney Boehm and Marvin H. Albert; Based on the novel "The Man In Black" by Marvin H. Albert; Director of photography: Russell Metty; Art directors: Alexander Golitzen and Frank Arrigo; Set decorations: John McCarthy and James S. Redd; Sound: Waldon O. Watson and Frank H. Wilkinson; Unit production manager: Hal Polaire; Assistant director: Joseph Kinny; Second unit director: James C. Havens; Associate producer: Alvin G. Manuel; Film editor: Ted J. Kent; Makeup: Bud Westmore; Hair stylist: Larry

Germain; Ladies' costumes: Rosemary Odell; Mens' costumes: Helen Colvig; Dialogue coach: Irvin Berwick; Matte supervisor: Albert Whitlock; Cosmetics by Cinematique; Music composer: Don Costa; Music supervision: Joseph Gershenson; "Hold Me Now And Forever" - music by Don Costa, lyrics by Phil Zeller, sung by The Kids Next Door; Technicolor; Techniscope

Cast: Dean Martin (Alex Flood); George Peppard (Dolan); Jean Simmons (Molly); John McIntire (Ben Hickman); Slim Pickens (Yarbrough); Don Galloway (Jace); Brad Weston (Torrey); Richard O' Brien (Ryan); Carol Anderson (Claire); Steve Sandor (Simms); Warren Vanders (Harvey); John Napier (McGivern)

Reviews: *VARIETY* 8/9/67
NEW YORK TIMES 11/9/67

Released by Universal in November 1967; color; 102 minutes

Movie Gross: $1,750,000

THE AMBUSHERS (1967)

Credits: Produced by Irving Allen; Directed by Henry Levin; Screenplay by Herbert Baker; Based on the book "The Ambushers" by Donald Hamilton; Directors of photography: Burnett Guffrey and Edward Colman; Music composed and conducted by Hugo Montenegro; Title song written by Herbert Baker and Hugo Montenegro, sung by Tommy Boyce and Bobby Hart; Art director: Joe Wright; Associate producer: Douglas Netter; Second unit director: James Havens; Film editor: Harold F. Kress; Second unit cameramen: Jack Marta and Tony Braun; Special effects: Danny Lee; Dress and costume designer: Oleg Cassini; Set decorator: Richard Spero; Assistant director: Jerome M. Siegel; Unit production manager: Howard Pine; Second unit assistant: Harold Lewis; Makeup supervision: Ben Lane; Hairstyles: Virginia Jones; Sound supervisor: Charles J. Rice; Sound: James Flaster and Jack Haynes; Choreography: Mary Jane Mangler; Property master: Max Frankel; Dean Martin's wardrobe designer: Sy Devore; Technicolor

Cast: Dean Martin (Matt Helm); Senta Berger (Francesca Madeiros); Janice Rule (Sheila Sommers); James Gregory (MacDonald); Albert Salmi (Jose Ortega); Kurt Kasznar (Quintana); Beverly Adams (Lovey Kravezit); David Mauro (Nassim); Roy Jenson (Karl); John Brascia (Rocco); Linda Foster (Linda); Yumiko Ishizuka, Ulla Lindstrom, Lena Cederham, Terri Hughes, Kyra Bester, Annabella Incontrera, Karin Fedderson, Marilyn Tindall, Susannah Moore, Penny Brahms, Jann Watson, Dee Duffy (Slaygirls)

Dean's Song: Everybody Loves Somebody (Voice Over)

Reviews: *VARIETY* 12/20/67
NEW YORK TIMES 12/23/67
AMERICA 1/13/68

Released by Columbia in December 1967; color; 102 minutes
Movie Gross: $4,700,000

HOW TO SAVE A MARRIAGE AND RUIN YOUR LIFE (1968)

Credits: Produced by Stanley Shapiro; Directed by Fielder Cook; Written by Stanley Shapiro and Nate Monaster; Director of photography: Lee Garmes; Production design: Robert Clatworthy; Costumes: Moss Mabry; Film editor: Philip W. Anderson; Production consultant: Bill O' Sullivan; Set decorator: George R. Nelson; Makeup supervision: Ben Lane; Sound supervisor: Charles J. Rice; Property master: Max Frankel; Assistant director: Ray Gosnell; Hairstylist: Virginia Jones; Sound: William Randall, Jr. and Jack Haynes; Color: Pathe; Musical score composed and conducted by Michel Legrand; "Winds Of Change" - lyrics by Mack David, music by Michel Legrand, sung by the Ray Conniff Singers; Panavision

Cast: Dean Martin (David Sloane); Stella Stevens (Carol Corman); Eli Wallach (Harry Hunter); Anne Jackson (Murie Laszlo); Betty Field (Thelma); Jack Albertson (Mr. Slotkin); Katharine Bard (Mary Hunter); Woodrow Parfrey (Eddie Rankin); Alan Oppenheimer (Everett Bauer); Shelley Morrison (Marcia Borie); George Furth (Roger); Monroe Arnold (Wally Hammond); Claude Stroud (Hall Satler)

Reviews:

NEW YORK TIMES	1/19/68
VARIETY	1/24/68
NEW YORKER	1/27/68
NEWSWEEK	1/29/68
COMMONWEAL	2/9/68
AMERICA	2/17/68

Released by Columbia in January 1968; color; 102 minutes
Movie Gross: $2,500,000

BANDOLERO! (1968)

Credits: Produced by Robert L. Jacks; Directed by Andrew V. McLaglen; Screenplay by James Lee Barrett; Based on a story by Stanley L. Hough; Music: Jerry Goldsmith; Director of photography: William H. Clothier; Art direction: Jack Martin Smith and Alfred Sweeney, Jr.; Set decorations: Walter M. Scott and Chester L. Bayhi; Special photographic effects: L. B. Abbott and Emil Kosa, Jr.; Stunt coordinator: Hal Needham; Orchestration: Herbert Spencer; Film editor: Folmar Blangsted; Unit production manager: Jack Stubbs; Assistant director: Terry Morse, Jr.; Sound: Herman Lewis and David Dockendorf; Makeup: Dan Striepeke and Del Acevedo; Hairstyling: Edith Lindon; Color: Deluxe; Panavision

Cast: James Stewart (Mace Bishop); Dean Martin (Dee Bishop); Raquel Welch (Maria); George Kennedy (Sheriff Johnson); Andrew Prine (Roscoe

Bookbinder); Will Geer (Pop Chaney); Clint Ritchie (Babe); Denver Pyle (Muncie Carter); Tom Heaton (Joe Chaney); Rudy Diaz (Angel); Sean McClory (Robbie); Harry Carey (Cort Hayjack); Donald Barry (Jack Hawkins); Guy Raymond (Ossie Grimes); Perry Lopez (Frisco); Jock Mahoney (Stoner); Dub Taylor (attendant); Big John Hamilton (bank clerk); Bob Adler (Ross Harper); John Mitchum (bath house customer); Joseph Patrick Cranshaw (bank clerk); Roy Barcroft (bartender)

Reviews:

VARIETY	6/5/68
NEW YORK TIMES	7/18/68
TIME	8/2/68

Released by 20th Century Fox in July 1968; color; 107 minutes

Movie Gross: $5,500,000

5 CARD STUD (1968)

Credits: Produced by Hal B. Wallis; Directed by Henry Hathaway; Screenplay by Marguerite Roberts; From a novel by Ray Gaulden; Music composed and conducted by Maurice Jarre; Title song sung by Dean Martin - lyrics by Ned Washington, music by Maurice Jarre; Director of photography: Daniel L. Fapp; Production design: Walter Tyler; Set decoration: Ray Moyer; Makeup artist: Adelbert Acevedo; Hairstylist: Carol Meikle; Sound recording: Harold Lewis; Editorial supervision: Warren Low; Costumes: Leah Rhodes; Unit production manager: Frank Beetson; Assistant director: Fred Gammon; "Mercy's Call" by W. H. Doane and F. C. Van Al Styne; Associate producer: Paul Nathan; Technicolor

Cast: Dean Martin (Van Morgan); Robert Mitchum (Reverend Rudd); Inger Stevens (Lily Langford); Roddy McDowell (Nick Evers); Katherine Justice (Nora Evers); John Anderson (Marshal Dana); Ruth Springford (Mama Malone); Yaphet Kotto (Little George); Denver Pyle (Sig Evers); Bill Fletcher (Joe Hurley); Whit Bissell (Dr. Cooper); Ted de Corsia (Eldon Bates); Don Collier (Rowan); Roy Jenson (Mace Jones); Jerry Gatlin (stranger); Chuck Hayward (O' Hara); Louise Lorimer (Mrs. Wells); Boyd "Red" Morgan (Fred Carson); George Robotham (Stoney); Hope Summers (customer)

Dean's Song: 5 Card Stud (Voice Over)

Reviews:

VARIETY	7/17/68
NEW YORK TIMES	8/1/68

Released by Paramount in August 1968; color; 101 minutes

Movie Gross: $3,500,000

THE WRECKING CREW (1969)

Credits: Produced by Irving Allen; Directed by Phil Karlson; Screenplay by William McGivern; Based on the book "The Wrecking Crew" by Donald Hamilton; Music composed and conducted by Hugo Montenegro; Song "House Of Seven Joys" by Mack David and

DeVol; Costume designer: Moss Mabry; Director of photography:
Sam Leavitt; Art director: Joe Wright; Property master: Max
Frankel; Film editor: Maury Winetrobe; Dean Martin's makeup:
Hank Edds; Set decorator: Frank Tuttle; Karate advisor: Bruce Lee;
Title design: Wayne Fitzgerald; Associate producer: Harold F.
Kress; Unit production manager: Ralph Black; Assistant director:
Jerome Siegel; Sound supervisor: Charles J. Rice; Sound: James
Flaster and Arthur Piantadosi; Makeup supervision: Ben Lane;
Hairstyles: Virginia Jones; Helicopter sequences: Frank Tallman;
Dean Martin's wardrobe designer: Sy Devore; A Meadway-Claude
Production

Cast: Dean Martin (Matt Helm); Elke Sommer (Linka Karinsky); Sharon Tate
(Freya Carlson); Nancy Kwan (Yu-Rang); Nigel Green (Count
Contini); Tina Louise (Lola Medina); John Larch (MacDonald);
John Brascia (Karl); Weaver Levy (Kim); Wilhelm Von Homberg
(Gregor); Bill Saito (Ching); Fuji (Toki); Pepper Martin (Frankie);
Ted H. Jordan (guard); David Chow (bartender); James Lloyd (desk
clerk); Chuck Norris (Garth); Allen Pinson (page); Bill M. Ryusaki
(Henri)

Dean's Songs: Anniversary Song; Cry; Exactly Like You; Glory Of Love; Let
Me Call You Sweetheart; On The Sunny Side Of The Street; Red
Sails In The Sunset; Melancholy Baby (All songs are Voice Overs)

Reviews: *VARIETY*   12/25/68
            NEW YORK TIMES   2/6/69
Released by Columbia in February 1969; color; 105 minutes

Movie Gross: $2,400,000

AIRPORT (1970)

Credits: Produced by Ross Hunter; Directed and screenplay by George Seaton;
From the novel by Arthur Hailey; Director of photography: Ernest
Laszlo; Art directors: Alexander Golitzen and E. Preston Ames; Set
decorators: Jack D. Moore and Mickey S. Michaels; Unit
production manager: Raymond Gosnell; Assistant director: Donald
Roberts; Film editor: Stuart Gilmore; Sound: Waldon O. Watson,
David M. Moriarty and Ronald Pierce; Technical advisors: John N.
Denen (F. A. A. Air Traffic Control) and Captain Lee Danielson;
Music editor: Arnold Schwarzwald; Makeup: Bud Westmore;
Hairstylist: Larry Germann; Script supervisor: Betty Abbott;
Cosmetics: Universal Pictures professional cosmetics; Special
photographic effects: Film Effect of Hollywood (Don W. Weld and
James B. Gordon); Costume designer: Edith Head; Music composed
and conducted by Alfred Newman; Associate producer: Jacque
Mapes; Technicolor

Cast: Burt Lancaster (Mel Bakersfeld); Dean Martin (Vernon Demerest); Jean
Seberg (Tanya Livingston); Jacqueline Bisset (Gwen Meighen);
George Kennedy (Joe Patroni); Helen Hayes (Ada Quonsett); Van
Heflin (D. O. Guerrero); Maureen Stapleton (Inez Guerrero); Barry
Nelson (Anson Harris); Dana Wynter (Cindy Bakersfeld); Lloyd
Nolan (Harry Standish); Barbara Hale (Sarah Demerest); Gary

With Jacqueline Bisset on the set of *Airport*
(Universal Pictures publicity photo)

Collins (Cy Jordan); John Findlater (Peter Coakley); Jessie Royce Landis (Harriet DuBarry Mosman); Larry Gates (Commissioner Ackerman); Peter Turgeon (Marcus Rathbone); Whit Bissell (Mr. Davidson); Virginia Grey (Mrs. Schultz); Eileen Wesson (Judy); Paul Picerni (Dr. Compagno); Robert Patten (Capt. Benson); Clark Howat (Bert Weatherby); Lew Brown (Reynolds); Lisa Gerritson (Libby Bakersfeld); Jim Nolan (Father Lonigan); Ena Hartman (Ruth); Sharon Harvey (Sally); Albert Reed (Ned Ordway); Jodean Russo (Marie Patroni); Dick Winslow (Mr. Schultz); Lou Wagner (Schuyler Schultz); Mary Jackson (Sister Felice); Shelly Novack (Rollings); Chuck Daniel (Parks)

Reviews:

VARIETY	2/18/70
NEW YORK TIMES	3/6/70
NEWSWEEK	3/16/70
AMERICA	3/21/70
NEW YORKER	3/21/70
SENIOR SCHOLASTIC	4/13/70

Released by Universal in March 1970; color; 137 minutes

Movie Gross: $12,378,259

something big (1971)

Credits: Produced and directed by Andrew V. McLaglen; Written by James Lee Barrett; Assistant director: Howard W. Koch, Jr.; Unit production manager: Robert M. Beche; Property: P. Dudley Holmes; Special effects: Logan Frazee; Sound: Jesus Gonzalez; Camera operator: Jack Whitman, Jr.; Second assistant director: Jerry Ziesmer; Stunt coordinator: Hal Needham; Casting: Hoyt Bowers; Script supervisor: Robert Forrest; Makeup: Don Schoenfeld and Hank Edds; Hairdresser: Esperanza Gomez; Costumes: Ray Summers and Richard Bruno; Dog trainer: Joe Hornok; Head wrangler: Dick Lundin; Supervising sound editor: Jack Finlay; Supervising music editor: Gene Feldman; Stills: Don Christie; Art director: Alfred Sweeney; Film editor: Robert Simpson; Director of photography: Harry Stradling, Jr.; Associate producer: Harry Bernsen; Musical score composed and conducted by Marvin Hamlisch; Title song - music by Burt Bacharach, lyrics by Hal David; Technicolor; A Cinema Center Films Presentation; A National General Release

Cast: Dean Martin (Joe Baker); Brian Keith (Colonel Morgan); Honor Blackman (Mary Anna Morgan); Carol White (Dover McBride); Ben Johnson (Jesse Bookbinder); Albert Salmi (Johnny Cobb); Don Knight (Tommy McBride); Joyce Van Patten (Polly Standall); Denver Pyle (Junior Frisbee); Merlin Olsen (Sergeant Fitzsimmons); Robert Donner (Angel Moon); Harry Carey, Jr. (Joe Pickens); Judi Meredith (Carrie Standall); Ed Faulkner (Captain Tyler); Paul Fix (Chief Yellow Sun); Armand Alzamora (Luis Munos); David Huddleston (Malachi Morton); Bob Steele (Teamster #3); Shirleena Manchur (stagecoach lady); Jose Angel Espinosa (Emilio Estevez); Juan Garcia (Juan Garcia); Robert Gravage (Sam); Chuck Hicks

(Corporal James); John Kelly (barkeeper); Enrique Lucero (Indian spy); Lupe Amador (woman in village); Scruffy (Tuffy)

Reviews: *VARIETY*   11/10/71
                 NEW YORK TIMES   1/22/72
Released by National General in January 1972; color; 107 minutes
Movie Gross Unavailable

SHOWDOWN (1973)

Credits: Produced and directed by George Seaton; Screenplay by Theodore Taylor; Story by Hank Fine; Director of photography: Ernest Laszlo; Art directors: Alexander Golitzen and Henry Bumstead; Set decorator: George Milo; Sound: Waldon O. Watson and John R. Carter; Cosmetics: Cinematique; Music supervision: Hal Mooney; Special photographic effects: Albert Whitlock; Film editor: John W. Holmes; Associate producer and unit production manager: Donald Roberts; Assistant director: Jim Fargo; Titles and optical effects: Universal Title; Costumes: Edith Head; Music: David Shire; Technicolor; Filmed in TODD-AO 35; In cooperation with the U. S. Forest Service and Cumbles and Toltec Scenic Railroad

Cast: Rock Hudson (Chuck Jarvis); Dean Martin (Billy Massey); Susan Clark (Kate Jarvis); Donald Moffat (Art Williams); John McLiam (P. J. Wilson); Charles Baca (Martinez); Jackson Kane (Clem); Ben Zeller (Jerry Williams); John Richard Gill (Earl Cole); Philip L. Mead (Jack Bonney); Rita Rogers (girl); Vic Mohica (Big Eye); Raleigh Gardenhire (Joe Williams); Ed Begley, Jr. (Pook); Dan Boydston (Rawls)

Reviews: *VARIETY*   5/23/73
                 NEW YORK TIMES   11/22/73
Released by Universal in November 1973; color; 90 minutes
Movie Gross Unavailable

MR. RICCO (1975)

Credits: Produced by Douglas Netter; Directed by Paul Bogart; Screenplay by Robert Hoban; Story by Ed Harvey and Francis Kiernan; Art director: Herman A. Blumenthal; Music: Chico Hamilton; Director of photography: Frank Stanley; Sound: Jerry Jost and Harry W. Tetrick; Set decoration: Don Sullivan; Wardrobe: James Linn and Nancy McArdle; Makeup: Frank Westmore; Hairstyles: Judy Alexander; Unit production manager: Phil Rawlins; Assistant director: Daniel J. McCauley; Second assistant director: Edward E. Vaughan; Action scenes coordinated by George Fisher; Property master: Carl Beonde; Music supervisor: Harry V. Lojewski; Metrocolor; Panavision

Cast: Dean Martin (Joe Ricco); Eugene Roche (George Cronyn); Thalmus Rasulala (Frankie Steele); Cindy Williams (Jamison); Denise Nicholas (Irene Mapes); Philip Thomas (Purvis Mapes); George

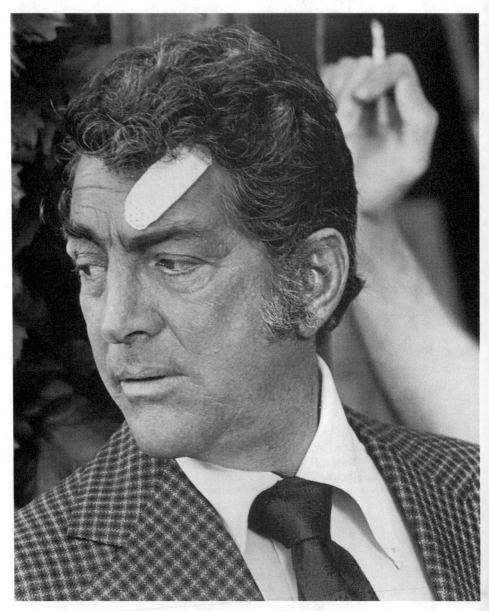

Dean's last starring role as *Mr. Ricco*
(United Artists/MGM publicity photo)

Tyne (Lt. Barrett); Robert Sampson (Justin); Michael Gregory (Tanner); Geraldine Brooks (Katherine Fremont); Joseph Hacker (Markham); Frank Puglia (Uncle Enzo); Ella Edwards (Sally); Rose Gregorio (Angela); Nicky Blair (Nino); John Quade (Arkansas); Nora Marlowe (Mrs. Callahan); Jay Fletcher (Lt. Harmon Jackson); Jason Wingreen (judge); Daniel Keough (doctor); H. B. Barnum III (Luther); Oliver Givens (Calvin Mapes); A. G. Vitanza (Patsy); Rick Richards (file officer); Dennis Lee Smith (Officer Hanley); David Buchanan (Officer Thompson); Tony Brubaker (Officer Wells); Mickey Caruso (Officer Riley)

Reviews: *VARIETY* 1/29/75
NEW YORK TIMES 1/30/75

Released by MGM in January 1975; color; 98 minutes
Movie Gross Unavailable

CANNONBALL RUN (1981)

Credits: Produced by Albert S. Ruddy; Directed by Hal Needham; Executive producer: Raymond Chow; Written by Brock Yates; Sound: Jack Solomon; Music supervision: Snuff Garrett; Associate producer and unit production manager: David Shamroy Hamburger; Production supervisor: Andre Morgan; Editors: Donn Cambern and William D. Gordean; Art director: Carol Wenger; Director of photography: Michael Butler; First assistant director: Bill Coker; Second assistant director: Frank Bueno; Special effects: Cliff Wenger, Sr.; Music arranged and conducted by Al Capps; Set decorator: Rochell Moser; Supervising sound editor: Milton Burrow; Sound re-recording: Donald O. Mitchell, Bill Nicholson and Rich Kline; Music editor: James Henrickson; Assistant film editors: Janice Parker, Steve Markovich and William Meshover; Sound effects editors: Robert A. Reich, David M. Liorton, Gordon Davidson, James Vant and Neil Burrow; Assistant sound effects editor: Scott Burrow; Script supervisor: Hope Williams; Stunt coordinator: Bobby Bass; Makeup: Tom Ellingwood and Ed Butterworth; Hairstylist: Gabe Borgo; Costume supervisor: Norman Balling; Mens' costumes: Don Vargas and Darryl Athons; Womens' costumes: Kathy O' Rear; Assistant to the producer: Adele Hadel; Assistant to Hal Needham: Kathy Shea; Production coordinator: Maureen Osborne Beall; Production assistants: Gwen Lawler and Chip Vucelich; Line producers: Stanley Brossette and Art Bano; Talent coordinator: Sheila Manning; Music editor: Grover Helsley; Assistant music editor: Chris McNary; Property master: Jerry Graham; Assistant property master: Gary Kieldrup; Transportation coordinator: Howard Small; Transportation captain: Michael Doyle; Lenses and optical effects: Pacific Title; Camera operator: Dick Colean; Boom operator: Glen Lambert; Gaffer: Bud Schindler; Still photographer: Richard Robinson; Nurse: Dorothy Vitale; Location services: Chris Karamanos; Location auditors: John W. Stuart and Jim McCarthy; Panaflex camera and lenses by Panavision; Technicolor; Songs: "Love Is On The Air" written by L. Henley, J. Hurt and J. Slate -

performed by Lou Rawls; "Cannonball Run" written and performed by Chuck Mangione; "Beauty's Theme" written by Durrill, Capps, Rofford and Garrett - performed by Al Capps; "Just For The Hell Of It" written and performed by Ray Stevens; "If And When" written by B. Peters - performed by Lou Rawls; "You've Gotta Have A Dream" written by Molinary, Capps and Garrett - performed by the California Children's Choir; Clip of "Behind The Green Door" with permission of Mitchell Brothers Film Group

Cast: Burt Reynolds (J. J. McClure); Roger Moore (Seymour); Farrah Fawcett (Pamela); Dom DeLuise (Victor); Dean Martin (Jamie Blake); Sammy Davis, Jr. (Fenderbaum); Jack Elam (doctor); Adrienne Barbeau (Marcy); Terry Bradshaw (Terry); Jackie Chan (Subaru driver number 1); Bert Convy (Brad); Jamie Farr (sheik); Peter Fonda (chief biker); George Furth (A. F. Foyt); Michael Hui (Subaru driver number 2); Bianca Jagger (sheik's sister); Molly Picon (Mom Goldfarb); Jimmy "The Greek" Snyder (The Greek); Mel Tillis (Mel); Rick Aviles (Mad Dog); Warren Berlinger (Shakey Finch); Tara Buckman (Jill); John Fiedler (desk clerk); Norman Grabowski (Paroski); Joe Klecko (Polish racing driver); Grayce Spence (chairperson); Bob Tessier (biker); Alfie Wise (Batman); Johnny Yune (talk show host); Lois Areno, Simone Burton, Finele Carpenter, Susan McDonald, Janet Woytak (Seymour's girls); Ben Rogers (Pennsylvania patrolman); Jan Lewis (Missouri patrolman number 1); Fred Smith (California patrolman number 1); Roy Tatum (Connecticut patrolman); Dudley Remus (New Jersey patrolman number 1); Hal Carter (New Jersey patrolman number 2); Brock Yates (organizer); Kathleen M. Shea (starting girl); Nancy Austn (phone booth lady); Vickie Reigle (car hop); Bob Stenner (California highway patrolman number 2); Ken Squier (California highway patrolman number 3)

Reviews:

TEEN	6/81
NEW YORK TIMES	6/20/81
VARIETY	6/24/81
SPORTS ILLUSTRATED	6/29/81

Released by 20th Century Fox in June 1981; color; 93 minutes

Movie Gross: $35,378,000

CANNONBALL RUN II (1984)

Credits: Produced by Albert S. Ruddy; Directed by Hal Needham; Written by Hal Needham, Albert S. Ruddy and Harvey Miller; Based on characters created by Brock Yates; Executive producers: Raymond Chow and Andre Morgan; Casting: Mike Fenton and Jane Feinberg; Music supervision: Snuff Garrett; Music: Al Capps; Editors: William Gordean and Carl Kress; Art director: Tho. E. Azzari; Director of photography: Nick McLean; Unit production manager: Bill Cohler; First assistant director: Tom Connors; Second assistant directors: John Peter Kousakis and Jan De Witt; Additional second assistant director: Jerry Ketcham; Set decorator: Charles M. Graffo; Special effects: Philip Cory; Construction coordinator: Larry Verne; Supervising sound effects: Don Hall; Sound editors: Virginia A. Cook, Terie Dorman, Kathleen Rose, Joey Ippilito, and Jack Schrader; Assistant sound editors: Carmen Baker and Laurey Condon; Assistant film editors: Janice Parker and Carol Ann Digiuseppe; Apprentice film editor: Maggie Ostrioff; Supervising music editor: Jim Henrikson; Music editor: Nancy Fogarty; Assistant music editor: Kathleen Fogarty; ADR editor: Jay Engel; Assistant ADR editor: Gael Chandler; Sound re-recording: Bill Varney, Gregg Landaker and Allen L. Stone; Assistant to executive producers: David Chan; Assistant to Mr. Ruddy: Adele Natell; Assistant to Hal Needham: Kathy Shea; Production coordinator: Judith Gill; Production secretary: Susan Elkins; Administrative assistants: Tom Ellison, Richard DeLabio and Douglas Liman; Production accountants: Robert Knoechel and Blanche Bisbing; Production comptroller: John Stuart; Costume supervisor: Norman Salling; Mens' costumes: Don Vargas; Womens' costumes: Kathy O' Rear; Camera operators: Michael D. O' Shea, Michael A. Genne and Ray De La Motte; Assistant camera operators: Steve Smith, Keith Peterman and Eric Engler; Sound mixer: Darin Knight; Boom operator: Don Bolger; Gaffer: Dick Hart; Best boy: Randy Glass; Key grip: Tim Ryan; Best boy: Carl Gibson, Jr.; Property master: Bill Petrotta; Assistant property masters: Gary Kieldrup and Richard Baum; Stunt supervisor: Hope Williams; Stuntcoordinator: Alan R. Gibbs; Stunt safety: Clay Boss; Makeup: Tom Ellingwood; Hairstylist: Judith Cory; Unit publicist: Stanley Brossette; Still photographer: Peter Sorel; Nurse: Dorothy Vitale; Negative cutter: Donah Bassett; Transportation coordinator: Donald Casella; Transportation captains: Michael Brum and William Myers; Transportation dispatcher: Charles Renfroe; Location manager: Jack Young; Additional casting: Marlene Goldman; Craft services: Klondike Jones; Titles and optical effects: Westheimer Company; Unit production supervisor: Marlene Rubenstein; Aerial sequences coordinated by Don Lykins (By-Air Corp); Special voice effects: Frank Welker; Greensman: Michael Hunter; Animation sequence: Ralph Bakshi; Music coordinator: Dave Pell; "Like A Cannonball" written by Milton Brown, Steve Dorff and Snuff Garrett - performed by Menudo; "Cannonball" written and performed by Ray Stevens; "Stop In The Name Of Love" written by Eddie Holland, Lamont Dozier and Brian Holland - performed by the Supremes; Production facilities and services provided by Intl. Producers Services, Hollywood, CA; Lamborghini provided by Celebrity Machine; Lenses and Panaflex camera by Panavision; Technicolor; The producers wish to thank Gov. Bruce Babbitt, the state of Arizona, the Arizona Film Commission and Old Tucson for their cooperation in the making of this film.

Cast: Burt Reynolds (J. J. McClure); Dom DeLuise (Victor/Captain Chaos); Dean Martin (Blake); Sammy Davis, Jr. (Fenderbaum); Jamie Farr (sheik); Marilu Henner (Sister Betty); Telly Savalas (Hymie);

Shirley MacLaine (Sister Veronica); Susan Anton (Jill); Catherine Bach (Marcia); Foster Brooks (fisherman number 1); Sid Caesar (fisherman number 2); Jackie Chan (Jackie); Tim Conway (CHP number 1); Tony Danza (Terry); Jack Elam (doctor); Michael Gazzo (Sonny); Richard Kiel (Arnold); Don Knotts (CHP number 2); Ricardo Montalbaum (king); Jim Nabors (Homer); Louis Nye (fisherman number 3); Molly Picon (Mrs. Goldfarb); Charles Nelson Reilly (Don Don); Alex Rocco (Tony); Henry Silva (Slim); Frank Sinatra (himself); Joe Theismann (Mack); Mel Tillis (Mel); Abe Vigoda (Caesar); Fred Dreyer (CHP number 3); Dale Ishimoto (Japanese father); Arte Johnson (pilot); Linda Lei (beautiful girl); Chris Lemmon (young cop); George Lindsey (Cal); Doug McClure (the slapper); Jilly Rizzo (Jilly); Jack Smith (announcer); Dub Taylor (police officer); Lee Kolima (Nicky); Shawn Wetherly (Dean's girl); John Worthington Stuart (bartender); Debi Greco (sheik's girl); John Zee (Sheldon); Bob Sheldon (policeman at lake); Fred S. Ronnow (pilot); Kai Joseph Wong (Japanese executive); Sandy Hackett (official); Sean Alexander (gas station attendant)

Dean's Song: Everybody Loves Somebody (Voice Over)

Reviews: *NEW YORK TIMES*   6/29/84
                    VARIETY   7/11/84

Released by Warner Brothers in June 1984; color; 106 minutes

Movie Gross: 14,400,000

CAMEO APPEARANCES
ROAD TO BALI
Released by Paramount in January 1953; color; 91 minutes

PEPE
Released by Columbia in December 1960; color; 195 minutes (later cut to 157 minutes)

ROAD TO HONG KONG
Released by United Artists in June 1962; black and white; 91 minutes

COME BLOW YOUR HORN
Released by Paramount in June 1963; color; 112 minutes

CANZONI NEL MONDO
(Also known as World By Night and 38-24-36)

Released in Italy by Gala; 1963; color; 98 minutes

"Return To Me" is heard as a voice over as clips of Dean driving his car are shown. He then lip-synchs portions of "On An Evening In Roma" while clowning around by the pool.

426

MARILYN

Released in 1963; 83 minutes

Clips of the aborted film *Something's Got To Give* are shown in this Rock Hudson-narrated documentary.

BIRDS DO IT

Released by Columbia in August 1966; color; 95 minutes

ROWAN AND MARTIN GO TO THE MOVIES

Released by MGM in 1968

PARAMOUNT NEWS REELS

2/23/50   WRESTLING: CHIMP, NO CHUMP, NEW CHAMP!

Jerry wrestles "Gorgeous Pierre" the chimp. Dean referees.

6/50   SCREEN STARS GO WEST WITH OUR FRIEND IRMA

Premiere of *My Friend Irma Goes West.*

7/12/51   MARTIN AND LEWIS STOP TRAFFIC IN TIMES SQUARE

Crowds of people block West 44th St. in New York City trying to catch a glimpse of Martin and Lewis who are breaking all previous engagement records at the Paramount Theatre.

8/51   STARRY NIGHTS IN CALIFORNIA AND NEW YORK

Dean attends the premiere of *A Place In The Sun.*

2/9/53   MARTIN AND LEWIS HONORED

The team receive the *Photoplay* award.

6/3/53   LAUGH ENVOYS BOUND FOR ENGLAND

Martin and Lewis board the *Queen Elizabeth* for a tour of England.

8/53   GOLF: THE CADDY HAS HIS DAY

At *The Caddy's* premiere, Dean pours popcorn on Perry Como and Eddie Fisher. Dean is also seen arriving by airplane and playing golf.

11/53   HOLLYWOOD HOST TO GREEK RULERS

While touring Paramount studios, King George and Queen Frederika of Greece are spotted by Martin and Lewis.

4/6/54   STARS IN YOUR EYES

Dean attends the premiere of *Knock On Wood.*

7/15/54   LIVING IT UP IN ATLANTIC CITY
            Premiere of *Living It Up* in Atlantic City, NJ. "Martin and
            Lewis Day" proclaimed in the city.

11/18/54   THE BATTLE OF THE CENTURY: MARCIANO VS. LEWIS
            To benefit MDA, Jerry "fights" Rocky while Dean referees.

3/11/55   FRIARS HONOR MARTIN AND LEWIS
            Dean and Jerry are honored for their MDA work.

10/29/55   MARTIN AND LEWIS CLOWN FOR CHARITY
            Dean and Jerry frolic poolside to raise interest in MDA.

3/21/56   ACADEMY AWARDS PRESENTED IN HOLLYWOOD
            Dean is shown at the ceremony.

6/26/56   PREVIEW ON ATLANTIC CITY BOARDWALK
            Premiere of *Pardners*

COLUMBIA SCREEN SNAPSHOTS

4/26/50   MEET THE WINNERS
            Dean and Jerry at the *Photoplay* Awards Banquet.

9/28/50   THIRTIETH ANNIVERSARY SPECIAL
            Dean attends the opening of Jerry's camera shop.

9/13/51   HOLLYWOOD AT PLAY
            Dean and Jerry at Barney's Beanery.

9/25/52   HOLLYWOOD FUN FESTIVAL
            Edited compilation of the above three shorts.

11/17/55   HOLLYWOOD PREMIERE
            Stock footage showing the opening of Jerry's camera shop.

3/22/56   HOLLYWOOD CITY OF STARS
            Stock footage of the *Photoplay* awards.

ADDITIONAL FILM PROJECTS

FILM VODVIL (SIC) #5

An eleven minute Columbia short (released April 4, 1946) that marked Dean's first film appearance. Backed by the Art Mooney Orchestra, Dean performs "San Fernando Valley" and "Temptation."

FAIRFAX AVE.

Dean "performs" the "title song" in this Jerry Lewis home movie filmed in 1950.

WATCH ON THE LIME

Dean appears as a German officer in this Jerry Lewis home movie filmed in 1950.

MOLLY TRAILER

Dean and Jerry appear in the theatrical trailer (late 1950.)

THE REINFORCER

Dean portrayed "Joe Lasagna" in this Jerry Lewis home movie filmed in October 1951.

WANNA BUY A RECORD?

A Capitol promotional film from 1952 "starring" Mel Blanc and Billy May with cameos by Dean (who is seen recording "Oh Marie") and Les Paul and Mary Ford.

STOOGE PREMIERE

Dean, Jerry, and Hal Wallis appear to promote the opening of the picture (12/29/52)

FOX THEATRE PROMO

During the filming of *Money From Home,* Dean and Jerry plugged their upcoming appearances at the Chicago Fox Theatre (4/22/53)

COME BACK LITTLE SHIKSA

Dean appeared in this Jerry Lewis home movie filmed in 1953.

COPA SHOW

Dean and Jerry's stage act was filmed in New York City on 2/3/54.

PARAMOUNT PRESENTS VISTAVISION

Clips of *Three Ring Circus* are shown in this short released on 3/9/55.

SANDS SHOW

Dean and Jerry's stage act was filmed in Las Vegas on 3/28/56.

SANDS SHOW

Dean, Frank Sinatra, and Sammy Davis, Jr. were filmed onstage in Las Vegas on January 23, 1963.

U. S. TREASURY BONDS APPEAL

Dean filmed this on the set of *Murderers' Row* in July 1966.

"Since I Met You Baby"

Warner Brothers; color; 1983; Produced and directed by Ricci Martin. Dean's first and only music video.

"L. A. Is My Lady"

Qwest/Warner Brothers; color; 1984; Dean is one of many celebrities briefly seen in this Frank Sinatra music video.

PROPOSED FILMS

SOMETHING'S GOT TO GIVE

20th Century Fox
Producer: Harry Weinstein
Director: George Cukor

Dean was to star with Marilyn Monroe in this remake of the 1939 Cary Grant film *My Favorite Wife.* Production started at the end of April 1962 and was shut down on June 11th due to Marilyn's fragile emotional and physical state. Monroe died on August 5th.

THE RAVAGERS

Columbia

This fifth Matt Helm movie was due to start filming in the Fall of 1969. The final shooting script, dated October 19, 1969, was written by Robert Kaufman. The far-fetched (even for a Matt Helm flick) plot concerned the assassination of a congressman by a Helm look-alike and Matt's attempt to find the impostor. The script called for Dean to disguise himself as a goateed hippie ice-cream man, a Clarence Darrow-type lawyer (complete with white fright wig), and as Helm's elderly mother!

Columbia Pictures promoted *The Ravagers* with a full-page ad in the September 20, 1969 issue of *Billboard,* but the film was never made. There was also talk of teaming Dean with Frank Sinatra in a "Matt Helm Meets Tony Rome" project, but nothing materialized.

Chapter 10

Home Video Releases

MOVIES

MY FRIEND IRMA
Paramount 4903

AT WAR WITH THE ARMY
Goodtimes 9195

JUMPING JACKS
Paramount 5732

THE STOOGE
Paramount 5212

SCARED STIFF
Paramount 5726

THE CADDY
Paramount 5302

ARTISTS AND MODELS
Paramount 5510

PARDNERS
Paramount 6501

HOLLYWOOD OR BUST
Paramount 5605

THE YOUNG LIONS
20th Century Fox 1057

SOME CAME RUNNING
MGM M3 00964

RIO BRAVO
Warner Brothers 11050

CAREER
Paramount 5907

BELLS ARE RINGING
MGM MV 700063

OCEAN'S 11
Warner Brothers 11158

ALL IN A NIGHT'S WORK
Magnetic 2017 (1978 release)
Starmaker 1049 (1990 release)

WHO'S GOT THE ACTION
Paramount 6207

TOYS IN THE ATTIC
MGM/UA M201637

4 FOR TEXAS
Warner Brothers 11090

ROBIN AND THE 7 HOODS
Warner Brothers 11369

KISS ME STUPID
MGM/UA M202362

THE SONS OF KATIE ELDER
Paramount 6729

MARRIAGE ON THE ROCKS
Warner Brothers 12058

THE SILENCERS
Columbia 83253

TEXAS ACROSS THE RIVER
MCA 45012

MURDERERS' ROW
Columbia 60066

ROUGH NIGHT IN JERICHO
MCA 81321

THE AMBUSHERS
Columbia 60726

HOW TO SAVE A MARRIAGE AND RUIN YOUR LIFE
Goodtimes 4551

BANDOLERO!
20th Century Fox 1203

5 CARD STUD
Paramount 6737

THE WRECKING CREW
Columbia 83273

AIRPORT
MCA 55031

SHOWDOWN
MCA 80029

CANNONBALL RUN
Vestron 6001 (Edited television version)
Video Treasures 9255 (Edited television version)
HBO Home Video 90609 (Original theatrical version)

CANNONBALL RUN II
Warner Brothers 11377

ROAD TO BALI
Burbank 590

ROAD TO HONG KONG
MGM 202078

COME BLOW YOUR HORN
Paramount 6535

MARTIN AND LEWIS GIFT SET
Contains *My Friend Irma, Jumping Jacks* and *Scared Stiff*
Paramount 12984

FRANK SINATRA RAT PACK COLLECTION
Warner Brothers
Contains *Ocean's 11, Robin and the Seven Hoods* and *Four For Texas.*

MATT HELM GIFT SET
Columbia
Contains *The Ambushers* and *Murderers' Row*

MATT HELM GIFT SET 2
Columbia
Contains *The Silencers* and *The Wrecking Crew*

MISC.

A&E BIOGRAPHY: DEAN MARTIN
A&E Home Video 14035
        1995 A&E special

BING CROSBY SPECIAL
Classic TV (No Number Listed)

BLOOPERS FROM THE WORLD'S GREATEST FUNNYMEN
Brentwood Home Video VS-078

BLUSHING BLOOPERS
Video Specials VS-012
        R-rated audio track of *Caddy* out-takes synched up with Martin and
        Lewis film clips.

BOB HOPE: UNREHEARSED ANTICS OF THE STARS
Guthy-Renker (No number listed)

CLASSIC COMEDY TEAMS
Goodtimes 8010

COLGATE COMEDY HOUR
Classic TV (No Number Listed)

COLGATE COMEDY SHOW/MDA TELETHON FOR MAIL CARRIERS
Classic TV (No Number Listed)

COLGATE COMEDY HOURS
Hollywood's Attic (No numbers listed)

Vol. 1:	Margaret Dumont/Mike Mazurki (12/30/51)	
Vol. 2:	Dorothy Dandridge (11/4/51)	
Vol. 3:	Rosemary Clooney (9/21/52)	
Vol. 4:	Polly Bergen/Bob Fosse (2/4/51)	
Vol. 5:	Jane Morgan/Fosse and Niles (5/20/51)	
Vol. 6:	Helen O'Connell/Bob Fosse (4/29/51)	
Vol. 7:	Connie Russell/Ray Malone (1/25/53)	
Vol. 8:	Burt Lancaster/Skylarks (10/4/53)	
Vol. 9:	Modernaires/Franklin Pangborn (1/10/54)	
Vol. 10:	Treniers/Dick Humphreys (5/2/54)	
Vol. 11:	Vera Miles/Milton Frome (12/19/54)	
Vol. 12:	Cameos by Jimmy Durante, George Raft and Tony Curtis (5/8/55)	

CROONERS OF THE CENTURY
Goodtimes 8060

> Dean performs "That's Amore" from a Colgate Comedy Hour.

DEAN MARTIN AND JERRY LEWIS - COLGATE COMEDY HOUR
Front Row Entertainment

Volume One:	5744	Guest: Burt Lancaster (10/4/53)
Volume Two:	5745	Guest: Rosemary Clooney (9/21/52)
Volume Three:	5746	Guest: Marilyn Maxwell (9/17/50)
Volume Four:	5747	Guest: Vera Miles (12/19/54)

Also available as a box set: 4028

DEAN MARTIN - HOLLYWOOD CLASSICS
Brentwood 0932 (2 Tape Set)

> Contains *At War With The Army* and a Dean Martin documentary.

DEAN MARTIN SHOW
Video Dimensions (No Number Listed)

> This is an edited black-and-white print of Dean's premiere show on NBC.

DINAH SHORE CHEVY SHOW
Shokus Video 451

DOM DeLUISE - EAT THIS, THE VIDEO #2
Bacchus Films, Inc. 8889

> Dean appears in brief sketch originally shown on Dom's 1987 syndicated television show.

GOLF GOOFS AND CELEBRITY MOMENTS
Parents Approved Video 1078
> Very brief clip of Dean teeing off in the 1950s.

HOLLYWOOD CLOWNS
MGM 300688

HOLLYWOOD HOME MOVIES
Maljack Productions CG 2059

JACK BENNY COMEDY HOUR
Goodtimes 5114

JOHNNY CARSON - HIS FAVORITE MOMENTS '60s AND '70s:
> HERE'S JOHNNY
Buena Vista 2733
> Classic 1969 clip of Dean with George Gobel and Bob Hope.

JOHN WAYNE STORY - THE LATER YEARS
Goodtimes 08543
> Dean welcomes John Wayne to his television show in 1965.

JUDY, FRANK AND DEAN - ONCE IN A LIFETIME
Kingworld 6802
> 1962 Judy Garland TV special.

MAGIC OF BING CROSBY
Vision Entertainment 50294-3
> Very brief clip of Dean singing "True Love" with Bing and Patti Page.

MARTIN AND LEWIS COMEDY CLASSICS
Passport International 3P-9 (3 Tape Set)
Contains *At War With The Army,* Martin and Lewis At The Movies (a collection of
film trailers) and a Colgate Comedy Show.

MARTIN AND LEWIS - MASTERS OF LAUGHTER
Goodtimes 8491
> Martin and Lewis documentary.

MARTIN AND LEWIS - THEIR GOLDEN AGE OF COMEDY (Disney Channel)
Video Treasures
Part One: SV 9745
Part Two: SV 9746
Part Three: SV 9747
Also available as a box set: SV 9827

MARTIN AND LEWIS
Diamond Entertainment
Vol. One: 42029 Guest: Rosemary Clooney (9/21/52)
Vol. Two: 42030 Guest: Polly Bergen (2/4/51)
Vol. Three: 42031 Guest: Burt Lancaster (10/4/53)
Vol. Four: 42032 Guest: Cameos by Jimmy Durante, George Raft and Tony Curtis
                          (5/8/55)
Also available as a box set: 11207

MILTON BERLE TEXACO STAR THEATRE
Sagebrush Enterprises (No Number Listed)

MILTON BERLE'S MORE MAD WORLD OF COMEDY
Rhino Home Video

OSCAR'S GREATEST MOMENTS 1971-1991
RCA/Columbia Home Video 50973
            Very brief clip of Dean with Raquel Welch at 1979 Academy Award
            Ceremony.

PREMIERE OF *A STAR IS BORN*
Video Yesteryear

READER'S DIGEST PRESENTS LEGENDS OF COMEDY; TV COMEDY
                    CLASSICS: THE '50s AND '60s
Reader's Digest Video RV45-116-GW/3

REEL MOMENTS: LAUGHTER
Karol Video

SPY THRILLERS, VOL. 1
Sinister Cinema
            Contains the trailers to *The Silencers, Murderers' Row* and
            The Wrecking Crew.

Surrounded by a bevy of "Slaygirls" on the set of *The Wrecking Crew*
(Columbia Pictures Corp. publicity photo)

Chapter 11

Periodicals

(Note: All of the following picture Dean on the front cover.)

1944

BILLBOARD	January 14

1950

TELE VIEWS	April 28
TV FORECAST	October 28
TV GUIDE	November 11-17

1951

TV GUIDE	June 23-29
LIFE	August 13
QUICK	October 8
TV GUIDE	November 2-8
TV DIGEST	November 3

1952

LOOK	January 29
THE VISITOR	February 23-March 1
TV GUIDE	March 7-13
CIRO'S MONTHLY	Spring
LOOK	April 22
TV DIGEST	August 16
1,000 JOKES	Summer
TV GUIDE	September 19-25
LOOK	December 16
MOVIE LIFE YEARBOOK	#14

1953

TV SHOW	January
TV GUIDE	June 5-11
TV TODAY	October 2
TEMPO	October 5
TV PEOPLE AND PICTURES	October
LEISURE TIME	November 29

1954

CUE	January 2
MUSIC VIEWS	February
TELEVISION LIFE	March
HOT ROD	July
TV	July
TV AND MOVIE SCREEN	July
TV GUIDE	August 14-20
MOVIE ANNUAL	

1955

COMPACT	January
MOVIE PREVUE	February
TV REVUE	March
TV MOVIE SCREEN	May
TV/RADIO-HERALD (NEW YORK TRIBUNE)	June 5-11
PARADE	August 28
TV FAN	December

1956

HIT PARADER	March
RECORD WHIRL	April
TV STAGE	June
CONFIDENTIAL	November

1957

MUSIC VENDOR	July 7
INSIDE STORY	August

1958

MUSIC VENDOR	April 14
HIT PARADER	October
TV/RADIO MAGAZINE	November 9-15

1959

PARADE	June 7
WASHINGTON POST AMERICAN WEEKLY	August 30

1960

FILM REVIEW	October

1961

SUNDAY NEW YORK NEWS COLOROTO MAG	April 30
MOVIE TV SECRETS	December

1962

NEW YORK JOURNAL AMERICAN	February 25
PARADE	August 12
TV MOVIE SCREEN	December

1963

TV GUIDE	December 14-20

1964

TV MAGAZINE	November 22-28

1966

TV GUIDE	April 2-8
LOOK	May 17
PHOTOPLAY	July
TV TIME AND CHANNEL	September 24-30
CASHBOX	November 12

1967

TV GUIDE	February 18-24
TV AND MOVIE SCREEN	March
TV TIME AND CHANNEL	March 4-10
ST. LOUIS POST DISPATCH TV MAGAZINE	March 26
TV STAR PARADE	April
CORONET	May
TV RADIO MIRROR	May
TV RADIO SHOW	May
PHOTO TV LAND	June
TV WORLD	June
MOVIE MIRROR	October
PHOTOSCREEN	October
MOVIE MIRROR	December

TV RADIO MIRROR	December
TV RADIO SHOW	December
LOOK	December 26
TV MAGAZINE	December 31-January 6
MOVIE SCREEN YEARBOOK	#16

1968

TV PICTURE LIFE	January
FILMS IN REVIEW	February
MOVIELAND AND TV TIME	February
MOVIE MIRROR	February
PHOTOPLAY	March
TV RADIO TALK	March
TV STAR PARADE	March
MOVIELAND AND TV TIME ANNUAL	Spring
ADAM FILM QUARTERLY #4	April
(Note: This is an "adult" magazine.)	
INSIDE TV	April
PHOTOSCREEN	April 1
TV MOVIE SCREEN	May
TV MOVIE PLAY	May
MOVIE LIFE	June
PHOTOPLAY	July
TV RADIO MIRROR	August
SCREEN STARS	August
INSIDE TV	September
TV STAR PARADE	September
TV GUIDE	September 28-October 4
MODERN MOVIES	October
MOVIE LIFE	November
TV YEARBOOK	#20
MOVIE TV FAMILY ALBUM	#4

1969

SCREEN STORIES	March
INSIDE TV	April
MOVIE MIRROR	April
TV RADIO MIRROR	May
TV RADIO TALK	September
MODERN MOVIES	October
SCREEN STORIES	October
TV MOVIES TODAY	October
MOVIE TV FAMILY ALBUM	#5
WHO'S WHO IN MOVIES	#4
TV STAR ANNUAL	#27

HOLLYWOOD SECRETS YEARBOOK	#18
MOVIE LIFE YEARBOOK	#46

1970

PARADE	February 22
MOTION PICTURE	March
MOVIELAND AND TV TIME	March
PHOTOSCREEN	March
RONA BARRETT'S HOLLYWOOD	March
SCREEN STARS	March
TV RADIO TALK	March
TV RADIO TIME	March
MOVIE WORLD	April
TV RADIO MIRROR	April
TV STAR PARADE	April
MOVIE LIFE	July
TV RADIO SHOW	July
MOVIE STARS	September
BILLBOARD	September 19
TV AND SCREENWORLD	October
TV PHOTO STORY	October
TV GUIDE	November 28-December 4
CORONET	December
MOVIE LIFE	December
TV NEWS	December 19-26
TV RECORD SUPERSTARS	December
MOVIE LIFE YEARBOOK	#47
WHO'S WHO IN MOVIES	#5
TV RADIO ALBUM	1970

1971

SCREENLAND	January
PHOTOPLAY	February
PHOTOSCREEN	April
MOVIE LIFE	July
MOVIE PARADE	July
PHOTOSCREEN	July
SILVER SCREEN	July
TV RADIO MIRROR	July
TV SCREEN WORLD	July
MOTION PICTURE	August
MOVIELAND AND TV TIME	September
PHOTOPLAY	September
SCREEN STARS	November
SILVER SCREEN	November

TV RADIO MIRROR	November
TV STAR ANNUAL	November
TV STAR PARADE	November
MOTION PICTURE	December
MOVIE MIRROR YEARBOOK	#14
MOVIE SCREEN YEARBOOK	#20
WHO'S WHO IN MOVIES	#6
SECRETS YEARBOOK	#20
TV YEARBOOK	#23

1972

RONA BARRETT'S HOLLYWOOD	January
TV RADIO SHOW	January
MOVIE WORLD	February
PHOTOPLAY	February
TV MOVIE SCREEN	February
MOVIELAND AND TV TIME	March
MOVIE MIRROR	March
TV STAR PARADE	March
MODERN SCREEN	April
TV RADIO MIRROR	April
TV RADIO SHOW	April
TV TIME AND CHANNEL	May 13-19
PHOTOPLAY	May
TV PICTURE LIFE	May
TV RADIO MIRROR	May
MOTION PICTURE	June
MOVIE WORLD	June
MODERN SCREEN	July
SILVER SCREEN	July
MOTION PICTURE	August
MOVIE MIRROR	September
MOVIE STARS	September
SCREEN STARS	September
CINEMASCREEN	October
SCREEN STORIES	October
TV STAR PARADE	October
TV RADIO TALK	November
MOVIELAND	December
TV RADIO SHOW	December
TV RADIO TALK	December
MOVIE MIRROR YEARBOOK	#15
MOVIE SCREEN YEARBOOK	#21
TV YEARBOOK	#24

| TV STAR DIRECTORY | #1 |
| WHO'S WHO IN MOVIES | #7 |

1973

MOVIE WORLD	January
POLICE GAZETTE	January
MOTION PICTURE	February
RADIO TALK	February
TV STAR PARADE	February
MOVIE LIFE	March
TV RADIO MIRROR	March
TV MOVIE SCREEN	April
MOVIEWORLD	May
MOTION PICTURE	June
TV RADIO MIRROR	June
TV RADIO SHOW	June
MODERN SCREEN	July
MOVIE STARS	July
PHOTOPLAY	July
MODERN SCREEN	August
MOVIE MIRROR	August
RONA BARRETT'S GOSSIP	August
SCREEN STARS	August
CHICAGO TV NEWS	October 20-27
TV RADIO MIRROR	October
TV GUIDE	November 10-16
TV MOVIE SCREEN	November
TV STAR ANNUAL	November (#41)
MOVIELAND AND TV TIME	December
PHOTOPLAY	December
SCREEN STARS	December
WHO'S WHO IN MOVIES	#8

1974

TV RADIO TALK	January
MOVIE MIRROR	February
MOVIE STARS	February
SILVER SCREEN	February
TV RADIO MIRROR	March
MOVIE LIFE	April
MOVIE STARS	April
MOVIE MIRROR	May
TV RADIO TALK	May
TV STAR PARADE	May
PHOTOSCREEN	June

SILVER SCREEN	June
MOVIE LIFE	July
MOVIE MIRROR	July
SCREEN STORIES	August
TV STAR PARADE	August
MOVIE LIFE	September
SCREEN AND TV ALBUM	September
MOVIE MIRROR	October
TV AND MOVIE SCREEN	November

1975

MOVIELAND AND TV TIME	April
SCREEN STORIES	June
SCREEN STORIES	October

1976

TV DAWN TO DUSK	January
MOTION PICTURE	June

1978

HIGH TIMES	June

1980

TV WEEK	December 14-20

1983

SHOWBIZ	October 16-22

1988

USA WEEKEND	March 4-6
JET	March 7
SPY	November

1989

DISCOVERIES	August

1990

YESTERDAY	#5

1995

MOVIE CLUB	Spring

1996

PEOPLE   January 6

1998

TV GUIDE   April 4

SELECT MAGAZINE ARTICLES

1949

NEWSWEEK   April 18
TIME   May 23

1950

TV GUIDE   November 11

1951

COLLIERS   February 10
TIME   July 23
NEW YORKER   July 28

1952

LOOK   January 29
CORONET   February
TV GUIDE   March 14

1953

TV GUIDE   June 26
TV GUIDE   October 16

1955

TV GUIDE   May 28
NEWSWEEK   August 15
COSMOPOLITAN   October

1956

TIME   January 9

1957

TV GUIDE   April 13

1958

TV GUIDE   February 22

LIFE	December 22

1959

NEWSWEEK	February 9

1960

LOOK	November 8

1961

SATURDAY EVENING POST	April 29

1963

LOOK	April 9

1965

TV GUIDE	September 18

1966

TIME	March 11

1967

NEWSWEEK	March 20
LIFE	May 26
GOOD HOUSEKEEPING	November

1968

LADIES HOME JOURNAL	November

1969

TV GUIDE	March 1
BILLBOARD	September 20

1970

TV GUIDE	April 18

1976

TV GUIDE	April 10

1978

ESQUIRE	July 4

1987

JET   December 21

1994

TV GUIDE   July 17

1996

TV GUIDE   January 6
NEWSWEEK   January 8
TIME   January 8
ENTERTAINMENT WEEKLY   January 12
ESQUIRE   March

COMIC BOOKS

1951

Movie Love (Famous Funnies Corporation)
December (#12)

1952

Adventures of Martin and Lewis (D. C. Comics)
July/August (#1)
September/October (#2)
November/December (#3)

1953

January/February (#4)
March/April (#5)
May/June (#6)
July/August (#7)
September/October (#8)
November/December (#9)

1954

January (#10)
February (#11)
April (#12)
May (#13)
July (#14)
August (#15)
October (#16)
November (#17)

1955

January (#18)
February (#19)
April (#20)
(Note: #20 is the first Martin and Lewis comic to carry
the "Approved By The Comics Code Authority" stamp.)
May (#21)
July (#22)
August/September (#23)
October (#24)
November (#25)

1956

January (#26)
February (#27)
April (#28)
May (#29)
July (#30)
August (#31)
October (#32)
November (#33)

1957

January (#34)
February (#35)
April (#36)
May (#37)
July (#38)
August (#39)
October (#40)
(Note: This comic book continued as "The Adventures Of Jerry Lewis" until 1971.)

1959

Rio Bravo **(Dell Comics)**
No month listed

1965

Sons of Katie Elder **(Dell Comics)**
September-November

BOOKS

Movie Tie-In Novels

Young Lions   Irwin Shaw   Signet

Some Came Running	James Jones	Signet
Rio Bravo	Leigh Brackett	Bantam
Career	James Lee	Dell
Ocean's 11	George Clayton Johnson/	Pocket
	Jack Golden Russell	
All In A Night's Work	Saul Cooper	Popular
Ada	Wirt Williams	Dell
Sergeant's 3	W. R. Burnett	Pocket
Who's Got The Action	Alexander Rose	Crest
Who's Been Sleeping In My Bed	Michael Milner	Dell
4 For Texas	Dan Cushman	Bantam
Robin and the 7 Hoods	Jack Pearl	Pocket
Marriage On The Rocks	Cy Howard	Popular
Silencers	Donald Hamilton	Fawcett
Murderers' Row	Donald Hamilton	Fawcett
Rough Night In Jericho	Richard Meade	Fawcett
Ambushers	Donald Hamilton	Fawcett
5 Card Stud	Ray Gaulden	Berkley
Bandolero!	Arnold Hano	Popular
Wrecking Crew	Donald Hamilton	Fawcett
Airport	Arthur Hailey	Bantam
something big	Grant Freeling	Award
Cannonball Run	Michael Avallone	Leisure

Biographies

Everybody Loves Somebody Sometime (Especially Himself)
                            Arthur Marx   Hawthorn

Dino - The Dean Martin Story   Michael Freedland   W.H. Allen
      (UK Only)

Dino - Living High In The Dirty Business Of Dreams
                            Nick Tosches   Doubleday
      (Paperback edition published by Dell)

Miscellaneous

Stoned Like A Statue   Howard Kandel and Don Safran   Kanrom
      Dean "wrote" the introduction to this book, which contains photographs
      of statues that are captioned with poor drinking jokes.

(Columbia publicity photo)

Chapter 12

Product Endorsements

ADVERTISEMENTS

1951
Dean, Jerry Lewis, Polly Bergen and Marion Marshall were featured in an ad
for the Magnavox "big-picture" television.

1952
Dean and Jerry along with Pauline Kessinger (manager at the Paramount Cafe
Continental) extolled the virtues of Chesterfield cigarettes.

1953
Dean and Jerry promoted PurOlater oil filters.

Circa 1954
Dean and Jerry are pictured on the back of Fab Detergent boxes.

1958
Dean pitched Rheingold beer.

1962
Dean promoted the Sands Hotel in Las Vegas.

1970
Dean illustrated his golfing technique in a television commercial for "Dino"
brand golf balls. They were manufactured by "Pro-Tel Products" and
were available exclusively at White Front stores. The cost was $9.97
for a baker's dozen.

They were issued with two different pictures of Dean on the box.

1981

Dean appeared in a series of print (and television) ads for Bell Telephone's credit card.

1983

Dean and Frank Sinatra appeared in a television commercial for the Golden Nugget Hotel in Atlantic City, NJ.

TOYS and NOVELTIES

The following Martin and Lewis items are known to exist:
    Money clip
    View Master reel for "Money From Home" (Paramount promotional item)
    Playing cards
    Matches
    Salt shakers
    Notebook
    Toy Watch
    Decals (2 different pictures)
    Drinking cup
    Vendor card
    Puppets (2 different kinds; one puppet has Dean and Jerry connected at the head and sharing one body. Individual puppets also exist and were part of a game called "TV Puppet Show" which came with a curtain backdrop, tickets, photo, etc.)
    Tuck tape (cellophane tape) and whiz tape (cloth-based). A tin display rack that depicts caricatures of Dean and Jerry on its header was produced.

The following Dean Martin items are known to exist:
    Photo button
    Rock and Roll card (#31)
    A notebook (possibly an NBC promotional item) that pictures Dean with Al Hirt and Eydie Gorme in a publicity pose from the television special "Your All-Time Favorite Songs" 1964
    Vendor card
    George Barris' "Way Out Wheels" card (Topps Chewing Gum) 1970
    "Cannonball Run" game by Cadaco #670 (Dean pictured on box) 1981